Professional Certificate in Marketing

PAPER 4:
MARKETING IN PRACTICE

For exams in December 2007 and June 2008

Study Text

In this July 2007 edition

- **User-friendly format** for easy navigation
- Regular **fast forward** summaries emphasising the key points in each chapter
- Recent examples of **marketing practice**
- Fully revised for recent **exams** and **developments**
- A full **index**

Sixth edition July 2007

ISBN 978075174170 4
(previous edition 0 7517 2247 2)

British Library Cataloguing-in-Publication Data
A catalogue record for this book
is available from the British Library

Published by

BPP Learning Media
BPP House, Aldine Place
London W12 8AW

www.bpp.com/learningmedia

Printed and bound in Great Britain by
William Clowes Ltd, Beccles, Suffolk

All our rights reserved. No part of this publication may be reproduced, stored in a retrieval system or transmitted, in any form or by any means, electronic, mechanical, photocopying, recording or otherwise, without the prior written permission of BPP Learning Media Ltd.

We are grateful to the Chartered Institute of Marketing for permission to reproduce in this text the syllabus, tutor's guidance notes and past examination questions. We are also grateful to Karen Beamish of Stone Consulting for preparing the assignment based assessment learning material, and to Claire Louise Wright for help in preparing the text.

©
BPP Learning Media Ltd
2007

Contents

Page

Introduction
The BPP Study Text – Syllabus – Websites – The exam paper – Preparing for the examination – Guide to the Assignment Route – Background to case study: The Needle Works .... v – xxx

Part A Gathering, analysing and presenting information
1. Information for marketing 3
2. The customer database 23
3. Basic research techniques 47
4. Investigating marketing opportunities 61

Part B Building and developing relationships
5. Working with others 83
6. The front line role 105
7. The supply chain 119
8. Practical PR skills 145

Part C Organising and undertaking marketing activities
9. Planning and scheduling 163
10. Event management 181
11. Venue selection 203

Part D Co-ordinating the marketing mix
12. Advertising media 217
13. Promotional activity 245
14. Mix decisions 267

Part E Administering the marketing budget (and evaluating results)
15. Understanding marketing budgets 289
16. Justifying the budget 305

Question and Answer bank 325

List of Key Concepts and Index 351

Review form and free prize draw

The BPP Study Text

Aims of this Study Text

> To provide you with the knowledge and understanding, skills and application techniques that you need if you are to be successful in your exams

This Study Text has been written around the *Marketing in Practice* syllabus.

- It is **comprehensive**. It covers the syllabus content. No more, no less.
- It is targeted to the **exam**. We have taken account of the pilot paper, guidance the examiner has given and the assessment methodology.
- It is designed to support integration of your learning from the other three modules at this stage (see our note on page xxii).

> To allow you to study in the way that best suits your learning style and the time you have available, by following your personal Study Plan (see below)

You may be studying at home on your own until the date of the exam, or you may be attending a full-time course. You may like to (and have time to) read every word, or you may prefer to (or only have time to) skim-read and devote the remainder of your time to question practice. Wherever you fall in the spectrum, you will find the BPP Study Text meets your needs in designing and following your personal Study Plan.

> To tie in with the other components of the BPP Effective Study Package to ensure you have the best possible chance of passing the exam

INTRODUCTION

Recommended period of use	Elements of the BPP Effective Study Package
3-12 months before exam	**Study Text** Acquisition of knowledge, understanding, skills and applied techniques
1-6 months before exam	**Practice & Revision Kit (9/2007)** Tutorial questions and helpful checklists of the key points lead you into each area. There are then numerous Examination questions to try, graded by topic area, along with realistic suggested solutions prepared by marketing professionals in the light of the Examiner's Reports. The September 2007 edition will include the December 2006 and June 2007 papers.
From 3 months before the exam until the last minute	**Passcards** Work through these short memorable notes which are focused on what is most likely to come up in the exam you will be sitting.

Settling down to study

By this stage in your career you may be a very experienced learner and taker of exams. But have you ever thought about *how* you learn? Let's have a quick look at the key elements required for effective learning. You can then identify your learning style and go on to design your own approach to how you are going to study this text – your personal Study Plan.

Key element of learning	Using the BPP Study Text
Motivation	You can rely on the comprehensiveness and technical quality of BPP. You've chosen the right Study Text – so you're in pole position to pass your exam!
Clear objectives and standards	Do you want to be a prizewinner or simply achieve a moderate pass? Decide.
Feedback	Follow through the examples in this text and do the Action Programme and the Quick Quizzes. Evaluate your efforts critically – how are you doing?
Study Plan	You need to be honest about your progress to yourself – don't be over-confident, but don't be negative either. Make your Study Plan (see below) and try to stick to it. Focus on the short-term objectives – completing two chapters a night, say – but beware of losing sight of your study objectives.
Practice	Use the Quick Quizzes and Chapter Roundups to refresh your memory regularly after you have completed your initial study of each chapter.

These introductory pages let you see exactly what you are up against. However you study, you should:

- **Read through the syllabus** – this will help you to identify areas you have already covered, perhaps at a lower level of detail, and areas that are totally new to you

- **Study the examination paper section**, where we show you the format of the exam (how many and what kind of questions and so on)

Key study steps

The following steps are, in our experience, the ideal way to study for professional exams. You can of course adapt it for your particular learning style (see below).

Tackle the chapters in the order you find them in the Study Text. Taking into account your individual learning style, follow these key study steps for each chapter.

Key study steps	Activity
Step 1 **Chapter Topic list**	Study the list. Each numbered topic denotes a **numbered section** in the chapter.
Step 2 **Introduction**	Read it through. It is designed to show you **why the topics in the chapter need to be studied** – how they lead on from previous topics, and how they lead into subsequent ones.
Step 3 **Explanations**	Proceed **methodically** through the chapter, reading each section thoroughly and making sure you understand.
Step 4 **Key Concepts**	**Key concepts** can often earn you **easy marks** if you state them clearly and correctly in an appropriate exam.
Step 5 **Exam Tips**	These give you a good idea of how the examiner tends to examine certain topics – pinpointing **easy marks** and highlighting **pitfalls**.
Step 6 **Note taking**	Take **brief notes** if you wish, avoiding the temptation to copy out too much.
Step 7 **Marketing at Work**	Study each one, and try if you can to add flesh to them from your **own experience** – they are designed to show how the topics you are studying come alive (and often come unstuck) in the **real world**. You can also update yourself on these companies by going on to the World Wide Web.
Step 8 **Action Programme**	Make a very good attempt at each one in each chapter. These are designed to put your **knowledge into practice** in much the same way as you will be required to do in the exam. Check the answer at the end of the chapter in the **Action Programme review**, and make sure you understand the reasons why yours may be different.
Step 9 **Chapter Roundup**	Check through it very carefully, to make sure you have grasped the **major points** it is highlighting
Step 10 **Quick Quiz**	When you are happy that you have covered the chapter, use the **Quick Quiz** to check your recall of the topics covered. The answers are in the paragraphs in the chapter that we refer you to.
Step 11 **Illustrative question(s)**	Either at this point, or later when you are thinking about revising, make a full attempt at the **illustrative questions**. You can find these at the end of the Study Text, along with the **Answers** so you can see how you did.

Developing your personal Study Plan

Preparing a Study Plan (and sticking closely to it) is one of the key elements in learning success.

First you need to be aware of your style of learning. There are four typical learning styles. Consider yourself in the light of the following descriptions. and work out which you fit most closely. You can then plan to follow the key study steps in the sequence suggested.

Learning styles	Characteristics	Sequence of key study steps in the BPP Study Text
Theorist	Seeks to understand principles before applying them in practice	1, 2, 3, 7, 4, 5, 8, 9, 10, 11 (6 continuous)
Reflector	Seeks to observe phenomena, thinks about them and then chooses to act	
Activist	Prefers to deal with practical, active problems; does not have much patience with theory	1, 2, 8 (read through), 7, 4, 5, 9, 3, 8 (full attempt), 10, 11 (6 continuous)
Pragmatist	Prefers to study only if a direct link to practical problems can be seen; not interested in theory for its own sake	8 (read through), 2, 4, 5, 7, 9, 1, 3, 8 (full attempt), 10, 11 (6 continuous)

Next you should complete the following checklist.

Am I motivated? (a)

Do I have an objective and a standard that I want to achieve? (b)

Am I a theorist, a reflector, an activist or a pragmatist? (c)

How much time do I have available per week, given: (d)

- The standard I have set myself
- The time I need to set aside later for work on the Practice and Revision Kit
- The other exam(s) I am sitting, and (of course)
- Practical matters such as work, travel, exercise, sleep and social life?

Now:

- Take the time you have available per week for this Study Text (d), and multiply it by the number of weeks available to give (e) (e)
- Divide (e) by the number of chapters to give (f) (f)
- Set about studying each chapter in the time represented by (f), following the key study steps in the order suggested by your particular learning style

This is your personal **Study Plan**.

Short of time?

Whatever your objectives, standards or style, you may find you simply do not have the time available to follow all the key study steps for each chapter, however you adapt them for your particular learning style. If this is the case, follow the Skim Study technique below (the icons in the Study Text will help you to do this).

Skim Study technique

Study the chapters in the order you find them in the Study Text. For each chapter, follow the key study steps 1–2, and then skim-read through step 3, Jump to step 9 and then go back to steps 4–5. Follow through step 7, and prepare outline Answers to the Action Programme (step 8). Try the Quick Quiz (step 10), following up any items you can't answer, then do a plan for the illustrative question (step 11), comparing it against our answers. You should probably still follow step 6 (note-taking).

Moving on...

However you study, when you are ready to embark on the practice and revision phase of the BPP Effective Study Package, you should still refer back to this Study Text:

- As a source of **reference** (you should find the list of key concepts and the index particularly helpful for this)
- As a **refresher** (the Chapter Roundups and Quick Quizzes help you here)

A note on pronouns

On occasions in this Study Text, 'he' is used for 'he or she', 'him' for 'him or her' and so forth. Whilst we try to avoid this practice it is sometimes necessary for reasons of style. No prejudice or stereotyping accounting to sex is intended or assumed.

Syllabus

Aims

The *Marketing in Practice* module is the application of marketing in context and also forms the summative assessment for the Certificate in Marketing. It aims to assist participants to integrate and apply knowledge from all the modules at this stage.

Participants will not be expected to have prior qualifications or experience in a marketing role. They will be expected to be conversant with the **content of the other three modules at this stage** before undertaking the module.

Learning outcomes

Participants will be able to:

- Collect relevant data from a variety of secondary information sources.
- Analyse and interpret written, visual and graphical data.
- Devise appropriate visual and graphical means to present marketing data.
- Make recommendations based on information obtained from multiple sources.
- Evaluate and select media and promotional activities appropriate to the organisation's objectives and status and to its marketing context.
- Calculate and justify budgets for marketing mix decisions.
- Develop relationships inside and outside the organisation.
- Apply planning techniques to a range of marketing tasks and activities.
- Undertake basic marketing activities within an agreed plan and monitor and report on progress.
- Gather information for, and evaluate marketing results against, financial and other criteria.

Knowledge and skill requirements

Element 1: Gathering, analysing and presenting information (20%) (Marketing Environment)	
1.1	Identify sources of information internally and externally to the organisation, including ICT-based sources such as intranet and Internet.
1.2	Maintain a marketing database, information collection and usage.
1.3	Investigate customers via the database and develop bases for segmentation.
1.4	Explain information gathering techniques available.
1.5	Source and present information on competitor activities across the marketing mix.
1.6	Investigate marketing and promotional opportunities using appropriate information gathering techniques.
1.7	Gather information across borders.

Element 2: Building and developing relationships (20%) (Customer Communications)	
2.1	Describe the structure and roles of the marketing function within the organisation.
2.2	Build and develop relationships within the marketing department, working effectively with others.
2.3	Explain the 'front line' role: receiving and assisting visitors, internal and external enquiries.
2.4	Represent the organisation using practical PR skills, including preparing effective news releases.
2.5	Explain the supplier interface: negotiating, collaborating, operational and contractual aspects.
2.6	Explain how the organisation fits into a supply chain and works with distribution channels.
2.7	Use networking skills in the business world.
2.8	Explain the concept and application of e-relationships.
2.9	Describe techniques available to assist in managing your manager.

Element 3: Organising and undertaking marketing activities (20%) (Marketing Fundamentals)	
3.1	Describe the scope of individuals' roles in marketing: meetings, conferences, exhibitions, outdoor shows, outlet launches, press conferences.
3.2	Identify alternative and innovative approaches to a variety of marketing arenas and explain criteria for meeting business objectives.
3.3	Demonstrate an awareness of successful applications of marketing across a variety of sectors and sizes of business.
3.4	Explain how marketing makes use of planning techniques: objective setting; and co-ordinating, measuring and evaluating results to support the organisation.
3.5	Appraise and select a venue based on given criteria and make appropriate recommendations.
3.6	Explain how an organisation should host visitors from other cultures and organising across national boundaries.

INTRODUCTION

Element 4: Co-ordinating the marketing mix (20%) (Marketing Fundamentals)	
4.1	Select media to be used based on appropriate criteria for assessing media opportunities, and recommend a media schedule.
4.2	Evaluate promotional activities and opportunities including sales promotion, PR and collaborative programmes.
4.3	Explain the process for designing, developing and producing printed matter, including leaflets, brochures and catalogues.
4.4	Analyse the impact of pricing decisions and role of price within the marketing mix.
4.5	Describe the current distribution channels for an organisation and evaluate new opportunities.
4.6	Describe how organisations monitor product trends.
4.7	Explain the importance of the extended marketing mix: how process, physical aspects and people affect customer choice.
4.8	Explain the importance of ICT in the new mix.

Element 5: Administering the marketing budget (and evaluating results) (20%)	
5.1	Demonstrate an ability to manipulate numbers in a marketing context.
5.2	Explain the process used for setting a budget and apportioning fixed and overhead costs.
5.3	Explain how organisations assess the viability of opportunities, marketing initiatives and projects.
5.4	Prepare, present and justify a budget as the basis for a decision on a marketing promotion.
5.5	Make recommendations on alternative courses of action.
5.6	Examine the correlation between marketing mix decisions and results.
5.7	Evaluate the cost effectiveness of a marketing budget, including a review of suppliers and activities.

Related skills for marketers

There is only so much that a syllabus can include. The syllabus itself is designed to cover the knowledge and skills highlighted by research as core to professional marketers in organisations. However, marketing is performed in an organisational context so there are other broader business and organisational skills that marketing professionals should also posses. The 'key skills for marketers' are therefore an essential part of armoury of the 'complete marketer' in today's organisations. They have been identified from research carried out in organisations where marketers are working.

'Key skills for marketers' are areas of knowledge and competency common to business professionals. They fall outside the CIM's syllabus, providing underpinning knowledge and skills. As such they will be treated as systemic to all marketing activities, rather than subjects treated independently in their turn. While it is not intended that the key skills are formally taught as part of programmes, it is expected that tutors will encourage participants to demonstrate the application of relevant key skills through activities, assignments and discussions during learning.

INTRODUCTION

Using ICT and the Internet

Planning and using different sources to search for and select information; explore, develop and exchange information and derive new information; and present information including text, numbers and images.

Using financial information and metrics

Planning and interpreting information from different sources; carrying out calculations; and presenting and justifying findings.

Presenting information

Contributing to discussions; making a presentation; reading and synthesising information and writing different types of document.

Improving own learning and performance

Agreeing targets and planning how these will be met; using plans to meet targets; and reviewing progress.

Working with others

Planning work and agreeing objectives, responsibilities and working arrangements; seeking to establish and maintain co-operative working relationships; and reviewing work and agreeing ways of future collaborative work.

Problem solving

Exploring problems, comparing different ways of solving them and selecting options; planning and implementing options; and applying agreed methods for checking problems have been solved.

Applying business law

Identifying, applying and checking compliance with relevant law when undertaking marketing activities.

Assessment

CIM will normally offer two forms of assessment for this module from which centres or participants may choose: written examination and continuous assessment. CIM may also recognise, or make joint awards for, modules at an equivalent level undertaken with other professional marketing bodies and educational institutions.

Marketing journals

In addition to reading core and supplementary textbooks participants will be expected to acquire a knowledge and understanding of developments in contemporary marketing theory, practice and issues. The most appropriate sources of information for this include specialist magazines eg *Marketing*, *Marketing Week*, *Campaign and Revolution*; dedicated CIM publications eg *Marketing Business*; and business magazines and newspapers eg *The Economist*, *Management Today*, *Business Week*, *The Financial Times*, and the business pages and supplements of the quality press. A flavour of developments in academic marketing can be derived from the key marketing journals including:

- Admap
- European Journal of Marketing
- Journal of the Academy of Marketing Science
- Journal of Consumer Behaviour: An International Research Review
- Journal of Consumer Research
- Marketing Intelligence and Planning
- Journal of Marketing
- Journal of Marketing Management

Websites

The Chartered Institute of Marketing

www.cim.co.uk	CIM website with information and access to learning support for participants
www.cim.co.uk/learningzone	Direct access to information and support materials for all levels of CIM qualification
www.cim.co.uk/tutors	Access for Tutors
www.shapetheagenda.com	Quarterly agenda paper from CIM

Publications on line

www.ft.com	Extensive research resources across all industry sectors, with links to more specialist reports (Charges may apply)
www.thetimes.co.uk	One of the best online versions of a quality newspaper
www.economist.com	Useful links, and easily-searched archives of articles from back issues of the magazine
www.mad.co.uk	Marketing Week magazine online
www.brandrepublic.com	Marketing magazine online
www.westburn.co.uk	Journal of Marketing Management online, the official Journal of the Academy of Marketing and Marketing Review
http://smr.mit.edu/smr/	Free abstracts from Sloan Management Review articles
www.hbsp.harvard.edu	Free abstracts from Harvard Business Review articles
www.ecommercetimes.com	Daily enews on the latest ebusiness developments
www.cim.co.uk/knowledgehub	3000 full text journals titles are available to members via the Knowledge Hub – includes the range of titles above – embargoes may apply
www.cim.co.uk/cuttingedge	Weekly round up of marketing news (available to CIM members) plus list of awards and forthcoming marketing events

Sources of useful information

www.1to1.com	The Peppers and Rogers One-to-One Marketing site which contains useful information about the tools and techniques of relationship marketing
www.balancetime.com	The Productivity Institute provides free articles, a time management email newsletter, and other resources to improve personal productivity
www.bbc.co.uk	The Learning Zone at BBC Education contains extensive educational resources, including the video, CD Rom, ability to watch TV programmes such as the News online, at your convenience, after they have been screened
www.busreslab.com	Useful specimen online questionnaires to measure customer satisfaction levels and tips on effective Internet marketing research
www.lifelonglearning.co.uk	Encourages and promotes Lifelong Learning through press releases, free articles, useful links and progress reports on the development of the University for Industry (UFI)
www.marketresearch.org.uk	The Market Research Society. Contains useful material on the nature of research, choosing an agency, ethical standards and codes of conduct for research practice
www.nielsen-netratings.com	Details the current levels of banner advertising activity, including the creative content of the ten most popular banners each week (within Top Rankings area)

INTRODUCTION

Sources of useful information

www.open.ac.uk	Some good Open University videos available for a broad range of subjects
www.direct.gov.uk	Gateway to a wide range of UK government information
www.srg.co.uk	The Self Renewal Group – provides useful tips on managing your time, leading others, managing human resources, motivating others etc
www.statistics.gov.uk	Detailed information on a variety of consumer demographics from the Government Statistics Office
www.durlacher.com	The latest research on business use of the Internet, often with extensive free reports
www.cyberatlas.com	Regular updates on the latest Internet developments from a business perspective
http://ecommerce.vanderbilt.edu	eLab is a corporate sponsored research centre at the Owen Graduate School of Management, Vanderbilt University
www.kpmg.co.uk www.ey.com/uk www.pwcglobal.com	The major consultancy company websites contain useful research reports, often free of charge
http://web.mit.edu	Massachusetts Institute of Technology site has extensive research resources
www.adassoc.org.uk	Advertising Association
www.dma.org.uk	The Direct Marketing Association
www.theidm.co.uk	Institute of Direct Marketing
www.export.org.uk	Institute of Export
www.bl.uk	The British Library, with one of the most extensive book collections in the world
www.managers.org.uk	Chartered Management Institute
www.cipd.co.uk	Chartered Institute of Personnel and Development
www.emerald-library.com	Article abstracts on a range of business topics (fees apply)
www.w3.org	An organisation responsible for defining worldwide standards for the Internet

Case studies

www.1800flowers.com	Flower and gift delivery service that allows customers to specify key dates when they request the firm to send them a reminder, together with an invitation to send a gift
www.amazon.co.uk	Classic example of how Internet technology can be harnessed to provide innovative customer service
www.broadvision.com	Broadvision specialises in customer 'personalisation' software. The site contains many useful case studies showing how communicating through the Internet allow you to find out more about your customers
www.doubleclick.net	DoubleClick offers advertisers the ability to target their advertisements on the web through sourcing of specific interest groups, ad display only at certain times of the day, or at particular geographic locations, or on certain types of hardware
www.facetime.com	Good example of a site that overcomes the impersonal nature of the Internet by allowing the establishment of real time links with a customer service representative
www.hotcoupons.com	Site visitors can key in their postcode to receive local promotions, and advertisers can post their offers on the site using a specially designed software package
www.superbrands.org	Access to case studies on international brands

The Exam Paper

Format of the paper

		Number of marks
Part A:	A case study or scenario Compulsory multi-part question relating to the case study (Answer generally required in report format)	40
Part B:	Three questions from a choice of six (20 marks each) relating to the case study (Answer in a variety of business and marketing communication formats)	60
		100

Analysis of past papers

The analysis below shows the topics which have been examined since the new syllabus was introduced.

December 2006

Part A (compulsory question worth 40 marks)

1. A rural Transportation Museum has planned to increase its entrance fees. A range of special events, corporate hospitality and the hosting of an international conference are also planned.

    (a) Calculate total income from admission ticket sales in current year (from data given).
    (b) Calculate projected income from admission ticket sales in following year (from data given).
    (c) Describe three methods of setting marketing budget and recommend one.
    (d) Explain the role of the 3Ps of the extended marketing mix at the Museum.

Part B (three questions, 20 marks each)

2. Use SOST + 6M for outline plan of conference; briefing on cultural issues of overseas visitors
3. Role of PR, direct marketing, personal selling; letter promoting corporate hospitality
4. Impact of environmental factors; information in customer database
5. Press release re special event; sales promotion activities
6. Media schedule for special events; justification; evaluation criteria
7. Info for website; use of website; feedback questionnaire for website

What the examiner said

Candidates show improvement in the use of formats such as letters, press releases, reports and media schedules, and up-to-date knowledge of areas such as websites and cultural issues.

However, previously complained of weaknesses remain a problem, especially:

- Wasted time providing unnecessary formats (eg report introduction) and repeating case study material.
- Inability to use addition, multiplication and percentages correctly. (The requirement for marketers to be able to use numbers is more important than ever, therefore candidates will continue to be tested for numeracy in the compulsory question!)

The examiner warned that sales promotion techniques (applied to specific case study contexts) will be regularly tested, and business-to-business (B2B) marketing will also be a recurring theme.

(Specific feedback on particular questions will be discussed in Exam Tips within the Study Text.)

June 2006

Part A (compulsory question worth 40 marks)

1. A car franchise is looking to increase hire prices, requiring an increase in promotional activity (including a launch event) to maintain business.

    (a) Calculate direct venue costs (from data given).
    (b) Identify indirect costs.
    (c) Recommend venue (from data given) in report format.
    (d) Marketing objectives and evaluation methods for the event.

Part B (three questions, 20 marks each)

2. Even invitation letter; guidance to event staff; international guest issues
3. News release; business networking
4. Customer database information; methods of information gathering
5. Extended marketing mix for customer service; promotional mix to boost demand
6. Calculation of income before and after hire price increase
7. Report on use of ICT for marketing mix, customer loyalty and sales generation

What the examiner said

Numerical questions were generally answered better than previously, and more candidates were able to contextualise their answer to the case study.

However, the application of ICT to the marketing mix was an area of weakness, and few candidates were able to write good news releases and letter formats: these are basic skills, and will be re-assessed in future papers.

(Specific feedback on particular questions will be discussed in Exam Tips within the Study Text.)

December 2005

Part A (compulsory question worth 40 marks)

1. A large arts/cultural festival has gown to the point of needing integrated marketing. There are plans for a number of key events, including a celebrity gala evening.

    (a) Calculate revenue, costs and profit of holding the gala at each of two venues (from data given).
    (b) Identify non-financial factors in venue selection.
    (c) Recommend and justify a choice of venue.
    (d) Draft a letter to potential sponsors of the festival.

Part B (three questions, 20 marks each)

2. Sales promotion techniques and PR activities to build festival audiences
3. Advantages/disadvantages of specified advertising media
4. How service mix elements differ between festival and financial services marketing
5. Issues hosting international guests; using networking and personal selling skills to attract sponsors
6. Use of website; techniques (on-time and off-line) to increase web hits
7. Event plan for festival (using any suitable planning model)

What the examiner said

Candidates show improvement in time management, numerical work and question interpretation. However, marks are being lost through failure to use appropriate formats (eg letters). There seems to be confusion between 'sales promotion' and 'promotion' (as an element of the marketing mix) and between the marketing mix (4Ps), extended marketing mix (7Ps) and service mix (3Ps: people, process, physical evidence). Such basic pitfalls must be avoided!

Candidates must be familiar with syllabus content, including those areas which build on the other three Stage 1 modules. One of the best ways of preparing for the whole examination is to use past papers and review specimen answers.

(More specific feedback on particular questions will be discussed in Exam Tips within the Study Text.)

June 2005

Part A (compulsory question worth 40 marks)

1   A new 'micro' railway franchise is about to be launched.

    (a)   Calculate current income and costs for the railway (from data given).
    (b)   Calculate projected income and costs for the new franchise (from data given).
    (c)   Extended marketing mix to support corporate hospitality product, and how customers would evaluate this product.

Part B (three questions, 20 marks each)

2   Information needed (about local residents) and how used to plan services
3   Key stakeholder groups and their contribution/expectations
4   Local media plan (from data given) and recommendations for nationwide media
5   Press release for local tourism office; employee letter about changes
6   Sales promotion techniques and how they can be evaluated
7   Role of customer service; guidelines for customer service

What the examiner said

General weaknesses included:

- Lack of ability to use addition, multiplication and percentages in the compulsory numerical questions.

- Failure to read question requirements accurately (including using full formal report format, with executive summaries/introduction/findings etc when not required to do so)

- Failure to answer all parts of a question

'Media scheduling, writing news releases or letters, good interpersonal skills and basic budgeting are essential skills at this level, so expect to see these in future papers. Future questions are likely to be broken down into more sub-sections in order to ensure that candidates appreciate what is expected, and what weighting is applied to each part of the question.'

The examining team is trying to help and support you in getting good marks: take note!

(Specific feedback on particular questions will be discussed in Exam Tips within the Study Text.)

December 2004

Part A (compulsory question worth 40 marks)

1. A long-established manufacturer of quality chocolate products is attempting to regain market share. There are plans for a price-based collaborative promotion with a supermarket, and the launch of a new outlet, which may be franchised.

    (a) Calculate sales and profit of two price promotion options from data given.
    (b) Explain how the promotional mix can maximise the sales promotion.

Part B (three questions, 20 marks each)

2. Media schedule (with justification) for the outlet launch
3. Selection of venue for franchise roadshow; presentation on franchise benefits
4. Information needed to appoint franchisees
5. Press release and employee letter promoting the promotion and outlet launch
6. Relationships and communication with franchise holders
7. Report on use of ICT to develop on-going customer relationships

What the examiner said

With improvements in numerical skills and syllabus knowledge, the emphasis must now be on *contextualisation*: students must really imagine themselves in the featured role/scenario.

June 2004

Part A (compulsory question worth 40 marks)

1. Small independent advertising agency, serving local small business clients: three current jobs described.

    (a) Calculate cost of leaflet/advertising work (from data given)
    (b) Identify key relationships
    (c) Calculate charges to leaflet/advertising (from data given)

Part B (three questions, 20 marks each)

2. Media schedule for nightclub launch; factors in media selection
3. Describe sales promotion options; recommend and justify for nightclub
4. Notes for presentation on ICT impact on business
5. Information requirements and use (winning and serving clients)
6. Letter to client evaluating campaign effectiveness
7. Brief new client on conference organisation

December 2003

Part A (compulsory question worth 40 marks)

1. Small marina and boat club, managed by a volunteer committee, membership has been dropping and income is insufficient to cover costs: proposals for change are now on the table.

    (a) Calculate the current annual income (from data given)
    (b) Calculate projected annual income of changes implemented (from data given)
    (c) Letter to club members, seeking support for changes

Part B (three questions, 20 marks each)

2 Relationship building, given part-time/volunteer working
3 Suitability of marina as a conference venue; points looked for
4 Information needed for, and use of, member database
5 Media plan (within set budget) for advertising the marina
6 Use of the extended marketing mix to promote a new venture
7 Role of ICT in marketing the marina

June 2003

Part A (compulsory question worth 40 marks)

1 Independent local radio station. There are plans to raise the station's role in the community and raise listener figures. The station stages live concerts annually and is planning next year's event.

   (a) Calculate the profit made by this year's concert (from data given)
   (b) Calculate projected revenue and profit for next year's concert (from data given)
   (c) Use of the full extended marketing mix by a radio station

Part B (three questions, 20 marks each)

2 Briefing notes: advantages and disadvantages of radio as an advertising medium
3 Use of ICT to build listener loyalty
4 Information needed to profile audience, and how obtained
5 Letter to local newspaper suggesting collaborative promotion
6 Key contacts and relationship building for marketing/promotions executive
7 Use of promotional mix to ensure success of next year's concert

December 2002

Part A (compulsory question worth 40 marks)

1 Ghana-based importer of cars for supply through appointed retailers Africa-wide. Marketing plans include: database marketing, improved advertising, a special anniversary event, and a new retailer.

   (a) Assess advantages and disadvantages of co-operative advertising by retailer and importer
   (b) Calculate monetary value of advertising under two options (from data given)
   (c) Calculate costs of both options (from data given)
   (d) Recommend one of the options

Part B (three questions, 20 marks each)

2 Venue selection criteria and planning Gantt chart for anniversary event
3 Draft response, and further information needs, for new retailer proposal
4 Guidelines for retailers on selecting advertising media
5 Use of full marketing mix to ensure success of new retailer relationship
6 Information needs for new database, and how obtained
7 Use of Internet in relationships with retailers and manufacturers

Pilot paper

Part A (compulsory question worth 40 marks)

1   Company providing an Internet portal for a range of business services and information for the foreign investors in Hungary. Expansion is planned into other countries, and the relationship with the current advertising agency is being reviewed.

   (a)   Calculate cost savings by changing agency (from data supplied)
   (b)   Sample briefing document to show info required in an agency brief
   (c)   Problems of dealing with a new agency/supplier

Part B (three questions, 20 marks each)

2   Competitor audit: how to identify them; information needed, how to obtain/verify the information
3   Steps and Gantt chart for planning a launch event in Turkey
4   Using all elements of promotional submix to promote a 'virtual' company
5   Calculate the company's most profitable business and the effect of changes (from data given)
6   Letter to potential web advertisers; other possible approaches
7   Information needed about website visitors, and how it can be used.

Guide to the Assignment Route

- Aims and objectives of this guide
- Introduction
- Assignment route, structure and process
- Preparing for assignments: general guide
- Presentation
- Time management
- Tips for writing assignments
- Writing reports
- Resources to support Assignment Based Assessment

Aims and objectives of this Guide to the Assignment Route

- To understand the scope and structure of the Assignment Route process
- To consider the benefits of learning through the Assignment Route
- To assist students in preparation of their assignments
- To consider the range of communication options available to students
- To look at the range of potential assignment areas that assignments may challenge
- To examine the purpose and benefits of reflective practice
- To assist with time-management within the assignment process

Introduction

At time of writing, there are over 80 CIM Approved Study Centres that offer the assignment route option as an alternative to examinations. This change in direction and flexibility in assessment was externally driven by industry, students and tutors alike, all of whom wanted a test of practical skills as well as a knowledge-based approach to learning.

At Stage 1, all modules are available via this Assignment Route. The Assignment Route is however optional, and examinations are still available. This will of course depend upon the nature of delivery within your chosen Study Centre.

INTRODUCTION

Clearly, all of the Stage 1 subject areas lend themselves to assignment-based learning, due to their practical nature. The assignments that you will undertake provide you with an opportunity to be **creative in approach and in presentation.** They enable you to give a true demonstration of your marketing ability in a way that perhaps might be inhibited in a traditional examination situation.

The Assignment Route offers you considerable scope to produce work that provides existing and future **employers** with **evidence** of your **ability.** It offers you a **portfolio** of evidence which demonstrates your abilities and your willingness to develop continually your knowledge and skills. It will also, ultimately, help you frame your continuing professional development in the future.

It does not matter what type of organisation you are from, large or small, as you will find substantial benefit in this approach to learning. In some cases, students have made their own organisation central to their assessment and produced work to support their organisation's activities, resulting in subsequent recognition and promotion: a success story for this approach.

So, using your own organisation can be beneficial (especially if your employer sponsors you). However, it is equally valid to use a different organisation, as long as you are familiar enough with it to base your assignments on it. This is particularly useful if you are between jobs, taking time out, returning to employment or studying at university or college.

To take the Assignment Route option, you are required to register with a CIM Accredited Study Centre (ie a college, university, or distance learning provider). **Currently you would be unable to take the Assignment Route option as an independent learner.** If in doubt you should contact the CIM Education Division, the awarding body, who will provide you with a list of local Accredited Centres offering the Assignment Route.

Structure and process

The **assignments** that you will undertake during your studies are normally set **by CIM centrally** and not usually by the study centre. All assignments are validated to ensure a structured, consistent, approach. This standardised approach to assessment enables external organisations to interpret the results on a consistent basis.

Each module at Stage 1 has one assignment, with four separate elements within it. This is broken down as follows.

- The **Core Section** is compulsory and worth 40% of your total mark.

- The **Elective Section** has four options, from which you must complete **two**. Each of these options is worth 25% of your total mark. Please note here that it is likely that in some Study Centres the option may be chosen for you. This is common practice and is done in order to maximise resources and support provided to students.

- The **Reflective Statement** is also compulsory. It is worth 10%. It should reflect what you feel about your learning experience during the module and how that learning has helped you in your career both now and in the future.

The purpose of each assignment is to enable you to demonstrate your ability to research, analyse and problem-solve in a range of different situations. You will be expected to approach your assignment work from a professional marketer's perspective, addressing the assignment brief directly, and undertaking the tasks required. Each assignment will relate directly to the syllabus module and will be applied against the content of the syllabus.

All of the assignments clearly indicate the links with the syllabus and the assignment weighting (ie the contribution each assignment makes to your overall marks).

Once your assignments have been completed, they will be marked by your accredited centre, and then **moderated** by a CIM External Moderator. When all the assignments have been marked, they are sent to CIM for further moderation. After this, all marks are forwarded to you by CIM (not your centre) in the form of an examination result. Your **centre** will be able to you provide you with some written feedback on overall performance, but **will not** provide you with any detailed mark breakdown.

Preparing for Assignments: general guide

The whole purpose of this guide is to assist you in presenting your assessment professionally, both in terms of presentation skills and overall content. In many of the assignments, marks are awarded for presentation and coherence. It might therefore be helpful to consider how best to present your assignment. Here you should consider issues of detail, protocol and the range of communications that could be called upon within the assignment.

Presentation of the Assignment

You should always ensure that you prepare two copies of your assignment, keeping a soft copy on disc. On occasions assignments go missing, or second copies are required by CIM.

- Each Assignment should be clearly marked up with your name, your study centre, your CIM Student registration number and ultimately at the end of the assignment a word count. The assignment should also be word-processed.

- The assignment presentation format should directly meet the requirements of the assignment brief, (ie reports and presentations are the most called for communication formats). You **must** ensure that you assignment does not appear to be an extended essay. If it does, you will lose marks.

- The word limit will be included in the assignment brief. These are specified by CIM and must be adhered to.

- Appendices should clearly link to the assignment and can be attached as supporting documentation at the end of the report. However failure to reference them by number (eg Appendix 1) within the report and also marked up on the Appendix itself will lose you marks. Only use an Appendix if it is essential and clearly adds value to the overall Assignment. The Appendix is not a waste bin for all the materials you have come across in your research, or a way of making your assignment seem somewhat heavier and more impressive than it is.

Time management for Assignments

One of the biggest challenges we all seem to face day-to-day is that of managing time. When studying, that challenge seems to grow increasingly difficult, requiring a balance between work, home, family, social life and study life. It is therefore of pivotal importance to your own success for you to plan wisely the limited amount of time you have available.

Step 1   **Find out how much time you have**

Ensure that you are fully aware of how long your module lasts, and the final deadline. If you are studying a module from September to December, it is likely that you will have only 10-12 weeks in which to complete your assignments. This means that you will be preparing assignment work continuously throughout the course.

Step 2   **Plan your time**

Essentially you need to **work backwards** from the final deadline, submission date, and schedule your work around the possible time lines. Clearly if you have only 10-12 weeks available to complete three assignments, you will need to allocate a block of hours in the final stages of the module to ensure that all of your assignments are in on time. This will be critical as all assignments will be sent to CIM by a set day. Late submissions will not be

INTRODUCTION

accepted and no extensions will be awarded. Students who do not submit will be treated as a 'no show' and will have to resubmit for the next period and undertake an alternative assignment.

Step 3 — Set priorities

You should set priorities on a daily and weekly basis (not just for study, but for your life). There is no doubt that this mode of study needs commitment (and some sacrifices in the short term). When your achievements are recognised by colleagues, peers, friends and family, it will all feel worthwhile.

Step 4 — Analyse activities and allocate time to them

Consider the **range** of activities that you will need to undertake in order to complete the assignment and the **time** each might take. Remember, too, there will be a delay in asking for information and receiving it.

- Preparing terms of reference for the assignment, to include the following.

    1. A short title
    2. A brief outline of the assignment purpose and outcome
    3. Methodology – what methods you intend to use to carry out the required tasks
    4. Indication of any difficulties that have arisen in the duration of the assignment
    5. Time schedule
    6. Confidentiality – if the assignment includes confidential information ensure that this is clearly marked up and indicated on the assignment
    7. Literature and desk research undertaken

    This should be achieved in one side of A4 paper.

- A literature search in order to undertake the necessary background reading and underpinning information that might support your assignment
- Writing letters and memos asking for information either internally or externally
- Designing questionnaires
- Undertaking surveys
- Analysis of data from questionnaires
- Secondary data search
- Preparation of first draft report

Always build in time to spare, to deal with the unexpected. This may reduce the pressure that you are faced with in meeting significant deadlines.

Warning!

The same principles apply to a student with 30 weeks to do the work. However, a word of warning is needed. Do not fall into the trap of leaving all of your work to the last minute. If you miss out important information or fail to reflect upon your work adequately or successfully you will be penalised for both. Therefore, time management is important whatever the duration of the course.

Tips for writing Assignments

Everybody has a personal style, flair and tone when it comes to writing. However, no matter what your approach, you must ensure your assignment meets the **requirements of the brief** and so is comprehensible, coherent and cohesive in approach.

Think of preparing an assignment as preparing for an examination. Ultimately, the work you are undertaking results in an examination grade. Successful achievement of all four modules in a level results in a qualification.

There are a number of positive steps that you can undertake in order to ensure that you make the best of your assignment presentation in order to maximise the marks available.

Step 1 Work to the brief

Ensure that you identify exactly what the assignment asks you to do.

- If it asks you to be a marketing manager, then immediately assume that role.
- If it asks you to prepare a report, then present a report, not an essay or a letter.
- Furthermore, if it asks for 2,500 words, then do not present 1,000 or 4,000 unless it is clearly justified, agreed with your tutor and a valid piece of work.

Identify whether the report should be **formal or informal**; who it should be **addressed to**; its **overall purpose** and its **potential use** and outcome. Understanding this will ensure that your assignment meets fully the requirements of the brief and addresses the key issues included within it.

Step 2 Addressing the tasks

It is of pivotal importance that you address **each** of the tasks within the assignment. **Many students fail to do this** and often overlook one of the tasks or indeed part of the tasks.

Many of the assignments will have two or three tasks, some will have even more. You should establish quite early on, which of the tasks:

- Require you to collect information
- Provides you with the framework of the assignment, i.e. the communication method.

Possible tasks will include the following.

- *Compare and contrast.* Take two different organisations and compare them side by side and consider the differences ie the **contrasts** between the two.
- *Carry out primary or secondary research.* Collect information to support your assignment and your subsequent decisions
- *Prepare a plan.* Some assignments will ask you to prepare a plan for an event or for a marketing activity – if so provide a step-by-step approach, a rationale, a time-line, make sure it is measurable and achievable. Make sure your actions are very specific and clearly explained. (Make sure your plan is SMART.)
- *Analyse a situation.* This will require you to collect information, consider its content and present an overall understanding of the situation as it exists. This might include looking at internal and external factors and how the current situation evolved.
- *Make recommendations.* The more advanced your get in your studies, the more likely it is that you will be required to make recommendations. Firstly **considering and evaluating your options** and then making justifiable **recommendations**, based on them.

INTRODUCTION

- *Justify decisions.* You may be required to justify your decision or recommendations. This will require you to explain fully how you have arrived at as a result and to show why, supported by relevant information. In other words, you should not make decisions in a vacuum; as a marketer your decisions should always be informed by context.

- *Prepare a presentation.* This speaks for itself. If you are required to prepare a presentation, ensure that you do so, preparing clearly defined PowerPoint or overhead slides that are not too crowded and that clearly express the points you are required to make.

- *Evaluate performance.* It is very likely that you will be asked to evaluate a campaign, a plan or even an event. You will therefore need to consider its strengths and weaknesses, why it succeeded or failed, the issues that have affected it, what can you learn from it and, importantly, how can you improve performance or sustain it in the future.

All of these points are likely requests included within a task. Ensure that you identify them clearly and address them as required.

Step 3 Information Search

Many students fail to realise the importance of collecting information to **support** and **underpin** their assignment work. However, it is vital that you demonstrate to your centre and to the CIM your ability to **establish information needs**, obtain **relevant information** and **utilise it sensibly** in order to arrive at appropriate decisions.

You should establish the nature of the information required, follow up possible sources, time involved in obtaining the information, gaps in information and the need for information.

Consider these factors very carefully. CIM are very keen that students are **seen** to collect information, **expand** their mind and consider the **breadth** and **depth** of the situation. In your *Personal Development Portfolio*, you have the opportunity to complete a **Resource Log**, to illustrate how you have expanded your knowledge to aid your personal development. You can record your additional reading and research in that log, and show how it has helped you with your portfolio and assignment work.

Step 4 Develop an Assignment Plan

Your **assignment** needs to be structured and coherent, addressing the brief and presenting the facts as required by the tasks. The only way you can successfully achieve this is by **planning the structure** of your Assignment in advance.

Earlier on in this unit, we looked at identifying your tasks and, working backwards from the release date, in order to manage time successfully. The structure and coherence of your assignment needs to be planned with similar signs.

In planning out the Assignment, you should plan to include **all the relevant information as requested** and also you should plan for the use of models, diagrams and appendices where necessary.

Your plan should cover your:

- Introduction
- Content
- Main body of the assignment
- Summary
- Conclusions and recommendations where appropriate

Step 5 Prepare Draft Assignment

It is good practice to always produce a **first draft** of a report. You should use it to ensure that you have met the aims and objectives, assignment brief and tasks related to the actual assignment. A draft document provides you with scope for improvements, and enables you to check for accuracy, spelling, punctuation and use of English.

Step 6 Prepare Final Document

In the section headed 'Presentation of the Assignment' in this unit, there are a number of components that should always be in place at the beginning of the assignment documentation, including **labelling** of the assignment, **word counts**, **appendices** numbering and presentation method. Ensure that you **adhere to the guidelines presented**, or alternatively those suggested by your Study Centre.

Writing reports

Students often ask 'what do they mean by a report?' or 'what should the report format include?'.

There are a number of approaches to reports, formal or informal: some report formats are company specific and designed for internal use, rather than external reporting.

For Continuous Assessment process, you should stay with traditional formats.

Below is a suggested layout of a Management Report Document that might assist you when presenting your assignments.

- *A Title Page* includes the title of the report, the author of the report and the receiver of the report

- *Acknowledgements* – this should highlight any help, support, or external information received and any extraordinary co-operation of individuals or organisations

- *Contents page* provides a clearly structured pathway of the contents of the report – page by page.

- *Executive summary* – a brief insight into purpose, nature and outcome of the report, in order that the outcome of the report can be quickly established

- *Main body of the report divided into sections, which are clearly labelled.* Suggested labelling would be on a numbered basis eg:
  - 1.0 Introduction
  - 1.1 Situation Analysis
  - 1.1.1 External Analysis
  - 1.1.2 Internal Analysis

- *Conclusions* – draw the report to a conclusion, highlighting key points of importance, that will impact upon any recommendations that might be made

- *Recommendations* – clearly outline potential options and then recommendations. Where appropriate justify recommendations in order to substantiate your decision

- *Appendices* – ensure that you only use appendices that add value to the report. Ensure that they are numbered and referenced on a numbered basis within the text. If you are not going to reference it within the text, then it should not be there

- *Bibliography* – whilst in a business environment a bibliography might not be necessary, for an **assignment-based report it is vital**. It provides an indication of the level of research, reading and collecting of relevant information that has taken place in order to fulfil the requirements of the assignment task. Where possible, and where relevant, you could provide academic references within the text, which should of course then provide the basis of your bibliography. References should realistically be listed alphabetically and in the following sequence

- Author's name and edition of the text
- Date of publication
- Title and sub-title (where relevant)
- Edition 1st, 2nd etc
- Place of publication
- Publisher
- Series and individual volume number where appropriate.

Resources to support Assignment Based Assessment

The aim of this guidance is to present you with a range of questions and issues that you should consider, based upon the assignment themes. The detail to support the questions can be found within your BPP Study Text and the 'Core Reading' recommended by CIM.

Additionally you will find useful support information within the CIM Student website www.cim.co.uk -: www.cimvirtualinstitute.com, where you can access a wide range of marketing information and case studies. You can also build your own workspace within the website so that you can quickly and easily access information specific to your professional study requirements. Other websites you might find useful for some of your assignment work include www.wnim.com - (What's New in Marketing) and also www.connectedinmarketing.com - another CIM website.

Other websites include:

Website	Description
www.mad.com	Marketing Week
www.ft.com	Financial Times
www.thetimes.com	The Times newspaper
www.theeconomist.com	The Economist magazine
www.marketing.haynet.com	Marketing magazine
www.ecommercetimes.com	Daily news on e-business developments
www.open.gov.uk	Gateway to a wide range of UK government information
www.adassoc.org.uk	The Advertising Association
www.marketresearch.org.uk	The Marketing Research Society
www.amazon.com	Online Book Shop
www.1800flowers.com	Flower and delivery gift service
www.childreninneed.com	Charitable organisation
www.comicrelief.com	Charitable organisation
www.samaritans.org.uk	Charitable organisation

Background to case study: The Needle Works

The following is background information for our Needle Works case study, which you will require to tackle Action Programmes throughout this Study Text. You may like to detach or photocopy it for ease of reference.

Background information

The Needle Works Ltd is a company retailing and distributing a wide range of products and services related to needlecraft. It currently has one large high street store and a small factory.

The Needle Works' products initially consisted of various kits, patterns and supplies (threads and yarns, needles, hoops) for common forms of needlecraft, sourced from designers and manufacturers in the UK and USA. These suppliers range from major corporations to small providers, especially in the emerging arena of hand-spun and naturally dyed materials.

In recent years, The Needle Works has diversified into

(a) more specialised craft niches, with materials, patterns and related products for particular forms such as silk embroidery, goldwork, beadwork and teddy-bear making;

(b) related retail areas such as instructional and coffee-table books and magazines, accessories (such as collectible thimbles, technical aids like magnifying lights and scissor-holders);

(c) related services, including finishing and framing of craft works (and pictures and posters), the design and manufacture of adjustable tapestry frames (on which work-in-progress is mounted and stretched), the valuation (for insurance purposes) of finished works, and the charting of designs.

The craft market is specialised, but surprisingly diverse. The customers at The Needle Works' London store include many women aged 50+, but also a small proportion of men, and an increasing number of young people of both sexes, due to a renaissance of interest in hand-made and decorated textiles in design and fashion colleges. Several ethnic communities (notably Middle-Eastern and central European) are regular customers, and tourists, particularly from the Far East, are major one-off customers. There are also some 'institutional' clients, such as old age homes and therapy units since traditional crafts are seen as a way of improving motor skills, increasing self-esteem and controlling stress.

The Needle Works is a family-founded and owned business, which has grown by word-of-mouth and specialist response to the market's needs over the years. It is relatively unstructured, since the management team is quite small.

INTRODUCTION

Mr and Mrs Smith founded the business. Their eldest son, Albert, has recently been appointed General Manager in order to modernise the business. He has now appointed you, with the title of Marketing Co-ordinator, to 'take in hand' the marketing of the store and its services.

Marketing has so far been rudimentary, and there is no 'marketing budget' as such: each task is tackled separately on the basis of need and cost-effectiveness. Some advertising used to be placed in specialised magazines in the craft sector, but a high-street presence, word-of-mouth and the boast of having 'the UK's largest range of needlecraft designs and supplies' has seen a steady level of business, without further promotion. This has been aided by:

(a) the gradual disappearance of small competitors, giving The Needle Works increasing status as a needlecraft 'Super Store', and increasing market share; and

(b) attractive in-store displays, promotions and seasonal sales.

Turnover is in the region of £2.6 million per year. (An average purchase is £20. Prices range from 60p for thread to £600 for a large kit.) There is a customer database, generated by a Visitor's Book in the store, in which all visiting customers are asked to enter their name, address and comments. (These are mostly of a 'love your store!' variety.) These names and addresses are periodically typed into a basic Microsoft Access database, together with order details entered into the store's point of sale computer. There are currently 10,000 names and addresses on this database.

Any promotional items (discount vouchers, mailing letters and so on) are produced in-house. The office computer has some basic DTP software. Susan Jones 'can design a bit', and Mr Smith is an accomplished calligrapher and illustrator.

Albert Smith has recently acquired the lease of additional floor space in the block of which The Needle Works showroom has the street-level frontage. This presents a significant opportunity to expand the business. Current ideas include a knitting supplies shop (a logical extension to a related craft area) and a craft education centre, running classes in the various crafts for which the business sells supplies (both a direct revenue-earner and a promotional, market-expanding tool).

This is the context in which you have been employed as Marketing Co-ordinator. Good luck!

The Needle Works
6-10 High Street
Old Town
London NW

Part A
Gathering, analysing and presenting information

Information for marketing

Chapter topic list

1. Integrated learning
2. The importance of information
3. Marketing research
4. Sources of information
5. Evaluating, presenting and using information

Syllabus content – knowledge and skills requirements

- 1.1 Identify sources of information internally and externally to the organisation, including ICT-based sources such as intranet and Internet
- 1.7 Gather information across borders

PART A   GATHERING, ANALYSING AND PRESENTING INFORMATION

Introduction

Part A of this Study Text deals with the gathering, analysing and presenting of information for marketing. This chapter introduces the idea that information is vital for decision making, and gives an overview of the types of information that can be obtained through marketing research. It also discusses the various sources of information. You can draw upon your studies of *Marketing Environment* here.

Chapters 2, 3 and 4 explore further aspects of information gathering. Chapter 2 focuses on the customer database as a source of information for marketing. Chapter 3 gives you some practical research skills for tapping into primary sources. Chapter 4 expands on the need and methodologies for gathering information about the marketing environment, competitor activity and marketing opportunities.

1 Integrated learning

FAST FORWARD

The assessment of *Marketing in Practice* by case study requires you to assimilate a body of information and to use that information in decision-making and in carrying out marketing tasks. You are also required to appreciate what further information might be needed in order to make decisions, and where it might be obtained.

This chapter should be regarded as an introduction to concepts and skills which underpin the whole *Marketing in Practice* syllabus and assessment.

(a) **Building and developing relationships** (as we will discover in Part B of this Text) requires the exchange of information and tapping into information sources.

(b) **Organising and undertaking marketing activities** (Part C) requires the gathering of information on options, costs, schedules, availability and a host of other strategic and operational matters.

(c) **Co-ordinating the marketing mix** (Part D) likewise requires the monitoring of the marketing environment and competitor activity, the strengths and weaknesses of the organisation's marketing plans, and the effects of pricing decisions, product developments and promotional messages on performance.

(d) **Administering the marketing budget and evaluating results** (Part E) requires detailed costing and performance feedback information.

Exam tip

The essential point to remember is the role that information plays in all marketing activity and decision-making. You may be tempted to take this for granted, but it is the core underlying theme of this syllabus.

2 The importance of information

2.1 Information flows

FAST FORWARD

Information (measurement, facts and data, analysis) is required for **rational decision making**, particularly for marketing, which requires a detailed, realistic understanding of the customer's needs and wants, the marketing mix and the marketing environment.

It would be impossible to list all the possible uses of information in a business organisation. In a sense, an organisation is a **system of information flows**: Figure 1.1

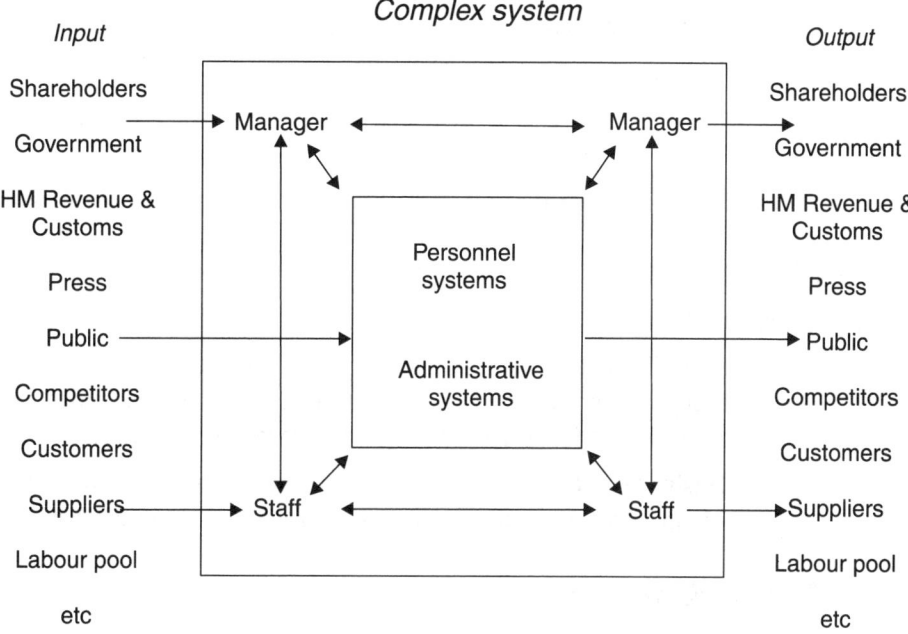

Figure 1.1: The organisation as an information system

All human action and decision-making is based, consciously or unconsciously, on information: about the **environment**, the **needs or wants** of the individual, the **likely outcomes** of the action or decision (based on past experience or the advice of others) and so on.

Since an organisation is defined as a 'social arrangement for **the controlled performance of collective goals**' (*Huczynski and Buchanan*, 2001) it is even more important that decisions should be rational and based on appropriate information about all the variables involved, about the goals to be reached, and about the performance process and results.

 Marketing at Work

Procter & Gamble have devised a Statement of Business Principles, setting out 10 guiding principles for all their activity. The top three are as follows:

1   *Plan all action in advance.* Always forecast business in relation to expenditure, always check that the business is reaching objectives according to forecast, and always be ready to adjust plans as necessary.

2   *Base all actions on facts.* One fact is worth many judgements. Strive always to find the factual truth as a subject before acting. This applies to all fields of business: product, packaging, advertising, promotions and expenditure.

3   *Always know the objective of your actions.* Know what advertising, individual promotions and sales plans are intended to do and judge their success by whether they achieve objectives.

Drucker (1955) wrote that: 'Marketing is the whole business seen from the point of view of its final result, that is from the **customer's** point of view'. A marketing orientation to business suggests that the purpose of business activity is to *find out what people want*, and to give it to them: to make what you can sell, not sell what you can make. This clearly requires the gathering and use of information.

2.1.1 How much information?

Having said that information is necessary for all decision making, some points must be recognised.

(a) Most decisions are based on **incomplete information**.

   (i) All possible information is not available

   (ii) Beyond a certain point, the gathering of more information would not be worth the extra time and cost of obtaining and analysing it

(b) **Too much information** makes decision-making harder rather than easier.

2.1.2 Where do we find information?

Information can be sourced:

(a) **Inside the organisation**. This is information we already have, such as sales figures, reports, price lists, literature, customer information etc. It may be stored electronically in a central database or in forms and files scattered throughout the organisation.

(b) **Outside the organisation**. Information we don't have, but can get access to, often at a cost – from customers, suppliers, research organisations, publishers, websites and so on.

2.2 The marketing information system

> **FAST FORWARD**
>
> The **marketing information system** is 'the framework for the day-to-day management and structuring of information gathered regularly from sources both inside and outside an organisation' (Dibb *et al.*, 2001).

As you will appreciate from your studies in *Marketing Environment*, a wide range of information is systematically gathered for marketing purposes. Some examples include:

- Prices
- Advertising expenditure
- Sales
- Competitor activity
- Distribution costs
- Stock levels
- Attributes of potential promotional/supply chain partners
- Buyer behaviour (and the social trends affecting it)
- PESTLE (Political, Economic, Socio-cultural, Technological, Legal and Environmental) factors affecting the marketing environment
- Internal audit (and/or SWOT analysis) of the organisation's marketing capabilities

Action Programme 1

Make a poster of the three Procter & Gamble business principles listed earlier.

Exam tip

Sources and *uses* of information are frequent areas of exam questioning. Make sure you can distinguish clearly between aspects such as:

(i) What sort of information is needed
(ii) Where the information can be obtained
(iii) How the information will be obtained
(iv) What it will be used for

3 Marketing research

FAST FORWARD

Marketing decisions are made under conditions of uncertainty and risk. Marketing research aims to **reduce the risk** by providing information about the variables involved in the decision, and the possible outcomes of particular decisions and actions.

(Dibb et al.)

Key concept

Marketing research is 'the process of gathering, interpreting and reporting information to help marketers solve specific marketing problems or take advantage of marketing opportunities'.

3.1 Research for marketing

FAST FORWARD

Marketing research can operate across the extended marketing mix and the marketing environment.

A wide variety of information may be relevant to marketing decisions.

(a) **Market research** involves the gathering of information about the market for a particular produce or service: consumer attitudes, environmental influences on supply and demand, competition, product usage and so on.

- Analysis of the market potential for existing products
- Forecasting likely demand for new products
- Sales forecasting for all products
- Study of market trends
- Study of the characteristics of the market
- Analysis of market shares

(b) **Product research** is concerned with the product – whether in development, new, improved or already on the market – and how customers respond (or are likely to respond) to it.

- Customer acceptance of proposed new products
- Comparative studies between competitive products
- Studies into packaging and design
- Forecasting new uses for existing products
- Test marketing
- Research into the development of a product line (range)

(c) **Price research**

- Analysis of elasticities of demand
- Analysis of costs and contribution or profit margins
- The effect of changes in credit policy on demand
- Customer perceptions of price (and quality)

(d) **Sales/promotion research**

- Motivation research for advertising and sales promotion effectiveness
- Analysing the effect of advertising or direct marketing on sales demand
- Analysing the effectiveness of individual aspects of advertising such as copy and media used
- Establishing sales territories
- Analysing the effectiveness of sales teams
- Analysing the effectiveness of other promotional methods and the promotional mix as a whole

(e) **Distribution research**
 - The location and design of distribution centres
 - The analysis of packaging for transportation and shelving
 - Dealer supply requirements
 - Dealer advertising requirements
 - The cost of different methods of transportation and warehousing

As you can see, information can be gathered across the 'four Ps' of the marketing mix (and indeed the 'seven Ps' of the extended marketing mix, as we will discuss in Chapter 14), and the marketing environment.

Exam tip

> A key theme of recent questions has been *'What information do you need for …?'*. In June 2003, it was for profiling the customer (audience) base of a local radio station. In December 2003, it was for a proposed database of current and future members of a small boat club. In June 2004: winning and serving clients of an advertising agency; in December 2005, selecting franchisees; in June 2005, tailoring a marketing mix to potential railway customers; in June 2006, segmenting the customer base of a car hire/sales company. Questions also tend to ask *'How could this information be obtained?'* (as in June 2003 and June 2006) and/or *'How could this information be used?'* (as in December 2003 and June 2005). Get used to asking these three questions in relation to decisions you make – or read about in your studies.

3.2 Primary and secondary research

FAST FORWARD

> Data may be derived from **primary** or **secondary sources**.

One way of classifying research approaches is by the nature of the sources of data they use.

Key concepts

> **Primary data** are data collected especially for a particular purpose, directly from the relevant source.
>
> **Secondary data** are data which have already been gathered and assembled for other purposes or general reference.

Primary sources of consumer information, for example, would be the consumers themselves. Primary research is usually '**field research**', involving surveys, interviews, questionnaires, observation or experiments. These techniques will be discussed in Chapter 3.

Secondary sources of consumer information would include published statistics and reports on consumer behaviour, books, Internet sites and so on. They are accessed by '**desk research**' which can often be carried out literally from the researcher's desk (given access to appropriate reference sources). We discuss these sources of information below.

3.3 Quantitative and qualitative research

FAST FORWARD

> Data may be **qualitative** (psychographic) and/or **quantitative** (statistical, demographic).

Another way of classifying research approaches is according to the type of data gathered.

Key concepts

> **Quantitative research** gathers statistically valid, numerically measurable data.
>
> **Qualitative research** focuses on information that is difficult to quantify, such as values, attitudes, opinions, beliefs and motivations.

1: INFORMATION FOR MARKETING

Quantitative research answers questions such as: How many? What percentage? How often? How many times? How much? Where? This is essentially *demographic*, statistical information, telling the marketer who buys what, and where, in what quantities and at what price.

While quantitative data may show that 75% of men aged 18-35 drive a car, *qualitative* data might reveal how they go about choosing a car, how they feel about their car, what would make them change cars and so on. This is essentially *psychographic* information.

As we will see in Chapter 3, quantitative data is usually gathered by survey, and qualitative data by personal interviews and discussion groups. Both types of data may be gathered from primary and/or secondary sources.

Action Programme 2

Give examples of qualitative and/or quantitative data that might be gathered in the following circumstances.

(a) The sales of a product appear to be declining in a particular region.
(b) You want to know whether customers would support night-time opening.
(c) You are about to schedule TV advertising.

4 Sources of information

FAST FORWARD

Secondary sources of information include:

- internal data records
- published information
- bought-in reports
- the Internet and intranet
- general environmental scanning

All these sources are available **internationally**, for gathering cross-border data.

As we saw above, **primary** sources of information are basically 'the horse's mouth', whoever that may be: customers, consumers, supply chain partners or other businesses. We will look at techniques for gathering primary data in Chapters 2 and 3 of this Text.

Here, we will look at **secondary** sources of information.

- Existing data generated and held by the organisation
- Published information, both general and industry specific
- Bought-in market research reports
- The Internet
- General 'environmental scanning'

4.1 Internal data records

The following information gathered in the course of operations and transactions may be relevant to marketing planning and control.

- Production data about quantities produced, materials and labour used etc
- Data about inventory
- Data about sales volumes
- Data about marketing, promotion and brand data
- All cost and management accounting data
- Financial management data

PART A GATHERING, ANALYSING AND PRESENTING INFORMATION

Such information often goes back several years, so that comparisons can be made and trends extrapolated.

4.2 Published information

The **government** is a major source of economic, industrial and demographic information. Examples of government publications are as follows.

(a) *The Annual Abstract of Statistics* and its monthly equivalent, the *Monthly Digest of Statistics*. These contain data about manufacturing output, housing, population etc.

(b) *Economic Trends* (monthly), *Social Trends* (annually) and *Labour Market Trends* (monthly).

(c) *Census of Population*. The Office for National Statistics publishes continuous datasets including the National Food Survey, the Household Survey and the Family Expenditure Survey.

(d) *Census of Production* (annual). This has been described as 'one of the most important sources of desk research for industrial marketers'. It provides data about production by firms in each industry in the UK.

(e) *British Business*, published weekly by the Department of Trade and Industry, gives data on industrial and commercial trends at home and overseas.

(f) *Business Monitor* (published by the Office for National Statistics), gives detailed information about various industries.

Official statistics are also published by other government bodies such as the European Union, the United Nations and local authorities.

Non-government sources of information include the following.

(a) Companies and other organisations specialising in the provision of economic and financial data (eg Reuters and the Thomson Extel Survey).

(b) Directories and yearbooks, such as Kompass or Kelly's Directory.

(c) Professional institutions (eg Chartered Institute of Marketing, Chartered Management Institute, Institute of Practitioners in Advertising).

(d) Specialist libraries, such as the City Business Library in London, which collect published information from a wide variety of sources.

(e) Trade associations, trade unions and Chambers of Commerce.

(f) Trade and professional journals, newspapers and commentaries (and their websites).

(g) Commercial organisations such as banks and TV networks.

(h) Surveys produced by research agencies (Gallup, MORI, Mintel, Euromonitor).

Marketing at Work

Euromonitor's website makes available (at cost) detailed **profiles of countries and markets**. Summaries can be viewed free. Links to relevant information sources are also provided. For example (latest available at May 2007):

Country factfile: Malaysia

Socio-economic indicators

	Unit	2005	2006	2007
Population aged 65+	'000	1,106.47	1,140.82	1,182.26
Annual disposable income	$US million	68,127.29	69,259.29	71,453.38
Consumer expenditure	$US million	47,951.41	49,438.32	
New registrations of passenger cars	'000			
Consumer expenditure on food	$US million	10,210.00	10,666.60	10,918.10
Internet users	'000	10,813.01	11,655.84	12,4128.84
Soft drink market	Million litres	970	1,012	1,053

Source

International Marketing Data and Statistics 2006
World Consumer Lifestyles Databook 2006
Consumer Asia 2006
World Consumer Spending 2006-2007
Bank Negara Malaysia (Central Bank of Malaysia)   (www.bnm.gov.my)
Jabatan Perangkaan Malaysia (Department of Statistics)   (www.statistics.gov.my)

www.euromonitor.com

While some of the above sources are general and others trade-, market- or profession-specific, bear in mind that general information may be applicable to your target market: keep an open mind and active 'antennae' for relevant data. Department of Transport budgets, for example, may be on the need-to-know list for car manufacturers.

Action Programme 3

Does your organisation, or individual department, have a library or libraries of published materials such as books, reference works, trade journals or newspapers? What titles are regularly stocked? How often is the information updated? How is the information categorised or indexed?

4.3 Bought-in reports

Much of the above published material is in the public domain. It is accessible and inexpensive to gather, but may need considerable analysis and processing in order to produce sufficiently targeted information for a specific organisation's needs. On the other hand, tailor-made information is only available by commissioning or undertaking primary research, which is a costly exercise.

A middle course may be to buy in reports prepared externally, whether as primary research for another organisation which is then syndicated, or as a commercial service to industry data users.

4.4 Audits

Various **audits** generate published reports which can also be bought by marketers.

4.4.1 Consumer panels or home audit panels

Consumer panels consist of a representative sample of consumers who have agreed to have their attitudes and buying habits monitored over a period of time. There are established panels for the purchase of groceries, consumer durables, cars, baby products and many others.

Audits of Great Britain (AGB) ran the Television Consumer Audit for 25 years which estimated the purchase of groceries and frozen foods for home consumption in a sample of 6,300 households in the UK. It has recently been replaced by the high-tech Superpanel, which allows the households to scan data directly from purchases into the database by means of barcodes after every shopping trip.

Consumer panels generate a vast amount of data which need to be sorted if they are to be digestible.

(a) Standard trend analysis shows how the market and its major brands have fared since the last analysis, grossed up to reflect the population.

(b) Special analyses depend on industrial preferences.
- Source of purchase analysis
- Frequency of purchase analysis
- Demographic analysis
- Tracking of individuals, to show their degree of brand loyalty

4.4.2 Trade and retail audits

Trade audits are carried out among panels of wholesalers and retailers, and the term **'retail audits'** refers to panels of retailers only. A research firm sends 'auditors' to selected outlets at regular intervals to count stock and deliveries, thus enabling an estimate of throughput to be made. Sometimes it is possible to do a universal audit of all retail outlets: EPOS (electronic point of sale systems) makes the process both easier and more universal.

The audits provide details of the following.

(a) **Retail sales** for selected products and brands, sales by different type of retail outlet, market shares and brand shares.

(b) **Retail stocks** of products and brands (enabling a firm subscribing to the audit to compare stocks of its own goods with those of competitors).

(c) **Selling prices** in retail outlets, including information about discounts.

4.5 The Internet – 'cyber research'

Key concepts

The **Internet** (or 'information superhighway', or 'World Wide Web') is a collection of computers and computer networks, via which users can access and share database information, and send and receive electronic messages world-wide at speed.

Information and Communication Technology (ICT) is a collective term for computer and telecommunication based technologies, used extensively in modern communication and data processing applications. ICT includes: the Internet, websites and email; mobile phone applications; digital TV and radio; database management and customer relationship management (CRM) software; and so on.

The Internet can be a fast, efficient way to search for and access secondary data world-wide.

(a) Governments, educational institutions, libraries, commercial organisations and agencies have websites which contain information and include links to other sites where information can be found. Well-designed sites typically have their own indexes and menus, as well as marked hypertext links that allow the browser to 'jump' to related areas and topics.

(b) **Search engines** (such as Google and Yahoo!) maintain large databases of web pages, and can be used to locate relevant sites by word search.

(c) '**Newsgroups**' and mailing lists act as a kind of bulletin board service, where people post messages and articles on various topics.

It can be difficult conducting an efficient data search unless you know what you are doing. However, the Internet is friendly enough for you to be able to **browse** in areas of interest and follow links. As you discover relevant sources of information, you can 'bookmark' them, or add them to your 'Favourites' list to create a shortcut for regular reference.

Exam tip

> When an exam question asks you to enumerate the 'uses of ICT' in marketing, you may immediately think of *promotional* uses (such as web-, email-based or SMS marketing) and/or *customer relationship management* uses (such as computer-telephony integration and databases). Don't forget the *information-gathering* applications of ICT: accessing databases and reports for market information, inviting customers to fill in online feedback forms, gathering e-mail contacts and so on. (The design of an online feedback questionnaire, asking users about their experience of the website itself, was set in the December 2006 exam, for example.)

4.6 Intranet

Intranets are mini versions of the Internet connecting computers within an organisation. Each employee or terminal has a browser which gives access to corporate information.

Intranets can be used to disseminate corporate information on a wide variety of topics, as well as to facilitate file-sharing and database access. Potential applications may be illustrated by the following examples.

(a) Silicon Graphics' intranet has 150,000 pages and is used daily by about 4,000 of the company's 8,000 staff. Besides being used as the company's daily newspaper the intranet has been found to be a particularly effective method of induction for new staff.

(b) One of the most successful intranet uses is the personnel Web page, which allows anyone in the firm to see what their colleagues are doing and how they are progressing.

(c) Extensive internal databases can be built, so that an employee can enter search words and bring up relevant files and data (eg on customers or suppliers, product availability, market research and so on).

(d) Intranets offer a new way of putting together '**groupware**' – software to support group working.

4.7 General 'environmental scanning'

Environmental scanning is simply the process of keeping your 'radar' switched on to what is going on in your market place. **Market intelligence** can be gleaned in many ways.

- Any newspaper, magazine, trade or academic journal
- Conferences, exhibitions, trade shows
- Personal contacts in the trade
- Personal experience and observation of the market

PART A GATHERING, ANALYSING AND PRESENTING INFORMATION

Action Programme 4

Here is a small selection of headlines from *The Daily Telegraph newspaper (UK)*.

(a) Two tube (London's underground rail system) strikes a week being planned by unions
(b) Inquiries pour in for jobs at Siemens
(c) Protesters halt royal tree felling
(d) Film comeback for Mickey Mouse at 67

In each case: what sort of organisations should take note of the articles as part of their environmental scanning for marketing threats and opportunities?

4.8 Gathering information across borders

Most of the secondary sources surveyed so far in Section 4 have their counterparts in other countries.

(a) Foreign **governments and international bodies** (such as the United Nations) publish reports and statistics.

(b) Foreign **trade associations** and industry bodies publish surveys. Many also have international links.

(c) **International news** and information agencies (such as Reuters) publish world-wide reports.

(d) **Resource guides** (such as the British Overseas Trade Board's *Market-Search*) provide links to recommended international sources of information.

(e) International **newspapers and journals** are available (in print, and frequently also on the Internet).

(f) **Internet sites** give access to foreign educational and governmental institutions and their databases, and to the websites of commercial organisations around the world. Access is not restricted to working hours (which helps when there are time differences) and information can be downloaded for later translation.

Marketing at Work

Check out some of the following sites. How helpful are they likely to be for (a) businesses in the local market and (b) researchers from overseas?

China

National Bureau of Statistics	www.stats.gov.cn
Ministry of Foreign Trade & Economic Co-operation	www.moftec.gov.cn
Department of International Co-operation, State Information Center, CEInet Data Co Ltd	www.ce.cei.gov.cn

Poland

Glowny Urzad Statystyczny (GUS) (Central Statistical Office)	www.stat.gov.pl
Narodowy Bank Polandi (National Bank of Poland)	www.nbp.pl

5 Evaluating, presenting and using information

5.1 Evaluating data

FAST FORWARD

Data must be **evaluated** for:

- relevance
- up-to-dateness
- accuracy
- the credibility and objectivity of the source
- corroboration/confirmation
- correct methodology in sampling and data collection
- cost-effectiveness

All data collected should be **evaluated** using the following criteria.

(a) Is the data **relevant** to the purpose for which it was collected?

(b) Is it **up-to-date**?

(c) Is it **reliable and accurate**?

(d) Is the source of the data **credible** and objective, or unbiased? Look for the following.

    (i) The source's **reputation**, and your own past experience of its accuracy and reliability.

    (ii) **Internal evidence** that the information is accurate, consistent, balanced and supported by evidence.

    (iii) The source's **interests, motives, values and purpose** in compiling the information. Is the source trying to persuade you of something, market something or disguise something?

(e) Is the data subject to **confirmation**, or comparison with data from other sources? Are you prepared to risk basing decisions on uncorroborated data?

(f) Is the data based on a large and representative **statistical sample** of the relevant population?

(g) Has the data been gathered in a way that makes it **meaningful and reliable**? Has the same question been put to all respondents? Were all terms consistently defined? Did researchers lead or suggest 'right' answers? Were the respondents influenced by the researcher, or each other, or the desire to be 'nice'?

(h) Has the data collection and analysis been worthwhile? Has it fulfilled its purposes at a **reasonable cost** in money, time and effort?

5.2 Analysis and presentation of research findings

FAST FORWARD

Data must be **analysed** and **presented** as information, accessible and relevant to the needs of the intended user.

As you may recall from the compulsory Part A question in the *Customer Communications* exam:

- Quantitative research quite often presents 'raw data': lists or tables of numbers, or ticks in boxes. This data must be analysed in order to identify key features, trends, probabilities and averages.

- Qualitative research also presents 'raw data' in the form of records of words in narrative form. This data must be analysed in order to summarise, interpret, categorise and measure the frequency of responses, for presentation in quantitative or statistical form.

Management information, or decision-support information, resulting from data analysis must be formatted for **presentation** to the target user.

- Printed tables
- Charts
- Graphs
- Narrative reports
- Oral presentation with visual aids
- Interpretation and recommendations

All these formats are covered in the *Customer Communications* module. Particular applications (such as using a Gantt chart to schedule advertising media or event planning) are also covered in relevant chapters of this Text.

Marketing at Work

Ten largest Internet markets in Europe, 2003 (in millions of Internet users)

Country	Users
Germany	37.8
UK	30.5
France	24.7
Italy	23.5
Poland	10.4
Netherlands	8.8
Spain	8.5
Russia	8.1
Turkey	7.2
Sweden	5.6

Note: Total of ten largest countries is 165.1 million Internet users comprising 79% of all European Internet users.

Source: eMarketer, February 2004

The way in which information will be processed and presented, as discussed in detail in *Customer Communications*, depends on:

- **Its intended audience**. Who will be required to use and understand the information? What types of data and formats will help them get the best use out of the information? What level of detail and/or sophistication will they be able to absorb and use?
- **Its intended purpose**. What will the information be used for? What does it need to demonstrate or prove most clearly? (A trend? A correlation between one variable and another? A frequency distribution, indicating the concentration of buyers in one market

segment or another? Key differences in buyer behaviour that might suggest a basis for market segmentation?) How (and how frequently) will it need to be accessed, in order to fulfil its purposes? (Eg Will it be used every time a customer calls, as part of a customer relationship management system?)

Exam tip

> These are key considerations when preparing reports, e-mails, advertisements, press releases and other communication tasks for the *Marketing in Practice* exam. One of the ways of ensuring that you properly *contextualise* your answers is to consider:
>
> - Who is the audience?
> - What is their information need?
> - What is my purpose (in the scenario) for this task?

5.3 Key uses of marketing information

FAST FORWARD

> Marketing information is used for a range of planning and control tasks.

We will be looking at this in more detail throughout this Text, but you should be aware from the outset of the range of uses to which information about markets, customers and the business environment can be put.

(a) **Segmenting markets**, so that 'groups' of customers and potential customers with similar characteristics can be *targeted* with effective marketing strategies and so that the organisation's offering can be appropriately *positioned* to appeal to relevant segments, to maximise return on marketing investment.

(b) **Marketing planning**: planning, organising and undertaking marketing activities which will be relevant to the needs, wants and preferences of the target market; taking into account environmental constraints, including competitor activity, legal regulation and consumer trends; supplying relevant information to employees.

(c) **Relationship marketing**: building databased records of customer buying activity and preferences, so that further contacts and follow-up offers can be tailored and even personalised accordingly (eg individually addressed letters/emails, special offers and loyalty incentives based on past transaction history).

(d) **Supply chain relationship management**: building similar records of contacts, transaction history and performance of suppliers, distributors and other partners in the value chain, so that their performance can be managed in future.

(e) **Managing the organisation's communications and profile**: using environmental data to drive change in the organisation's culture and image (eg responding to increasing consumer pressure towards corporate social responsibility in regard to the environment, fair employment practices and so on).

(f) **Evaluating marketing activity**, using feedback from customers and other stakeholders to assess the effectiveness of marketing plans and adjust them where required.

PART A GATHERING, ANALYSING AND PRESENTING INFORMATION

Action Programme 5

The Needle Works

As the new Marketing Co-ordinator of The Needle Works, you decide you quickly need to get a handle on the commercial craft supply trade, and needlecraft in particular. You also need to get some sense of how The Needle Works' sales break down by product group.

(a) Make a list of some of the information sources you will tap into most easily and with least cost, in order to gain some general market intelligence.

(b) The only immediately available sales information comes from the EPOS print-out used by Loshini Lawal to motivate the sales assistants.

Week *Commencing:*
Sales by assistant by product

	Thread (units)	Kits (units)	Frames (units)	Patterns (units)	Accessories (units)	TOTAL
Loshini	40	20	5	25	30	120
Jane	15	10	-	-	5	30
Sarah	10	5	-	10	15	40
Tom	20	7	3	-	-	30
Sarina	5	10	-	10	10	35
Rafi	10	10	-	5	20	45
TOTAL	100	62	8	50	80	300

Required:

(i) If the profits generated by each product are as follows, which sales assistant has generated the least profit?

Thread	£2
Kits	£1
Frames	£3
Pattern	£2
Accessories	£1

(ii) You would like to know which products are doing better than others. Present this information in diagram form, so you can show the rest of the management team.

(iii) What does your analysis so far *not* take into account?

(iv) Suggest ways of improving overall team performance, from the information given.

Chapter Roundup

- The assessment of **Marketing in Practice** by case study requires you to assimilate a body of information and to use that information in decision-making and in carrying out marketing tasks. You are also required to appreciate what further information might be needed in order to make decisions, and where it might be obtained.
- **Information** (measurement, facts and data, analysis) is required for **rational decision making**, particularly for marketing, which requires a detailed, realistic understanding of the customer's needs and wants, the marketing mix and the marketing environment.
- The **marketing information system** is 'the framework for the day-to-day management and structuring of information gathered regularly from sources both inside and outside an organisation' (Dibb *et al.*, 2001).
- Marketing decisions are made under conditions of uncertainty and risk. Marketing research aims to **reduce the risk** by providing information about the variables involved in the decision, and the possible outcomes of particular decisions and actions.
- **Marketing research** can operate across the extended marketing mix and the marketing environment.
- Data may be derived from **primary** or **secondary** sources.
- Data may be **qualitative** (psychographic) and/or **quantitative** (statistical, demographic).
- **Secondary sources** of information include:
    - internal data records
    - published information
    - bought-in reports
    - the Internet and intranet
    - general environmental scanning

    All these sources are available **internationally**, for gathering cross-border data.
- Data must be **evaluated** for:
    - relevance
    - up-to-dateness
    - accuracy
    - the credibility and objectivity of the source
    - corroboration/confirmation
    - correct methodology in sampling and data collection
    - cost-effectiveness
- Data must be **analysed** and **presented** as information, accessible and relevant to the needs of the intended user.
- Marketing information is used for a range of planning and control tasks.

Quick Quiz

1. How much information is required to make a decision?
2. What is product research?
3. Give five examples of internal data that could be used for marketing research.
4. Give three examples of industry/trade specific publications.
5. What information is generated by a consumer panel?
6. Give three examples of sources of information on the Internet.
7. Give five examples of sources of overseas market intelligence.
8. How can you evaluate the credibility and objectivity of a data source?
9. How is raw quantitative and qualitative data converted into management information?
10. List three uses of customer data.

PART A GATHERING, ANALYSING AND PRESENTING INFORMATION

Answers to Quick Quiz

1. The right amount! Most decisions are based on incomplete information in conditions of uncertainty. Data reduces risk of the unknown, but the future is unpredictable. Gathering and analysing data costs money.

2. How customers respond (or might respond) to a given product.

3. Production data, sales volumes, management accounting statistics, financial and management reports and information on marketing, promotion and brand.

4. There are examples from every industry. Our examples include *Marketing Week* for marketers (make sure you have a copy!), *The Bookseller* for booksellers and publishers and the *Building Services Journal* for those who serve the construction industry.

5. Consumer panels give information about consumer attitudes and buying habits over a period of time.

6. You could have suggested: the homepages of government institutions, educational establishments, libraries or agencies, newsgroups or Internet search engines.

7. Examples include reports and statistics published by foreign governments and agencies, the surveys compiled by international news and information agencies, resource guides, international newspapers and Internet sites.

8. You should refer to the checklist of criteria in Paragraph 5.1.

9. Qualitative and quantitative raw data (words or figures) becomes management information when it is analysed and presented in a meaningful way. In order to make it accessible to the intended user it may be summarised, interpreted, categorised and presented in an easily understood form.

10. Market segmentation/targeting; customisation/personalisation of messages for relationship marketing; evaluating the effectiveness of marketing activity via customer feedback and purchase behaviour.

Action Programme Review

1. If you think this is a frivolous exercise, consider that:
   - these three principles are the key to all the marketing activities discussed in this Study Text, and a useful checklist for effective action
   - the presentation of information is an important marketing skill in itself

2. (a) Quantitative data on sales volume comparing region-on-region and year-on-year to establish amount (units, value, %) and rate of decline. Qualitative data on why consumers are less happy with the product.

   (b) Quantitative data on volume of sales in comparable times/markets during night hours, percentage support among sample groups. Qualitative data about people's attitudes to night shopping, possible fears (related to area?).

   (c) Quantitative data on audience figures at scheduled times, demographics of audience, cost of advertising. Qualitative data on audience response to the ad.

3. This is important information for any workplace research you may have to do – not least, for assessment of your skills in this area of the syllabus!

4   Here are some suggestions. You may have other ideas.

    (a)   Coach firms, car park owners, environmental groups, regional competitors of organisations likely to be adversely affected in London.

    (b)   Competitors of Siemens, recruitment consultants.

    (c)   Land developers, environmental groups.

    (d)   Makers of T-shirts, watches, toys, nostalgia-related goods.

    It is a good idea to get into the habit of playing this game whenever you read a newspaper. One day you may spot a golden opportunity for your organisation that all competitors miss.

5   (a)   Some sources you may have identified include: women's magazines and specialist craft/needlecraft magazines; craft suppliers' and guilds' Internet sites; and personal contacts (including colleagues and customers).

    (b)   (i)

	Thread	Kits	Frames	Patterns	Accessories	Profit
Loshini	40 × 2	20	5 × 3	25 × 2	30	**195**
Jane	15 × 2	10			5	**45**
Sarah	10 × 2	5		10 × 2	15	**60**
Tom	20 × 2	7	3 × 3			**56**
Sarina	5 × 2	10		10 × 2	10	**50**
Rafi	10 × 2	10		5 × 2	20	**60**

    Jane generated the least profit £45

    (ii) We have chosen a pie chart.

PRODUCT SALES (w/c: [date])

Frames 2.6%
Patterns 16.7%
Thread 33.3%
Kits 20.7%
Accessories 26.7%

Thread : 100/300 = 33.3%

Accessories: 80/300 = 26.7%

Kits: 62/300 = 20.7%

Patterns: 50/300 = 16.7%

Frames: 8/300 = 2.6%

(iii) The staff sales chart does not take into account that Loshini is the only full-time staff member (given in the background information): the others are only part-time. Neither the staff sales chart nor the product sales chart take into account the relevant values of the products. The frames are expensive items, whereas the high-performing threads are very cheap. Overall, for example, kits may have brought in most revenue, and Tom may have performed better in terms of sales value than sales units.

(iv) Ways of improving overall team performance may include:
(1) Giving incentives to boost sales of certain products.
(2) Organising product training (some staff do not sell any of certain products).
(3) Organising staff rotas to give the best coverage of product expertise at all times.
(4) Training on sales technique.

> Now try Question 1 at the end of the Study Text

The customer database

Chapter topic list

1. Database
2. Building a database
3. Investigating customers via the database
4. Customer relationship management
5. Segmentation
6. Using database information

Syllabus content – knowledge and skills requirements

- 1.2 Maintain a marketing database, information collection and usage
- 1.3 Investigate customers via the database and develop bases for segmentation

PART A GATHERING, ANALYSING AND PRESENTING INFORMATION

Introduction

In Chapter 1 we outlined some of the many sources of information that can be used to support marketing decisions. In this chapter, we look at how that information can be stored and accessed, in the form of a database. It will help you to:

- Understand the structure and use of database systems
- Collect information on customers and leads for input to the database
- Appreciate how the customer database can be used for market analysis
- Use basic segmentation as a practical marketing tool
- Appreciate the scope and limitations of database usage

1 Database

1.1 What is a database?

FAST FORWARD

A **database** is a comprehensive structured collection of data (usually computerised) which can be accessed by different users for different applications.

Key concept

A **database** is a comprehensive, structured collection or file of data which can be accessed by different users for different applications.

In theory, a database is simply a coherent structure for the storage and use of data. It involves the centralised storage of information.

- **Common data** for all users to share
- Avoidance of **data duplication** in files kept by different users
- **Consistency** in the organisation's use of data
- **Flexibility** in the way in which shared data can be queried, analysed and formatted

Such a structure could be fulfilled by a centralised file registry or library, or a self-contained data record like a master index card file. In practice, however, large scale databases are created and stored on **computer** systems, using **database application packages**, such as Microsoft Access.

1.2 Data storage

FAST FORWARD

Databases allow for the **collection and storage of data**, and also for **interaction** with data through various forms of interrogation, calculation and report formatting.

Computer database packages allow data to be stored in a coherent structure, in one place.

(a) **Data** are the raw components of information: names, dates, item descriptions, prices, colours, addresses.

(b) **Fields** are the labels given to types of data. *Kaufeld* (1996) refers to them as 'places for your data to live'. A customer database, for example, might include fields such as: title (data = Mr), first name (data = Joseph), last name (data = Bloggs), Company (data = Anon Ltd), Address, Phone Number, Fax Number, Contact Type (data = customer), interests (data = widgets).

- (c) **Records** are the collections of fields relevant to one entry. (Kaufeld suggests 'all the homes on one block.') So all the above data fields for a particular customer (Mr Bloggs) make up one customer record.

- (d) **Tables** (or database files) are collections of records that describe similar data ('all the blocks in one neighbourhood'). All the customer records for a particular region or product may be stored in such a file.

- (e) **Databases** (or catalogues) are collections of all the tables (and other formats which can be created from them) relating to a particular set of information ('a community of neighbourhoods'). So your customer database may include tables for various regions' customers, product customers and customer contacts, plus various reports and queries that you use to access different types of information.

There are two basic kinds of database.

- (a) A **flat file system** lumps all the data into single table databases, like a phone directory where names, addresses, phone numbers and fax numbers are stored in the same file.

- (b) A **relational database** system allows greater flexibility and storage efficiency by splitting the data up into a number of tables, which can nevertheless be linked and integrated together. For example, one table may contain customer names and addresses/contact details, while others track sales transactions by outlet or product and another, customers' payment histories. A linking field such as a customer number would allow you to interrogate all three tables, generate an integrated report on a particular customer's purchases and payments, or a list of customers who had made multiple purchases with a poor payment record.

Flat systems are easy to build and maintain, and are quite adequate for applications such as mailing lists, or membership databases. **Relational systems** integrate a wider range of business functions, for invoicing, accounting, inventory and marketing analysis. If your organisation already operates a relational system, learn how to use it. If you are required to set up or build a relational system, get help: use a 'wizard' or template (in the database package) or ask an expert – at least the first time.

1.3 Data manipulation

Basic features of database packages allow you to do many things.

- (a) **Find particular records**, using any data item you know.
- (b) **Sort records alphabetically**, numerically or by date, in ascending or descending order.
- (c) **Filter records**, so that you 'pull out' and view a selection of records based on specified criteria (all addresses in a certain postcode, for example, or all purchasers of a particular product).
- (d) **Interrogate records**, generating the selection of records based on a complex set of criteria, from one or more linked tables. For example, you might specify that you want all customer records where the field 'City' equals 'London' or Birmingham' AND where the field 'Product' equals 'Widget' AND where the field 'Purchase Date' is between 'Jan 2007' and 'Jan 2008'. The query would generate a table consisting of customers in London and Birmingham who purchased Widgets in 2007.
- (e) **Calculate and count** data entries. For example, if you wanted to find out how many customers had purchased each product, you could run a query that asked the database to group the data by the field 'product' and then count by field 'Customer ID' or 'Last Name'. It would count the number of customer ID numbers or names linked to each product. You could also ask to 'sum' or add up all the values in a field: total number of purchases, or total purchase value.
- (f) **Format** selected data for a variety of uses such as reports, forms, mailing labels, charts and diagrams.

You will probably be working with a database that has already been created for you, using a particular software package. It is up to you to get to know how to use it and how your organisation wants its data structured and formatted.

As we proceed to talk about 'building a database' we will mainly focus on the gathering of the data, rather than database design: if you want to know more about the latter, talk to IT experts in your organisation, or borrow the handbook to one of the popular database packages.

Action Programme 1

Find out what type(s) of database your organisation (or college) uses, and for what applications. If possible, get access to the database and browse through the index, directory or switchboard to see what databases/catalogues contain what database files or tables, queries, reports and forms, with what fields.

2 Building a database

2.1 Feasibility study

> **FAST FORWARD**
>
> The **feasibility** and **cost-effectiveness** of building an in-house database should be studied. For direct marketing purposes, alternatives include rented or bought-in mailing lists.

A survey entitled *Impact of Computerised Sales And Marketing Systems In The UK* (by the Hewson Consulting Group) found significant agreement that effective marketing databases can be the key to successful marketing. However, it also found that ineffective databases are a drain on resources and morale. There are several barriers to the effective use of database systems in sales and marketing.

- **Lack of motivation** by key players
- **The high costs** of the system
- The **limitations** of software/hardware capability
- **Resistance to change**, coupled with lack of confidence in the perceived benefits
- Problems with **internal communications** and complex implementation issues
- The **lack of business experience** among IT specialists

2.1.1 Costs of database systems

The **direct** costs of setting up a sales and marketing system (the cost of hardware and software) only amount to about 45% of the total cost. **Indirect** and often hidden costs include consultancy, the time spent training staff, loss of selling time while training and on-going costs of maintenance.

2.1.2 Benefits of database systems

However, there are potential benefits!

(a) Increased **sales and/or market share** (due to enhanced lead follow-up, cross-selling, customer contact and so on)

(b) Increased **customer retention** (though better targeting and contact)

(c) Better **use of resources** and cost reduction (through targeting, less duplication of information-handling)

(d) Better **decision-making** (through quality management information)

(e) **Competitive advantage** arising from any of the above.

This can be represented diagrammatically as follows: Figure 2.1.

```
Central database of
prospects/customer records
         ↓
Better profiling of prospects/customers
         ↓
Better understanding of
prospects/customers' needs
         ↓
More effective
segmentation
         ↓
Better targeting of
prospects/customers
         ↓
Better chance of prospects/ customers
responding
         ↓
Better chance of
securing sales
         ↓
Better chance of
increasing revenue
```

Figure 2.1: Benefits of a central customer database

2.2 A customer database

FAST FORWARD

A comprehensive customer database may include a variety of data relevant to the customer: contact details; transaction details; purchase history; contact history; and any special data gathered as part of loyalty schemes.

Action Programme 2

Can your organisation's database answer the following questions?

- Who are our customers?
- What do they want?
- Where do they come from?
- Why do they come to us?
- What do they buy?
- How much do they spend?
- When do they buy?
- How often do they buy?

Maybe it has other information fields, not listed here.

Marketing at Work

It is important to use data obtained via the Internet with the subject's full knowledge and permission. **'Permission marketing'** encourages the seeking of an individual's consent before he or she is marketed to. In practice, companies often provide 'opt in' or 'opt out' boxes for the customer to tick. The UK Privacy and Electronic Communications Regulations 2003 requires proactive (opt-in) acceptance of electronic communications, such as e-mail marketing. Backing up personal information requests with some kind of incentive (eg entry in a prize draw) will increase the likelihood of continued interaction and permission from the customer.

2.2.1 Contents of the database

A comprehensive customer database might include the following.

(a) **Customer titles**, names, addresses and contact (telephone, fax, e-mail). E-mail addresses should be linked with other known attributes, because an email address on its own usually says nothing about the customer.

(b) **Professional details** (company; job title; responsibilities), especially for business-to-business marketing

(c) **Personal details** (sex, age, number of people at the same address, spouse's name, children, interests, and any other relevant data known, such as newspapers read, journals subscribed to)

(d) **Transaction history** (what products/services are ordered, how often, how much is spent)

(e) **Call/contact history** (sales or after-sales service calls made, complaints/queries received, meetings at shows/exhibitions)

(f) **Credit/payment history** (credit rating, amounts outstanding, aged debts)

(g) **Current transaction/details** (items currently on order, dates, prices, delivery arrangements)

(h) **Special account details** (membership number, loyalty or incentive points earned, discount awarded), where customer loyalty or incentive schemes or valued customer cards are used.

Exam tip

> The June 2006 exam asked what information a company would want in its customer databases (to segment its market and assist future marketing activity). The examiner was disappointed the candidates (a) wasted time by describing databases and segmentation and (b) neglected the potential of information such as transaction and contact history. The first is an exam technique problem – the second, a knowledge problem (tested again in December 2006, with the same shortfall): take note!

2.2.2 Structuring the data

Each of these items will be in a separate field (and, in a relational database, perhaps separate tables) in your database. When designing new tables, the following procedure is recommended.

(a) List and briefly describe the reports, lists, mailing labels and whatever else you want to come out of the system. **What will you want to use the data for** and in what form will it be most useful? What combinations of information will you want to pull together? How will you want them sorted?

(b) **Sketch out samples** of the above reports, lists, mailing labels and so on. This will give you an idea of the format and content of the fields you will require in your table(s).

(c) **List and name all the fields you will require**. If you are designing the table from scratch, you will also need to specify the type of field (date, numbers, text and so on) and other technical details. Include a 'primary key', a field in which the data will be unique for each record (such as a customer ID number or product code) for indexing purposes.

(d) **Organise the fields** into one or more tables. For a flat system, pick a logical order that will make data input easy. For a relational database, group together data that naturally goes together (for example, name, address, telephone, fax, e-mail for a contacts or mailing list table) and link together tables that are related (as most of the tables suggested in Paragraph 2.2.1 might be).

2.2.3 Where does customer information come from?

FAST FORWARD

> **Customer and contact details** can be sourced from a wide range of transactions, feedback mechanisms, promotional mechanisms and secondary sources. All data must be periodically reviewed for **accuracy** and **up-to-dateness**.

Customer information may come from the following sources.

(a) **EPOS** (Electronic Point of Sale) recorded data on all sales transactions and orders. Transaction details may be input manually, or by bar code reader or 'swiping' of magnetic-stripped customer cards.

(b) **Transaction documents**, such as order forms, invoices, credit applications and customer account records.

(c) **Details gathered by telemarketers** (incoming and outgoing calls) and salespersons on every contact with customers.

(d) Details provided by customers on customer care, feedback and market research **forms/questionnaires**.

(e) Details provided by customers on on-pack coupons, entry forms or phone lines for **promotional competitions**, prize draws or incentives.

(f) Details provided by customers when applying for credit accounts, discount schemes, valued customer cards and other **loyalty and incentive schemes**.

(g) Details provided by customers who visit **shows and exhibitions**.

2.2.4 Websites as sources of customer data

A very important source of customer information is the company's website on the Internet. Few major brands do not have their own web pages. Most advertisements in other media (press, TV or radio) direct consumers to web addresses for further information or online ordering.

Exam tip

A question on the Pilot paper asks about the information that a company might need to gather about its website visitors, and how such information may be used to build the business. Here is a brief answer.

Questions to ask web visitors	Possible uses
1. Why did you visit our site?	Understanding reasons for visits will help in improving services/generating traffic
2. What information did you look for?	Are we providing the information that we should?
3. Did you find it?	Customer satisfaction – is the site user friendly and comprehensive?
4. Which pages did you visit?	Demonstrating 'hit' rates to potential advertisers
5. Did you find the information relevant?	Customer satisfaction/likelihood of repeat visits
6. Was the site easy to use?	As above
7. What did you particularly like or dislike?	Suggestions for future development of the site
8. What is your area of business?	Market research into customer profiles
9. Where are you based?	Potential for expansion may be indicated
10. Would you be interested in receiving regular updates?	Promotion of new services and events

This could also have formed the basis for an answer to a question in December 2006, asking you to draft a feedback questionnaire for website users (asking for feedback on their experience of the website) and state how the information would be used to improve the website.

People have become used to giving various geographical and lifestyle details on websites as they browse around, often as part of personalisation features, site registrations and so on. A trail of the **'clicks'** performed by a visitor to a site will show what pages they are most interested in, while 'cookies' software can be used to record browsing preferences over time.

The gathering and use of such data is covered by data protection and privacy legislation. In most countries of the world, there is now some form of *'opt in' requirement*, for customers/contacts to agree to receive further information from the organisation or third parties.

Marketing at Work

- AutoTrader has a second-hand car-search website which asks users to enter their name, postal and e-mail addresses before it will look for a car to match their specifications. This enables **geographic profiling**, not possible on e-mail addresses alone.

- 'Give an individual something of real value in **exchange** for their data, be upfront about what you intend to do with it and they will let you into all sorts of personal secrets . . . The VirginConnect WebPlayer allows users to surf the Net and use e-mail. To receive the device customers must log onto a website and complete a questionnaire covering topics such as shopping preferences, music and entertainment interests and web usage . . . And in accepting the machine, customers are also agreeing to receive targeted banner ads and emails from Virgin and other marketers.'

Marketing Business, June 2000

On-line or e-mailed questionnaires can also be used to gather customer **feedback** on products and services. The following is a specimen questionnaire for online feedback collection by a retail company.

'Shopping Experience' Evaluation

1. How often do you visit one of our stores?

   ○ Every day
   ○ Several times a week
   ○ About once a week
   ○ Several times a month
   ○ About once a month
   ○ Less than once a month

2. How would you rate our stores in the following areas?

	Excellent	Very Good	Good	Fair	Poor
Ease of access	○	○	○	○	○
Quality of merchandise	○	○	○	○	○
Availability and helpfulness of staff	○	○	○	○	○
General attractiveness	○	○	○	○	○

3. How likely are you to:

	Very Likely	Somewhat Likely	Somewhat Unlikely	Not at all Likely
Return to our stores?	○	○	○	○
Recommend our stores?	○	○	○	○

4. What do you like most about our stores?

5. What do you like least about our stores?

6. What features would you like added or changes you would like made to our stores?

Thank you for taking the time to give us your feedback.

2.3 Contacts databases

FAST FORWARD

As well as a database of existing customers, the organisation may wish to build a database of sales leads, prospects and other contacts as a **mailing list**.

A typical contacts database may include:

- **Contact titles**, names, addresses and contact (telephone, fax, e-mail) details

- **Professional details** (company name, address, contact details, job title) in a business-to-business context

- **Contact 'type'** – exhibition visitor, referral, existing customer, enquirer, 'cold' contact, bought-in list

- **Contact's interests** in a particular product/service area

- **Contact history** (whether called/mailed, whether responded, whether followed up, whether purchased)

2.3.1 Where does contact information come from?

Contact or mailing list information may come from various sources.

(a) **Recommendation** and referrals from customers (whether spontaneous or through 'introduce a friend' schemes or referral requests)

(b) **Enquiries** for further information, in response to advertising, promotion and PR (via telephone, mail, 'hits' on website)

(c) Enquiries compiled at **exhibitions** and fairs

(d) **Leads** brought back by salespeople, not yet converted into sales

(e) Details provided in response to **promotional competitions**, prize draws and incentives. Every 'send in for your chance to win' or 'send in to claim your discount' coupon should be a vehicle for capture of mailing list data: this will often be their primary purpose

(f) Relevant **secondary sources**

(g) Specialist **mailing list suppliers**. Lists can be hired or bought from commercial list owners: they can often be appropriately segmented (we discuss this further below)

(h) The **in-house database** of non-competing organisations in the same market, who may be willing to swap or rent lists. If you buy anything by post, you end up on a mailing database, and are often given the opportunity to receive, or decline to receive, information on related products.

Action Programme 3

What secondary sources might provide relevant names, addresses, company and contact details?

It may not be worthwhile building an in-house contact list, or relying on it to reach a wide range of potential customers. Most direct marketing is based on lists rented from **list brokers**, who generate mailing labels or conduct mailings themselves. There is a large catalogue of lists varying from specific magazine subscribers, to consumer and business lists across all market sectors. The cost of renting a list ranges from £50 per thousand to hundreds of pounds per thousand, with an additional charge for any selection criteria you require when they generate the list (geographical area, age) and any handling they undertake on your behalf.

List brokers can be found in the Direct Marketing Press or via the Direct Marketing Association.

2.3.2 Maintaining the database

If the customer database is linked to **online transaction processing** (for example, via EPOS), purchase data will automatically be updated with each new transaction. However, a typical contacts database will have to be regularly and systematically **maintained**.

(a) Contacts who become customers should be transferred to the customer database.

(b) Any up-dated or altered information (such as change of address) should be entered in the database.

(c) Additional information obtained from contacts should be added to the relevant records.

(d) New names and records should periodically be added to the database, and names which have received no response should be deleted.

(e) Requests from customers or members of the public to have their details erased from the database should be honoured.

(f) New fields can be added to the database design as new types of information become available.

(g) Remember that in **business-to-business** markets, contacts often move to different companies. This represents a **networking opportunity**.

3 Investigating customers via the database

> **FAST FORWARD**
>
> Customer databases can be **interrogated** to identify profitable customers, buying patterns and trends, marketing opportunities and market segments.

There are a number of ways in which a database can be interrogated to derive information for marketing planning.

3.1 Identifying the most profitable customers

The Italian economist Vilfredo Pareto was the first to observe that in human affairs, 20% of events result in 80% of outcomes. This has become known as Pareto's law, or the 80/20 principle. It shows up quite often in marketing. In general, a small number of existing customers are 'heavy users' of a product or service and generate a high proportion of its sales revenue.

A customer database which allows purchase frequency and value per customer to be calculated indicates to the marketer who the potential heavy users are, and therefore where the promotional budget can most profitably be spent.

Action Programme 4

Suggest three strategies for getting revenue from frequent or loyal users of your products.

3.2 Identifying buying trends

By tracking purchases per customer (or customer group, as we will discuss below), you may be able to identify certain customer types.

(a) **Loyal repeat customers** who cost less to retain than new customers cost to find and attract.

(b) **'Backsliding'** or lost customers, who have reduced or ceased the frequency or volume of their purchases.

(c) **Seasonal or local** purchase patterns may be identified, to support promotion planning (to boost 'off-peak' sales) and production/distribution planning (meeting seasonal peaks in demand).

(d) Purchase patterns are often in response to **promotional campaigns**. Increased sales volume or frequency following promotions is an important measurement of their effectiveness.

3.3 Identifying marketing opportunities

More detailed information (where available) on customer likes and dislikes, complaints, feedback and lifestyle values may offer useful information and guidance, for:

- **Product** improvement
- **Customer care** and quality programmes
- New **product development**
- **Decision-making** across the marketing mix

Simple data fields such as 'contact type' will help to evaluate how contact is made with customers, of what types and in what numbers. Business leads may be generated most often by trade conferences and exhibitions. Light or one-off users will be attracted by promotional competitions and incentives, and loyal customers by personal contact through representatives.

Customers can be investigated using any data field included in the database. How many are on e-mail or the Internet? How many have spouses or children? These parameters allow the marketer to **segment** the customer base for marketing purposes.

4 Customer relationship management

> **FAST FORWARD**
>
> **CRM systems** are used to integrate customer data from multiple sources. This enables the data to be used:
> - to enhance customers' experience of contact with the firm
> - to enhance customer loyalty
> - to increase efficiency

Customer Relationship Management (CRM) is big business, driven by Internet and database developments. It is covered in detail in the *Customer Communications* module. The following summary (Figure 2.2) should refresh your memory:

```
   Website                          Call Centre
   [With Web                        [With Computer
   Personalisation                  Telephony
   Technology]                      Integration]
              \                    /
               \                  /
                Central Customer Database
               /                  \
              /                    \
   Field Sales Team                 Despatch
   [Using SFA (Sales                Customer service
   Force Automation)                Accounts
   software]
```

Figure 2.2: CRM systems

CRM should be regarded first and foremost as an **integrated business process** which integrates individual customer data from multiple sources.

2: THE CUSTOMER DATABASE

Exam tip

> This exam always contains an ICT-themed question, often in the form: *'What role could ICT play in ...?'* or *'How can the firm make best use of ICT to ...?'*. There are a couple of things to note with such questions.
>
> (a) ICT includes IT (computers, databases) *and* CT (networks, phones): ICT applications therefore embrace a wide range of applications – not just the Internet. In the context of CRM, ICT includes sales force automation, computer-telephony integration, databases and so on.
>
> (b) Consider carefully *what ICT is being asked to do*. If it is to 'build the business' or 'market the business', the scope is wide: you'll need to think about communications, promotions, advertising (e-mail, SMS, web) and so on. In June 2003, you were asked to discuss how ICT could be used 'to build the loyalty' of radio listeners: this is more of a relationship marketing/CRM question. In December 2004, it was 'developing on-going customer relationships' in a chocolate manufacturer.
>
> In December 2005, it was 'supporting [an event], before, during and after it takes place' – giving a wide scope for discussion (in this case, specifically of *website* usage). In June 2006, it was 'enhancing the marketing mix to generate sales and encourage customer loyalty': again, a wide scope focused on the 4Ps of price, product, place and promotion.

4.1 The process of CRM

A CRM system contains four distinct sub-processes: Figure 2.3.

Stage	Description
Data gathering	Data is selectively gathered and organised by segment according to customer motivations.
↓	
Analysis of data	Using both quantitative and qualitative analysis, a new set of market segments (and how to satisfy them) can be identified.
↓	
Value delivery	Changes are made to the marketing mix based upon the newly defined segments.
↓	
Monitoring, feedback and control	Test the system for its strategic sense and financial viability.

Figure 2.3: The use of CRM in marketing planning

Marketing at Work

Niewierski (2004) offers the following advice on how to make **best use of a customer database** (through *postcard marketing*).

'It's a fact that your customers are your best leads – the people most likely to purchase your products and services are the ones who have paid for them before and been happy with the results. Profit is not just about acquiring new customers, it is about fostering the relationships you already have. And it is also a fact that it costs far less money to retain customers by building loyalty than it does to go out and acquire new ones. ... There are a few rules to bear in mind when marketing to contacts in your company database.

'Rule#1 Collect all of your customers' information

It sounds like a no-brainer but you would be surprised. The more information that you can gather on your customers, the more you will be able to select and target individual customers with relevant specials. ...

'Rule#2 Don't treat your customers like prospects

When you collect the information in your database, make sure that you differentiate between people who have placed an order in the past and people who have not. Customers want to feel like you are paying attention to them and so when they have placed a few orders with you they will not appreciate a "10% discount for first-time buyers" postcard.

'Rule#3 Don't let your designs get stagnant

'When you are mailing to databases of people that you have never spoken to before it is acceptable to send them the same postcard multiple times. This strategy can help to increase recognition and eventually increase your response rate. However, when dealing with existing customers, you need to mix things up a bit. Your mailings should be attention grabbing and informative to stand out in their mail.'

4.2 Use of customer data for CRM

The key point about CRM is that it enables the use of customer data to be more readily converted into competitive advantage.

(a) **To enhance customers' experience of doing business with the firm**. Linking the sales force to a central database, for example, gives customers real time product/price/availability/delivery information. Computer-telephony integration (CTI) allows telephone operators to address customers by name and to have account details to hand.

(b) **To enhance relationship with the customer**, fostering customer loyalty. Customisation and personalisation of marketing messages and offers makes the customer feel known and valued – as well as increasing the likelihood of purchase (because of effective targeting).

(c) **To target the organisation's offerings** on the basis of actual buying patterns and preferences of individual consumers – not just segment characteristics (*Peppers and Rodgers*, 1993; *Postma*, 1999).

(d) **To capture increasingly detailed and up-to-date customer information**. Starting with name and address details (allowing direct marketing), the organisation may use subsequent contacts to elicit information about buying or media preferences (allowing targeted offers) or more personal details (such as birthdays, for 'special' relationship-building messages).

(e) **To enable all of the above as efficiently and cost-effectively as possible**, by integrating data storage and interrogation.

Marketers need to evaluate results to examine what went right (and wrong), so that the information can be used for future activities. Often customer feedback is gathered, but not acted upon.

Action Programme 5

It has been suggested that CRM fails to meet customer expectations 55-70% of the time. Why might this be?

We look further at customer relationship management in the context of **'e-relationships'** in Chapter 6.

5 Segmentation

FAST FORWARD

Segmentation allows marketers to target sub-groups within a given market with an appropriate marketing mix for their particular characteristics.

Key concept

Segmentation is the process by which consumers are grouped together according to identifiable characteristics that are relevant to their buying behaviour, thereby allowing marketers more effectively to target one or more segments of the market with the marketing mix.

Effective segmentation offers a number of benefits for consumer and marketer alike.

- The organisation is in a better position to **spot and service customer needs** and wants
- The **marketing mix can be adjusted** to the particular requirements of each segment
- Consumers should benefit from **increased choice**, and more closely tailored products
- Targeted marketing should lead to **lower cost of sales**

5.1 Bases for segmentation

FAST FORWARD

Segmentation can be done on any basis that is measurable, accessible, substantial and homogeneous.

5.1.1 What makes a usable segment?

Clearly, there are very many possible characteristics of buyers which could be used to segment markets, because people and groups are complex entities. Whatever characteristic or criterion is selected as a basis for segmentation, the resulting market segment needs to have certain attributes.

(a) **Measurable**. Information must exist or be obtainable (cost effectively) about the defining characteristic. The location and age of customers, for example, is more readily identified than their personality traits.

(b) **Accessible**. The organisation must be able to reach the defined segment by marketing methods. No mailing list or telesales strategy would be available, for example, for blue-eyed people, but wearers of tinted contact lenses could effectively be reached via opticians and chemists.

(c) **Substantial**. The defined segment should be large enough to be worth separate consideration and targeting of marketing effort, not just in size, but in potential profitability. Over 65-year olds in the lowest socio-economic bracket may not be as profitable as the group of 18 year olds in the same bracket, who are likely to have a larger spending span and potential for upward mobility.

(d) **Homogeneity**. The defined group should act broadly as a group for marketing purposes! A segment is not really a segment if individuals and groups within it react very differently to price changes or promotional messages. Segmentation by age or gender alone might cover a wide range of buying patterns, depending on spending points, lifestyle, education and ethnic origin.

(MASH might be a useful acronym to use as a checklist.)

5.1.2 Common bases for segmentation

Some of the main variables on which market segmentation is carried out at the strategic level include the following.

(a) **Demographics**. Statistics on the age, gender, marital status, family and household size, income, occupation and education of a population. These data are quantifiable, accessible and relatively cost-effective, and can readily identify potential markets and trends such as shifts in age and income distributions. In practice, demographic segmentation is carried out on the basis of age, gender and income/occupation, or combinations, such as 'the affluent elderly', 'young adult males' or 'yuppies'.

> **Key concept**
>
> **Demography** is the study of measurable statistics of a population, such as age, sex, family structure, income, occupation and education.

(b) **Social status and social class**. In the UK, there is a popular stratification into 'working class', 'middle class' and 'upper class', but objective measures of social class consist mainly of socio-economic variables such as income, education and occupation and residential area. There are various classifications, of which the National Readership Survey (formerly JICNAR) Social Grades (A, B, C1, C2, D, E) are most commonly used for marketing purposes.

(c) **Family life cycle (FLC)**, which reflects the structure, membership and pre-occupations of the family over time, and correlates to changes in income, expenditure and consumption priorities. Developmental stages include bachelorhood, newly-married couple, parenthood ('full nest'), post-parenthood ('empty nest') and solitary survivor. In addition, there are now models to take account of later marriages, childless couples, single parents and non-family households.

(d) **Psychographics**. Lifestyle or AIO (Activities, Interests and Opinions) analysis. Psychographic segmentation classifies people according to their values, attitudes and motivations. 'Lifestyle' refers to distinctive choices about how to live that are made by communities. 'Upwardly mobile' and 'security and status seeking' are two examples of lifestyle categories.

> **Key concept**
>
> **Psychography** is a form of consumer research which builds up psychological or psycho-social profiles of consumers or consumer groups.

5.2 Databases for segmentation

> **FAST FORWARD**
>
> The four main **strategic bases for segmentation** are demographics, psychographics, social class and family life cycle, but simpler bases such as gender, age, location, purchases, contact source and purchase volume/frequency/loyalty may be used through database queries.

A customer database may be sophisticated enough, and sufficiently subject to detailed analysis, to contain socio-economic, geo-demographic or other classifications.

(a) Residential post-codes, for example, can be cross-referenced to ACORN, targeting classifications of residential areas by affluence or demographic composition.

(b) Occupational or job title details may be cross-referenced to JICNAR social groupings, such as ABC1.

(c) Age, spouse and children details may be cross-referenced to family life cycle stages.

However, more basic segmentation is available through the simplest database, and may be equally valuable as an everyday marketing tool. Common bases for segmentation which can be built into database fields include the following.

(a) **Gender**. Products generally targeted by gender include cosmetics, clothing, cars and even financial services.

(b) **Age**. The 'youth market' has emerged strongly as a distinct target group for clothes, media, music and even banks. Other products are targeted at the 'grey' spending power of older people, such as special health insurance and retirement leisure activities.

(c) **Geographic location**. Despite sophisticated classifications of geo-demographics, the simple location of customers can be of great practical use to database marketers when advertising the launch of a retail outlet in a particular area, or selecting local media such as cinemas, outdoor poster sites and radio stations.

(d) **Socio-economic group**. The NRS grade is useful information because it is used throughout the marketing industry by market researchers and the media.

Social Grade	Description of occupation	Example
A	Higher managerial and professional	Company director
B	Lower managerial and supervisory	Middle manager
C1	Non-manual	Clerk
C2	Skilled manual	Electrician
D	Semi- and un-skilled manual	Labourer
E	Those receiving no income from employment and casual workers	Unemployed

(e) **Interests and previous purchases**. This is one of the most obvious bases for segmentation, and one of the most practical uses of the database. If enquirers have asked about particular products or services, or customers have purchased one or more products in a related group, then they can be segmented by product, for the purposes of information on promotions, new products in the same line or product improvements.

(f) **Contact type and source**. If the database includes a field corresponding to 'where did you hear about us/our product?', customers can also be segmented as consumers of particular media (for the purposes of advertising planning) or frequenters of particular retail outlets (for the purpose of in-store sales promotions).

(g) **Purchase volume, frequency and loyalty**, eg heavy and light users.

Action Programme 6

The Needle Works

From the background information you have been able to glean as the new Marketing Co-ordinator of the Needle Works, answer the following questions.

(a) How might the company usefully segment its customer database, and for what purposes?
(b) How might you improve the data-gathering process in order to achieve this?

5.3 Segmenting business databases

While industrial markets are usually smaller, more easily identified and more easily reached than consumer markets (via trade media, conferences, shows and directories), they can still usefully be segmented.

(a) **By location**

(b) **By size**, giving a broad indication of the need for products and services such as management training or human resource consultancy

(c) **Usage rates**: supply planning will be carried out on the basis of heavy, medium or light consumption of raw materials and parts

(d) **Trade/industry classification**: eg manufacturing, media, finance and publishing which may use different products and services, or use them in different ways, and will be targeted through different media

(e) **By product use**: the needs of an organisation for cars for use by its sales force may be different to those of an organisation hiring cars out to the public

5.4 Beyond segmentation

> **FAST FORWARD**
>
> **New technology** has supported the targeting of marketing not just to groups (segments) of customers, but to individual customers, based on their *actual* buying preferences and specific profiles. This is often called 'one-to-one' marketing.

Peppers and Rogers (1993) argue that: 'In the one-to-one future, it won't be how much you know about *all* of your customers that's important, but how much you know about *each* of your customers.' They emphasise the need for two-way communication vehicles and feedback mechanisms – interactive communication and dialogue – as a way of learning about customers and developing customer relationships.

6 Using database information

> **FAST FORWARD**
>
> **Database information** can be used for a variety of sales support, direct marketing, promotion management and marketing analysis applications.

6.1 Uses of database information

We have already mentioned many of the ways in which database information can be used. The following is a summary of the main ones.

(a) Uses of **direct mail**

- To maintain customer contact between (or instead of) sales calls
- To generate leads and 'warmed' prospects for sales calls
- To promote and/or sell products and services direct to customers
- To distribute product or service information

(b) **Transaction processing**. Databases can be linked to programmes which generate order confirmations, despatch notes, invoices, statements and receipts.

(c) **Marketing research and planning**. The database can be used to send out market surveys, and may itself be investigated to show purchasing patterns and trends.

(d) **Contacts planning**. The database can indicate what customers need to be contacted or given incentives to maintain their level of purchase and commitment. A separate database may similarly be used to track contacts at conferences and trade shows and invitation lists to marketing events.

(e) **Product development and improvement.** Product purchases can be tracked through the product life cycle, and weaknesses and opportunities identified from records of customer feedback, complaints or warranty/guarantee claims.

6.2 Data security and controls

> **FAST FORWARD**
>
> Certain **constraints on data use** exist to protect the individual, including the Data Protection Act and Mailing Preference Service.

Most customers, and consumers in general, are by now aware that when they supply their names and addresses they will be used in various ways. Most would accept that the details will be kept on file or in a mailing list, and many would expect to be sent information about goods and services by the same company. They may, however, be irritated to find that their details have been passed on to other companies, or that they are on a list for frequent or wide-ranging promotional information.

Direct marketers in most countries must now state clearly, when inviting customers or respondents to provide name and address details, the use to which the details will be put. It is also common to offer an opt-out from details being re-used or passed on.

Legislation and regulation exists to protect consumers from misuse of personal details held on computer, unsolicited mail and tele-marketing, and invasion of privacy.

(a) There are now stringent **trading practices and regulations** in the direct mail industry, administered by the Direct Mail Services Standards Board (DMSSB) and Mail Order Protection Scheme (for display advertisements in national newspapers that ask for money in advance).

(b) **The Mailing Preference Service** allows customers to state whether they would – and more often, would not – be willing to receive direct mail on a range of specific areas. (Similar 'Do not call' registers are kept in the USA and Australia, for telemarketing.)

(c) The UK **Privacy and Electronic Communication Regulations 2003** require proactive acceptance (opt in) to receive electronic direct mail communications (such as e-mail newsletters or offers).

(d) **The Data Protection Act 1998** (and related codes of practice) provides that data controllers (organisations who control the contents of files of personal data and the use of personal data) must register with the Data Protection Registrar. They must limit their use of personal data (defined as any information about an identifiable living individual) to the uses registered. *Exemptions* from the requirements include data relating to the membership of an unincorporated club and contact details for supplying articles or information.

Data Protection Principles

Personal data held by data users

(1) The information to be contained in personal data shall be obtained, and personal data shall be processed, **fairly and lawfully**. (In particular, information must not be obtained by deception.)

(2) Personal data shall be held only for one or more **specified** (registered) and lawful purposes.

(3) Personal data shall be **adequate, relevant and not excessive** in relation to its purpose or purposes.

(4) Personal data shall be **accurate** and, where necessary, **kept up-to-date**. ('Accurate' means correct and not misleading as to any matter of fact.)

(5) Personal data shall not be kept for **longer than is necessary** for its purpose or purposes.

(6) An individual shall be entitled at reasonable intervals, and without undue delay or expense:

   (i) to be **informed** by any data controller whether it holds personal data of which that individual is the subject, and for what purpose(s) the data is held

   (ii) to **access** to any such data held by a data controller

   (iii) where appropriate, to have such data **corrected or erased**

(7) Appropriate **security measures** shall be taken against unauthorised access to, or alteration, disclosure or destruction of, personal data.

(8) Data may not be **exported** outside the European Economic Area, except to countries where the rights of data subjects can be adequately protected.

Action Programme 7

Write to the Mailing Preference Service and ask to be put on the mailing list for business services, whatever product or industry sector you work in, or anything else that interests you. See how many direct marketers there are out there – and how accurate their mailing list labels and general targeting are!

The extent of regulation (and/or voluntary self-regulation) of direct marketing activity is a 'hot issue' worldwide: you may like to follow the debates (about spam control, use of contact information, 'Do not call' registers and so on) in the quality and marketing press.

Chapter Roundup

- A **database** is a comprehensive structured collection of data (usually computerised) which can be accessed by different users for different applications.
- Databases allow for the **collection and storage of data**, and also for **interaction** with data through various forms of interrogation, calculation and report formatting.
- The **feasibility** and **cost-effectiveness** of building an in-house database should be studied. For direct marketing purposes, alternatives include rented or bought-in mailing lists.
- A comprehensive customer database may include a variety of data relevant to the customer: contact details; transaction details; purchase history; contact history; and any special data gathered as part of loyalty schemes.
- **Customer and contact details** can be sourced from a wide range of transactions, feedback mechanisms, promotional mechanisms and secondary sources. All data must be periodically reviewed for **accuracy** and **up-to-dateness**.
- As well as a database of existing customers, the organisation may wish to build a database of sales leads, prospects and other contacts as a **mailing list**.
- Customer databases can be **interrogated** to identify profitable customers, buying patterns and trends, marketing opportunities and market segments.
- **CRM systems** are used to integrate customer data from multiple sources. This enables the data to be used:
    - to enhance customers' experience of contact with the firm
    - to enhance customer loyalty
    - to increase efficiency
- **Segmentation** allows marketers to target sub-groups within a given market with an appropriate marketing mix for their particular characteristics.
- Segmentation can be done on any basis that is measurable, accessible, substantial and homogeneous.
- The four main **strategic bases for segmentation** are demographics, psychographics, social class and family life cycle, but simpler bases such as gender, age, location, purchases, contact source and purchase volume/frequency/loyalty may be used through database queries.
- **New technology** has supported the targeting of marketing not just to groups (segments) of customers, but individual customers, based on their actual buying preferences and specific profiles. This is often called 'one-to-one' marketing.
- **Database information** can be used for a variety of sales support, direct marketing, promotion management and marketing analysis applications.
- Certain **constraints on data use** exist to protect the individual, including the Data Protection Acts and Mailing Preference Service.

Quick Quiz

1. What are (a) fields, (b) records and (c) tables in database terminology?
2. How might (a) customer and (b) contact information be gathered?
3. What factors make a good external mailing list?
4. What should be done with 'undeliverable' mailshot items?
5. How does the '80/20 rule' apply to marketing; and how can the database be used to capitalise on it?
6. What are (a) demographics and (b) psychographics?
7. List the NRS scale of social grades.
8. What are the main purposes of direct mail?

Answers to Quick Quiz

1. (a) Fields: labels given to different types of data
   (b) Records: collections of fields relevant to one entry
   (c) Tables: collections of records that describe similar data

2. (a) Electronic point of sale, transaction documents, telemarketers and salespeople, customer care feedback and market research.
   (b) Enquiries through a website, mailshot, exhibitions or trade fairs; recommendations from other customers; relevant secondary data; or swapped, rented or bought-in lists.

3. A good external mailing list comprises targeted leads with full personal information – name, contact details, position (for business-to-business customers) and their history of contact with your company: everything, in other words, to help you demonstrate their (potential) custom is valued and that you are efficient and pleasant to deal with.

4. This is valuable information in keeping your customer database up-to-date.

5. The 80/20 Principle (or Pareto's Law) is that 20% of events result in 80% of outcomes. In marketing terms, a high proportion of revenue is received through a relatively small base of customers.

6. (a) The study of measurable statistics of a population.
   (b) A form of customer research which builds up a psychological or psycho-social profile of consumer groups.

7. NRS scale: A – higher managerial and professional; B – Lower managerial and supervisory; C1 – Non-manual; C2 – Skilled manual; D – Semi-skilled and unskilled manual; E – Those receiving no income from employment/casual workers.

8. There are four main functions for direct mail.
   - To maintain customer contact between (or instead of) sales calls
   - To generate leads and warm prospects for sales calls
   - To promote and/or sell products and services direct to customers
   - To distribute product or service information

Action Programme Review

1. If you can't get access to a database at work, try the local library, where you may find that the 'index card' system has been computerised as a database. Or use an Internet search engine or browser to interrogate some online databases. This is not really something you can learn from books – have a go!

2. Your own research.

3. Some suggestions: The Yellow Pages, Business Pages, membership lists of clubs and trade/professional organisations, catalogues of attendees at conferences, exhibitions and trade shows, subscription lists for relevant journals, directories of directories and other industry 'who's who' lists, advertiser contact details in various media.

4. (a) Encouraging them to buy more on each purchase occasion (for example, by offering a suite of related products and services)

    (b) Encouraging them to buy more frequently (for example, by offering incentive discounts)

    (c) Encouraging them to stay with you longer, or customer retention (for example, by offering loyalty incentives like frequent flyer programmes)

5. There may be poor understanding of customers, such as a failure to realise that customer needs have changed. CRM programmes need to ensure that the right customers are targeted with the right information and promotions.

6. (a) The customer base could usefully be segmented along the lines of the market as a whole, targeting groups such as women 50+, middle-eastern and central European customers (heavy users, loyal), 18-25 year olds in fashion and design courses (a new market to be developed), and age care therapy institutions (long-term customers). These should also be segmented according to whether they are local to the store and are therefore potential regular *retail* customers, and those more distant and even international (eg tourists) as future mail order or e-commerce prospects. The EPOS system should be investigated to see whether there are distinct segments or buying patterns for particular styles of needlework, and for various product lines: yarns, patterns, accessories, frames or services. The regular customer groups could be targeted with additional purchase incentives or loyalty/reward schemes (perhaps a Needle Works Club Card?). The new youth market should be accessible via colleges, and targeted with a more youthful design-focused message.

    (b) No current database information directly taps into the above segments, especially interest in knitting or classes. Launch information on these areas can be segmented only by locality, since they will require personal presence at the showroom.

    The EPOS system gives good quality information about sales per product per week and where customers place orders, (eg for frames or framing services) per customer. Most customer data is captured via the Visitors' Book. It would be impractical for sales staff to input customer data for every non-account, over-the-counter transaction, so it is recommended that the Visitors' Book system be kept – but upgraded to collect better quality information.

    Instead of an open 'comments' section, it should have columns that customers can tick to express interest and request more information on particular crafts, products and most importantly on knitting supplies and educational activities/classes. These interests could be added as a field to the customer database ('interests') to trigger selective mailings to interested customers. Gender information could also be derived from the titles and names supplied, and added to the database.

7. You can always get your name taken off again later if your mailbox won't stand the strain!

Now try Question 2 at the end of the Study Text

PART A GATHERING, ANALYSING AND PRESENTING INFORMATION

Basic research techniques

Chapter topic list

1. Research planning
2. Questionnaires
3. Qualitative research
4. Other research techniques
5. Gathering information across borders

Syllabus content

- 1.4 Explain information gathering techniques available
- 1.7 Gather information across borders

PART A GATHERING, ANALYSING AND PRESENTING INFORMATION

Introduction

In Chapter 1, we discussed the various sources of information available to organisations when researching customers, market opportunities, competitor activity, the marketing environment and consumer behaviour. We looked in detail at secondary sources of information, used in desk research. In Chapter 2, we went on to focus on customer research via the database.

In this chapter, we look at how primary sources of information can be tapped via field research.

Remember that *marketing* research aims to collect, analyse, interpret and use data on the marketing organisation and its environment, while *market* research is a narrower activity focusing on specific markets.

1 Research planning

FAST FORWARD

Research planning involves:

- defining the need for information
- specifying research objectives
- evaluating data available
- defining relevant types and sources of data
- deciding on the data collection vehicle
- planning and briefing

Research involves the following basic steps.

- Defining the question or problem
- Defining the range of options available
- Designing the research project
- Collecting the data
- Analysing and interpreting the data
- Presentation of findings and recommendations

The first three steps form the **planning stage** of the research.

Effective planning is crucial to getting the right answers to the right questions. **Poor research planning** may result in:

- Inadequate briefing of researchers
- Poor problem/question/decision definition
- Neglect of available sources, or poor selection of sources
- Poor research design, using an inappropriate vehicle or using it ineffectively
- Lack of ownership of the project – and therefore failure to implement findings

1.1 Defining the problem

FAST FORWARD

Marketing and market research will only be worthwhile and cost effective if it is designed to address **real and relevant** marketing and sales issues: opportunities, threats, strengths or weaknesses, or real problems.

Some clarification of possible answers or options may be helpful in designing the research. If there is a decline in sales, for example, the research may focus on the likely effects of **pricing** decisions, the choice of **distribution** channels, alterations to the **product**, or an increase in **promotional activity**. Questions can then focus on relevant areas.

- Who buys what, in what quantity and where from?
- Who doesn't buy, and why?
- What are the shopping habits/buying power of those buying or not buying?
- What products are selling best?
- How aware are people of the promotional message?
- What effect does a price rise have on sales?

1.2 Designing the research

Once the researchers know what question is to be answered, or problem resolved, they can determine other issues.

(a) The specific **objectives** of the research: for example, to interview customers in a region with declining sales to determine the reasons for the decline.

(b) What **data is already available** previously collected by research, available from existing records or feedback from existing marketing activities, or from secondary sources.

(c) What **type of data** is needed: secondary or primary, quantitative or qualitative or a blend of both.

(d) What **sources of data** (secondary or primary) will be most appropriate?

(e) What **sample** of what **population** will be interviewed? (For example, should the question be asked of customers, or potential customers who don't buy the product, or those who consume the product and/or influence the purchase decision, but are not actually buyers?) A population is all the items or individuals who fall into the specified target group. A sample (often intended to be a random cross-section) of the population can then be used for research. The larger the sample, and the more genuinely representative of the population, the more valuable the data will be.

(f) What **mechanism** will most effectively and efficiently collect the data: postal survey, personal interview, focus group?

(g) **Who** will carry out the data collection: in-house or external services? (This is discussed further below.)

(h) Precisely what **format**, questions and incentives the research mechanism (questionnaire, interview, discussion guide) will have. A badly worded or designed questionnaire, for example, may fail to gather the answers required. (This is discussed in Sections 2 and 3.)

1.3 Who will do the research?

FAST FORWARD

Research may be carried out in-house or using **external specialists**.

The decision of whether to plan and carry out research in-house, or use management consultants or a specialist research agency, depends on several factors.

(a) External agencies offer several benefits.

- **Trained and experienced** staff, who can design appropriate vehicles
- **Objectivity**, which may produce a clearer view of the questions to be asked
- **Security** and confidentiality: screened questioners, and respondent anonymity
- **Cost-effectiveness**, where the above are critical to the research's effectiveness

PART A   GATHERING, ANALYSING AND PRESENTING INFORMATION

Marketing at Work

Marketing research moves online

Some websites, aimed at particular user profiles, are offering partner companies access to target demographic groups. Given the low cost and speed of response of online surveys, plus the ability to reach hard-to-find groups, such methods are likely to become increasingly popular.

'The teenage girls' website Mykindaplace.com has been using online surveys for the past 12 months to help its sponsorship partners to find answers to questions quickly. In 2001, it ran a beauty survey for Maybelline ... the survey drew around 4,000 responses over a weekend, and, with the incentive amounting to no more than the chance to win one of 100 Maybelline Lipliners, the total cost of running the survey came in at around £35 ... Furthermore, responses to each of the questions were broken down by age and region, giving the client a clearer picture of age-related and regional differences in the perception of the brand.'

Marketing Business, April 2002

(b) **Do-it-yourself research** often makes sense:

- Where **data is readily available** to in-house staff
- Where in-house staff **understand** the nature of the problem and target audience
- Where the **budget is very limited**
- Where the **confidentiality** of the research is crucial

In the rest of this chapter we take a practical approach: guiding you in designing and doing research yourself. If you do use a consultancy, you will need to provide them with a detailed **written brief.**

- The **research problem** to which an answer is required
- The **intended use** of the data collected
- The **budgetary** constraints
- Any **background information** which will put the problem in context

2 Questionnaires

2.1 Structured or unstructured?

FAST FORWARD

> **Questionnaires** for use in surveys may be structured or unstructured, and questions correspondingly closed or open.

A **questionnaire** is essentially a **data capture instrument**, as are diaries and recording devices discussed later in this chapter. It lists all the questions to which the researcher wants the respondent to answer, and it records the response of the interviewee.

(a) A **structured questionnaire** lists all questions to be asked in a logical sequence, specifying the precise wording to be used in the response (eg through multiple choice), and providing categories for recording the replies (eg using tick boxes or rating scales).

(b) An **unstructured questionnaire**, by contrast, may simply be a set of open-ended questions to which the respondent can write replies in his or her own words.

There are two main ways in which questions can be asked: **open-ended** (unstructured) and **closed/set-choice** (structured).

(a) Does the question allow the respondent to finish his own answer, in his own words? Open questions introduce variety and allow the full range of possible responses and new information (rather than the respondent merely selecting from your assumptions). An open question may be worded like this:

'How did you travel to work today?'

Alternatively, the questionnaire could offer a range of possible responses, making the data easier to process by both respondent and research analyst.

(b) Does the question make it as easy as possible for the respondent to answer, in terms of time and effort required? Avoid questions that require respondents to perform calculations or write long responses. Try to offer lists of options, tick boxes or scales.

Action Programme 1

What types of problem can you envisage arising from the use of multiple choice questions? How can such problems be overcome?

2.2 How are questionnaires administered?

> **FAST FORWARD** Questionnaires may be administered by phone, post, on-line or personal face-to-face interview.

Questionnaires can be administered by any of the following means.

(a) **Telephone surveys**. Where the questionnaire is conducted as an interview over the phone, and results recorded by the interviewer, this offers speedy, interactive responses over a wide geographical area. Questions will have to be even shorter and simpler to allow for the absence of visual support.

   (i) Have a list of at least twice as many interviewees as you require respondents (because of no-answers and do-not-wish-to-be-interviewed responses).

   (ii) Allow sufficient time per call. Getting hold of the right person takes time, and respondents typically reply at greater length than required in order to explain choices.

(b) **Postal surveys**. The questionnaire is sent to the respondent to complete and return: this may be done by conventional post, fax or e-mail or by logging on and completing the survey on-line. Self-administered questionnaires are a cheap method of reaching a large sample, and avoid the bias inherent in personal contact, but attention will need to be given to some areas.

   - The ease of completion by the respondent
   - The unambiguous nature of questions in order to produce quality answers
   - Incentives to complete and return the survey

(c) **Personal interviews** in homes, on the streets, or at retail outlets. Interviewer bias and leading becomes a factor, but so does the personal interaction, which can motivate quality responses. Being labour intensive, personal interviews are costly for large samples, but secure a high response rate compared to other survey vehicles.

2.3 Survey response rates

Survey response rates vary widely. Anything from 12-70% is 'normal' for consumer surveys. Your customer database will elicit higher responses than a 'cold' mailing. In addition, the Institute of Direct Marketing has suggested the following techniques to boost the response to a postal survey.

Technique	Percentage response increase
A clean customer file for sample selection	+150
A first reminder (letter)	+26
A second reminder (phone)	+25
Introductory questions of high interest to respondent	+19
Incentive	+18
Second reminder (letter and questionnaire plus reply envelope)	+12
Second class post	+8
First class post	+5
Questionnaire on yellow paper	+4

Source: *The Practitioner's Guide to Direct Marketing*

3 Qualitative research

FAST FORWARD

Qualitative research elicits narrative, subjective data, via depth interviews, group discussion (focus) groups and/or projective techniques.

Qualitative research is the process which aims to collect qualitative primary data, although qualitative data are also collected in the process of quantitative research, primarily questionnaires.

(a) Its main **methods** are the open-ended interview, whether this be a depth interview (one-to-one) or a group discussion (focus group), and projective techniques.

(b) The **form** of the data collected is narrative rather than isolated statements reduceable to numbers.

(c) Its main **purpose** is to understand consumer behaviour and perceptions.

The key to qualitative research is to allow the respondents to say what they feel and think in response to flexible, 'prompting' questioning, rather than to give their responses to set questions and often set answers in a questionnaire.

3.1 Depth interviews

In a depth interview the key line of communication is between the interviewer and the respondent. They have an open-ended conversation, not constrained by a formal questionnaire, and the qualitative data are captured as narrative by means of an audio or video tape.

(a) **What type of interview?** Although depth interviews are usually one-to-one, there may be more than one respondent and there may also be an informant, there to give information about tangible things (eg how big the organisation's purchase budget is) but not about his own attitudes.

(b) **How long should it be?** Genuine depth interviews interpret the meanings and implications of what is said and can therefore take some time. By contrast, a mini-depth interview may take only 15 minutes, because it can focus on one, predefined topic like a pack design.

(c) **How structured should it be?** It can be totally open-ended, ranging over whatever topics come up, or it can be semi-structured with an interview guide and perhaps the use of show material.

(d) **Should show material be used?** The type of material that is commonly used includes mock-ups or prototypes, storyboards or concept boards, narrative tapes and animatics, a form of cartoon.

(e) **Where should the interview take place?** Usually at home or in the workplace.

3.2 Focus groups

When planning qualitative research using group discussions, a number of factors need to be considered.

(a) **Type of group.** A standard group is of 7-9 respondents, but other types may also be used.

(b) **Membership.** Who takes part in the discussion depends on who the researcher wants to talk to (users or non-users, for instance) and whether they all need to be similar (homogeneous). A focus group is typically demographically balanced, in line with the target population.

(c) **Number of groups.** Having more than 12 groups in a research project would be very unusual.

(d) **Recruitment.** Usually on the basis of a quota sample: respondents are screened by a short questionnaire to see whether they are suitable. In order to persuade them to join in, the members are usually given an incentive plus expenses.

(e) **Discussion topics.** These will be decided by the researcher with regard to the purpose of the group discussion, and the data required.

(f) **Easing the respondents into the process.** There should be an introductory section (10 minutes).

- The purpose of focus groups
- Instructions
- The discussion is being taped/observed
- Round-robin introductions by the group

The advantages and disadvantages of group discussions and depth interviews are as follows.

Group discussions	
Advantages	**Disadvantages**
• Less intimidating • Easily observed • Range of attitudes can be measured • Social aspect reflects real world • Dynamic and creative • Cheaper	• Participants may not express what they really think – they may be inhibited or they may be showing off • Views may be unrealistic – meaningful in a group context but not for the individual

Depth interviews	
Advantages	**Disadvantages**
• Decision making processes can be analysed • Majority and minority opinion can be captured • Sensitive topics more easily discussed • Unusual behaviour can be discussed	• Time consuming • Less creative • More expensive • Gives depth, but not breadth (compared to surveys, questionnaires)

'Focus groups are used ... especially in the areas of brand image monitoring or development, brand positioning, with products and services that are more complex or emotive in nature, and where qualitative data is more important than quantitative data. The strength of the focus group methodology is in depth. It can never replace professionally designed structured surveys, by questionnaire, phone, or interview for breadth. A moderator can probe when information provided is shallow or superficial, which is an inherent problem with structured surveys or mail questionnaires. The *real* reasons for consumer decision making can often be elicited that traditional surveys cannot hope to uncover. For brand-image generation, the data elicited by a professionally conducted focus group is generally far more useful than the less personal survey method' (*Davies*, 2002).

Marketing at Work

'**Focus groups** are particularly useful in Asia, where:

- The exchange of information by word of mouth is central to not only to our cultures, but also the way business is done. Business means building up a relationship, and only when you have met and talked to people over an extended time do relationships move to the level of more open exchange of views that are central to good business. And the same applies for consumers.

- Many countries like China, Taiwan, Indonesia, Thailand, Malaysia and the Philippines are multi-cultural. Many consumers in Asia are at least bilingual and more often than not people can talk and converse in certain dialects, while to read or write in those dialects is far more difficult. Translating questionnaires often results in changes in the 'meaning' of questions, resulting in misunderstanding and invalid results. The focus group setting can reduce a lot of these difficulties.

'On the other hand, difficulties include:

- A casual way of life – and urban traffic jams – making it difficult to get focus groups together! (Invite extra people.)

- Conditioning to keep one's opinion to oneself in order not to cause others to 'lose face'. (Requires a longer warm-up period.)

- Different languages and dialects. (Allow more time for discussion, transcription and analysis.)

- Gender/age values, which may inhibit younger people or women from giving feedback. (Consider segregated groups.)'

Davies (2002)

3.3 Projective techniques

Projective techniques provide stimuli to which interviewees respond, in such a way as to reflect their unconscious beliefs and motivations.

A number of techniques might be employed.

(a) **Third person**, or 'friendly Martian' as it is sometimes called, is designed to get the respondent talking about issues. The researcher asks the respondent to describe what someone else might do. For example; 'If someone wanted to buy a house, what would they need to do?'

(b) **Word association** is based on an assumption that if a question is answered quickly, it is spontaneous and sub-conscious thoughts are therefore revealed. The person's conscious mind does not have time to think up an alternative response. ('What immediately comes into your mind when you hear the following?' etc).

(c) **Sentence completion** is a useful way to get people to respond quickly so that underlying attitudes and opinions are revealed.

Men who watch football are ....
Women wear red in order to ....

(d) In **thematic apperception tests** (TAT tests), people are shown a picture and asked to describe what is happening in the picture. They may be asked what happened just before or just after the picture. It is hoped that the descriptions reveal information about deeply held attitudes, beliefs, motives and opinions stored in the sub-conscious mind.

The major drawback with projective techniques is that the answers require skilled analysis and interpretation. The techniques are most valuable in providing **insights** rather than answers to specific research questions.

4 Other research techniques

> **FAST FORWARD**
>
> **Other research techniques** include observation, experimentation and data recording.

Other research techniques that you should be aware of, although you are less likely to carry them out yourself, include the following.

(a) **Experiments**

Laboratory experiments set up an artificial environment in which factors can be manipulated and compared to a 'control' so as to isolate the effects of particular factors. This is most often used for measuring response to advertisements and packaging, before (pre-testing) and after (post-testing) release.

Field experiments test out products and promotions in realistic surroundings, to give an idea of how they will perform. Examples include **in-house placement tests** (where a sample or panel of consumers tries out and evaluates the product at home), **store tests** (where sample stores trial products or point-of-sale material) and **test marketing** (where the marketing plan is carried out in a limited area).

(b) **Observation**

Interviews give information on what people say they will do and even what they think they will do: they cannot tell the researcher what people will actually do. Observation involves watching and recording behaviour.

Direct observation has a watcher observing (or even interacting with) the target population, as it reacts to product displays in store, for example.

Behaviour can also be **recorded** by mechanical devices which measure eye movement or emotional reactions (in response to ads) or track movement through retail space (in response to displays) or websites (tracking browsing patterns).

(c) **Recorded data**

Questionnaires are a way of recording data. Other examples may be found.

(i) **Diaries** completed by the sample of respondents are used to record consumer behaviour or media behaviour (how TV, radio and other media are used). This is time-consuming for the subject, so should be confined to short periods.

(ii) **Electronic recording systems** such as EPOS (Electronic Point of Sale systems) or video recording in stores.

4.1 The use of the Internet

Company websites can be used to assess the effectiveness of marketing on the Internet. Any such research should adhere to the usual principles:

- Define objectives
- Collect the data
- Analyse the data
- Report the results
- Take the necessary action

Log files on web servers enable companies to see which pages and items each visitor selects. This provides a wealth of market research information. Analysing these files will show which contact leads to a successful outcome, such as a sale. Different customer profiles can be set up, using **online registration** and questionnaires.

Marketing at Work

Dell Computers (www.dell.com) records online sales, as well as telephone orders generated by site visits. They can do this because they have a unique telephone number advertised on the website to use when placing orders.

Traditional market research techniques can also be used on the Internet:

- Questionnaires (such as the example in Chapter 2)
- Troubleshooting
- Online focus groups

5 Gathering information across borders

FAST FORWARD

There are added complexities to gathering primary data from **international sources**.

As with secondary research (discussed in Chapter 1), there are certain added complexities to gathering primary data from international sources.

(a) **Language barriers**. Questionnaires may have to be translated. Particular care should be given to the implications of trigger words in rating scales, such as **semantic differential scales**, in translation. (The differentials between poor-fair-good-excellent may be altered in direct translation to another language.)

(b) **Cultural differences**. Assumptions about people, for example, in sampling and question design, should be challenged. Qualitative research in particular will be subject to interpretation, and cultural assumptions (even with regard to simple matters such as body language and facial expression) may distort the results.

(c) **Demographics**. Demographic information (used in sampling, for example, to ensure proportional representation) will have to be obtained and analysed for each country in which research will be carried out. In some countries, this information may be less sophisticated or less readily available.

(d) **Distance and time**. If you are using personal methods of data gathering, travel distances and even telephone costs and time-differences may make the delays and costs of running the research from the home office prohibitive. Researchers will have to be selected and briefed in the overseas region.

(e) **Secondary sources**, available through international agencies, the Internet or international branches of your organisation, may be more attractive than commissioning overseas research.

(f) **Overseas partners**. Information sources should include overseas agents and distributors, foreign branches of the organisation's bank, consultancies or ad agencies, UK embassies and trade delegations and foreign sections of professional bodies. International trade shows and exhibitions in which the organisation is taking part may be a good opportunity to gather information.

Action Programme 2

The Needle Works

You have just got your database sorted out. Albert Smith sends you the following memo.

Memo

To: [your name]
From: Albert Smith
Date February 2007
Re: Education Programme

Now that we have a marketing person on board, I'd like to tackle the Education Programme we started work on last year and never got off the ground.

We decided that, since our competitors were offering various needlecraft classes, and from time to time our customers asked us whether we intended to do so, we would put together a class programme. We selected and scheduled a range of classes: tapestry, cross stitch, creative stitchery, candlemaking and crewel embroidery on weekday evenings for 3 hours. We had a very poor response – the times were wrong, or the class was the wrong level or type: in the end we cancelled the classes. We also had trouble finding teachers.

However, we promised the customers who asked that we would give them classes, and I would like to reactivate the proposal.

Since you talked about database marketing last week, I've been thinking: perhaps we could have a real 'student club', doing not just classes but activity days – or even weekend breaks – and appreciation evenings, talks, gallery visits, drop-in times, a newsletter – that sort of thing. I'm not sure exactly what our customers would want, or how much they'd be prepared to pay. I suppose that depends on what else is available, and people's preferences for small groups, doing a whole craft project in class or just working on their own.

How could we gather some real information on what people want from classes: something we can really use for planning a proper programme that our customers will attend?

What ideas might you suggest?

PART A GATHERING, ANALYSING AND PRESENTING INFORMATION

Chapter Roundup

- **Research planning** involves:
    - defining the need for information
    - specifying research objectives
    - evaluating data available
    - defining relevant types and sources of data
    - deciding on the data collection vehicle
    - planning and briefing

- Marketing and market research will only be worthwhile and cost effective if it is designed to address **real and relevant** marketing and sales issues: opportunities, threats, strengths or weaknesses, or real problems.

- Research may be carried out in-house or using **external specialists**.

- **Questionnaires** for use in surveys may be structured or unstructured, and questions correspondingly closed or open.

- Questionnaires may be administered by phone, post, on-line or personal face-to-face interview.

- **Qualitative research** elicits narrative, subjective data, via depth interviews, group discussion (focus) groups and/or projective techniques.

- **Other research techniques** include observation, experimentation and data recording.

- There are added complexities to gathering primary data from **international sources**.

Quick Quiz

1   Why should an organisation not merely collect all the data it can?

2   What are the advantages of doing research 'in-house'?

3   What are the effects of poor research planning?

4   What are the three types of question in terms of what they seek to find out?

5   List three ways in which a respondent can be motivated to return a questionnaire.

6   What are the advantages and disadvantages of qualitative research groups?

7   How might language and cultural differences affect the gathering and interpretation of research data?

Answers to Quick Quiz

1. Targeting the data most relevant for decision making and processing it effectively ensures good value for the time and money resources committed to its collection.

2. Where the data is available, the advantages are: staff knowledge, cost and confidentiality.

3. Paragraph 1 lists five key problems.

4. The three main types of question are behavioural, attitudinal and classification.

5. Three from: clean customer file for sample selection, reminders by letter and telephone, high interest introductory questions, incentives, eye catching presentation.

6. Refer to the table in Paragraph 3.2.

7. Great attention has to be paid to avoid different connotations being accidentally introduced through translation or by different cultural outlooks.

Action Programme Review

1. Here are some ideas. You may have thought of others.

    (a) Capturing a full range of possible responses to a question such as 'In which store do you buy the majority of your clothes?' can be impractical. This problem can be overcome by listing the most popular stores and using an 'other (please specify)' option.

    (b) The position of the alternative responses may introduce bias. This problem can be overcome (but not entirely) by producing different versions of the questionnaire.

    (c) An unbalanced set of alternative responses could be provided such as the following.

    Q: What do you think of TV programme 'XXX'?

A:	1	2	3
	Too boring	Very dull	Indifferent

    Obviously such response sets should not be used.

2. Given existing resources, the most obvious suggestion might be a questionnaire, for mailing to customers in the local area, asking: what classes would interest them; when they should be held; what price would be considered appropriate; which other activities they would like to be involved in; and so on. Alternatively, a focus group (using representative samples of customers and store visitors) could be used.

Now try Question 3 at the end of the Study Text

Investigating marketing opportunities

Chapter topic list

1. Integrated learning
2. Internal marketing audit
3. External appraisal
4. The competitor intelligence system
5. Investigating marketing and promotional opportunities

Syllabus content – knowledge and skills requirements

- 1.5 Source and present information on competitor activities across the marketing mix
- 1.6 Investigate marketing and promotional opportunities using appropriate information gathering techniques
- 5.3 Explain how organisations assess the viability of opportunities, marketing initiatives and projects

PART A GATHERING, ANALYSING AND PRESENTING INFORMATION

Introduction

The Chartered Institute of Marketing identifies **marketing strategy** and its components as a key business process.

- Reviewing the company's **competitive position**
- The systematic collection and use of **market information**
- Involvement of **all levels of staff** in collecting market information

In this chapter, we deal with the gathering of some of the information required for strategic marketing planning.

(a) Information on competitors' activities

(b) Information about the company's own strengths and weaknesses

(c) Information about the marketing environment, and factors that pose threats or opportunities to marketing activity

(d) Information about specific opportunities to launch or competitively position products

So, on completion of this chapter, you should be able to:

- Source and present information on competitor activity across the marketing mix (including competitor pricing comparison)
- Undertake a basic SWOT analysis of the marketing organisation and its environment
- Gather and evaluate information on marketing and promotional opportunities

1 Integrated learning

We do not cover the purposes, theory and processes of strategic planning here: it is dealt with in detail in the *Marketing Environment* and *Marketing Fundamentals* syllabuses (and corresponding BPP Study Texts).

Nor do we discuss, in this chapter, the kinds of policy decisions and actions that might be taken in response to the information gathered on competitors, on the company's current marketing performance and on emerging opportunities and threats. This is the subject of Part D of this Text, and particularly Chapter 14, which discusses the use of such information across the extended marketing mix. Again, that material builds on *Marketing Fundamentals*.

Instead, we focus on the information gathering process.

2 Internal marketing audit

2.1 Marketing audit

FAST FORWARD

A **marketing audit** is a systematic analysis of the organisation's marketing position and performance. It includes marketing objectives, capabilities and competitive effectiveness.

Key concept

A **marketing audit** is 'a comprehensive, systematic, independent and periodic examination of a company's – or business unit's – marketing environment, objectives, strategies and activities, with a view to determining problem areas and opportunities and recommending a plan of action to improve the company's marketing performance.' (*Kotler et al.*, 1999)

At the level of planning and co-ordinating marketing activities, the *internal* part of a marketing audit will pay attention to several issues.

(a) **Marketing capabilities**: what resources, strengths and weaknesses does the marketing organisation have to build on?

(b) **Marketing performance**: how effective is marketing activity across the marketing mix, compared to objectives?

(c) **Competitive effectiveness**: what are the actual and potential sources of the organisation's competitive advantage?

> **Key concept**
>
> A **capability profile** is a description of the potential ability of an organisation to operate in its markets: the assets on which it can build, in terms of skills, knowledge, reputation, organisation and management, infrastructures and attitudes.

The purpose of the analysis is to express, qualitatively and quantitatively, which areas of marketing activity have strengths to be exploited and which have weaknesses to be minimised or eliminated. Key areas which significantly affect the department or organisation's objectives should be highlighted for attention.

2.2 Audit data

FAST FORWARD — A systematic audit should be undertaken as a quantitative and qualitative research exercise.

A number of sources of **internal data** are available for gathering the above information, including past internal and market research reports, forecasts, budgets and performance data (sales, revenue and profit figures, customer feedback records, cost analysis, personnel performance appraisals). By looking at trends (worsening or improving over time) or by comparing measures or ratios with other firms in the same sector (benchmarking), it may be possible to identify key strengths and weaknesses.

Data can be gathered by questionnaire, canvassing a wide variety of opinions at all levels of the organisation, plus selected supply chain partners and customers.

2.3 Specimen audit questions

A checklist of some of the areas for evaluation is as follows. If you added a rating scale for each (1-10, say, or poor-fair-good-excellent) you would have the basis of a questionnaire or discussion guide.

1   Capabilities

(a) To what extent does the organisation as a whole have a marketing orientation? Is the customer genuinely the focus of our plans and objectives?

(b) What is our public image/reputation?

(c) How effectively are the customer's needs understood and conveyed throughout the firm by the marketing function?

(d) How flexible/responsible/efficient is the organisation of the marketing department?

(e) Are there clear, realistic, measurable marketing objectives?

(f) Are sufficient resources being committed to marketing to enable the objectives to be achieved? Is the division of costs between different products and activities sensible and supportive?

(g) Are our procedures for gathering data, formulating marketing plans and evaluating performance efficient and effective? Have planning and control been successfully carried out?

PART A GATHERING, ANALYSING AND PRESENTING INFORMATION

- (h) Is our marketing information system adequate and effective?
- (i) Are we in a strong or weak bargaining position in relation to sources of supply, quality, delivery and price of materials and services?
- (j) What is the size, skill base, and efficiency of our marketing function and sales force? Do we motivate, train and develop marketing personnel?
- (k) Do we encourage communication, innovation and feedback at all levels of the organisation?
- (l) Is our management style strong or weak, and in what ways? Is it suited to the business culture?
- (m) What is the strength of our key brands?
- (n) What is the strength of customers' brand loyalty?
- (o) How widely do we develop networks and build trade and customer relationships?

2 *Performance* (4 Ps or 7 Ps)

- (a) Are sales revenue and profit or contribution meeting forecasts?
- (b) Is the product mix 'healthy'? Is product demand growing, stable or likely to decline? Are we well placed in growth markets? Are products being developed or improved in line with customer needs and product trends?
- (c) How successful are our new product launches? How effective is our research and development?
- (d) How does our product and process quality measure up to standard?
- (e) Is the product reaching consumers effectively and efficiently? Are delivery lead times and standards as planned?
- (f) Are the sales teams and/or direct marketing campaigns successful in winning orders?
- (g) Are our price levels appropriate (for supply and demand, customer attitudes, competitor pricing)?
- (h) Is the marketing message reaching the target audience? How effective are our advertising and promotional campaigns?
- (i) Are we retaining and focusing marketing effort on profitable customers? As sales revenue rises, is contribution, or profit, also increasing?
- (j) Have we reached target levels of customer/client service? Are we still improving?
- (k) Do all marketing activities show returns on investment?

3 *Competitive effectiveness*

- (a) What markets are competitors targeting?
- (b) What competitor products are in direct competition with ours?
- (c) What market segments or niches do we serve uniquely or strongly?
- (d) How are our products differentiated from those of competitors? How are they unique in areas which are highly regarded by consumers?
- (e) How do our product/service/delivery quality standards compare with our competitors?
- (f) How effective are our R & D schedules? Do we beat competitors to new product launches?
- (g) Are we gaining/retaining or losing market share in contested markets?
- (h) How effectively and efficiently do we gather data about our competitors?

Action Programme 1

Use the above checklist as an interview discussion guide for an impromptu marketing audit. Use it on yourself, to appraise your own organisation (set up a suitable rating scale) or ask a fellow student or colleague to work through some or all of the questions with you.

3 External appraisal

FAST FORWARD

External appraisal is aimed at identifying environmental changes which may represent threats or opportunities for the organisation.

We mentioned **environmental scanning** in Chapter 1. Information on the external environment can be gathered from a wide variety of sources.

- Primary sources at the interface between the organisation and the environment (ie customers, suppliers and distributors).
- Secondary sources (outlined in detail in Chapter 1).

Action Programme 2

Just to test your knowledge from *Marketing Environment*, what are 'SLEPT' factors, and what *other* areas would a marketing organisation want to be aware of?

3.1 Gathering environmental intelligence

It is easy to be overwhelmed by the volume of relevant environmental information on offer. However, the following may be helpful, as a process for creating usable intelligence

Stage	Description
PRIMING	Define key areas in which change will be significant (competitor pricing, consumer attitudes)
MONITORING	Scan external data sources
SENSING	Identify appropriate external indicators of change in a key area (rumours of price change, new fashion)
GATHERING	Collect relevant and reliable information from sources (using methodologies discussed in Chapters 2-3).
PROCESSING	Analyse information for trends and implications. Organise in a useable format.
COMMUNICATING	Package, summarise, illustrate and/or offer conclusions/recommendations.

Figure 4.1: A process for environmental scanning

The first stage is particularly important. Even in environmental scanning, with the best will in the world you cannot find what you don't know you're looking for! The research equivalent is doing a keyword search in an index, or database, or on the Internet.

3.1.1 Classifying environmental factors

As you should recall from your *Marketing Environment* studies, the PEST, SLEPT or PESTLE model is the most popular framework for classifying factors in the macro or external environment.

- *Political factors* include government policy, political stability/instability in overseas markets, foreign trade policy and so on.

- *Economic factors* include business cycles (boom, recession, recovery), interest and foreign exchange rates, inflation, employment figures and energy costs. Such factors affect both the costs of doing business and the disposable income of consumers.

- *Socio-cultural factors* include demographics (age, location, socio-economic status and other structural factors in the population as a whole); lifestyle and fashion trends; consumption, shopping and media use; business and social customs; and consumer values and concerns (eg 'green' consumerism).

- *Technological factors* include new products (eg digital music), new processes (eg e-procurement and e-commerce); risk of product obsolescence; increasing global competition; and virtual teamworking and organisation.

- *Legal factors* include law and regulation on employment (eg health and safety, equal opportunities), marketing (eg advertising standards and restrictions), consumer rights, product safety/labelling and so on.

- *Environmental/ethical factors* include sustainability of energy/resource use, recyclable products/packaging, pollution control, ethical trading with suppliers, ethical investment and so on.

Exam tip

> In December 2006, you were asked to explain how a range of macro and micro (competitive) environment factors could impact on a given organisation. The examiner noted that this required learning from the *Marketing Environment* syllabus – but was still disappointed that candidates showed so little understanding of how (for example) interest, inflation and unemployment rates might impact on discretionary spending by consumers. We have only summarised the PESTLE model here: make sure you can apply it in detail!

Action Programme 3

Square Wheels plc is a UK firm producing pedal bicycles. It has a major factory in the UK, and has also acquired a plant in Tijuana (Mexico) near the US border, and another in Romania, formerly a state-run concern, and still managed by the same team. Square Wheels sells all over Europe and the Americas and also in India and China, where it has a licensing agreement with local manufacturers, enabling it to have a presence in the market. Bikes are perceived as leisure goods in Europe and North America, whereas they are essential means of transport in India and China. The R & D department has recently come up with a new product idea: a battery-powered motor which can be affixed to the bike for extra power going up hill! It is thought that this might encourage a wider audience in hilly areas and among older users.

From the mini-scenario given:

(a) How complex is Square Wheels' environment?

(b) Identify the political/legal risks to which it is vulnerable.

(c) What might be some implications of (i) population growth in China and India and (ii) the changing age structure of the populations of Europe (fewer young people)?

(d) What ecological or environmental concerns should Square Wheels monitor?

3.2 Opportunities and threats

FAST FORWARD

Organisational **strengths and weaknesses** are significant if they:

- are important and relevant to customers and/or
- affect the organisation's ability to compete

External appraisal has two main purposes.

- To identify **profit-making opportunities** which can be exploited by the company's strengths
- To identify **environmental threats** against which the company must protect itself

Opportunities

- What opportunities are posed by changes or existing conditions in the business environment?
- What is their profit-making potential?
- What is our capability profile compared with that of competitors? Who is better placed to exploit the opportunities?
- What is our performance potential in the field of opportunity?
- What are the costs and risks of exploiting the opportunity?

The opportunity may involve product development, market development, market penetration or diversification. No realistic opportunity should be ignored.

Threats

- What threats might arise to us or our business environment?
- How will competitors be affected?
- How will we be affected?
- Do we have strengths to deal with the threat, or do weaknesses need to be corrected in order for us to survive the threat?
- What contingency plans are required?

Marketing at Work

The following is an example (in executive summary form) of the kind of market data available from research and database organisations, in this case Euromonitor.

Why buy this report

- Get insight into trends in market performance
- Pinpoint growth sectors and identify factors driving change
- Identify market and brand leaders and understand the competitive environment

Executive Summary

Poor performance again in 2004

Although Polish cosmetics and toiletries went through a recession at the start of the review period, it merely stagnated from 2002-2004, with constant value growth of 1% expected in 2004 over the previous year. This poor performance resulted from a recession in Poland and resulting low disposable incomes for Polish consumers. At the end of the review period, there was a noticeable increase in demand for cheaper cosmetics and toiletries and a lowering of unit prices by manufacturers to generate sales. Both factors were behind the weak constant value sales performance.

Direct appeal for Avon

The review period saw the dynamic expansion of direct selling companies in Polish cosmetics and toiletries. Direct selling company Avon is expected to be the overall leader in 2004 in cosmetics and toiletries, overtaking multinational giants like Procter and Gamble, L'Oréal Groupe and Unilever. Avon is expected to grow its share of overall cosmetics and toiletries by two percentage points from 2001-2004. Its leading position in colour cosmetics, fragrances and skin care will underpin its success.

Modern distribution channels lead retail revolution

The review period saw a retail revolution. There was a notable shift of sales from drugstores and specialist shops to supermarkets/hypermarkets. This is due to the increasing popularity of modern retail formats, which offer a wide variety of goods at a cheaper price. Direct selling companies also considerably improved their performance, mainly due to a strong position in colour cosmetics and skin care. Sales through department stores, outdoor markets and "others" experienced a decline.

Optimistic prognoses for cosmetics and toiletries in Poland

Estimates regarding the growth of Polish cosmetics and toiletries look much more positive for the forecast period. Accession to the EU in May 2004 resulted in increased imports and exports and a larger number of products on offer. Higher disposable incomes among Polish consumers are expected to create a shift towards mid-priced and premium products. The most dynamically developing will be fragrances and colour cosmetics, with such cosmetics and toiletries being viewed as a good means of stating an improved economic position.

www.euromonitor.com/cosmetics_and_toiletries_in_Poland 10 May 2006

4 The competitor intelligence system

> **FAST FORWARD**
>
> **Competitor analysis** involves identifying the relative strengths and weaknesses of the organisation, compared to those of competitors and potential competitors.

Key concept

> **Competitor analysis** is the identification and qualification of the relative strengths and weaknesses (compared with competitors or potential competitors), which could be of significance in the development of a successful competitive strategy.

The **competitor intelligence system** is a formal term for the procedures used to obtain data for competitor analysis. We will look at three aspects of competitor intelligence-gathering.

- **Who** are your competitors?
- **What** should you know about them?
- **Where** do you get the information?

4.1 Who are your competitors?

Organisations need to be aware of the following.

(a) **Who are their existing and potential competitors?**

Competitors need not be producers of similar products or directly competing brands, nor similar types of organisation operating in the same market or market segment. The competitors of book publishers, for example, include not only other book publishers, but producers of alternative products (CD-Rom publishers, video producers, audio books, computer packages) and producers of other products which absorb people's discretionary spending on leisure and gifts.

Look at the following diagram:

[Venn diagram showing three overlapping circles labelled Competitor C, Competitor A, and Competitor B]

Competitor B is clearly a key 'head-to-head' competitor of A, because their markets overlap. However, competitor C – despite its serving a different market in general – has a product or promotional angle that brings it into competition with A and B.

(b) **Who are their key competitors?**

In a market where there is one or more competitors, marketing decisions may be influenced by what a competitor does or is about to do. (A price war, in which competitors successively undercut each other until one of them withdraws, is the simplest example.) Some competitors will have more power in the market than others, and it will be important to know who they are. Key competitors will be those with a **large or growing market share**, those with highly **differentiated or focused** products or services and those with a **capability profile** that would allow them to capitalise on opportunities.

Marketing at Work

Coca Cola defines its **competitors** as:

- Pepsi, in the cola market
- All other soft drinks
- Tea and coffee
- Tap water

Coca Cola's chief executive has declared that 'the main competitor' is tap water: any other share definition is too narrow.

Action Programme 4

Whom would you list as the competitors of

(a) a bank?
(b) a petrol station?

4.2 What do you need to know about competitors?

FAST FORWARD

Influential competitors should be **profiled** in the same way as the organisation's own marketing position and performance.

You need to know how they compare with you in terms of goals, capabilities, performance and competitive effectiveness. Anything you do, ask yourself whether they do it differently, and if so, how?

Marketing at Work

One of the best ways of gathering information about a competitor is to undertake a **mystery shopper** exercise. This is where you pretend to be an actual prospective customer of an organisation, but are actually collecting information about

- the organisation
- its products/services
- its prices
- the way it treats customers

Some organisations, particularly retail chains, employ mystery shoppers to find out information about their own company and use this as a source of measurement, just like customer satisfaction surveys.

Some companies *(Ansells* in the UK, *Coles Supermarkets* in Australia) even featured a mystery shopper in their advertising campaigns, to reassure customers that there was constant checking of service quality.

4.2.1 Competitor profile

A capability and strengths and weaknesses profile of a competitor should include the following areas.

(a) **Future goals**

   (i) What are their stated goals and real priorities?

   (ii) How satisfied are they with their present position in the market, and what changes are they most likely to attempt?

   (iii) What is the management like? (Strong or weak? United or divided? Risk-taking or risk-averse? Good at change? Locked into a particular strategy?)

(b) **Capabilities**

   (i) What are their **core competencies**: what do they do distinctively well?

   (ii) What **resources** do they have to build on? (Production capacity, established distribution channels, flexibility and innovation, capital, staff skills and motivation, reputation, brand strength.)

   (iii) What are their special **competitive advantages**? (Relationship with key distributors, cheap production, access to government?)

(c) **Current strategy and performance across the extended marketing mix**

   (i) **Managerial ability**, and the ability, loyalty and motivation of employees.

   (ii) **Product mix**: product/service quality, diversity, positioning and specifications, new product development, leaders or followers on product design?

   (iii) **Operations**: research and engineering capacity, up-to-dateness and development potential of plant and machinery.

   (iv) **Distribution channels**: including the effectiveness of the sales force and direct marketing.

   (v) **Price strategy**: product/service prices, leaders or followers on price?

   (vi) **Financial strength**: cost of sales, debt position and sources of new finance, profitability, ability to develop new products or sustain competition on price.

   (vii) **Promotional strategy:** preferred messages and media, 'unique selling points' and promotional platforms or themes, expenditure on advertising, promotion and selling, effectiveness of PR, customer care/service programmes.

   (viii) **Organisation**: ability to gather market intelligence and respond flexibly, organisation culture, marketing orientation, efficient processes and systems.

   (ix) **Customer/consumer perception** of all the above.

4.2.2 Formatting competitor data

This data can be used in two main ways.

(a) **A competitor analysis** compares the strengths, weaknesses and capabilities of the competitor with those of the organisation doing the analysis.

(b) **A competitor response profile** indicates:

   (i) the competitor's **vulnerability** to environmental forces, downturns in sales and competitor activity (if you can analyse your company's vulnerability to such factors, you can also model that of your competitors)

   (ii) the most potentially advantageous '**battle ground**' on which to take on the competitor. This may be a market where the competitor is weak, or a product range which is low-priority for the competitor.

4.3 Where do you get the information?

> **FAST FORWARD**
>
> There are many open and ethical **sources of competitor information**, including published material, advertising, media coverage, customers, suppliers, distributors and the competitors themselves (products and services).

The very phrase 'intelligence system' has a ring of 'espionage' about it. The more useful competitor information is, the more sensitive it is, and the more closely guarded it will be: however, by definition, it is also information that competitors will be very keen to obtain!

However, there are plenty of ethical and completely open sources of information about competitors.

(a) **Competitors' products and services**. If you want to know about the product, you can see it on store shelves (which gives additional information about point-of-sale display, promotion and impact), or buy it for analysis. Members of the organisation might also use the competitor's services and report back on the experience or bring back relevant literature.

(b) **Competitors' promotional and informational literature**. Monitor advertising, point-of-sale information and direct mail packages (put yourself on the mailing list). Public companies also issue annual reports and accounts, which give a wide range of financial and non-financial information, including goals for the future. Don't forget job advertisements and application forms: they give data on personnel policies and capabilities.

(c) **Press/media coverage**. Monitor articles in trade and general press and press releases. Internet databases are an efficient way of running a cuttings search, or a media monitoring agency may be retained to gather relevant clippings for you.

(d) **Exhibitions, conferences and meetings of trade/professional associations**. Network with third parties who know and are willing to discuss competitors, and even competitors themselves. Even if information is tightly controlled, a sense of the organisation's culture, style and staff can be gleaned.

(e) **Internet**. Monitor the competitor's website. How sophisticated is it? What does it offer?

(f) **Sales rep activity**. The competitor's customers and retail outlets may discuss visits and offers made by representatives. Your own reps will be a useful source of feedback.

(g) **Competitors' suppliers**. Suppliers of services or products to the company may disclose some information about their relationship with another, especially if it is openly available. Many retailers and wholesalers get information on competitors' pricing from suppliers.

(h) **Retailers** may be a source of information such as share of sales volume, customer feedback and scheduled promotions.

(i) **Customer research** is often used to elicit information about the customer's experience with, awareness of and attitude to competing products.

(j) **Other secondary sources**. The competitors' directors may be in *Who's Who* or the *Directory of Directors*. The company may feature in a local history. Advertising may be reviewed in *Campaign*.

4.3.1 Ethical issues in competitor monitoring

All of the above can be researched via open networking, desk research and field research. Be aware, however, that there are more covert means of gaining information, especially from competitors and their suppliers. People may issue bogus requests for tenders/proposals to get competitors to submit product/service/costings details, or make bogus calls to competitors. Variations on this theme include calls from job seekers, market researchers, and marketing students doing a project, wanting details about the company and its plans.

There is nothing at all unethical about an employee of a restaurant, say, eating in another restaurant and bringing back impressions of its decor, service, menu and food. But what if the same employee called the restaurant and claimed to be a food journalist preparing a profile for 'The Good Food Guide', in order to get more in-depth information on recipes, or the chef, or the restaurant's plans for the future? Use research strategies you feel comfortable with, in accordance with your organisation's ethical objectives.

Exam tip

> The questions we have just asked in Paragraphs 4.1 – 4.3.
>
> - Who are your competitors?
> - What do you need to know about competitors?
> - Where do you get the information?
>
> ... mirror precisely the requirements of a question set in the Pilot Paper.

Action Programme 5

Where would you go for information on competitors' prices?

4.3.2 A simple competitive intelligence system

Taylor (1997) suggests a simple two-step system for efficient competitive intelligence gathering.

(a) **Use the Internet**. Set up a group of key words (the name of competitors, brand names, prominent figures). You could do database searches yourself, or use a news scanning service, which scans for you. You should also review relevant online databases such as the *Financial Times*' FTPROFILE or AC Nielsen's marketing information.

(b) **Use a network**. Select one individual in every major operating group or department in your organisation as the competitive intelligence specialist for that area. Ask that individual to gather and e-mail you any piece of market intelligence that may be valuable.

Exam tip

> It is useful to commence any report with a brief situation analysis, and conclude by bringing all of your information together. Below is a suggested format for a **competitor analysis**.
>
> - An **overview of your organisation**, identity, business role, product and service offering, size and turnover.
> - An outline of **who your competitors are**, comparing them with your own organisation in terms of product and service offers, the size and turnover of the organisation.
> - Identification of your own organisation's **strengths**, and those of the competitor.
> - A grid that compares your own organisation with two or three other competitors, focusing on the **marketing mix**. Set up headings in the grid that enable you to identify key competitive areas.
>
>   - Price
>   - Product
>   - Distribution outlets
>   - Promotional activity
>   - Customer services activity
>   - Service levels
>   - Customer profile
>   - Market share

> As an added dimension, look at the broader issues affecting competition, such as **SLEPT factors**. How do they affect pricing? How do environmental issues affect packaging? How does your organisation respond to external forces? How do your competitors respond to the same forces?
>
> From the information you have drawn together, make some **key comparisons** and conclusions. Fully explain where your organisation could **add more value** to the product or service proposition.
>
> **Identify and recommend** some possible tactical activities for the marketing mix to help the organisation be more competitive (not just in the short term, but to sustain the **competitive advantage**). Don't forget to **justify your recommendations**.
>
> Beware wasting time in an exam, however, if you have not been *asked* to write a full report, or you have only been asked for specific elements of analysis!

5 Investigating marketing and promotional opportunities

FAST FORWARD

> **Evaluating a marketing or promotional opportunity** requires the gathering and analysis of information about the objectives of the opportunity, its feasibility (SWOT analysis), cost-benefit analysis and performance measures for control.

This area of the syllabus represents one of the key purposes to which customer, marketing and competitor research (covered in Part A of this Study Text) are put. We will look at specific examples in Part D of the Text, but here we will give a general framework.

5.1 Opportunities

There are many occasions when opportunities arise which are not preplanned or part of some previously agreed marketing strategy. The most frequent type of 'opportunity' is that of being offered advertising space or airtime. On other occasions there may be an approach from another organisation to join in a joint promotion.

Tactical decisions are relatively low-key and made quickly in response to opportunities or changes. However, any tactical decision on whether to engage in an activity should fit in with the organisation's overall direction or **strategy**. Clearly, advertising in an inappropriate journal because the space was half price, or having a joint promotion with a company whose reputation is poor, are not good ideas!

5.2 'Scorpion' – a tool for assessing opportunities

FAST FORWARD

> The **SCORPION model** can be used as a tool for assessing the merits of a wide range of options.

The acronym SCORPION can be used as a tool for assessing the merits of a wide range of options, whether this be a change in price, opening a new outlet, renting a poster site, advertising on the back of bus tickets, or anything else for that matter.

Synergy	Is this opportunity one which fits in with what the organisation is trying to achieve, in terms of reputation, branding, market share etc?
Customers	Will this activity positively impact on our customers, or even attract new ones?
Objectives	Does this fulfil any of our business objectives?
Rivals	Is this the sort of activity that would allow us to gain advantage over our rivals?
Profit	Perhaps most importantly: will this make us money?
Information	Do we have enough information on which to base a decision?
Other actions	How well does this stand up against other things we could do with the same amount of money, which may be better value?
Needs	Does this match a need we have? Or does it help fulfil our customers needs?

4: INVESTIGATING MARKETING OPPORTUNITIES

Exam tip

> Using a model such as SLEPT, SCORPION or SWOT analysis can be very useful in an exam situation as it steers you to making structured, intelligent comments against a set range of criteria. Don't forget, though, that a model by itself is unlikely to be sufficient: you need to be able to ask the questions from the perspective of the particular scenario given!

Action Programme 6

Hall Faull Downes Ltd produces components for manufacturers in the engineering industry. It has been in business for 25 years, during which time profits have risen by an average of 3% per annum, although there have been peaks and troughs in profitability due to the ups and downs of trade in the customers' industry. The increase in profits until five years ago was the result of increasing sales in a buoyant market, but more recently, the total market has become somewhat smaller and Hall Faull Downes has only increased sales and profits as a result of improving its market share.

In recent years, the company has developed many new products and currently has 40 items in its range compared to 24 only five years ago. Over the same five-year period, the number of customers has fallen from 20 to nine, two of whom together account for 60% of the company's sales.

Give your appraisal of the company's future, and suggest what it is probably doing wrong.

Action Programme 7

The Needle Works

Your market research questionnaire on educational activities has had a very good response (53%). Research shows that most of your customers are in favour of such an initiative, particularly those in your local region. Direct competitors (smaller craft shops) already run classes which are very popular and inexpensive (under £5 per hour), but do not offer a wide range of topics, do not run very often, and are generally held during shopping hours only, which working customers are unable to attend. Cost and small group sizes are particularly important to potential students, as is the timing/convenience of classes. Expensive classes are accepted by people who want individual tuition and a high-quality class environment or 'celebrity' tutors. Your suggestions of social activities and a membership club were almost unanimously welcomed (95% of respondents).

Draw up a suitable visual representation of these results (plus any detail you want to add) which will highlight a possible opportunity or competitive advantage. Add notes on the factors you would take into account in evaluating the feasibility of the opportunity you identify. Think about all 7 Ps of the extended marketing mix.

[*Key skill for Marketers: Presenting information*]

Chapter Roundup

- A **marketing audit** is a systematic analysis of the organisation's marketing position and performance. It includes marketing objectives, capabilities and competitive effectiveness.
- A systematic audit should be undertaken as a quantitative and qualitative research exercise.
- **External appraisal** is aimed at identifying environmental changes which may represent threats or opportunities for the organisation.
- Organisational **strengths and weaknesses** are significant if they:
  - are important and relevant to customers and/or
  - affect the organisation's ability to compete
- **Competitor analysis** involves identifying the relative strengths and weaknesses of the organisation, compared to those of competitors and potential competitors.
- Influential competitors should be **profiled** in the same way as the organisation's own marketing position and performance.
- There are many open and ethical **sources of competitor information**, including published material, advertising, media coverage, customers, suppliers, distributors and the competitors themselves (products and services).
- **Evaluating a marketing or promotional opportunity** requires the gathering and analysis of information about the objectives of the opportunity, its feasibility (SWOT analysis), cost-benefit analysis and performance measures for control.
- The **SCORPION model** can be used as a tool for assessing the merits of a wide range of options.

Quick Quiz

1. What is a 'capability profile'?
2. What questions might be asked to analyse an organisation's competitive effectiveness?
3. What is the purpose of (a) internal and (b) external analysis?
4. Outline the sequence for creating market/environmental intelligence.
5. Who are the 'key' competitors of a business?
6. What information might you gather about a competitor's (a) future goals, and (b) capabilities?
7. What is a 'competitor response' profile?
8. List eight sources of information about competitor activity.
9. What issues should be considered when evaluating the feasibility of a marketing opportunity?

Answers to Quick Quiz

1. A description of the potential ability of an organisation to operate in its markets in terms of its assets, skills, knowledge, reputation, management, infrastructures and attitudes.

2. A full list of questions relating to competitive effectiveness is found in Section 2.3.

3. Both internal and external analyses are vital information gathering tools if an organisation is to fend off challenges and exploit opportunities. SWOT analysis deals with both aspects: the strengths and weaknesses identified are a good indication of how fit the organisation is to deliver its objectives or respond to changes in the market place. The perceived opportunities and threats enable the organisation to deal early with potential problems from the macro environment and to profit from new openings in the market.

4. This is shown in Figure 4.1.

5. Key competitors are those who have already established a large or growing market share, highly differentiated product and a capability profile that allows them to capitalise on opportunities.

6. Future goals: their stated goals; satisfaction with present position and market share objectives; their management style/culture, particularly how innovative, responsive and united they are. Capabilities: what they do very well with what level of resources; untapped resources; main competitive advantages.

7. A competitor response profile indicates the competitor's vulnerability in relation to environmental and market forces, and suggests in which arenas you might successfully compete.

8. A full list is provided in Section 4.3.

9. SCORPION is a useful mnemonic (Section 5.2).

Action Programme Review

1. This is a useful intelligence gathering tool on *any* marketing organisation. If you are using it, however informally, with a fellow student or someone from an organisation not your own, check for conflict of interests, confidentiality issues and so on.

2. You may be more familiar with the acronym PEST (Political, Economic, Social and Technological). SLEPT adds 'legal' as a separate factor. Additional factors include: interest and pressure groups like professional bodies, the CBI, trade unions, consumers' associations, and the physical environment, ecology and the 'Green' movement (PESTLE adds the extra 'E' for Environmental). Since we did not specify the 'macro' environment, you might also have listed 'micro' factors such as customers, competitors, suppliers and distributors.

3. (a) Square Wheels' environment is fairly complex, because it operates in so many different countries, but the basic technology is fairly simple – a bicycle is not a complex product.

   (b) To identify the political risks in any of the areas mentioned, read a newspaper! Hong Kong reverted to Chinese sovereignty in 1997: but this is unlikely to raise the risk profile of the business, since it already has substantial operations in China, and there is no evidence that the Chinese government is going to nationalise profitable businesses. There may be other risks with the labour force in Tijuana, and problems of economic and business management in Romania.

   (c) The implication of population growth is an increased market. However, if accompanied by increases in prosperity, customers may be able to afford other means of transport for commuting (eg motor scooters and cars). The new battery technology may be useful in developing countries, rather than in Europe. In Europe, the changing age structure may affect the use of bikes: fewer young people will buy them, so the aim might be to promote them on the grounds that they offer health-giving exercise.

PART A GATHERING, ANALYSING AND PRESENTING INFORMATION

- (d) In ecological terms, the push-bike is energy-efficient, and so is a prime example of an ecologically friendly product. Other issues include energy efficiency in its factories, and how hazardous materials are dealt with (with EU directives on the use and recycling of certain types of batteries).

4 (a) The bank's competitors would include the other banks: indeed, this was the only way the market was perceived for a long time. However, building societies have now emerged as a major competitor in the wider 'financial services' sector, follows by supermarkets and retailers offering financial services (advice, loans, insurance, cash).

   (b) Similarly, petrol companies were so busy competing among themselves that they were wrong-footed by supermarkets, who now sell petrol at out-of-town stores as part of a larger package of services.

5 Price information is available from a variety of sources. Most manufacturing firms get the data from customers. In retail, prices are readily available at point of sale and in price listings, advertisements and catalogues, as well as from customers and suppliers. Many firms use sales agents to monitor prices. There may also be feedback available from competitive tendering.

6 A general interpretation of the facts as given might be sketched as follows.

   (a) Objectives: the company has no declared objectives. Profits have risen by 3% per annum in the past, which has failed to keep pace with inflation but may have been a satisfactory rate of increase in the current conditions of the industry. Even so, stronger growth is indicated in the future.

   (b)

Strengths	Weaknesses
Many new products developed.	Products may be reaching the end of their life and entering decline.
Marketing success in increasing market share.	New product life cycles may be shorter.
	Reduction in customers.
	Excessive reliance on a few customers.
	Doubtful whether profit record is satisfactory.
Threats	**Opportunities**
Possible decline in the end-product.	None identified.
Smaller end-product market will restrict future sales prospects for Hall Faull Downes.	

   (c) Strengths: the growth in company sales in the last five years has been as a result of increasing the market share in a declining market. This success may be the result of the following.

   - Research and development spending
   - Good product development programmes
   - Extending the product range to suit changing customer needs
   - Marketing skills
   - Long-term supply contracts with customers
   - Cheap pricing policy
   - Product quality and reliable service

   (d) Weaknesses:

   (i) The products may be custom-made for customers so that they provide little or no opportunity for market development.

   (ii) Products might have a shorter life cycle than in the past, in view of the declining total market demand.

   (iii) Excessive reliance on two major customers leaves the company exposed to the dangers of losing their custom.

(e) Threats: there may be a decline in the end-market for the customers' product so that the customer demands for the company's own products will also fall.

(f) Opportunities: no opportunities have been identified, but in view of the situation as described, new strategies for the longer term would appear to be essential.

(g) Conclusions: the company does not appear to be planning beyond the short term, or is reacting to the business environment in a piecemeal fashion. A strategic planning programme should be introduced.

(h) Recommendations: the company must look for new opportunities in the longer term.

　(i) In the short term, current strengths must be exploited to continue to increase market share in existing markets and product development programmes should also continue.

　(ii) In the longer term, the company must diversify into new markets or into new products and new markets. Diversification opportunities should be sought with a view to exploiting any competitive advantage or synergy that might be achievable.

　(iii) The company should use its strengths (whether in R & D, production skills or marketing expertise) in exploiting any identifiable opportunities.

　(iv) Objectives need to be quantified in order to assess the extent to which new long-term strategies are required.

7　You may have come up with a different way of representing a different opportunity, but as an example:

Position map of available craft classes

(Position map: vertical axis from Inexpensive to Expensive, horizontal axis from Low to High topic/frequency range. Upper-left quadrant: Exclusive tuition. Upper-right quadrant: Universities, design colleges. Lower-left quadrant: Craft shops.)

Strengths	Weaknesses
Quality premises	High overheads
Strong customer loyalty	Staff availability evenings
Finance/size	
Networks	
Customer database	
Opportunities	**Threats**
Evening classes	Competitor classes cheap
Wide topic range	Local area at night: perception of elderly customers?
Large/frequent programme	
Membership Club	Customer demand for small class/low cost

PART A GATHERING, ANALYSING AND PRESENTING INFORMATION

Your notes might include observations such as:

(a) There is an apparent opportunity for a reasonably-priced programme offering a wide variety and high frequency of classes: demand seems to be supportive.

(b) The apparent opportunity for evening classes. However, other factors include the threatening perception of the city at night, particularly for an elderly customer group and the costs of staffing the premises after hours. An alternative proposal – lunchtime short classes – might be advisable.

(c) The mathematics of small class numbers and low cost does not immediately add up, given the need to pay tutors per hour. The quality of the premises might allow a higher price, relative to competitors. The 'club' activities could be pursued in larger numbers to support small class rolls.

(d) The Needle Works' strengths in database and customer loyalty provide cost-effective access to the target market, and the Club and class programme support each other.

> Now try Question 4 at the end of the Study Text

Part B
Building and developing relationships

Working with others

Chapter topic list

1. Working relationships
2. The marketing function within the organisation
3. Roles and relationships at work
4. Interpersonal skills and managing others
5. Working effectively in teams

Syllabus content – knowledge and skills requirements

- 2.1 Describe the structure and roles of the marketing function within the organisation
- 2.2 Build and develop relationships within the marketing department; working effectively with others
- 2.9 Describe techniques to assist in managing your manager

PART B BUILDING AND DEVELOPING RELATIONSHIPS

Introduction

In this chapter, we will look at working relationships within the marketing department and between the marketing department and the rest of the organisation. In the chapters that follow, we go on to consider relationships with customers and visitors, suppliers of services, partners in the supply chain, and finally the wider business and social community.

Many of the general principles of building relationships are discussed in this chapter. Interpersonal skills, conflict management and team roles and dynamics will be relevant to customer and supplier relationships too. This section of the Text links closely with your *Customer Communications* studies.

1 Working relationships

> **FAST FORWARD**
>
> A **working relationship** can be established with anyone with whom you come into contact for the fulfilment of a transaction or task: colleagues, suppliers, customers or clients.

How might you describe a 'good working relationship'? A precise definition would include different things for different for different people, but there are two main components.

(a) **Good working**

A good working relationship allows or facilitates work transactions, the completion of tasks and the fulfilment of objectives.

(b) **Good ... relationships**

A good working relationship allows or facilitates ongoing and mutually satisfying interpersonal relations.

Elements in (a) might include prompt and willing service, co-operation and co-ordination, communication, expertise, teamworking skills and mutual reward or benefit.

Elements in (b) might include politeness, friendliness, trust, openness, respect and the ability to resolve conflict.

2 The marketing function within the organisation

2.1 The role of the marketing assistant

> **FAST FORWARD**
>
> The **role of marketing assistant** involves a variety of tasks, relationships and responsibilities.

When the syllabus for *Marketing in Practice* was being researched, the role or job title most closely related to it was that of marketing assistant. Although by no means a senior role, this job involves a variety of tasks, relationships and responsibilities.

The role can sometimes be an extension of a secretarial job, and a position as secretary to the marketing manager is often the route in to a career in marketing.

There is no standard job description for a marketing assistant, although it is likely to involve:

- Advertising, but not with large budgets
- Organising events, such as exhibitions, stands or conferences
- Some responsibility for budget administration

The above are recognisable as sections of the MIP syllabus, and as such feature in each exam set so far.

However, there is often a very 'ad hoc' element to such jobs, meaning that every day is different and you get called on at short notice to undertake a variety of projects.

2.2 The organisation of marketing

FAST FORWARD

The relationship of marketing to **other organisational functions** will depend on the formal structure of the organisation, and the extent to which the organisation has adopted a marketing orientation.

Kotler *et al* (1999) note that there has been both an absolute and a relative rise in the importance of marketing in the organisation.

(a) The **responsibility** of marketing has increased due to the increasingly complex environment, the slow-down of demand in existing product fields and the rise in competition.

(b) Companies have been forced to move from a product or production orientation to a **marketing orientation**, making marketing one of the critical management functions.

Kotler suggests that as a business grows, it moves from basic functions (finance, production, sales) to an increasingly evolved view of marketing: Figure 5.1.

The simple sales department   *The separate marketing department*

The modern marketing company

Figure 5.1: The evolution of marketing organisation

Of course, organisation structures are more complex than that, and the precise relationship of the marketing function to other functions (such as production, finance, human resources, research and development) will depend on whether the organisation is structured by function, geographical/national territories or more marketing oriented divisions by market or product.

Product management or **brand management** systems have become popular with organisations producing a range of products. This is a type of **matrix organisation**, which overlays functional management with resource management: Figure 5.2. Product or brand managers have several responsibilities.

- Developing **marketing plans** for their product/brand
- Developing **promotional campaigns**
- **Stimulating support and interest** among the salesforce and distributors
- **Gathering feedback** on the product/brand's performance
- **Initiating product improvements** to meet market needs

Figure 5.2: A matrix structure

2.3 Interdepartmental relations

> **FAST FORWARD**
>
> Interdepartmental **conflict** stems from genuine clashes of emphasis as well as prejudice and politics, and the marketing department needs to exercise internal promotion and employee relations in order to integrate its activities with those of other departments.

'In principle, business functions should mesh harmoniously to achieve the overall objectives of the firm. In practice, departmental interfaces are often characterised by deep rivalries and misunderstandings... Some inter-departmental conflict stems from differences of opinion about what lies in the best interests of the firm; some from real trade-offs between departmental well-being and company well-being; and some from unfortunate departmental stereotypes and prejudices'. (*Kotler*, 2002).

The **marketing concept** is designed to foster a deeper appreciation by all departments of the value and benefits of a **customer orientation**, but how much influence should marketing have over other departments to bring about co-ordinated effort in customer service, say, or product development? Other departments naturally stress their own special contribution to company goals, and view problems and opportunities in the light of their own expertise and culture.

Kotler *(ibid)* summarises the potential for conflict as follows.

Other Departments	Their Emphasis	Marketing Emphasis
R & D	Basic research Intrinsic quality Functional features	Applied research Perceivable quality Sales features
Engineering	Long design lead time Few models Standard components	Short design lead time Many models Custom components
Purchasing	Narrow product line Standard parts Price of material Economical lot sizes Purchasing at infrequent intervals	Broad product line Non-standard parts Quality of material Large lot sizes to avoid stockouts Immediate purchasing for customer needs
Manufacturing	Long production lead time Long runs with few models No model changes Standard orders Ease of fabrication Average quality control	Short production lead time Short runs with many models Frequent model changes Custom orders Aesthetic appearance Tight quality control
Finance	Strict rationales for spending Hard and fast budgets Pricing to cover costs	Intuitive arguments for spending Flexible budgets to meet changing needs Pricing to further market development
Accounting	Standard transactions Few reports	Special terms and discounts Many reports
Credit	Full financial disclosures by customers Low credit risks Tough credit terms Tough collection procedures	Minimum credit examination of customers Medium credit risks Easy credit terms Easy collection procedures

So what can you do as a member of the marketing department to overcome such obstacles to co-operative working? You may not be able to influence orientation or policy but you will be involved in **communication** and **co-ordination**.

The following paragraphs suggest some brief guidelines for working with individuals and teams from other departments.

2.3.1 Networking

The more you have contact with people in other functions, learn what they do and show that you appreciate their problems and capabilities, the more likely you are to develop co-operative relationships.

(a) Attend organisation-wide and interdepartmental events and meetings.

(b) Join quality circles and other multi-disciplinary teams and committees that focus on joint objectives.

(c) Use your contacts in other departments to arrange visits and briefings so you learn about each other's functions.

2.3.2 The internal customer concept

As the term suggests, the internal customer concept implies the following.

(a) Any unit of the organisation whose task contributes to the task of other units (whether as part of a process or in an advisory or service relationship) can be regarded as a **supplier of a service** like any other supplier used by the organisation.

(b) **Customer choice** operates within the organisation as well as in the external market environment.

(c) The unit's objective thus becomes the efficient and effective **identification and satisfaction of customer needs**, wants and expectations within the organisation as well as outside it.

(d) The unit must 'create, build and maintain mutually beneficial **exchanges and relationships'** within the organisation, as well as outside. In other words, customer relations are important internally, too.

Action Programme 1

Who are the internal customers of the marketing function? What are their needs/expectations?

2.3.3 Internal promotion and communication

Every organisation has a major internal target audience for its promotional message. The PR function includes employee relations. These are important for various reasons.

- **Public relations**, since employees are also representatives of the company
- Employee **morale and productivity**
- **Innovation** and **quality control**

As a marketing communicator, you should recognise the importance of getting production staff excited about an upcoming launch (which might soften the blow of the launch deadlines) and encouraging branch managers and sales staff to feel energised by your marketing support of their efforts. You may have to brief front line staff on customer likes and dislikes.

Be prepared to use a wide range of internal **promotional media and activities**. This may include meetings, factory tours, presentations, internal newsletters, intranet messages, competitions and suggestion schemes, letters, memos and reports.

Exam tip

> 10 marks were available in the June 2005 exam for writing a letter to employees, informing them of management changes (in such a way as to highlight the benefits to them). The question made this point explicit – but you should bear it in mind for future questions. The purpose of internal communications is often to *promote* decisions, changes or events – just as you would to *external* customers.

2.3.4 Co-ordination

One of the main purposes of organisational communication is co-ordination.

Key concept

> **Co-ordination** is 'planning, or taking action to improve, the inter-relationships (especially of timing and methods of communication) between a number of various activities, which contribute to the achievement of a single objective, so that they do not conflict and the objective is achieved with a minimal expenditure of time and effort.'
>
> *(Dictionary of Management)*

You need to ensure that departments whose work depends on yours, or on whose work yours depends, are kept informed.

- **Plans and schedules**
- **Changes** to plans and schedules
- **Feedback** on the results or completion of plans and schedules

This may seem like common sense. It seems obvious that you should check with the design or production department before you advertise product specifications, and inform them of the planned date of a new product launch, and monitor their readiness as the date approaches. Failure to monitor progress, adjust plans and communicate between units are common problems, and sources of conflict and chaos.

3 Roles and relationships at work

3.1 Roles

FAST FORWARD

People adopt a number of different **roles** and relate to each other in those roles, as well as interpersonally.

Roles are sometimes described as parts that people play (like actors) or hats that people wear.

- People adopt different roles in different circumstances.
- Roles define 'who a person is' in these circumstances and in relation to others.
- Roles have certain signs or characteristics associated with them, so that a style of behaviour is expected of a person in a given role.

In the marketing department, you adopt your '**work role**', as opposed to your role as student, member of a family, sports enthusiast (or whatever). Within your work role may be more specific roles, such as co-ordinator of marketing activity, event organiser, assistant to your superior and colleague to your peers – depending upon what function you are performing and what other people require and expect from you.

There are important skills in working with others.

- Identifying what roles other people are in, and what your role should be
- Identifying the behaviours and role signs expected of you in a given role

This will help you to avoid inappropriate behaviours such as over-familiarity in a professional context, lack of leadership in an authority role or insubordination in a subordinate role.

3.2 Structural relationships

FAST FORWARD

Relationships in work organisations are structural (based on authority and function), interpersonal (or human) and contractual/legal.

Roles exist **in relation to each other**. In the work environment, there are three basic relationships between roles.

- **Subordinate role** working for and reporting to others
- **Equal or peer role** working with others towards a shared goal
- **Authority role** with people working for and reporting to you

These are essentially relationships of **power, authority** and **influence**. Within this structure, there are also **functional** relationships: what you and others do, to contribute to your shared tasks objectives.

Authority and functional relationships are built into the formal structure, communication and procedures of the organisation. Its **culture** dictates the way in which these relationships are regarded and expressed.

Structural relationships shape two key aspects of working with others.

(a) **The scope and limits of authority**

Each person and team needs to know what areas they have authority over, and how far that authority extends. For example, you may have responsibility for controlling local advertising, but refer national advertising decisions to your boss.

(b) **Co-ordination and communication**

Since your work objectives will be achieved for or through other people, you need to ensure an efficient flow of work, resources and information towards overall objectives. Your plans and schedules need to dovetail with those of other individuals and teams with whom your work is linked.

Politics flows from **authority relationships** in an organisation.

Key concept | **Politics** are activities concerned with the acquisition of power and the exercising of influence in relation to others.

Organisations are political systems.

(a) Individuals have their own **agendas**, priorities and goals.
(b) They compete for their share of the organisation's **limited resources**, power and influence.
(c) They form **cliques**, alliances, pressure groups and blocking groups centred around values and objectives which may be opposed by others.

3.3 Interpersonal relationships

Overlaid on structural factors in relationships, there are interpersonal or human factors such as individual personalities, interpersonal skills, whether people have rapport, personal differences, attitudes and values, perceptions, communication and group behaviour.

When we talk about **building relationships**, we are mainly talking about developing rapport, trust and effective communication, which, although complicated by structural factors and politics, are essentially **interpersonal skills**.

3.4 Contractual and legal relationships

Some aspects of work relationships are covered by **contract, law and regulation**.

You have a general duty, for example, of **faithful duty to your employer** under your contract of employment.

- Duty to obey lawful and reasonable orders
- Duty to use skill and care
- Duty not to disclose confidential information

You also have specific responsibilities, under **health and safety legislation**, to work in such a way as to avoid injury to yourself and others.

Similarly, there are laws and regulations covering how your employer should treat you, including disciplinary situations, dismissal and redundancy, grievance handling, health and safety, working terms and conditions (pay, holiday entitlements) and so on.

3.4.1 Discrimination

Among the formal aspects of work relationships, you should be aware that you have responsibilities under **equal opportunities legislation** not to discriminate or show prejudice against people on grounds such as sex, sexual orientation, race, religion or disability. This applies to how you deal with colleagues and members of the public.

Key concept

> **Discrimination** is giving less favourable terms or treatment to a particular individual or group because of some characteristic that they are assumed to have, or some category to which they are assumed to belong.

There are legal provisions against discrimination in the UK.

(a) The **Sex Discrimination Act** outlaws certain types of discrimination on the grounds of sex, marital status (that is, whether the person is single, married or divorced) and sexual orientation.

(b) The **Race Relations Act** outlaws certain types of discrimination on grounds of colour, race, nationality or ethnic origin. (Additional regulations cover religious beliefs.)

(c) The **Disability Discrimination Act** outlaws certain types of discrimination on grounds of physical or mental disability.

(d) The **Employment Equity (Age) Regulations** (introduced in October 2006) outlaws certain types of discrimination on grounds of age.

There are two main types of discrimination under the Acts.

(a) **Direct discrimination** occurs when one interested group is treated less favourably than another.

(b) **Indirect discrimination** occurs when requirements or conditions are imposed, with which a substantial proportion of the interested group could not comply. If you were serving a queue of people and gave a discount only to those who could say 'Happy Christmas' to you in Welsh, you would be guilty of indirect discrimination!

Another current issue in the workplace is **sexual harassment**, which has been ruled to be unlawful sexual discrimination. Under 2003 regulations on sexual orientation and religious belief, a wider range of jokes, 'banter' and potentially harassing behaviours in the workplace may have to be addressed. All employees (and marketers) must recognise the increasing diversity of the workforce (and consumer base) in this regard.

Action Programme 2

Find out what policies your organisation has to define the relationships, rights and responsibilities between its individuals and groups. Check:

- the organisation or office manual or handbook
- your contract of employment
- policy statements and notices to staff
- the personnel or human resources department

3.5 Recognising 'key relationships'

FAST FORWARD

> **Key relationships** are those with people whose information, input or authority are essential to your working effectively.

PART B   BUILDING AND DEVELOPING RELATIONSHIPS

You cannot invest the same amount of time and energy in every person you deal with, and the fact is that some individuals and groups will be more useful or necessary to you in accomplishing your personal and work goals than others. We are not saying you should not bother with social or friendly relationships, or that you need to become a manipulator of people! In your work role you need to establish effective **working relationships**.

> **Exam tip**
>
> Developing relationships inside and outside the organisation is one of the learning outcomes of this syllabus. The June 2003 case study set you up in a team at a radio station, including marketing management, sales team and shared administrative assistants: you are involved in event organising, and collaboration with other local media. In this complex scenario, you are asked to identify your *'key contacts'* and how you can build effective working relationships with them. A similar question (set within an advertising agency) was set in June 2004.
>
> A slightly different aspect was set in December 2003, addressing particular *difficulties* likely to be experienced in a setting where the management committee are unpaid volunteers and your own appointment is part time.
>
> The examiner noted that 'there is no easy mnemonic or framework here, and candidates needed to really think about what the issues might be'. He also reminded candidates that ways to build relationships or overcome difficulties 'needed to be practical and low cost': resist the temptation to have daily meetings or weekly parties!

There are some key individuals with whom you need to manage your relationship with particular care.

(a) **People on whom you rely for information** or input to your own work, in order to fulfil your objectives

   (i) **People whose work precedes yours in the flow of work or project sequence**. For example, the market researcher who has to gather and supply data before you can compile a report and recommendations.

   (ii) **People to whom you have delegated tasks:** that is, people through whom you get things done. This includes subordinates and colleagues as well as agencies to whom you contract aspects of a task. For example, the office assistant you rely on to get your reports typed, copied and bound for the departmental meeting.

   (iii) **People with whom you must collaborate in order to complete a project**. You may not have delegated or contractual authority over other people involved in a project: relationships will be key to co-ordination and co-operation. A product launch, for example, will involve many units of the marketing and production functions: who can you talk to for progress checks?

   (iv) **People who have information or expertise you regularly require**. Sources of expert knowledge and advice need to be identified and cultivated. For example, the information technology officer who can be relied on to get the system working again when it has crashed on the morning when a report is due.

(b) **People who have authority over you and your work**

   Your relationships with your team leader, immediate boss and department head are vital.

   (i) They control your salary and career prospects, and the quality of your working life in general.

   (ii) They set the objectives and give the instructions that define your work.

   (iii) They control access to the resources (budget, information, staff, space), that you need to do your job.

(c) **Other people who can mobilise influence and resources on your behalf**

In Chapter 8 we discuss the importance of **networking**, both within and outside the organisation. It is important to build relationships with powerful allies, supporters, information sources and controllers of budgets. Not all influential people are in high positions of authority. A personal assistant may know more than anyone, and have access to the right people.

These relationships should be particularly cultivated, on a regular basis, or at least for the duration of the project to which they are key. We discuss how they can be built and developed in the next section.

Attention!

> Having said all the above, it is also important not to neglect or destroy relationships with non-key players. Without people like receptionists, telephonists, post room staff, maintenance and security staff, your job would be a lot harder!

Action Programme 3

The Needle Works

As a result of your market research and competitor comparison (Chapters 3 & 4), you have drafted a recommendation that The Needle Works set up an educational and activities programme, for submission to Albert Smith. Thinking about the history and culture of the business, and about how the programme would need to be organised, it occurs to you that Albert will not be the only 'key player' in the decision-making and implementation processes.

Make a list of who has influence, and in what area. Whose support and input might you require to get your programme (a) approved and (b) up and running?

Marketing at Work

What 'type' of people are you likely to find in your marketing department? Have you geared your relational style to the stereotypical marketing person: extraverted, creative, fast-talking, enthusiastic?

Marketing and the Small Firm asked small firms which **skills** they considered most vital for *effective* marketing.

Skill	%
Know the product/market well	~26
Communicate well	~18
Understand people/customers	~14
Be enthusiastic/motivated	~5
Have the gift of the gab	~4
Be creative	~4
Show confidence in company/products	~4
Be outgoing/extravert	~3

PART B BUILDING AND DEVELOPING RELATIONSHIPS

4 Interpersonal skills and managing others

FAST FORWARD

> **Interpersonal skills** are essential for relationship management. They include rapport building, influencing, building trust and co-operation and managing conflict and disagreement.

Key concept

> **Interpersonal skills** are skills used in establishing and maintaining relationships between people. They are essentially communication skills, used in an interactive situation such as a face-to-face or telephone discussion.

Interpersonal skills include:

- The ability to build **rapport**, or a sense of relationship, with another person
- The ability to **persuade** or **influence** another person
- The ability to gain the **trust**, **confidence** and **co-operation** of another person
- The ability to **resolve conflict or disagreements**

Obviously, these are not things you can really learn in a book. You need to develop your communication skills, and to practise applying and adjusting them in every interaction that you encounter, until you consistently get the results you want.

We will look briefly at each of the areas listed above: they are the building blocks of relationships.

4.1 Building rapport

Key concept

> **Rapport** is the process of establishing and maintaining a relationship of mutual trust, understanding and responsiveness between two or more people.

Rapport is the sense of 'being in tune with' another person, or 'getting on' with them. Building rapport is like building a bridge to the other person: creating a point of understanding and contact, on which meaningful communication and relationship can be based. So how is it achieved?

(a) **Matching**, or mirroring, the other person's non-verbal signals: posture, gestures, eye contact and volume and pace of speaking.

(b) Demonstrating **respect and understanding** for the other person's viewpoint, emotions or culture.

- Talking about **topics of interest** to the other person
- Using a **vocabulary** the other person shares
- **Empathising** with the person's feelings
- Wearing **clothes** and adopting **manners** which will not alienate the other person
- **Appreciating** the person's views, even if not agreeing with them

4.2 Influence

Influencing is a process whereby some form of 'pressure' is applied to change other people's attitudes or behaviours. *Gillen* (1999) distinguishes between what he calls:

(a) **Manipulative** influencing, using tactics designed around dishonest logic or negative feelings. This is a 'push' approach which attempts to dismiss, override or get around the other person's point of view.

(b) **Positive** influencing: 'non-manipulative, persuading behaviours that demonstrate that you are treating people openly, honestly and respectfully'. This is a 'pull' approach which:

- attempts to understand the other person's point of view
- attempts to help the other person to understand your point of view
- invites or leads the other person to appreciate or agree with your point of view (through persuasion).

In addition, influence may be exerted through **power**. Power is an aspect of the relationship between people: how the power holder is perceived by others and what (s)he is able to offer them. *French and Raven* (1958) classified power as follows.

(a) **Legitimate power**: the ability of a leader or manager to exercise authority, based on his or her position in the organisation.

(b) **Expert power**: the ability of a leader to exert influence based on others' recognition of his or her knowledge or expertise in an area in which they need help.

(c) **Reward power**: the ability of a leader to exert influence based on access to, and control over, resources which others value (pay, assistance, information, contacts and so on).

(d) **Referent power**: the ability of a leader to exert influence based on his or her 'charisma' or leadership qualities.

(e) **Coercive power**: the ability of a leader to exert influence based on his or her ability to apply negative sanctions if people don't comply.

4.3 Trust and co-operation

Rapport and influencing skills can be used to facilitate **encounters**. In order to develop a **relationship**, further investment is required.

Cultivating a relationship is a bit like cultivating a garden: it requires regular time, effort, nourishment and creativity, even at work, where you might think that sharing an office all day would be sufficient!

(a) **Keep in contact**. Communicate regularly. (This may be a challenge in 'virtual' teams which do not share office space, or with part-time workers.)

(b) **Be dependable**. Trust is built on trustworthiness. Don't let people down, break promises or violate confidentiality.

(c) **Showing willing**. Offer or agree to give information, collaboration, help or support whenever appropriate. This builds up a credit bank of co-operation.

(d) **Utilise social and informal opportunities**. Lunch breaks, after-hours activities, even a quiet chat over the coffee machine, are designed to allow colleagues to get to know and trust each other as people, building a relationship that will benefit co-ordination and communication at work.

(e) **Avoid or mend conflict**. Unresolved personality clashes, hostilities and rivalries ruin working relationships.

(f) **Maintain appropriate roles**. However friendly you get with people outside work, or in informal situations, remember to behave appropriately in business contexts.

4.4 Managing conflict and disagreement

Key concepts

> **Co-operation** is working or acting together.
>
> **Conflict** is the clash or opposition of opposing 'forces', which may include the interests, opinions or beliefs of individuals or groups. Conflict often arises at work from competition for scarce resources and power, the incompatible goals and priorities of individuals and teams, lack of communication, and incompatibility of individual or team personalities or styles of working.

One useful model of conflict resolution is the **win-win model**. This states that there are three basic ways in which a conflict or disagreement can be worked out.

Method	Frequency	Explanation
Win-lose	This is quite common.	**One party gets what (s)he wants at the expense of the other party**: for example, Department A gets the new photocopier, while Department B keeps the old one (since there were insufficient resources to buy two new ones). However well-justified such a solution is (Department A needed the facilities on the new photocopier more than Department B), there is often lingering resentment on the part of the 'losing' party, which may begin to damage work relations.
Lose-lose	This sounds like a senseless outcome, but actually **compromise** comes into this category. It is thus very common.	**Neither party gets what (s)he really wanted**: for example, since Department A and B cannot both have a new photocopier, it is decided that neither department should have one. However 'logical' such a solution is, there is often resentment and dissatisfaction on both sides. (Personal arguments where neither party gives ground and both end up storming off or not talking are also lose-lose: the parties may not have lost the argument, but they lose the relationship …) Even positive compromises only result in half-satisfied needs.
Win-win	This may not be common, but working towards it often brings out the best solution.	**Both parties get as close as possible to what they really want**. How can this be achieved?

It is critical to the **win-win** approach to discover what both parties really want. For example, Department B may want the new photocopier; because they have never found out how to use all the features (which do the same things) on the old photocopier because they just want to have the same equipment as Department A; or because they fear that if they do not have the new photocopier, their work will be slower and less professionally presented.

There are important questions in working towards win-win.

- What do you want this for?
- What do you think will happen if you don't get it?

These questions get to the heart of what people really need and want.

In our photocopier example, Department A says it needs the new photocopier to make colour copies (which the old copier does not do), while Department B says it needs the new copier to make clearer copies (because the copies on the old machine are a bit blurred). Now there are options to explore. It may be that the old copier just needs fixing, in order for Department B to get what it really wants. Department A will still end up getting the new copier but Department B has in the process been consulted and had its needs met.

Action Programme 4

Suggest a (i) win-lose, (ii) compromise and (iii) win-win solution in the following scenarios.

(a) Two of your team members are arguing over who gets the desk by the window: they both want it.

(b) You and a colleague both need access to the same file at the same time. You both need it to compile reports for your managers, for the following morning. It is now 3.00pm, and each of you will need it for two hours to do the work.

(c) Manager A is insisting on buying new computers for her department before the budgetary period ends. Manager B cannot understand why – since the old computers are quite adequate – and will moreover be severely inconvenienced by such a move, since her own systems will have to be upgraded as well, in order to remain compatible with department A. (The two departments constantly share data files.) Manager B protests, and conflict erupts.

[*Key skill for Marketers: Problem solving*]

4.5 Managing your manager

'Managing upwards' is an important skill for several reasons.

(a) To manage the expectations of superiors, ensuring that deadlines and success measures are realistic and adequately resourced.

(b) To avoid poor time management through 'interruptions' and changes of plan from above.

(c) To keep superiors informed, and to get them used to reporting by exception (reporting only when necessary, because of a deviation from plan or an unforeseen contingency): this avoids micro-management and unnecessary interference by poor delegaters.

(d) To gain authorisation and support to put your plans and ideas into action.

(e) To promote your ideas and achievements, so your ability and potential will be noticed (self-marketing).

4.5.1 Techniques for managing your manager

Some of the techniques you could use to manage upwards are as follows.

- Negotiate and agree **work goals**, targets and methods with your boss: clarify expectations.

- Negotiate (if necessary) **reporting by exception**: having agreed goals and targets, you should have discretion to manage your work until or unless problems occur. Agree ground rules for what matters require supervision/reporting and which don't.

- Support reporting by exception by **limiting your availability** to interruptions: limit the number of times you check your e-mail, use voice mail etc.

- Develop **assertive communication** techniques: learn to state your case (and, when necessary, say 'no') calmly, straightforwardly but firmly.

- Use **upward influencing** tactics. Rational argument works well: present logical reasons for your suggestions (if possibly, with a business case: how your idea will further the objectives of the marketing department or organisation as a whole).

- Cultivate **personal trust and rapport**, which increases your ability to communicate with and influence your boss.

PART B BUILDING AND DEVELOPING RELATIONSHIPS

- **Respect** the organisation's cultural values about status and manager subordinate relationships. Use appropriate channels of communication. Respect formality where necessary.
- Be your own **PR agent**. Do not be shy to draw your boss's attention to your achievements and ideas, or those of your team: this increases trust and respect, and may earn you greater autonomy and/or responsibility.

5 Working effectively in teams

Key concept

> A **team** is 'a small number of people with *complementary skills* who are committed to a *common* purpose, performance goals and approach for which they hold themselves *mutually accountable*.'
>
> *(Katzenbach & Smith)*

5.1 Uses of teams

FAST FORWARD

Teams are particularly useful where the sharing and testing of ideas is required.

The basic work unit of organisations has traditionally been the **functional department** (such as marketing or sales). In more recent times, businesses have adopted smaller, more flexible and responsive units: teams. **Teamworking** allows work to be shared among a group, so that it gets done more quickly and with a sharing of skills and information, while allowing people to keep sight of the 'whole' task. Teams are particularly effective for increasing communication, generating new ideas and evaluating ideas from different view points.

(a) **Brainstorming groups** generate creative ideas for problem-solving, or innovative promotional campaigns.

(b) **Quality circles** draw people together from different disciplines to share ideas about quality issues.

(c) **Project teams** can be set up to handle particular tasks or projects, cases or customer accounts or product launches.

(d) **Study and discussion groups** explore issues from different points of view.

(e) **Team briefings** present information and instructions.

5.2 Team roles

FAST FORWARD

Effective teams need a **mix of people** who are good at getting things done and getting on with others.

Belbin (1993) drew up a list of the necessary functions which must be performed to keep a team functioning effectively.

Member	Role
Co-ordinator	Presides and co-ordinates. Balanced, disciplined, good at working through others.
Shaper	Highly strung, dominant, extravert, passionate about the task itself, a spur to action.

Member	Role
Plant	Introverted, but intellectually dominant and imaginative. Source of ideas and proposals but with disadvantages of introversion.
Monitor-evaluator	Analytically intelligent. Dissects ideas, spots flaws. Possibly aloof, tactless – but necessary.
Resource-investigator	Popular, sociable, extravert, relaxed. Source of new contacts, but not an originator. Needs to be made use of.
Implementer	Practical organiser, turning ideas into tasks. Trustworthy and efficient, but not exciting. Not a leader, but an administrator.
Team worker	Most concerned with team maintenance – supportive, understanding, diplomatic. Popular but uncompetitive – contribution noticed only in absence.
Finisher	Chivvies the team to meet deadlines and attend to details. Urgency and follow-through important, though not always popular.

The **specialist** joins the team to offer expert advice when needed: legal experts, PR consultants or design consultants, say.

Action Programme 5

The Needle Works

What difficulties can you anticipate in building working and supplier relationships at the Needle Works? How might these be overcome?

[*Key skill for Marketers: Working with others*]

5.3 Effective teamworking

> **FAST FORWARD**
>
> While groups are extensively used in decision-making (eg committees and task forces), there are **drawbacks** as well as **advantages** to team working.

5.3.1 Team decisions

Group decision-making can be of **benefit**.

(a) Pooling skills, information and ideas – perhaps representing different functions, specialisms and levels in the organisation – could increase the **quality of the decision.** Groups have been shown to produce better evaluated decisions than individuals working separately. Even the performance of the group's best individual can be improved by having 'missing pieces' added by the group.

(b) Participation in the decision-making process makes the decision **acceptable** to the group, whether because it represents a consensus of their views, or simply because they have been consulted. Acceptance of the decision by the group may be important if it affects them, and/or they are responsible for carrying it out.

There are, however, **problems** in group decision-making.

(a) Group decisions **take longer** to reach than individual decisions – especially if the group seeks consensus by working through disagreement.

(b) Group decisions tend to be **riskier** than individual decisions.

    (i) **Shared responsibility** blurs the individuals' sense of responsibility for the outcome of the decision.

    (ii) **Contradictory information** may be ignored, to protect the group's consensus or pet theories.

    (iii) **Cohesive groups** tend to feel infallible and they get over-confident.

    (iv) Group cohesion and motivation may be founded on **values** like innovation, boldness and flexibility – which support risk-taking.

5.3.2 Factors in team performance

Some of the factors affecting the performance of teams are as follows.

(a) **Co-operation and conflict resolution.** Since teams are made up of a number of individuals, it is important that they get on and work well with each other. Two team members who are hostile or non-communicative are likely to have a negative effect on the whole team.

(b) **Clearly defined goals and responsibilities.** Teams should be briefed on a regular basis so that they know what is expected of them. The goals of individual team members should if possible be made to coincide with those of the group as a whole.

(c) **Clear and regular feedback.** The team must be given information on progress and results so that it can learn, correct or adjust its performance – or celebrate.

(d) **Group motivation.** As with individuals, if teams are encouraged to work hard, and rewarded for doing so, then this is likely to have a positive effect on performance.

(e) **Communication.** In general, the greater the communication between team members and team leaders, the greater and more effective the performance.

Action Programme 6

What teams are you currently a member of? What makes them feel like 'teams', rather than just groups of people? See if you can identify which of Belbin's team roles are fulfilled in your team, and where there are gaps which need to be filled.

Chapter Roundup

- A **working relationship** can be established with anyone with whom you come into contact for the fulfilment of a transaction or task: colleagues, suppliers, customers or clients.
- The **role of marketing assistant** involves a variety of tasks, relationships and responsibilities.
- The relationship of marketing to **other organisational functions** will depend on the formal structure of the organisation, and the extent to which the organisation has adopted a marketing orientation.
- Interdepartmental **conflict** stems from genuine clashes of emphasis as well as prejudice and politics, and the marketing department needs to exercise internal promotion and employee relations in order to integrate its activities with those of other departments.
- People adopt a number of different **roles** and relate to each other in those roles, as well as interpersonally.
- **Relationships in work organisations** are structural (based on authority and function), interpersonal (or human) and contractual/legal.
- **Key relationships** are those with people whose information, input or authority are essential to your working effectively with different people in different contexts.
- **Interpersonal skills** are essential for relationship management. They include rapport building, influencing, building trust and co-operation and managing conflict and disagreement.
- **Teams** are particularly useful where the sharing and testing of ideas is required.
- Effective teams need a **mix of people** who are good at getting things done and getting on with others.
- While groups are extensively used in decision-making (eg committees and task forces), there are **drawbacks** as well as **advantages** to team working.

Quick Quiz

1. Give one example of incompatible emphases between marketing and another department.
2. What is the internal customer concept?
3. Give three examples of the benefits of internal promotion/member relations.
4. How can an awareness of roles help you to work with others?
5. Why is there 'organisational politics'?
6. Give four examples of legal, contractual or policy provisions governing interpersonal behaviour at work.
7. Give six examples of 'key players' in your job situation.
8. What are the sources of power or influence in an organisation?
9. List five steps you can take to cultivate relationships.
10. List Belbin's team roles.

PART B   BUILDING AND DEVELOPING RELATIONSHIPS

Answers to Quick Quiz

1   Kotler's conclusions are listed in Paragraph 2.3.

2   Your internal customers are anyone in the organisation whose work is affected by your own. It is your role to develop relationships, satisfy colleagues' needs, market your competence and communicate with them as effectively as with customers external to the organisation.

3   By creating excitement about the company's objectives and projects, you create personal motivation in staff and 'buy in'. By creating involvement and pride you increase the company's productivity and quality. Being informed helps make staff realise their contribution to the bigger picture and can help the organisation pull together by removing some of the inter-departmental friction (which Kotler describes).

4   Professional behaviour is appropriate to your role or roles. Understanding what others expect from you will prevent you from making mistakes.

5   Organisations are political systems. Individuals have their own goals, and have to compete with others for the organisational resources to achieve them. Individuals can form interest groups in order to exert more power in influencing the outcome of decisions which may be based on self-interest rather than the company's well-being.

6   You have a contractual obligation to show 'loyal duty' to your employer. There is legal enforcement of indirect and direct discrimination through the Race Relations, Disability and Sex Discrimination Acts over the previous three decades. Many companies issue a policy against bullying, harassment and discrimination.

7   This will depend on your own circumstances. Remember that key relationships are those which impact on you most directly.

8   Legitimate power, expert power, reward power, referent power and coercive power.

9   Refer to Paragraph 4.3.

10 Refer to Paragraph 5.2

Action Programme Review

1   (a)   Senior management and shareholders, who expect the strategic objectives of the organisation to be met through effective and efficient marketing activity.

    (b)   The production function, which expects to be given practicable product specifications and production schedules and expects its efforts to be justified by the success of the product in the market place – to feel that output is being effectively 'sold'.

    (c)   The accounting and administrative function, which expects clear and accurate budgets, forecasts and records of expenditure, sales and so on, for the required financial control and reporting and record-keeping systems.

    (d)   The members of the organisation as a whole, who expect to be given information – and particularly 'good news' – by the organisation, to be able to feel pride in the organisation's image to the outside world, to identify with it and to feel that the marketing function is 'getting it right' and that:

          (i)   they are not wasting effort on a product that nobody wants; and

          (ii)   their efforts are being properly communicated to the market: the marketing 'does justice to' the products/organisation they are committed to.

2   Your findings might have included a wide range of policies from dress codes to passive smoking, sexual harassment, age discrimination, the rights of gays and lesbians, discipline and grievance, general conduct in the work place and so on. If no such policies were accessible, how are 'norms' of roles and relationships defined in the organisation?

3   Albert Smith has the organisational authority to approve your recommendation. However, Mr and Mrs Smith still exercise informal cultural and expert power in the business, as the founders – and heads of the family. You are likely to have to get their support. Mrs Smith will be particularly important as a source of expert knowledge and experience, as you develop your programme – and also of contacts, since you will need to source teachers. It is not clear how the programme would be organised, or under whose authority: it may well come under the umbrella of 'Administration' once it has been launched, so you will need to get Amy Chan's support and involvement at an early stage. It is also worth bearing in mind that the Sales Assistants – in their front line role – will be the ones who promote, explain and welcome people to the programme, so you will need to involve and educate them – probably through their senior.

4   (a)   (i)   **Win-lose**: one team member gets the window desk, and the other does not. (Result: broken relationships within the team.)

        (ii)   **Compromise**: the team members get the window desk on alternate days or weeks. (Result: half satisfied needs.)

        (iii) **Win-win**: what do they want the window desk for? One may want the view, the other better lighting conditions. This offers options to be explored: how else could the lighting be improved, so that both team members get what they really want? (Result: at least, the positive intention to respect everyone's wishes equally, with benefits for team communication and creative problem-solving.)

    (b)   (i)   **Win-lose**: one of you gets the file and the other doesn't.

        (ii)   **Compromise**: one of you gets the file now, and the other gets it later (although this has an element of win-lose, since the other has to work late or take it home).

        (iii) **Win-win**: you photocopy the file and *both* take it, or one of you consults his or her boss and gets an extension of the deadline (since getting the job done in time is the real aim – not just getting the file). These kind of solutions are more likely to emerge if the parties believe they *can* both get what they want.

    (c)   (i)   **Win-lose**: Manager A gets the computers, and Manager B has to upgrade her systems.

        (ii)   **Compromise**: Manager A will get some new computers, but keep the same old ones for continued data-sharing with Department B. Department B will also need to get some new computers, as a back-up measure.

        (iii) **Win-win**: what does Manager A want the computers for, or to avoid? Quite possibly, she needs to use up her budget allocation for buying equipment before the end of the budgetary period: if not, she fears she will lose that budget allocation. Now, that may not be the case, or there may be other equipment that could be more usefully purchased – in which case, there is no losing party.

5   Some of the potential areas of difficulty you may have noted are as follows.

    (a)   The family involvement in the business: there may be a tendency to under-communicate with other staff because family members know each other so well (and because power is concentrated in the family). You will need to be assertive in ensuring that your expertise is heeded and valued. Your role may also involve ensuring that information flows to non-family members of the team.

    (b)   Part-time sales assistants: particular efforts will have to be made to keep part-timers 'in the loop' as things change, and to help them to feel part of the team. Staff meetings will be difficult, as members will be in the store at different times. Notice boards – and a communicative management style – may be used, and occasional staff get-togethers arranged.

PART B   BUILDING AND DEVELOPING RELATIONSHIPS

(c) Two worksites: factory staff may feel quite separate from store staff. Measures may have to be taken to bring them together: for example, site visits or all-staff quarterly meetings. A staff bulletin or news sheet might also be used.

(d) The prospect of external trainers/demonstrators: relationships will need to be set up and managed so that they are involved (and therefore dependable), informed (so that they project the right image, and promote the right products for the firm) and able to co-operate with store staff. Regular phone, email or newsletter contact, plus face-to-face meetings when they are in-store may be used to maintain contact.

6 What makes a team feel like a team? Perhaps a name, behavioural or dress norms, shared stories and successes (or heroic failures), 'badges' of some kind, its own space: there are many ways of building a team identity. As for the Belbin roles, you may have noticed that an individual can play more than one role.

Now try Question 5 at the end of the Study Text

The front line role

Chapter topic list

1. Front-line customer care
2. Receiving visitors
3. Assisting visitors
4. E-relationships

Syllabus content – knowledge and skills requirements

- 2.3 Explain the 'front line' role; receiving and assisting visitors, internal and external enquiries
- 2.8 Explain the concept and application of e-relationships

Introduction

In this chapter, we look more closely at face-to-face (and virtual) encounters between representatives of the marketing organisation and its customers and visitors. We cover both:

(a) the **'front-line' role** of providing information and assistance and
(b) the 'virtual' interface between the organisation and its stakeholders, through **e-relationships**.

1 Front-line customer care

FAST FORWARD

Customer care is everybody's job, because every individual and team in an organisation contributes to the products, services or general impression of the organisation that customers, clients and visitors take away with them.

Business organisations are increasingly recognising two things about customers.

- They have an ever-widening **choice** of products and services available to them
- **Service** is of major importance in winning and retaining customers

Key concept

Customer care is: 'the management and identification of 'moments of truth', with the aim of achieving customer satisfaction.' (*Thomas*, 1986)

All employees who come into contact with people from outside the organisation are ambassadors of the organisation.

This is particularly true of those employees who have responsibilities which put them regularly in contact with customers and clients. Again, do not think just in terms of sales and delivery people. Your job as a marketing assistant may be a 'front line' customer contact position.

- Assisting in the **reception** of visitors to the premises, or to your department
- Answering **enquiries** from customers, or members of the public
- Providing **information** about the organisation's products and services
- Handling **complaints** or **queries** from customers about products or services

Marketing at Work

According to the *Citizen's Charter Complaints Task Force* (*Putting Things Right*), it is much more cost effective to **handle customer complaints at the front line** than to pass them on for review by staff higher up the organisation. According to the survey, the following public sector organisations reported these costs per complaint.

	Handled informally by front line staff	Formally reviewed by senior staff
NHS Trust	£3.45	£370
Local Authority	£17	£110
HM Revenue & Customs	£30-70	£78-£650
Electricity company	£5.10	£80-£140

6: THE FRONT LINE ROLE

Exam tip

> This element of the syllabus may form part of a skills audit in your workplace. You may need evidence of your ability to greet visitors in the workplace, determine their needs and, where appropriate, meet their needs, either personally or through appropriate persons. If you still think customer service 'isn't your job', you will at least have to **make it your job** to this extent!
>
> The June 2005 exam offered 20 marks for explaining how good customer service could increase business (for a railway), and preparing a set of customer care guidelines for staff.

2 Receiving visitors

FAST FORWARD

> A **visitor** is a person who visits a person or a place. *Internal* visitors are the other people who work in your organisation, whereas *external* visitors include customers and clients (those people who do not work in your organisation).

There are many general rules on dealing with people, such as effective oral and non-verbal communication, and **courtesy**. These should of course be applied when dealing with anybody with whom you came into contact in the course of business.

Dealing with visitors to the workplace involves **direct interpersonal contact**. Personal contact is the most direct and flexible way of communicating.

(a) **Each party gets an overall impression of the other**: hearing and seeing aid interpretation, and help to confirm it through feedback.

(b) **Personality can be brought into play**, especially in persuasive contexts encouraging customers to buy or reassuring them that their business is being dealt with efficiently.

(c) **Immediate exchange is possible**: question and answer, action and reaction, feedback and modification.

(d) **Greater sensitivity is encouraged**: tact, trust, understanding, sympathy or co-operation can be exchanged in face-to-face situations.

We discuss some of the 'practical PR' skills involved in dealing with people, and how they affect the organisation's image, in Chapter 8. Here, we discuss some of the human, procedural and legal aspects of the front-line reception and assistance role.

2.1 Greeting people

FAST FORWARD

> Whatever type of visitor you are receiving, you should always be **polite**, **courteous** and display **good manners**.

First impressions are vital: if you do not get it right first time you may never deal effectively with that person.

(a) **Smile**. It actually takes fewer muscles to smile than to frown, so give your face a rest! Forget about your own troubles and concentrate on the matter in hand.

(b) **Make eye contact**. Don't gaze intently into people's eyes – in some cultures, this is threatening and uncomfortable – but don't keep looking down or away, otherwise they will think that you are not interested in them and they may not trust you.

(c) If the visitor offers to **shake hands** with you, never decline the offer.

If you are greeting somebody you know you must gauge the **formality** or otherwise of your greeting according to your relationship to date. Do not be overfamiliar, but make sure that you use their name once or twice (their first name if the relationship has developed that far).

PART B BUILDING AND DEVELOPING RELATIONSHIPS

Remember that pleasantries ('How are you?', 'Did you have a good journey?') are useful in establishing rapport, but do not waste time in getting down to business. (If clients are inclined to gossip do not cut them dead, but say 'Well, what can I do for you today?' at the earliest opportunity.)

2.2 Receiving external visitors

These are certain standard **reception procedures** which should be carried out when receiving all visitors. These may be summarised as follows.

- Greet the visitor politely
- Sign the visitor in for identification, security and safety purposes
- Notify the person that (s)he has come to see that the visitor has arrived
- Stay with the visitor until (s)he is collected
- Direct the visitor to the office of the persons he has come to see

Here are some further guidelines whether you are on reception duty or welcoming a visitor to a meeting.

(a) **Don't keep visitors waiting unnecessarily.** They should be made comfortable whilst waiting.

(b) **Greet visitors by their name** (if known) and with a handshake.

(c) If dealing with **sensitive or personal matters**, wait until you are behind closed doors before beginning such discussions.

(d) **Direct visitors** to the office or interview room where the meeting is to be held.

(e) **Maintain a courteous and interested tone** during all dealings with external visitors.

(f) If you have to take a **phone call** whilst waiting with a visitor, or whilst in a meeting with one, keep it very brief.

Action Programme 1

Consider the following scenario in the Customer Service office of Baddley & Co Bank.

MRS WEAVER: [*Timidly, glancing at her watch*] Um...excuse me...that young man knows that I've arrived, doesn't he?

RECEPTIONIST: [*Not looking up*] Oh yes. He said he'll be along in a minute.

[*Several minutes pass by*]

PETER: [*Ambling out of the reception area and winking at the receptionist.*] Ah. Mrs...um. I see you've found some magazines! Would you like to finish reading that?

MRS WEAVER: [*Putting down* Banking World *and looking rather frightened.*] Hello. I had an appointment to see a Mr Benton. I hope I'm...

PETER: That's me – you can call me Peter. Mrs...[*flicks through file*] Weaver, ah yes, that's right – problems with loan repayments. Would you like to come this way?

[*PETER walks quickly down the corridor, pausing half way down to check that MRS WEAVER is following.*]

PETER: [*In doorway, to three junior staff in suits, smoking and laughing*] Could you clear out for ten minutes, please guys: I've got an F104.

[*MRS WEAVER arrives in the room. The three 'guys' pick up their papers, put out their cigarettes and leave. PETER leans his head out of the door before closing it and makes an inaudible remark which is greeted with loud laughter.*]

PETER:	Well Mrs Weaver. How can we help you?	
MRS WEAVER:	Well actually *you* wrote to me and asked me to come in and see you. I'm sorry.	
	[*The phone rings.*]	
PETER:	Oh, put him through. John! How are you? How's business?... Yes I did ring you, its about that ten grand you were after. I just wanted to say, no problem mate. Yes, I thought you'd be pleased. How's Caroline? [*Lengthy silence while PETER listens to the person on the other end of the line.*] I'm sorry... I had no idea, mate. So it's completely... um... there's no chance of you getting back together? ... Well, give it time, you know what they say. Look, I've got to go – I'll see you Friday, OK? Bye.	
	[*Peter now looks down at the file on the table and leafs through it for some time.*]	
	Now then, Mrs Weaver...	

Peter clearly does not deal with Mrs Weaver very well. What criticisms would you make of his handling of this case?

3 Assisting visitors

There is a balance between what you can reasonably be expected to know about your organisation and knowing the **limits within which you are able to deal with enquiries**. Nevertheless, the way that you deal with visitors and their enquiries is crucial to the success of the relationship and of your organisation.

Action Programme 2

The Needle Works

You have recommended an 'open evening' for regular customers in the refurbished showroom, partly as a public customer contact exercise and partly to show off the new knitting department. You have organised a festive in-store display, a string quartet and a buffet and drinks, with waiter service. Albert Smith wants you to attend on the evening itself because you are frequently the first point of contact with clients on the telephone, and because you organised the open evening, and might be needed to supervise arrangements. You know that your presence will (thanks to excellent pre-planning) not be required once things have been set up. You will not be paid to attend. You had arranged to see some friends that evening.

Who will gain if you attend the open evening, and in what ways?

3.1 Meeting visitors' information needs

FAST FORWARD

You may have to answer a variety of routine and non-routine **enquiries** as part of your job.

If a visitor or caller requests **information** about the products or services of the organisation, you may well have the information to hand, although the degree of knowledge you need to have will depend on the nature of your involvement and the complexity of the organisation's activity.

Be sure that you can give an answer to the following questions.

(a) What does your organisation do? What does your own department do, and what other departments are there?

(b) Does your organisation supply to other businesses, to domestic clients or to both? Does it export its product or services?

(c) Is there a brochure describing your organisation's products/services? There may be many such brochures – are you aware of all of them?

(d) What new products or services are going to be introduced? Are the old versions to be discontinued?

(e) Who are your organisation's major competitors? How are your organisation's products/services different from theirs?

(f) If you did not know the answer to a question about your organisation, who could help you or deal with the query?

Exam tip

> **Learn as much as you can** about your organisation's business: it will make you more effective in your job and it will help your prospects. You will learn by experience from doing your own job and you can also learn by talking to colleagues, especially those who are more experienced than you are. You could also glance through trade journals – even if the detailed articles are too complex or specialised for you, the advertisements will be very informative. In a similar way, *note and use* details about your (imagined) employer in the exam case study scenario.

Asking other people is an acceptable option. Recognise your own limits and get help. You should have a telephone list of departments and individual colleagues you can consult. Use your common sense.

- Who is the most appropriate person to consult?
- When and how might you consult them?

3.2 To whom should you give information?

FAST FORWARD

> Be aware of **data security** constraints on your ability to give information.

Whether or not you give information about your organisation's products or services in response to unsolicited queries depends very much upon the sort of product or service that you supply. You may, for example, need to know something of the circumstances of prospective customers to determine whether its products or services are suitable for that customer's needs.

In cases where the product/service is more limited in its availability or more sensitive in its nature, the organisation may require certain formal checks to be carried out to verify an enquirer's **identity** and **eligibility** to receive information.

(a) Some companies operate a policy of replying **only in writing** to requests for information that could be sensitive.

(b) Banks, for example, will not tell you your own bank balance unless you have agreed some **password** known only to you and them in advance.

3.3 Confidentiality

FAST FORWARD

> **Confidentiality** should always be maintained where considered necessary. The affairs of your own organisation and its clients are confidential and should not be disclosed to others unless the circumstances are appropriate.

The information you give out will also be limited by the principles and procedures of **confidentiality**. You do not expect the staff of your bank to discuss your personal financial circumstances with anybody who happens to walk into the branch. Everybody has a right to expect the organisations that they deal with to respect the privacy of their affairs.

(a) **Do not discuss the detailed affairs of one client with another.** You might sometimes need to say 'I dealt with a very similar case last week, and the way we solved the problem there was...', but you should never give names or other details that would identify one client to another.

(b) If you are asked for the **names of some of your other customers** – for example, if a potential customer wants a second opinion on the worth of your products – make sure you get permission from the other customers to use them as **references**.

(c) **Within your organisation use the 'need to know' principle**. If people in other departments do not need to be given all of the information that you possess about a particular client, do not give it to them. There may be organisational rules that forbid certain information from being passed between departments.

> **Key concept**
>
> **Confidentiality** is the keeping of information, given 'on confidence' to particular parties, between those parties: not disclosing information to those not authorised to have access to it.

Do not forget that the affairs of your own organisation are confidential. Do not gossip about your organisation to clients, or malign your colleagues.

4 E-relationships

> **FAST FORWARD**
>
> **E-relationships** are relationships mediated by repeated contacts using electronic or ICT media.

Marketers can take steps towards promoting effective e-relationships with customers. We look at relationships with **suppliers** in the context of 'e-procurement' in the next chapter. You will probably notice that the principles which are explored would hold true for 'offline' customers as well, and that human interaction will never be fully replaced.

4.1 E-relationships with customers

> **FAST FORWARD**
>
> E-relationships can be **developed** in a number of ways, including:
> - Improving customer interaction
> - Identifying segments and processes that suit e-relationships
> - Creating new relationships

4.1.1 Improving customer interaction

The first thing for the organisation to do is to **upgrade the interaction with its existing customers**.

(a) Create **automated responses for the FAQs** (Frequently Asked Questions) posed by customers, so that customers become conditioned to electronic communication.

(b) Set **fast response standards**, at least to match anything offered by the competition.

(c) **Use e-mail** in order to confirm actions, check understanding, and reassure the customer that their business is being taken forward.

(d) **Establish ease of navigation** around your website and enhance the site's 'stickiness' so that there is a reduced likelihood that customers will wander away.

Marketing at Work

A study conducted by Rubic Inc in the USA ('Evaluating the 'Sticky' Factor of E-Commerce Sites') found that the majority of websites fail to communicate effectively with customers. Only 40 per cent had a strategy of personalisation for their e-mail messages to customers. When customers responded to follow-up offers, only one quarter of websites recognised the fact that they were dealing with a repeat customer. Forty per cent of e-mail enquiries went unanswered despite promises of replies within two days.

4.1.2 Selecting segments and processes for automation

The organisation should **understand its customer segments** and the likelihood that they will be receptive to the Internet.

(a) Some will be eager to transfer to the new technology, others will do so if persuaded, and residual groups will prefer to remain as they are.

(b) Efforts should be made to **automate** the provision of customer service to low-value customers.

(c) The organisation should establish **personalised service relationships** with high value customers.

The organisation must also **understand its customer service processes** in order to see those which can safely be automated, and those which have to be delivered in other ways.

(a) Customers are often conscious about **time** and timeliness. Getting on to the Internet sometimes takes longer than a telephone call, so the customer will want more value from the process. Remember that a short simple transaction is often better conducted over the telephone!

(b) **Live interaction** may be very useful if there is scope for cross-selling and the conversion of enquiries into sales. It is essential for customers who have a strong preference for human contact. The availability of service supplied by human intervention can also be appropriate if the organisation needs to build trust (eg it is a new brand) and secure information from the customer.

(c) **E-mail** may not be sufficient as a communication tool, especially if it involves a delay before replies are forthcoming.

Marketing at Work

Many banks offer **personal, phone and Internet banking**; some (like First Direct) have single-channel accounts (phone or Internet only), whilst others (like *egg*) allow constrained choice: *egg* (the Internet and telephone banking arm of the Prudential Assurance Company) will allow telephone and Internet customer interaction, but only permits new customers to enrol via the web.

One reason why *Charles Schwab* (specialists in stock and share dealing) is able to charge much bigger fees than some of its rivals is that it combines an **online service** with a low-cost branch network and a telephone service. They have recognised the web has certain virtues and weaknesses. The web is lousy if you have a complex question. Likewise, it does not allow for people's need for relationships. Not everyone feels happy about sending a cheque to a broker they have never seen.

4.1.3 Creating new relationships

The organisation should exploit ICT developments in order to create **new relationships** and **experiences** for customers.

(a) **E-mail marketing** can be used to give product and offer updates.

(b) **E-zines** and newsletters can be used to make regular value-added contacts with customers.

(c) The corporate **website** should be designed to prompt multiple visits: offering new/updated content; entertaining interactive features (eg quizzes and testers, games etc); helpful links and database/search features; special offers and so on.

(d) Special areas of the website may be set up for **key account customers**, or to customers who choose to register as 'members' (thereby giving permission for relationship marketing), with special offers, facilities or perceived exclusivity.

(e) **Virtual communities** of customers can be set up (using discussion groups, message boards and so on) to create word-of-mouth promotion and referral, elicit feedback and enhance the 'stickiness' of the website.

(f) **Self-service elements** (database searches, e-commerce transactions) can be used to empower customers and cement relationships: eg an online grocery store which allows past shopping lists to be saved for next time, making recommendations and offers on previously bought items etc.

(g) **Web links** and banner advertisements can be used to provide added value to customers through collaborative promotions and referrals.

Other ICT tools for relationship marketing include mobile phone text-messaging, which has become a key promotional tool in the youth market in recent years.

> **Exam tip**
>
> An interesting twist on e-relationships emerged in the June 2004 exam, where you were asked to suggest how ICT could impact on a night club. The examiner applauded answers which recognised that a 'club' can go 'way beyond its physical boundaries', recommending strategies such as extending the club to digital music radio and Web playlist forums.
>
> Similarly, in December 2005, you were asked how a website could be used to support the marketing of a cultural festival, both before, during and after the event. (You were also asked to recommend on-line techniques – such as those listed above – and off-line techniques for getting more people to visit or 'hit' your website. *Off-line* techniques would include advertising your website address and features, such as promotional competitions.)
>
> In December 2006, you were asked to suggest information that should be featured on the website of a museum – and how the website could be used to increase visitor numbers.

> **Marketing at Work**
>
> *M&Ms*
>
> The major 2004 challenge for MasterFoods main confectionery brand, M&Ms, was to surpass their innovative 'global colour vote' campaign of the previous year (in which consumers were asked to pick a new M&Ms colour). The result was 'a campaign that exemplifies the concept of **integration**: that is, an advertising campaign successfully supported by on-line, SMS and in-store promotion to raise consumer interest'. The campaign – 'Money 4 Mates' – featured a competition in which the more mates you get to enter, the better your chance of winning. Friendship connections are crucial for M&Ms' core target market of 14-24 year olds, a demographic that is also the heaviest user of the Internet and SMS as forms of peer group communication. To reinforce the benefit of the promotion, the entire campaign concept was to create the attraction of sharing with friends.
>
> *BRW*, March 17, 2005

4.2 E-relationships within the organisation

FAST FORWARD

> Many organisations now operate using **'virtual' teams**: interconnected groups of people who may never be present in the same office – and may even be on different sides of the world – but who share information and tasks, make joint decisions and fulfil the collaborative functions of a 'physical' team.

The development of ICT has enabled communication and collaboration among people in different locations via:

(a) Teleconferencing, videoconferencing and webcasts, allowing 'virtual' meetings.

(b) Locally networked PCs and the World Wide Web, with email, instant-messaging, shared access to databases and so on, allowing fast, interactive communication and data sharing.

(c) Meeting manager systems, with electronic 'white boards' (for making notes), bulletin boards and data sharing. Virtual meeting participants can use teleconference lines to talk to each other, while showing charts and data on their PCs.

(d) Intranets, or employee-only areas of the corporate website, allowing online handbooks, journals, staff information and so on to be exchanged.

4.2.1 Virtual teamworking

'Virtual teams may be composed of full-time or part-time employees. They might have a global reach, or involve combinations of local telecommuting members and more traditional in-house workers. A senior executive might be on one planning committee for a product release, for example, another for identifying minority vendors, another to study relocating a plant, and another to evaluate software tracking. He may deal with key players who not only are out of the country but also are working for another company, or perhaps as suppliers who are on the virtual team to add information and technical support.' (*Solomon*, 2001)

Localised virtual teams have been used for some time in the form of **'teleworking'**: the process of working from home, or from a satellite office close to home, with the aid of computers, facsimile machines, modems or other forms of telecommunication equipment. The main benefits cited for such work include savings on office overheads and the elimination of the costs and stresses of commuting for employees.

4.2.2 Benefits of e-collaboration

More recently, however, the globalisation of business, the need for fast responses to marketplace demands and the increasing sophistication of available technologies has brought about an explosion in global virtual teamworking. More and more organisations are attempting to conduct business 24 hours a day, seven days a week, with people on different continents and in different time zones. Electronic collaboration allows organisations to:

- Recruit and collaborate with the **best available people** without the constraints of location or relocation. A team can 'co-opt' a Specialist when required, from a global pool of skills.
- Offer more **scheduling flexibility** for people who prefer non-traditional working hours (including the handicapped and working parents, for example).
- Maintain close **contact** with customers throughout the world.
- Operate **24-hour** 'follow the sun' working days (for example, for global customer support) – without having to have staff on night shifts.

Marketing at Work

Is **virtual team working** all about the technology? Solomon (Managing Virtual Teams, *Workforce*, June, 2001) argues otherwise.

'Effective managers of virtual teams understand critical non-technological skills. "Trust is a very important component of virtual teams. Managers have to trust that people will perform when they're away from direct supervision. Individual team members need to develop trust across different media, such as e-mail and telephone, which may be difficult to do."

'Developing a productive virtual team begins with selecting the right people. A successful team member is self-motivated and doesn't need a lot of detailed instructions or structure. Ideally, he or she is a strong communicator, a quality that helps counter-balance the anonymous nature of technology. In addition, [experts recommend] people who are adaptable, technically self-sufficient and results-oriented.

'Managers should set up regular virtual meetings to share expectations and debriefings. It is their task to frame the team's objectives so members clearly understand their roles. They emphasise the consequences of team decisions and provide ongoing monitoring and honest feedback about how the team is doing.

'Virtual teams offer an opportunity to work with the best talent throughout an organisation. But to accomplish this, managers must actively work to create a sense of connectedness and shared space, to use technology effectively and to know when to forgo technology for personal communication.'

For reflection:

How does your own experiences of virtual team working reflect the management challenges discussed in this article?

Chapter Roundup

- **Customer care** is everybody's job, because every individual and team in an organisation contributes to the products, services or general impression of the organisation that customers, clients and visitors take away with them.

- A **visitor** is a person who visits a person or a place. *Internal* visitors are the other people who work in your organisation, whereas *external* visitors include customers and clients (those people who do not work in your organisation).

- Whatever type of visitor you are receiving, you should always be **polite**, **courteous** and display **good manners**.

- You may have to answer a variety of routine and non-routine **enquiries** as part of your job.

- Be aware of **data security** constraints on your ability to give information.

- **Confidentiality** should always be maintained where considered necessary. The affairs of your own organisation and its clients are confidential and should not be disclosed to others unless the circumstances are appropriate.

- **E-relationships** are relationships mediated by repeated contacts using electronic or ICT media.

- E-relationships can be **developed** in a number of ways, including:
    - Improving customer interaction
    - Identifying segments and processes that suit e-relationships
    - Creating new relationships

- Many organisations now operate using **'virtual' teams**: interconnected groups of people who may never be present in the same office – and may even be on different sides of the world – but who share information and tasks, make joint decisions and fulfil the collaborative functions of a 'physical' team.

Quick Quiz

1. What sort of information does a visitors' signing-in book usually record?
2. What are the guidelines that should be followed when dealing with external visitors?
3. What can you do in order to create a good impression when greeting visitors?
4. What options do you have if you do not know the answer to an enquiry?
5. What is an e-relationship?
6. What are the advantages of virtual teamworking?

Answers to Quick Quiz

1. A visitors' book usually records the visitor's name, the name and department of the person they have come to see and the purpose of their visit. Sometimes signing in procedures include a time of arrival and exit or a car registration number for security and administration purposes.

2. They should be welcomed, asked to sign in, the person they intend to visit should be notified and reception should stay with the visitor until the host is available.

3. Show that you respect their time, their privacy, their comfort and are interested in them. Good manners dictate you should welcome by name if possible and that you should not keep visitors waiting unnecessarily or leave them to their own devices while you deal with other business.

4. Be honest and let the visitor know that you do not know the answer without making excuses. Let the visitor know what you are going to do about it and then do it or check that it has been followed up by a colleague.

5. An e-relationship is one maintained by electronic contact through an Internet site.

6. See Paragraphs 4.2.1 and 4.2.2 for a full answer.

Action Programme Review

1. Peter (and the organisation generally) handle Mrs Weaver badly from start to finish.

    (a) Mrs Weaver is kept waiting for some while after the appointed time before she receives any attention. Even the receptionist is offhand with her.

    (b) When he does arrive Peter does so in a very unbusinesslike manner. He does not greet Mrs Weaver by name. He does not apologise for being late.

    (c) His tone of friendliness ('you can call me Peter') is belied by his complete lack of interest in Mrs Weaver's case.

    (d) He is quite oblivious to any desire that Mrs Weaver may have for her business to be handled confidentially. He blurts out her financial problems in front of the receptionist.

    (e) He is most discourteous in not showing Mrs Weaver the way to the interview room. He should have let her go first and made some attempt to put her at her ease.

    (f) He is more polite to the three juniors who appear to be wasting time than he has so far been to his customer. He becomes conspiratorial in referring to her, mysteriously, as 'an F104'. This tells Mrs Weaver that the organisation regards her as a number and that her case, however harrowing its circumstances may be, are about to be swallowed up by bureaucracy.

    (g) Peter's private joke with his colleagues may have nothing to do with Mrs Weaver, but by now she is likely to be feeling that, when the organisation is not being seriously inconvenienced by her, it regards her as a laughing matter.

    (h) Once more Peter's lack of preparation is shown by his 'How can I help you?'

    (i) He should not have accepted the telephone call – it could have been diverted to a colleague or he could have called back later.

    (j) The organisation's time and Mrs Weaver's is wasted by the discussion of the caller's domestic circumstances. Mrs Weaver will hardly be able to feel that her own affairs are being handled confidentially if Peter is prepared to have conversations about his friend's circumstances in front of her.

PART B BUILDING AND DEVELOPING RELATIONSHIPS

2 (a) You can gain from the evening in a number of ways.

 (i) You may learn more about The Needle Works – about its overall aims and the way its various services are linked and complement each other. This will help you to market it more effectively.

 (ii) You will extend and develop your networks of people within the company. This is valuable networking, PR *and* market research: you are likely to find out more about how your customers view The Needle Works and its services.

 (iii) You will get feedback on your organisation of the open evening: both positive (hopefully) and negative (indicating areas of learning and improvement) which is good market research.

 (iv) Albert will be impressed by your loyalty to the company: good personal 'PR', enhancing your image with a person of influence in your workplace.

 (v) You will get a free meal!

 (b) The Needle Works and its customers will gain in the following ways.

 (i) You will have gathered information that will make you more effective in tailoring the marketing message to the customers.

 (ii) Your customers will be able to put a face to your name. They will feel more comfortable when dealing with you over the telephone or receiving direct mail from you.

 (iii) Your customers may be inclined to use a wide range of the company's services, if they are dealing initially with a known quantity. This should be to the benefit of both parties.

Now try Question 6 at the end of the Study Text

The supply chain

Chapter topic list

1. Supply chain relationships
2. Negotiating
3. Suppliers of marketing services
4. Working with advertising agencies
5. Working with distribution channels
6. E-procurement

Syllabus content – knowledge and skills requirements

- 2.5 Explain the supplier interface; negotiating, collaborating, operational and contractual aspects
- 2.6 Explain how the organisation fits into a supply chain, and works with distribution channels
- 2.8 Explain the concept and application of e-relationships

PART B BUILDING AND DEVELOPING RELATIONSHIPS

Introduction

In this chapter, we will look primarily at the **operational**, **procedural** and **contractual** aspects of working with the supply chain, particularly from the point of view of the marketing department's relationships.

(a) **Suppliers of marketing services** (advertising agencies, PR consultancies, creative freelancers)

(b) **Retailers and other distribution channels** which require marketing support. (If you're in the marketing department of a retail outlet, say, you can consider this section 'in reverse'!)

1 Supply chain relationships

FAST FORWARD

Supply chain relationships require interpersonal and business skills. As well as the human aspects discussed in other chapters, they involve:

- contracts
- systems and procedures
- in the context of business objectives or purpose

In many ways, relationships with suppliers and distribution channels are the same as those with colleagues, customers, visitors and other business contacts and require many of the same features. We will not be dealing again in detail with the 'human' aspects of relationships in this chapter.

In other respects, however, relationships with suppliers and distributors are different to those with colleagues and visitors. As **business relationships**, they raise a number of other issues.

(a) They involve dealings with other business organisations which have their own aims and objectives: these may or may not be in harmony with yours.

(b) They involve dealings with representatives of other business organisations, who have a dual responsibility to you (as client) and (primarily) to their employers.

(c) They are governed by legal terms and constraints, expressed in contracts.

(d) They are subject to commercial and competitive pressures: if one party is not satisfied, they can break the relationship.

(e) They are shaped by the operational requirements of the work for which the relationship was formed.

1.1 Collaborating

Key concept

Collaboration simply means 'working with', but is used in the stronger sense of working *jointly* or sharing tasks and responsibilities with another party.

There are **three main elements** to collaborating effectively with other business organisations and their representatives.

- Contracts
- Systems and procedures
- Purpose

1.1.1 Contracts

In basic terms, a contract or legally binding agreement exists between two parties if there is:

- The **intention to create a legal relationship** (as opposed to a purely personal one)
- **Offer and acceptance** (agreeing to supply or receive goods or services)
- **Consideration** (some payment given or promised for the goods or services to be supplied)

This covers most of the transactions you will come across in marketing activity. A contract does not have to be a formal legal document: it can be a letter, or even a strong **verbal understanding** (as long as the three basic elements can be proved). Be aware that when you ask a designer or printer to do work for you and they agree to do so, and you negotiate a price, that you are entering into a contract.

A contract may set out **express terms**, or clearly stated terms.

- Delivery/completion dates
- Description of the goods/services to be provided
- Quality standards below which the goods/services will not be accepted
- The amount to be paid, and when, and what it covers and does not cover
- Any conditions and caveats either party wishes to impose: for example, that they will not be liable for errors arising from faulty components or information provided by the other party; that in the event of cancellation of the project, they will be paid for all work done up to the date of cancellation.

Action Programme 1

Get hold of a copy of the terms and conditions of any service supplier you may do business with. (Printers often put them on the back of quotation stationery: advertising media, with their rate card. You can find them in Photo Library catalogues and order forms. Use your research skills.) Note the main issues covered by contract terms and identify areas where your procedures and practices may need adjusting to comply more securely.

[*Key skill for Marketers: Applying Business Law*]

A contract also has **implied terms**, which are 'understood' from the context of the business relationship. If not expressly stated, for example, it is still implied that goods and services should be of reasonable quality, provided to specification and within a reasonable timescale.

When working with other organisations, it is helpful to exchange a contract, letter or purchase order, which:

- Is in **writing** (even if only to confirm a verbal agreement)
- Defines the **products/services** to be supplied, and the delivery schedule
- Defines the **division of responsibility** between the parties
- Confirms the negotiated **terms and conditions** for payment

1.1.2 Systems and procedures

Procedures for collaborative working should include:

- briefing
- joint planning
- negotiation of terms
- sharing of information and resources
- monitoring, checking and approval
- feedback
- payment

The procedures to be followed will be dictated by the particular task or project in hand. Be aware that simply following recommended **procedures** correctly and efficiently is a major element in working smoothly and successfully with other organisations, who have usually developed ways of working for a reason!

In general, however, a **systematic approach** to collaboration should include the following.

(a) **Clear and specific briefing on requirements**. Be clear what you want suppliers/collaborators to do for you. Objectives, schedules, budgets and job specifications make everyone's job easier.

(b) **Joint planning**. The brief sets out what you want to achieve: how you get there (together) is best decided collaboratively, since the other party has input to offer, and their own aims, procedures and constraints to take into account. Define clearly the scope and limit of everyone's activity, and establish how to implement any recommendations agreed on.

(c) **Negotiation of terms**. (This will be discussed in more detail below.)

(d) **Sharing of information and resources**. Helping others to help you requires the provision or availability of any information, materials and other resources they may require. (A designer working on an ad for example, may require product samples, catalogues, existing corporate literature, corporate identity specifications and contacts with the company's printers.)

(e) **Monitoring, checking and approval**. Liaison and accountability is the way to ensure your objectives are met. Collaboration with marketing service providers requires submission of plans of work for checking and approval by the client at each stage of the process. If this is not built into the procedure, initiate it yourself.

(f) **Exchanging feedback**. Developing on-going relationships requires mutual adjustment. Regular feedback meetings allow both parties to reinforce positive aspects, identify and solve problems and celebrate collaborative successes. Balance constructive criticism and complaints.

(g) **Paying debts**. Nothing sours a commercial relationship like non-payment or persistent late payment. Accounts departments may resist for cash-flow reasons, but be prepared to champion legitimate demands.

1.1.3 Purpose

Here, we are referring to more than the job specification or task objectives which govern the activity of a relationship. If you want to develop an effective collaboration, consider what it is *for*: what is the purpose of collaborating rather than doing the work yourself?

(a) Your purpose in **retaining an advertising agency** or other consultancy service is to take advantage of the expertise, experience, contacts, facilities and synergy they offer. Your organisation is paying for specialist skills and objectivity and wide experience which it ignores to its loss – and to the detriment of the professional relationship. Moreover, it is unfair to force a supplier to perform against his judgement and advice especially if, as in the highly visible world of advertising and PR, it may affect his reputation in the industry.

(b) Your purpose in **working with retail outlets**, wholesalers, sales representatives and other distribution channels is to motivate them to stock and sell your products ('**push**') and/or to support them by promoting products to consumers ('**pull**').

Marketing at Work

Quinn (1988) tells the story of an **advertising agency** which has a major banking organisation as its client. The bank 'had a habit of running its agency like it would run any other department of its organisation, and the agency let it' (because it was frightened of losing a multi-million pound account). A UK television campaign was being planned, when the bank called in the agency to show them an American TV ad, which bank executives had seen and fallen in love with. In spite of the agency's opposition, the bank insisted that the campaign simply be re-shot in the British idiom. The agency argued that what works for US audiences (especially in terms of humour) does not work with British audiences. They were overruled, and though they did their best, the campaign was a disaster: the bank lost its claimed number one market position within weeks.

2 Negotiating

FAST FORWARD

Negotiating is a bargaining process through which commitments and compromises are reached, which are acceptable to both parties.

Negotiating is, simply, a process whereby two parties came together to confer with a view to concluding a jointly acceptable agreement. *Gennard and Judge* (2003) suggest that this process involves two main elements:

- **Purposeful persuasion**: whereby each party attempts to persuade the other to accept its case by marshalling arguments, backed by factual information and analysis.
- **Constructive compromise**: whereby both parties accept the need to move closer toward each other's position, identifying the parameters of common ground within and between their positions, where there is room for concessions to be made while still meeting the needs of both parties.

Such an approach can be applied to a number of different situations.

- Agreeing **contract terms**. For example: negotiating price, specifications and trading terms for purchase contracts; negotiating terms and conditions in employment contracts; and negotiating industrial relations agreements.
- **Conflict resolution**: reducing resentment and preserving relationship, by allowing both parties to obtain at least some of their desired outcomes.
- **Group decision-making** and **problem-solving**: integrating different viewpoints and interests so that the decision or solution is high on quality (from diverse relevant input) *and* acceptability (from joint consultation and commitment), enhancing the likelihood of effective implementation. People are increasingly expecting to participate in decisions that affect them, particularly at work.

Dobler et al. (1990) define negotiation in the purchasing context as: 'a process of planning, reviewing and analysing used by a buyer and a seller to reach acceptable agreements or compromises [which] include all aspects of the business transaction, not just price.'

They cite five major objectives in commercial negotiation:

- To obtain a fair and reasonable price for the quality specified
- To get the supplier to perform the contract on time
- To exert some control over the manner in which the contract is performed
- To persuade the supplier to give maximum co-operation to the buyer's company
- To develop a sound and continuing relationship with competent suppliers.

2.1 The negotiation process

FAST FORWARD

The **negotiation process** requires preparation, interaction, closure and follow-up.

The following figure (Figure 7.1) is a general overview of the negotiation process.

PREPARATION
Data gathering and analysis
Identifying key issues
Planning strategy and tactics
Preparing the meeting

INTERACTION
Opening
Presentations
Identifying common ground
Making concessions

CLOSURE
Final offer
Conclusion

FOLLOW UP

Figure 7.1: The negotiation process

Marketing at Work

In general, Asian **cultural preferences** in relation to conflict and negotiation reflect their collectivist values and high-context communication styles. Research into conflict strategy and face by Ting-Toomey *et al.* (1991) found that Asian subjects tended to use mutual face-saving strategies, including given others room to manoeuvre in negotiation, allowing them to recover face. They used consensus-seeking, integrative strategies. American subjects, in contrast, tended to focus on saving their own face (interpreted in a more individualistic sense as pride, reputation and self-respect), adopting control-focused and win-lose conflict/negotiation strategies.

2.2 Negotiating strategies

FAST FORWARD

A **'win-win' (or integrative) approach** to negotiation is generally regarded as the most ethical, relationship-building and long-term effective approach.

The aim of negotiating is not to get the best position for yourself or your organisation at the expense of the other party (a **win-lose outcome**). This can cause resentment, under-motivated performance by the 'losing' collaborator, or even the breaking of the relationship.

A basic 'win-win' approach to negotiating (*Cornelius & Faire*, 1989) is as follows.

(a) **Map out**, in advance, what the needs and fears of both parties are. This outlines the psychological and practical territory.

(b) **Define your desired outcome** and estimate the worst, realistic and best case scenarios. ('If I can pay £500, it would be ideal, but I'd settle for £600. Above £700, it's just not worth my while.') Start with the best case and leave room to fall back to the realistic case. Keep your goal in sight.

(c) **Look for mutual or trade-off benefits**. How might you both gain (for example, by getting a higher discount in return for longer or pre-booked series of ads or providing camera ready copy)? What might be cheap for you to give that would be valuable for the other party to receive, or vice versa?

(d) **Spell out the positive benefits** to the other party and support them in saying 'yes' to your proposals by making it as easy as possible. (Offer to supply information or help with follow-up tasks, for example.) Emphasise areas of agreement and common ground.

(e) **Overcome negativity** by asking questions

- What will make it work for you?
- What would it take to make this possible?

(f) **Overcome side-tracks** by asking questions such as: ' How is this going to get us where we want to go?'

(g) **Be hard on the problem but soft on the person**. This is not personal competition or antagonism: work together on problem solving (eg by using flip chart or paper to make shared notes). Show that you have heard the other person (by summarising their argument) before responding with your counter argument.

(h) **Be flexible**. A 'take it or leave it' approach breaks relationships. (However, saying 'no' repeatedly to sales people is a good way of finding out just how far below the list price they are prepared to go!) Make and invite reasonable counter offers.

(i) **Be culturally sensitive**. Some markets thrive on 'haggling'. Some cultures engage in a lot of movement up and down the bargaining scale (eg Asian and Middle Eastern), while others do their homework and fix their prices (eg German). In the former cultures, much emphasis is placed on building relationships and extending hospitality before getting down to terms.

(j) **Take notes**, so the accuracy of everyone's recollection of what was proposed and agreed can be checked.

(k) Summarise and **confirm the details** of your agreements to both parties (by memo, letter, contract) and acknowledge a mutually positive outcome.

Experience, **knowledge** and **expertise** count in negotiation: they add up to bargaining power, which is important even in a win-win approach. If there is someone in your department who has experience in a particular field (such as advertising sales), or your organisation retains an agency or consultancy, be prepared to let them handle negotiations for you.

PART B BUILDING AND DEVELOPING RELATIONSHIPS

Action Programme 2

Get together with fellow students (or friends) in pairs or teams to prepare and role-play a negotiation.

You are looking to purchase advertising space in (any appropriate) magazine for a colour advertisement for your product. You have not previously advertised in this magazine, but have identified it as one which is targeted for your market and high circulation: it could be the key to your up-coming campaign. The copy deadline for the next issue is approaching and the magazine had an unsold colour page which it needs to fill. Rate card price for the colour page is £2,000 (£2,800 for the inside front cover, £2,500 for the inside back cover: highly contested positions, (which you would love to secure). Standard discounts include 10% media buyer's commission, 10% for a series of six ads. You pay 5% extra for bleed colour (running off the page edge). You and the magazine representative(s) should separately (without telling each other) decide what your necessary outcomes are: you should decide what you have to spend from your space budget, and how many ads you think you will need; the magazine rep(s) should decide that the minimum price they will accept, given their need to see space filled. Negotiate a deal!

If you really can't find role-play partners, make notes on the possible strategies, win-win potential, and best-realistic-worst positions for all participants.

[Key skill for Marketers: Working with others]

3 Suppliers of marketing services

FAST FORWARD

There are many **suppliers** of **marketing-related services**, providing advice on or implementation of market research, advertising, promotions, PR, direct marketing, brand identity, sponsorship, creative process and many more areas.

3.1 Why use external marketing services?

There are a number of reasons why you might want to use external marketing services, rather than plan or carry out marketing activities in-house.

(a) Professional marketing agencies **specialise** in communications, media and consumer trends, and stay **up-to-date**.

(b) They have wide **experience** with a range of clients, which they can bring to bear on problems and opportunities.

(c) They supply specialist organisational and creative talent with **specialist facilities** (for example, for filming, sound recording and editing).

(d) They are **objective** about the client's needs and position, and may be better able to view the product from the consumer's point of view.

(e) The **cost** of using external services, past a certain level of sophistication, is usually cheaper than attempting to perform the same functions in-house.

In the last few decades, marketing techniques have increased dramatically in range and complexity. Standard '**above-the-line**' marketing (where media space is paid for), handled by large advertising agencies, has been augmented by '**below-the-line**' (promotional) activities. Agencies specialising in sales promotion, direct marketing, e-marketing and PR have sprung up as independent operations and divisions of large advertising agencies. Many companies now use more than one agency to handle a **portfolio** of techniques above- and below-the-line, or to cover local and on-going work as well as national strategic campaigns.

In addition, the complexities of **new media** (such as e-marketing) have created technical specialisms such as Web page design, datamining, and digital media buying.

3.2 Marketing service providers

We will discuss the various marketing techniques (above- and below-the-line) in Chapters 12 – 14. Here we will briefly outline some of the **service providers** with whom you may have to deal.

3.2.1 Market researchers

Market researchers can be commissioned to gather and analyse information on any aspect of the business, market or environment, as discussed in Chapter 3.

3.2.2 Advertising agencies

Advertising agencies are still the most commonly used marketing service. Agencies come in a range of sizes and specialisms to reflect the increasingly fragmented and diverse range of media.

- (a) '**Media only**' service (where the agency selects schedules and books advertising space at a discount, which is in part passed onto the client)
- (b) '**Full service**' (where the agency creates the whole campaign from concept through production to press/air).

Many larger, integrated agencies now have divisions specialising in various areas:

- Sales promotion
- Direct marketing
- Public relations
- E-marketing (Internet, CD-ROM, mobile phone, podcast)
- Design.

We will discuss relationships with advertising agencies in detail in section 4 below.

3.2.3 Promotion agencies

Promotional activities – collaborations between brands, competitions and incentives – have been a huge growth area in marketing. Some agencies specialise in these areas:

- Sourcing promotional incentive products and merchandise
- Devising links and negotiating deals between brands
- Organising competitions
- Designing and producing promotional packaging and information material.

PR consultancies handle several areas.

- (a) **Media or press relations** (keeping the media informed, in order to manage the company's portrayal and secure 'free' coverage of product/service information)
- (b) **Corporate relations** (promoting a corporate image to the public, market and business world, through a range of PR techniques)
- (c) **Marketing support** (promoting specific products or services via publicity, events, press coverage and so on)
- (d) **Government relations** (lobbying on behalf of the company's interests)
- (e) **Community relations** (targeted at the general public or local residents, via communication and social programmes, community involvement, sponsorship etc)
- (f) **Financial relations** (communicating with shareholders, financial media, the Stock Market)

(g) **Employee relations** (communicating with staff)

PR agencies are less easy to manage than advertising agencies, because their activity and output is often less tangible. The major cost is their time plus expenses. In order to make cost effective use of their services you need to consider the following.

- Set clear **objectives** for the on-going PR plan or specific project
- Set a project **fee** where possible
- **Brief** comprehensively
- **Monitor activity** perhaps via an independent cuttings or media monitoring agency
- Monitor **expenditure**

3.2.4 Direct marketing services

Direct marketing agencies (and separate specialists) offer a range of services from database and mailing list development, analysis and segmentation to telemarketing, direct mail package design, copy writing, mailing and fulfilment – and their electronic equivalents (e-mail, text messaging and so on).

3.2.5 Brand identity

There are specialist agencies which perform specific brand-related services:

- Design and produce product **packaging** and display
- Orchestrate the up-dating of **brand identity** and style
- Research, devise, market-test and register **brand names**

3.2.6 Sponsorship

Agencies undertake negotiations for:

- **Sponsorship agreements**
- **Product endorsements** by celebrities
- **Product placement** (the inclusion of branded products in films or TV programmes)

3.2.7 Creative services

Agency, freelance and corporate help is also available (independent of advertising agencies) with:

- Design and layout, artwork and illustration
- Concept development and copy writing
- Print buying and print production
- Photography
- Film, video and audio production
- Web-page design

Action Programme 3

Go out and buy or borrow a copy of *Campaign* (the journal of the advertising industry) and *Marketing Week*. Browse through them: you can ignore the 'who's moved where' and 'who won what account' material, but you will gather lots of useful ideas on the kinds of services and consultancies that are out there, and what they are doing. Add any interesting details to your list of potential useful contacts.

3.2.8 Other services

In addition to all the above, the marketing department may deal with many providers of services related to promotional events and activities:

- Event organisers, venue managers, hotel/restaurant staff
- Exhibition organisers, stand constructors and removalists
- The postal service and mailing houses
- Model agencies, prop/costume hirers – and so on.

4 Working with advertising agencies

4.1 Why use an agency?

FAST FORWARD

> Many advertisers use an **agency** for mass consumer-market advertising, because of the special expertise required.

Most companies which advertise use an advertising agency:

- for national or international campaigns
- for consumer markets.

In addition, large agencies offer a wide portfolio of marketing and corporate/brand identity services which may be utilised as a full-service package.

However, some companies prefer to arrange their own advertising.

(a) **Issues to consider in adopting a 'do it yourself' approach.**

Factors to consider	Questions	Directions
Experience	Do I know about advertising?	If 'yes', do-it-yourself is a possibility.
The task	Is it simple?	If simple, do-it-yourself is a possibility.
	Am I sure what it is?	If 'no', you probably need an agency.
Money	Would my account interest an agency?	If 'no', consider do-it-yourself.
	Can I afford it?	
Confidence	Do I need a second opinion on my selling approach?	If 'yes', try an agency.
Workload	Is there likely to be a lot of detailed follow-up?	If 'yes', try an agency.
People	Do I have people who can do it in-house?	If 'no', try an agency or specialist.

(b) **Advantages and disadvantages**

	Agency	Do it yourself
Advantages	Skills Experience Media contacts/discounts Outsider's point of view You can learn from other's mistakes.	Everything in your control Full understanding of your problems Learn as you go along May be faster and cheaper
Disadvantages	Lack of specific knowledge of your business Cannot devote all their time May do a poor job for a small client Probably expensive	Easy to make mistakes Lack of required skills Lack of specialised know-how Limited view – no outside knowledge

Adapted from Wilmshurst (1999)

Exam tip

The Pilot Paper covered a range of agency issues, including:

- What should be covered in an agency brief (with sample briefing document)
- What problems are likely to arise with a new supplier (especially in a specialised, international market) and how they can be overcome.

In December 2002, you were asked to evaluate a new advertising strategy from the point of view of relevant 'stakeholders': the agency required to carry out the strategy would be one of these 'stakeholders'!

It may not always be stated in a scenario whether the firm has engaged an agency: you may wish to consider engaging one, as one of the tools that may be appropriate in the context given.

4.2 Selecting an advertising agency

FAST FORWARD

Most firms retain an advertising agency after a careful **selection process** and with the intention of an on-going relationship (within a contracted period).

If you are using an agency for the first time, or are changing agencies, it is useful to have a list of section criteria such as the following:

Size	Is the agency's size/status comparable to our organisation?
Creativity	Do these people do creative imaginative work (if that is what we want)?
Full service	Can the agency source all our needs eg print, TV conference organisation?
Experience	Do they have suitable experience, as an agency, and as individuals?
Confidentiality	Do they work for our competitors? Might this be a problem?
Location/logistics	Are they nearby (if this is necessary)?
Personal factors	Can we work with them?
Billing/admin arrangements	Are they to our satisfaction?

Most firms retain their advertising agency after a careful selection process and with the intention of an on-going relationship. Involvement in a firm's marketing is a more 'intimate' relationship than providing legal or financial advice: the agency will be communicating for the company, so it has to 'immerse' itself in the company's culture. It would be impossible to brief and acclimatise a different agency to this extent for each campaign.

The agency will appoint an '**account executive**', who liaises with the appropriate person (marketing assistant or advertising co-ordinator) within the client organisation. These two individuals represent the interface between the two organisations and are responsible for the co-ordination of work traffic between them.

4.3 Briefing the agency

FAST FORWARD

> The **agency brief** is the initial and most important stage of any project undertaken. The planning and creative teams of the agency need initially to get to know the client, its products, brands, market and customers, and its culture, style, self-image and designed image.

Key concept

> A **brief** (in advertising agency terms) is 'an interpretation of a given market in relation to the product, plus every usable detail about the features and benefits of that product.' (*Quinn*, 1988)

A comprehensive brief will include the following details.

(a) **The product**, including its design and marketing history, and current 'life cycle' stage, its technical specifications, pack sizes, shelf-life, packaging/distribution arrangements and associated after-sales services.

(b) **The market**: who uses the product, how, when and why, how it is distributed (via wholesale, retail or direct selling), the product's current and desired market share, pricing and discount/margin policies for the product, and sales strategies.

(c) **Previous advertising**: the previous advertising budget (if any), competitors' advertising spend, breakdown of spend above- and below-the-line.

(d) **Current advertising policy**: budget available, desired image for the product and company, objectives of advertising.

(e) The brief may also contain the company's current ideas about the theme for advertising: what it believes is the key concept or **unique selling proposition (USP)** of the product or brand.

The brief is usually given to the agency account executive who relays it to the relevant agency personnel.

An example of a proforma for an Advertising brief is set out below.

PART B   BUILDING AND DEVELOPING RELATIONSHIPS

ADVERTISING BRIEF

Agency

Briefing date

Company

Contact name

Project name

Project description

Budget

Key deadlines

Company background

Business objectives

Background to the brief

Communications objectives

Target audience

Proposition

Here are some brief notes as a simple aid to filling in each section.

(a) **Project name and description**

Give the project a meaningful name to refer to. The specifics of the product along with the style (punchy, slick and so on) are needed.

(b) **Budget**

You need to be clear about what the budget covers. For example, how many new photographs need to be shot? This will have a bearing on the production costs. The budget for media will determine the choice for media selection. The agency can alter the resources according to the job. All budgets need to be agreed formally before proceeding.

(c) **Key deadlines**

List important key deadlines and ask the agency to draw up a timetable for presentation of design concepts, proofs, final proofs and so on.

(d) **Company background**

A brief description of the company will assist the agency in getting a 'feel' for an appropriate design.

(e) **Business objectives**

This will help the agency position the campaign (or whatever the project involves).

(f) **Background to the brief**

For example, is this a complete redesign, or just a freshen up? You need to be clear.

(g) **Communications objectives**

The primary objective may be to increase sales. This can be incorporated in the design.

(h) **Target audience**

The agency needs a full description of the characteristics of the audience. This will enable them to design the campaign (or whatever) with them in mind.

(i) **Proposition**

Be clear what the USP is. For example, you cannot have high quality, cheap products, top brands and commodity goods all in the same catalogue. With a clear picture, the agency will be able to focus on producing what is required without constantly referring back to the client.

4.4 Who's who in the agency?

FAST FORWARD

As a client, you will generally deal with an **account executive** within an agency.

Each agency may be structured in different ways.

The simplest form of **agency structure** is as follows.

```
                          General Manager
                          PLANS BOARD
    ┌─────────────────┬───────────┴──────────┬──────────────────┐
  Account Director  Creative Director     Media Director    Research Director
CLIENT↔Account Executive  Creative Teams    Media Planners   Market Research team
                     Art Director  Copywriter
                                         Traffic/Production Team
                  Visualisers  Designers  (workflow co-ordination)
```

Figure 7.2: Simple agency structure

- The **account executives** service the clients on a day-to-day basis
- The **account director** monitors work on given accounts
- The **creative team** 'produces' the ad
- The **traffic/production team** plans and schedules agency workflow, monitors progress against deadlines and 'chases' work

PART B BUILDING AND DEVELOPING RELATIONSHIPS

A large full service agency might look more like the organisation chart below.

Figure 7.3: Large agency structure

4.5 Flow of work through the agency

> **Checking and approving** work in progress is a key responsibility of the client.

The flow of work through the agency can be depicted as follows.

```
BRIEFING FROM CLIENT → FACT GATHERING ABOUT THE PRODUCT AND ITS PLACE IN THE MARKET (Responsibility: A/c executive) → CREATIVE ARRANGEMENT OF FACTS, OPPORTUNITIES: PRECISE WRITTEN STATEMENT OF A STRATEGY AND AN ADVERTISING OBJECTIVE (Responsibility: A/c executive) → REVIEW A/C DIRECTOR

→ FIRST REVIEW: Plans board comprising: General Manager, A/c Director - Creative Director. Is this strategy correct? Is the advertising objective, appropriate and fruitful? → CLIENT AGREEMENT WITH OBJECTIVE (Responsibility: A/c executive) → CREATIVE UNIT BRIEFED (Responsibility: A/c executive) → PRODUCE ADVERTISING (Responsibility: Creative unit)

→ REVIEW CREATIVE DIRECTOR → SECOND REVIEW: Plans board comprising General Manager, A/c Director - Creative Director. Does the advertising communicate effectively? Does it fulfil the brief? → BRIEF A/C EXECUTIVE (Responsibility: Creative unit) → PRESENT TO CLIENT AS APPROVED (Responsibility: A/c executive)
```

(Source: Hearne, 1987)

Figure 7.4: Agency work plan

Note the **client's responsibilities** implied by the above flow-chart.

(a) The advertising co-ordinator (or marketing department head) briefs the agency.

(b) The marketing department head approves the agency's assessment of the advertising objective, strategy, schedule and cost estimates.

(c) The advertising co-ordinator provides the agency with all available materials and information to help the creative team to produce effective ads.

(d) The advertising co-ordinator is the first one to see work that comes back from the agency at each stage of production (copy, story boards, sketches), and will probably check, correct and recommend any necessary changes before the ad is finally approved by the marketing department head.

(e) The ad is returned to the agency for typesetting, final art, filming and sound production, programming – or whatever format is being used.

(f) The advertising co-ordinator carries out final checks, and gets final approval before giving the agency clearance to release the ad to the media.

4.6 Agency costs

Advertising agencies traditionally charge the following fees.

- A fee for **advice/creativity** (usually around 15% of the value of the media space booked)
- **Design and production** costs, marked up by an agreed percentage

Commission or media discounts raise issues of conflict of interest. Many services are now fee-based: hourly, per project, or hourly up to an agreed maximum per project. This gives greater accountability. Production costs should still be separately budgeted, monitored and accounted for.

4.7 Avoiding problems

For the relationship between client and advertising agency (or any other supplier, for that matter) to be a **productive and harmonious** one, there are some rules to follow.

Behaviour	How?
'Give and take'	Provide each other with all the information they can, and trust each other
Constructive partnership	Be aware of the contributions each can make, and respective levels of authority
View the relationship as a long-term one	Invest time and resources getting to know one another and the market
Co-operative effort to attain high standards	Review the relationship to see if anything is going wrong, and to assess strengths and weaknesses and iron out small problems early on
Build a 'joint team'	Staff drawn partly from client and partly from agency to manage the relationship
Clarity of costs	Agree remuneration in writing

5 Working with distribution channels

We will be discussing 'place' as part of the marketing mix and the evaluation and management of distribution channels in Part D of this Study Text. Here we will briefly discuss distribution channels as another category of working relationship. Once again, all the interpersonal aspects already covered (collaborating, negotiating, courtesy, communications skills) apply.

5.1 Points in the chain of distribution

> **FAST FORWARD**
>
> Depending on the organisation's **supply chain (or distribution) strategy**, the marketing department may deal with retailers, wholesalers, dealers, agents, franchisees or direct sales agencies.

Potential distributors with whom the marketing department might deal include the following.

(a) **Retailers**: traders operating outlets which sell goods directly to consumers. These may be large or small, independent or part of a chain or co-operative, specialist or variety.

(b) **Wholesalers**: intermediaries who buy in and stock a range of products to sell on to other organisations such as retailers. Economies of scale allow them to buy and sell at discount prices.

(c) **Distributors and dealers**: intermediaries who contract to buy goods and promote and sell them to customers at a profit. They usually specialise in a particular product or brand.

(d) **Agents**: intermediaries who sell goods on the manufacturer's behalf, earning commission on the sales.

(e) **Franchisees**: independent organisations which in exchange for an initial fee and a share of sales revenue are allowed to trade under the name of the parent organisation.

(f) **Direct sales service providers**: telemarketing agencies and TV/Internet/direct mail marketing agencies. These functions may be carried out within the sales and marketing department of the organisation.

You should have covered these options in your studies for *Marketing Fundamentals*.

5.2 Factors in relationships with distribution channels

> **FAST FORWARD**
>
> **Distributors** are commercial organisations which have their own objectives.

In working with **distributors**, the marketer needs to bear in mind the following points.

(a) **The independent commercial objectives of the distributor**. Distributors are business organisations with their own requirements for efficiency and profitability. They do not stock products or run promotions as a 'favour' to the supplier!

   (i) You need to negotiate and contract terms.

   (ii) You need to promote the benefits of the product or collaboration to the distributor. We will discuss this further below.

   (iii) You need to work efficiently and with professionalism in order to maintain the working relationship.

(b) **The distributor's relationship with competitors**. Bear in mind that a retailer or wholesaler may well be stocking and promoting competing products. You will need to be discreet, to differentiate your product and promotions, and to be aware of opportunities to gain useful market intelligence.

(c) **The distributor's knowledge of the consumer**. Distributors are in the front line of contact with consumers. Be prepared to seek and respect their research or sense of what will work in terms of product and promotion.

(d) **The distributor's power in the market**. Major distributors have considerable buying power over suppliers, and good working relationships must be preserved with them, usually at the expense of autonomy and control over promotions. A major distributor may ask for exclusive rights to sell a product, or ask to sell it under an 'own brand' label. It may control all point-of-sale and media promotions regarding its sale of the product, charging a fee for promotional space and collaboration.

(e) **The mutual benefit of promotional collaboration**

   (i) If the supplier promotes the product to consumers through PR, advertising and consumer incentives, the distributor selling the product to consumers will benefit.

   (ii) If the distributor promotes the product to consumers – through advertising its availability through the distributor, or through in-store display and incentives – the supplier will benefit.

PART B BUILDING AND DEVELOPING RELATIONSHIPS

Marketing at Work

Top tips for franchisers

Before franchising your business, follow this checklist to make sure your business is ready and that it's destined to be one of the winners.

- Business must be pilot tested with company-owned and operated outlets.
- It must be successful, distinctive and replicable.
- Get professional advice from a solicitor, banker, accountant and possibly a franchise consultant.
- The franchise agreement must be written by an experienced franchise solicitor.
- Take the time to write an operations manual.
- Choose franchisees very carefully and slowly.
- Avoid overselling and forecasts.
- Have first-class training.
- Maintain good ongoing relationships.
- Focus on franchisee satisfaction and profitability.
- Keep developing the franchise and maintain standards.
- Ensure marketing, advertising and PR is first class.

Source: Franchise Council of Australia
Daily Telegraph, 8/3/05

Exam tip

The December 2004 exam featured a range of tasks centred around the selection and management of *franchises*: a presentation on the benefits of franchising; information needed to select a franchisee; relationships and communication with franchise holders. You needed to apply your skills from *this* syllabus to your knowledge of franchises (from *Marketing Fundamentals*). Other useful areas of *Marketing Fundamentals*, for this topic, include logistics and supply management.

5.3 'Push' and 'Pull' activity

FAST FORWARD

'Push' and 'pull' techniques (aimed at 'selling in' and 'selling through') should be carefully planned and negotiated to the mutual benefit of supplier and distributor.

In terms of marketing activity, the supplier will be involved in both 'push' and 'pull' promotion.

Key concept

'Push' or **'sell in'** techniques are designed to promote the product to the *distribution network* in order to get the product into the market place.

Unless the supplier has its own distribution outlet, it has to persuade distributors that stocking and selling the product will be worthwhile using various methods: this requires **'push' promotion**.

(a) **Trade advertising and promotion**, focused on the product's sales potential and the marketing support offered by the supplier.

(b) Offering **incentive** discounts or sale-or-return terms, to reduce the distributor's risk.

(c) Offering **product support**, such as guarantees, efficient after-sales, exchange or repair service, in-store stock checking and maintenance.

(d) Offering **marketing/promotional support**, such as point-of-sale display materials, sales force incentives, joint promotions and the demonstration of an aggressive 'pull' campaign.

7: THE SUPPLY CHAIN

Key concept

> **'Pull' or 'sell through'** techniques are designed to promote the product to the *consumer*, so that forecast or actual enquiry/sales volume encourages distributors to stock and re-stock the product.

Pull is achieved through the range of promotional methods: consumer advertising, promotional incentives, merchandising, packaging and PR: Figure 7.5.

```
                    'PUSH'                        'PULL'
   ┌──────────┐             ┌──────────────────┐          ┌───────────┐
   │ Supplier │ ──────────→ │Distribution Channel│ ──────→ │ CONSUMERS │
   └──────────┘   SELL IN   └──────────────────┘ DRAW OUT └───────────┘
        ▲                            ▲
        │  Orders in response to demand   Purchases, enquiries, feedback
        └──────────────────────────┘
            (TRADE DEMAND)               (CONSUMER DEMAND)
```

Figure 7.5: Promotion through the supply chain

Marketing at Work

IBM established the IBM Gold Logo Dealer award scheme, as a non-monetary **incentive scheme for dealers**. A number of computer dealers who exceed incentive-level volume and quality targets are annually awarded the title, which they are allowed to display on signage, stationery, advertising and so on. As if the recognition and prestige were not enough, surveys showed that *consumers* value this award and most major dealerships say it boosts their sales.

On the other hand, MacNamara (1993) tells of another major computer manufacturer who wanted to offer a new car or holiday to the dealership sales rep who sold the most machines. A communication audit was carried out to test dealers' responses – 'thank goodness', says MacNamara, because many dealerships refused outright to support such a supposed 'push' technique. ('If our customers know we are in the running to get a new car or holiday for selling them a certain brand of computer, they will question our motives. It will jeopardise our credibility!') In other words, 'push' can *damage* 'pull': information-sharing, monitoring and feedback saved this set of supply chain partnerships.

Action Programme 4

The Needle Works

The craft field seems to be characterised by small specialist suppliers: Mrs Smith sells equipment and accessories, patterns, books, magazines and kits from many different designers and manufacturers, locally and overseas. However, there is one major UK manufacturer of yarns, called Threadlines: they have a high profile in the market, and many needlework and knitting patterns specify their wool and threads as a guide to colour, amount required and so on. You carry an extensive range of Threadlines stock, which does well for you – and for Threadlines, since The Needle Works is the largest independent outlet for its products.

Write a memo to Albert Smith, the General Manager, and copied to Mrs Smith, suggesting some ideas for a collaborative promotion between the Needle Works and Threadlines. Emphasise the benefits to the former, but describe the benefits which could be offered to the latter, as an incentive to them to support the promotion.

[key skill for Marketers: Presenting information]

6 E-procurement

> **E-procurement** is business-to-business (B2B) e-commerce, whereby businesses conduct their purchasing (and often logistics and payment) over the Internet or direct data-sharing links (such as EDI: electronic data interchange).

6.1 E-sourcing

E-sourcing is defined by the Chartered Institute of Purchasing and Supply (CIPS) as: 'using the Internet to make decisions and form strategies regarding how and where services or products are obtained'. It therefore includes purchasing research, tendering, supplier appraisal and selection and so on.

Some of the tools available for e-sourcing include:

- Electronic catalogues, in which suppliers exhibit their products. Buyers are authorised to access product information and buy online.
- Electronic tendering, using online requests for quotation, specifications posted online or sent to supplier, and bids received and evaluated electronically.
- E-auctions, where suppliers offer goods and buyers bid competitively on line (as on E-Bay, for example – but this is now a popular tool for business procurement).
- Online data for supplier evaluation and selection: third party reports, customer feedback, approved/accredited supplier lists, benchmarking reports and so on.

6.2 E-procurement

E-procurement is 'using the Internet to operate the transactional aspects of requisitioning, authorising, ordering, receipting and payment processes for the required services or products' (CIPS).

Some of the tools available for e-procurement include:

- Electronic Data Interchange (EDI): documents can be exchanged in standardised electronic form, direct from computer to computer, for transactions.
- Online track-and-trace: barcode/RFID tagging of items allows their location to be tracked for delivery checking and expediting.
- Electronic payment systems: self-billing, electronic invoice generation, funds transfer and so on.
- Electronic point of sale (EPOS) systems: giving feedback from point of sales terminals to automatically generate re-ordering (and management information).
- Electronic contract management: updating e-contracts for changes, reporting by exception on delivery discrepancies etc.

Marketing at Work

Companies using e-procurement

- General Electric – via its Trading Partner Network of electronic supplier catalogues
- In the US, companies including Kellogg's and Prudential Insurance form a $17 billion Internet buying group
- Sainsbury's Efficient Consumer Response initiative uses an Internet-based system to share information between the retailer and its suppliers, allowing better estimation of required stock levels.

Action Programme 5

Check out some websites that allow you to shop online (eg *amazon.co.uk*) or trade deliveries (eg *dhl.com*) to get a flavour of e-procurement.

6.3 Benefits of e-procurement

The Internet and other ICT-enabled networks have enabled business buyers of goods and services to take advantage of:

(a) **A wider choice of suppliers**, including international and smaller suppliers they might not otherwise have access to.

(b) **Savings in procurement costs**, through electronic transaction processing, documentation exchange and information search.

(c) **Low inventory** and efficient stock turnover (such as Just In Time supply systems), because of quicker order turnaround times.

(d) **Improved relationships** down the supply chain, thanks to data sharing. The Internet makes it possible to set up 'virtual partnerships' between customers and suppliers.

Chapter Roundup

- **Supply chain relationships** require interpersonal and business skills. As well as the human aspects discussed in other chapters, they involve:
    - contracts
    - systems and procedures
    - in the context of business objectives or purpose

- **Procedures for collaborative working** should include:
    - briefing
    - joint planning
    - negotiation of terms
    - sharing of information and resources
    - monitoring, checking and approval
    - feedback
    - payment

- **Negotiating** is a bargaining process through which commitments and compromises are reached, which are acceptable to both parties.

- The **negotiation process** requires preparation, interaction, closure and follow-up.

- A **'win-win' (or integrative) approach** to negotiation is generally regarded as the most ethical, relationship-building and long-term effective approach.

- There are many **suppliers** of **marketing-related services**, providing advice on or implementation of market research, advertising, promotions, PR, direct marketing, brand identity, sponsorship, creative process and many more areas.

- Many advertisers use an **agency** for mass consumer-market advertising, because of the special expertise required.

- Most firms retain an advertising agency after a careful **selection process** and with the intention of an on-going relationship (within a contracted period).

- The **agency brief** is the initial and most important stage of any project undertaken. The planning and creative teams of the agency need initially to get to know the client, its products, brands, market and customers, and its culture, style, self-image and designed image.

- As a client, you will generally deal with an **account executive** within an agency.

- **Checking and approving** work in progress is a key responsibility of the client.

- Depending on the organisation's **supply chain (or distribution) strategy**, the marketing department may deal with retailers, wholesalers, dealers, agents, franchisees or direct sales agencies.

- **Distributors** are commercial organisations which have their own objectives.

- **'Push' and 'pull' techniques** (aimed at 'selling in' and 'selling through') should be carefully planned and negotiated to the mutual benefit of supplier and distributor.

- **E-procurement** is business-to-business (B2B) e-commerce, whereby businesses conduct their purchasing (and often logistics and payment) over the Internet or direct data-sharing links (such as EDI: electronic data interchange).

Quick Quiz

1 What are the three basic requirements for a contract to exist?
2 Outline the importance of (a) monitoring and (b) feedback in supply relationship.
3 Why should you take the advice offered by an advertising agency or other external marketing consultancy?
4 What is a 'full service' advertising agency?
5 How can an organisation ensure that it makes cost-effective use of a PR agency?
6 What should the 'brief' to an advertising agency contain?
7 Describe the flow of work to, through and from an advertising agency.
8 Give five examples of types of distribution channel.
9 What are 'push' and 'pull' techniques?
10 What is e-procurement?

Answers to Quick Quiz

1 The intention to create a legal relationship; offer and acceptance; and consideration.
2 Monitoring ensures that your objectives are being met at every stage of the process. Feedback is necessary to developing an ongoing working relationship and overcome problems.
3 Agencies specialise in communication and media and they are up-to-date. They have wide experience, objectivity, specialist knowledge and expensive production facilities.
4 A full service agency takes control of the whole campaign from concept through to press/air.
5 Ensure cost effectiveness by: setting clear objectives; negotiating a project fee; briefing fully; monitoring activity and expenditure.
6 Background to the company, market information and previous advertising strategies, campaign objectives, desired image, relevant policies, ball park budget.
7 This is summarised in Figure 7.4.
8 Your answer may have included: retailers, wholesalers, distributors, agents and franchises.
9 Push techniques work through promoting a product to the distribution network to get access to the market. Pull techniques promote direct to the consumer who put pressure on the distributors to stock the desired goods.
10 E-procurement means buying goods and services online.

Action Programme Review

1. Depending on what service you chose, terms may cover such issues as: delivery, variations of quality/quantity, payment dates and penalties, responsibility for additional costs, liability (for loss or destruction of property, problems, costs etc), ownership of materials, cancellations and delays, copyright ownership and rights, disclosure of information. Do take seriously the part of the exercise where you evaluate your own procedures in the light of contract terms. Just as an example, if you routinely ask printers or reprographics houses for the films of an ad or leaflet 'back', so you can use it again elsewhere, you might notice that your contract with them specifies that *they own* the films they have produced for you: you will need to state in your initial job contract that you want them at the conclusion of the job.

2. Do this exercise: it's useful – and great fun. In the marketing scenario, you may have come up with trade offs gaining you extra discount, free bleed, guaranteed cover positions etc in return for a pre-booked series.

3. Get into the habit of doing this regularly.

4. Your answer should be in proper memo format (and don't forget to 'c.c: Mrs Smith'). Your suggestions may have included activities such as: a one-off 'Threadlines' promotion in store, with exclusive window space and displays for two weeks, the cost to be offset by a 5% extra trade discount during the promotion. Threadlines to provide demonstrators of needlecraft or knitting in-store as PR and to draw customers in – with the understanding that they would use and promote Threadlines materials; joint advertising ('Threadlines – available from the Needle Works') in the local region; or Threadlines financial contribution to a Needle Works mail order catalogue or direct mail campaign in return for exclusive promotion of their materials. Benefits to the Needle Works would be extra sales of Threadlines materials at extra discount, sharing the costs of wider promotion and PR, and building on Threadlines' existing customer base and name to boost the Needle Works' own. Benefits to Threadlines would include increased pull-through, advantage over competitors through exclusivity, good relations with major distributor.

5. Your own research.

> Now try Question 7 at the end of the Study Text

Practical PR skills

Chapter topic list
1 Public relations
2 Representing the organisation
3 Networking

Syllabus content – knowledge and skills requirements
- 2.4 Represent the organisation using practical PR skills, including preparing effective news releases
- 2.7 Use networking skills in the business world

PART B   BUILDING AND DEVELOPING RELATIONSHIPS

Introduction

Public relations is 'the planned and sustained effort to establish and maintain goodwill and mutual understanding between an organisation and its publics' (*Institute of Public Relations*). It involves a range of corporate activities such as publicity, press/media relations, lobbying or representations to government and trade bodies, community projects and communicating with consumer groups. In its broadest sense, however, PR is simply the interface of groups in society: marketing organisations interface continually with their members, with the public, with consumers, with suppliers, with competitors and with governments.

In this chapter, we look at various ways in which you, as a marketing co-ordinator, may interface with other people and groups in a positive way.

1 Public relations

FAST FORWARD

The organisation's **image** is an important factor in whether it attracts and retains **members**, whether **consumers** buy its products/services, whether the **community** supports or resists its presence and activities and whether the **media** reports positively on its operations.

Some examples of an organisation's 'publics' are shown in Figure 8.1 below. Your organisation may have a PR, Corporate Affairs, Public Affairs, Community Relations, Media Relations or Public Information department or it may employ an **external PR agent** or **consultancy** to manage these relationships.

Figure 8.1: A company's target audiences

Since an organisation will inevitably project an image in its dealings with the outside world, and the costs of a negative image can be high, it makes sense to manage the messages being projected.

You are 'doing PR' when you send press releases or supply editorial articles, greet and assist visitors, deal with suppliers and distributors, design and send promotional messages or organise and participate in marketing activities.

Exam tip

> PR skills may be examined via the case study, in which you might need (or decide) to draft a press release or editorial/advertorial as part of your marketing strategy in the given scenario. They may also be included in a basic skills or communications audit, so each time you draft PR-related documents or recommendations, keep a copy for your portfolio.

Action Programme 1

According to Wilmshurst (1999), public relations has seven stages. These are listed in the table below. For each stage, think of an applicable example from your own work experience or organisation with which you are familiar.

1 State the problem or aim	
2 Research	
3 Identify the publics	
4 Select the media	
5 Monitor effects	
6 Plan the future	
7 Maintain financial checks	

2 Representing the organisation

2.1 When do you represent your organisation?

FAST FORWARD

> Marketing professionals are called upon to **represent the organisation** in a variety of contexts.

You need to be able to recognise situations in which you represent your organisation, because in those situations your behaviour, attitudes and messages have PR consequences for the organisation.

The word **represent** means:

- to stand as an equivalent or substitute for someone/something
- to portray or act as a picture or expression of someone/something
- to exemplify or typify the characteristics of someone/something

PART B BUILDING AND DEVELOPING RELATIONSHIPS

Action Programme 2

Before you read further, brainstorm your own list of situations in which you might represent an organisation. (A group brainstorming session also allows you to practise a range of interpersonal, planning and creative skills.) Go through your list and give examples of how you could create a positive or negative image in each situation. If you are in a group, role-play any examples that sound interesting: let observers and participants comment on the PR impact of different behaviours.

The following table suggests some of the contexts in which you might represent your organisation, as a marketing professional.

Context	Example	Affects image of
You **exercise authority** delegated to you by the organisation	You discipline or instruct a subordinate You make a contract with a supplier	Organisation's attitude to employees Organisation's integrity/professionalism
You **issue communications** on behalf of the organisation	You write or approve advertising copy, press releases, editorial articles	The organisation's products/services, aims – or whatever the topic of the message
You **identify yourself** as a member of the organisation	You sign your name to a communication on a company letterhead, or answer the telephone with the company name You present a business card You tell someone informally whom you work for	Whatever what you say or do implies about the organisation.
You are **associated in people's minds** with the organisation	You handle a customer complaint You give a presentation You are on the organisation's stand at an exhibition	The organisation's attitude to customers/quality The organisation's expertise

In many of these situations, you would be strongly aware of representing the organisation: they might take place in the work environment, or you might be acting clearly in your professional role.

So how can you **manage the organisation's image** in all these circumstances? We will consider some basic principles.

2.2 Conveying a positive image

FAST FORWARD

> Key factors in conveying a **positive image** of the organisation include: awareness; attitude; appearance; integrity; professionalism; crisis and issue management; good news.

2.2.1 Awareness

The first step in image management is being aware that you are projecting an image.

Be aware of the positive or negative **attitude** implied by words, behaviour and work outputs. Consider what you would assume about the attitude of someone who missed deadlines, issued advertising copy with errors or misleading promises, failed to return telephone calls, worked in an untidy or unhygienic environment, or spoke disrespectfully to you or about you. Consider what you would assume about the organisation that person represented.

2.2.2 Integrity

Illegal, dishonest or unethical behaviour (not to mention its legal consequences) creates powerful negative PR, in the business and wider community – and within the organisation itself.

- (a) **Abide by law and regulation in the areas of your responsibility.** Find out as much as you need to about contracts relating to the sale of goods and services, truth in advertising and product labelling standards, discrimination, defamation, health and safety at work, sexual harassment and so on.
- (b) **Abide by the terms of contracts**. Remember that letters and verbal agreements as well as legal documents may constitute a binding arrangement.
- (c) **Keep your promises**. Promises may not be legally binding, but going back on them repeatedly destroys trust, breaks relationships and loses co-operation.

The boundaries of what constitutes **ethical behaviour** by a corporation are extremely flexible. The organisation may want to project a positive image in areas such as the following.

- (a) **Fairness** is important in dealings with business contacts, employees and customers. For example, adjusting complaints when not legally obliged to do so, or negotiating non-exploitative terms with suppliers and employees.
- (b) **Social responsibility** may include not using anti-social promotional messages, being environmentally friendly and promoting positive images of minority groups.
- (c) **Respect for cultural differences**, especially when doing business overseas, is fundamental. Attitudes to the role of women, the exchange of gifts, religious beliefs and other customs and taboos should be carefully researched in international markets.

Marketing at Work

'Brands with a conscience'

An international think-tank on branding (the Medinge Group: www.medinage.org) annually evaluates brands on principles of sustainability, humanity and ethics, rather than financial worth. On its 2006 Top Brands list:

- ABN AMRO/Banco/Banco Real: banking group committed to sustainable investment [www.banco.se]
- BP: sustainable energy – 'green' oil [www.bp.com]
- First Mile Solutions (FMS): providing internet access to communities lacking communications infrastructure [www.firstmilesolutions.com]
- Slow Food Movement: promoting local growers and food preparers, valuing quality over speed [www.slowfood.com]
- Toyota Prius: petrol-electric hybrid car, licensing technology to rivals [www.prius.com]
- Watabaran: paper recycling for gift/card production in Nepal: employee shareholders for 'fair trade' [www.watabaran.com]

'Compassionate branding is a winning strategy for business today.'

For reflection: How can you communicate a 'compassionate brand'?

2.2.3 Professionalism

What is understood by the term 'professionalism' will depend on the context and culture of the organisation. In terms of practical PR, we suggest three dimensions of professionalism that create a positive image.

(a) **Courtesy**. This is a bare minimum requirement of all business communication.

(b) **Expertise**. Professionalism implies a level of competence which justifies financial remuneration. Incompetence is bad PR. Work out what range and standard of performance people are reasonably entitled to expect from you, and ensure that you can achieve it.

(c) **Efficiency**. Transactions take time, and invariably cost someone money. Professionals place a value on their time, energy, money and other resources, and recognise that others do the same. Be organised, prompt to appointments, deadline driven and budget conscious.

Action Programme 3

Imagine that your manager has asked you to give a presentation to Customer Services Staff entitled: 'Conveying Professionalism: Everyday PR'. Prepare a visual aid which illustrates the main points of your presentation. (If you are in a study group, you may even take the opportunity to give this presentation: useful experience for your portfolio.)

[Key skill for Marketers: Presenting information]

2.3 Crisis and issues management

FAST FORWARD

The management of potential negative messages (**crises and issues**) is a key part of PR activity.

Key concepts

Crisis communication is public communication in the face of a potential PR disaster, through which the organisation initiates damage control, to minimise or counter the negative PR effects.

Issues management is an on-going process of being aware of potential controversies and sensitive matters in relation to the business, and initiating communication programmes which can defuse or head off issues before they become crises.

2.3.1 Crisis management

Examples of **PR crises** include the withdrawal of a product from the market due to unforeseen safety defects, an ecological disaster such as the running aground of an oil tanker, or the enforced withdrawal of an advertising campaign deemed offensive by complaints to the Advertising Standards Authority.

Marketing at Work

FOOD RECALL

PASTA – PUMPKIN RAVIOLI 600 GRAMS

Best before date: May 15th 2005

Pasta Time is voluntarily recalling the above product because it has identified that pumpkin and walnut ravioli was incorrectly packaged into the pumpkin ravioli packets. Only product with the above best before date is included in this recall.

Consumers who suffer from a walnut allergy or intolerance should not consume this product. Consumers concerned about their health should consult their medical practitioner.

Apart from the packing irregularity, there is no other fault with this product.

We ask anyone with family and friends who may have purchased this product to contact them in case they may not be aware of this recall.

We apologise to our consumers for any inconvenience.

Consumers are asked to return any of the recalled product to the store of purchase for a full refund. For further information, please call (02) 9558 0132.

Pasta Time
Unit 4/3 Wood Street
Tempe NSW 2044

Effective crisis communication involves the following.

(a) **Planning**: being aware of areas of risk, identifying audience groups that will need to be communicated with, and preparing a response

(b) Recognising and **responding** to the likely level of public concern

(c) **Explaining** what has happened (telling the organisation's 'side of the story'), demonstrating openness and giving consistent messages (which includes keeping employees informed)

(d) Showing that the organisation **cares** about the problem. (A rule of thumb is: talk about people first, the environment second, property third and financial consequences fourth)

(e) **Demonstrating** that steps are being taken

(f) Using independent, authoritative '**champions**' who could speak out in support of the organisation.

2.3.2 Issues management

Examples of **issues** which require careful handling include public concerns about food additives, the environment and ethical investment. Issues management endeavours not just to fight fires as they arise, but to initiate communication, express general responsibility and openness, educate the public in the organisation's position and establish networks of goodwill and political support.

2.3.3 Positive 'spin'

The opposite of suppressing bad news is spreading good news. The purpose of all promotional communication is, essentially, to spread a positive message about the organisation, its products and services. Formal PR activities seize a range of opportunities for good news spreading, many of which do not overtly 'sell' anything: networking and lobbying, press and media releases, editorial articles and interviews, sponsorship and customer newsletters provide examples.

You can also contribute informally. If you are drafting a letter to customers, for example, take the opportunity to inform them of any recent or on-going successes. Generate positive '**word of mouth**' in your dealings with people: a very powerful tool, because it works through personal communication networks.

PART B BUILDING AND DEVELOPING RELATIONSHIPS

2.4 Press or media releases

FAST FORWARD

The press or media release is one of the most frequently used tools of public relations, aiming to achieve **advantageous editorial coverage** in the press or other media. The content and format of press releases were covered in detail in the *Customer Communications* module.

Exam tip

The December 2004 exam explicitly asked you to *draft a press release* to promote an outlet launch and promotion: in June 2005, it was a news release by a new railway franchise to a tourism office; in June 2006, a local news release describing the success of a launch event; and in December 2006, a press release to promote a transport museum in a regional paper. (Think about the different audiences these tasks imply.) In each case, the examiner was disappointed that some students did not know press release format or style: this needs to be addressed, as this format is a regular feature of this paper: you have been warned!

Even if you aren't asked for a media or press release, don't neglect it as one option for *'using the promotional mix'* or supplementing an advertising budget, or building relationships (with the media). In December 2005, for example, you were simply asked to 'recommend three public relations activities' to gain awareness of an event: media releases (targeted to an appropriate audience) would certainly be one option.

An example of a press release is set out below.

PRESS RELEASE

10 March 2003

WWF HONG KONG LAUNCHES NEW ECOWOODASIA WEBSITE TO GENERATE INTEREST AND FACILITATE INFORMATION FLOW ON FOREST CERTIFICATION

World Wide Fund For Nature Hong Kong (WWF Hong Kong) today launches a new website at www.ecowoodasia.org to generate interest and facilitate information flow on forest certification. We believe that this new website can provide useful information on certification and serve as a platform for exchanging opinions.

Forest certification may seem an irrelevant topic to Hong Kong people. Yet our daily lives are closely related to the forests – wooden furniture, office paper, toilet tissue, newspapers and magazines are probably all made from wood fibre. Every year we import approximately 7.8 million cubic metres of timber, which rank amongst top 20 in the world. This implies that Hong Kong has a vital role to play in conserving world forest resources.

WWF Hong Kong takes the lead in promoting credible certification schemes such as Forest Stewardship Council (FSC) certification and generating market demand on certified forest products by setting up EcoWood@sia. It is a voluntary group comprising of visionary companies which support credible certification schemes such as the FSC. Yet only a handful of people understand certification. "A web-based information tool like the EcoWood@sia website, is a powerful and effective way to get the message across. It is bilingual in Chinese and English and can reach thousands of audience members in different sectors," says Joyce Lam, EcoWood@sia Coordinator.

This new website is an interactive web-based information tool for anyone interested in certification. It not only contains information on forest certification and EcoWood@sia, but also invites stakeholders to share their views and suggestions on certification issues. The site includes sections on "web polling" and a "forum" where people can express their opinions and initiate discussions. "We believe that this new website can further spark off interest in certification among other Asian regions such as China and Taiwan, where awareness on certification is growing," says Joyce Lam.

- END -

> For further information, please contact Joyce Lam, Programme Officer of WWF Hong Kong at (852) 2526 1011 [tel.], (852) 9738 2930 [mobile], (852) 2845 2734 [fax], jlam@wwf.org.hk [e-mail], or visit EcoWood@sia website at www.ecowoodasia.org
>
> Notes to Editors
>
> 1. Forest Stewardship Council (FSC) The FSC is an independent, non-profit international organisation supporting environmentally appropriate, socially beneficial and economically viable forest management. The FSC accredits certification bodies which are responsible for certifying forests according to Council's Principles and Criteria.
>
>   http://www.fscoax.org
>
>   [posted at *www.wwf.org.uk/pdf/references/pressreleases_hongkong*]

Action Programme 4

(a) What is 'newsworthy' about the news release shown above?
(b) How does the press release appeal to its dual audiences?

3 Networking

FAST FORWARD

> **Networking** is the process of making, focusing and maintaining contacts which may be mutually beneficial sources of information and influence.

Key concept

> **Networking** is identifying, establishing and maintaining personal contact with individuals and groups who may be able to provide information, referrals or resources for one's business or personal development.

The importance of networking is reflected in the saying: 'It's not what you know: it's who you know'. Networks of contacts may be used for all sorts of reasons.

- **Market research**, or intelligence gathering about an industry and how it operates
- **Sourcing particular items** of information
- **Locating** service providers and collaborators, through recommendation
- **Self-promotion**, or raising awareness of your identity and services
- **Gathering sale prospects** or 'leads', recommendations and referrals (known as 'network marketing')
- **Establishing yourself** in the industry/professional 'community'
- **Widening your circle** of communication and influence.

'Using' contacts can sometimes be perceived in an unpleasant light. However, business dealing through personal relationships has a long and natural history: people are more likely to support the known than the unknown, especially if it comes with a personal recommendation. Business networks in particular are understood to be mutually beneficial. Everyone involved has the opportunity to gain from the relationship.

PART B　BUILDING AND DEVELOPING RELATIONSHIPS

Exam tip

> You may think of this as a 'soft' syllabus topic, but the December 2005 exam asked you to explain how you could use personal networking (and personal selling skills) to attract and retain sponsors for a cultural festival. A similar question in December 2006 asked what objectives you might have, and what skills you might use at a business networking event. Your answer might have covered areas such as: generating contacts and leads; building rapport; using influencing skills; deepening relationships; and so on.

Marketing at Work

The CIM advises you as a student to list the individuals and groups that you have **contact** with in your organisation and sphere of work. Which ones are particularly useful? Do you have their business card?

Your list may include:

- Departmental colleagues
- Colleagues in other divisions
- Customers/end users
- Suppliers
- External agencies
- Subcontractors
- Media editors/journalists
- Competitors
- Professional institutes
- Local business networks
- Trade associations

You will also meet useful contacts when you attend conferences, seminars, meetings, exhibitions and training courses.

3.1 Making contacts

Formal or targeted contacts can be made in many ways.

(a) **Gathering information**. Each time you identify and tap an expert source of information, regard the person as a potential on-going source to be cultivated.

(b) **Recommendations and referrals**. Each time you make a contact, ask about other people whom it might be useful for you to talk to. (This applies to prospective suppliers, collaborators and clients/customers.)

(c) **Joining organisations and attending events** where people relevant to your aims are likely to gather: professional bodies, training courses, seminars and conferences, trade exhibitions – and also Internet Discussion Groups. Don't forget to regard your own work organisation as a source of contacts. Membership of the 'club' not only opens doors, but reduces the number of doors you have to open to find the right people!

(d) **Secondary sources**. Trade/professional journals, contacts lists and even the Yellow Pages are good sources of leads. Each call can generate both an active member of your network and further personal referrals.

Informal or social contacts should not be underestimated. The people you meet outside work are just as likely to be, or to know, work-relevant contacts. Listen and learn!

Action Programme 5

Making a contact is, initially, simply a matter of intent. Following on from the Marketing at Work example above, for all relevant people you meet or talk to, ensure that you write down core information or collect their business card.

- Their name and contact details
- Their organisation, job title or area
- The nature and date of your latest contact with them

Use a notebook, index card system, electronic organiser or database to categorise and cross-reference your contacts in a range of relevant areas.

[*Key skill for Marketers: Improving own learning and performance*]

3.2 Focusing contacts

FAST FORWARD

Focusing a contact involves linking your name with a relevant 'tag' or piece of information that will enable other people to file you appropriately in their own contact database.

Good rapport is not in itself sufficient to create a useful contact: people may be glad to know you, as an individual, but your name will not necessarily come to mind when they are looking for a particular service or asked to recommend someone.

(a) **Swap information** about what you do, or (if you are job-seeking or sponsor-seeking, for example) what you are looking for. When making informal, social contacts, this can be done in a casual way, but it helps you to feel out who might be of use to you (and vice versa).

(b) **Exchange business cards**, so that the contact has an aide-memoire immediately linking your name with the relevant organisation if something comes up later.

(c) When seeking **referrals or leads**, give contacts as much information as they need to identify or select relevant prospects, and to jog their memory when things crop up later.

(d) **Gain a profile**. For example, give presentations to business or educational groups in the area of your expertise.

Action Programme 6

The marketer in a front line PR role must possess the following characteristics:

- Skilled communicator
- Good interpersonal skills
- Enjoy networking
- Enjoy meeting new people

How might you use these characteristics to co-operate fully with the **media**, and achieve your objectives? Think about the following areas of work.

Objective	How can this be achieved via your relationships with media contacts?
• Produce good copy	
• Be reliable	
• Keep yourself informed about events	
• Be co-operative at all times	

PART B BUILDING AND DEVELOPING RELATIONSHIPS

3.3 Building relationships

FAST FORWARD

Contacts have to be **maintained and mutually beneficial**, in order to turn them into useful relationships.

Contacts can be developed into 'live', on-going relationships by a variety of means, but the following are key principles.

(a) **Follow up**. Maintain contact, recollection and focus by 'touching base' every so often. If you encounter someone who might be useful to you, suggest that you meet 'to discuss it' – and do so. Report back to people on the result of any help or information they have given you. Or simply maintain social contact: you do not need an excuse to do this, and it can increase the trust and motivation for someone to put opportunities and information your way. If you thought the sending of corporate Christmas cards, and more creative variations on the theme, were a waste of time: think again.

(b) **Reciprocity**. Don't be a user: if you are requesting help, advice or information from a contact, consider what you are able to offer in return, and keep an eye on the 'net balance' over time. It may be a straight swap of information, recommendations or referrals, an incentive or reward, a mutually beneficial collaboration, or simply your recognition and gratitude, with the potential for later 'returning the favour' .

(c) **Pace and lead**. These terms refer to the need to meet people where they are, and build trust, before attempting to influence them. When developing contacts, you need to be open about your objectives, but not pushy. If you are seeking a favour, for example, you might initially approach contacts by stating that you are seeking their 'advice'. You might also ask: 'May I call you from time to time for further advice?'

Action Programme 7

The Needle Works

From your organisational efforts so far, on The Needle Works' behalf, you are aware that while you are increasingly able to 'talk the language' of marketing with the various service-providers you deal with, you are not yet fluent in the language of needlecraft. This places a barrier between you and your customers and colleagues. You are also aware that there seems to be a clash of culture between the various Craft Guilds which preserve and promote traditional skills through education and teacher accreditation, and the commercial retailers of craft supplies. There are rumours that the General Secretary of the Needleworkers' Guild disapproves of The Needle Works.

How will you address these issues? What information will you need? What contacts will you pursue, and where? How can you begin to build bridges? Jot down an immediate Action List for yourself.

[*Key skill for Marketers: Working with others*]

Chapter Roundup

- The organisation's **image** is an important factor in whether it attracts and retains **members**, whether **consumers** buy its products/services, whether the **community** supports or resists its presence and activities and whether the **media** reports positively on its operations.

- Marketing professionals are called upon to **represent the organisation** in a variety of contexts.

- Key factors in conveying a **positive image** of the organisation include: awareness; attitude; appearance; integrity; professionalism; crisis and issue management; good news.

- The management of potential negative messages (**crises and issues**) is a key part of PR activity.

- The **press or media release** is one of the most frequently used tools of public relations, aiming to achieve advantageous editorial coverage in the press or other media. The content and format of press releases were covered in detail in the *Customer Communications* module.

- **Networking** is the process of making, focusing and maintaining contacts which may be mutually beneficial sources of information and influence.

- **Focusing a contact** involves linking your name with a relevant 'tag' or piece of information that will enable other people to file you appropriately in their own contact database.

- Contacts have to be **maintained and mutually beneficial**, in order to turn them into useful relationships.

Quick Quiz

1. Can an organisation *avoid* having a 'profile' or public image?
2. Give six examples of poor image management by an individual.
3. What types of behaviour convey 'professionalism'?
4. What does effective crisis communication entail?
5. Give six examples of sources of contacts for a marketer seeking an advertising agency.
6. What is meant by 'focusing' contacts, and how can it be achieved?
7. Explain what is meant by 'reciprocity' in networking.
8. How might you use networking skills on your own behalf?

PART B BUILDING AND DEVELOPING RELATIONSHIPS

Answers to Quick Quiz

1. All actions, relationships and physical manifestations – as well as deliberately transmitted communications – convey a marketing message.

2. Your image is suggested by your words, your behaviour and your work outputs: poor image could be conveyed by missed deadlines, carelessly presented work, unfulfilled promises, disrespectful comments about colleagues, untidy environment, or unreturned phone calls.

3. Professionalism: courtesy, expertise, efficiency.

4. Crisis communication is trying to minimise the negative PR effects in the face of an operational disaster.

5. Sources of contacts: trade fairs and exhibitions; word-of-mouth recommendations; specialist press; networking events; suppliers.

6. Focusing a contact involves linking your name with a relevant tag or piece of information that will enable other people to file you appropriately in their own contact database.

7. Reciprocity means offering something back to your contacts for the assistance that you have sought from them.

8. Networking skills, deployed on your own behalf are an invaluable tool in managing your career and personal development. Make friends and influence people!

Action Programme Review

1 We have used the example of a customer service department.

1	State the problem or aim	There have been complaints from customers about delayed responses by sales staff. How well are we handling customer queries?
2	Research	The sales manager may ring in to the sales office and pretend to be a customer.
3	Identify the publics	Having found that service could be improved, and having trained his staff, the sales manager is eager to tell the customers all about it and other employees.
4	Select the media	The company issues advertising flyers, and a company newsletter.
5	Monitor effects	The cost of this activity needs to be balanced against the need to improve customer service.
6	Plan the future	How will customer needs change? A website and online ordering may be needed soon.
7	Maintain financial checks	'It is difficult to quantify the effects of PR, but unless this is undertaken seriously, much money can be wasted.' (Wilmshurst)

2 The main point of the exercise was the brainstorming process, but if you were stuck for ideas, see Paragraph 2.1

3 The following is just our suggestion, which may provide you with a more memorable way of remembering the issues involved.

Show enthusiasm — **P**OSITIVE

Show courtesy — **P**OLITE

Show your best — **PR**ESENTATION

PR = PROFESSIONALISM

PRODUCT — Know your stuff

PERSONALITY — Know your people

PRESSURE — Keep your cool

PART B BUILDING AND DEVELOPING RELATIONSHIPS

4   (a)   The news is *local,* appealing directly to Hong Kong people.
         It is current – posted on the day of launch.
         It links its subject matter to daily life.

    (b)   *For the end audience:*
         It appeals to people likely to be interested in WWF's activities.
         It positions Hong Kong as a world leader, appealing to the local audience.
         It appeals specifically to the forestry industry.

         For the media audience:
         It gives clear date, relevance, information contacts and editorial notes.
         It is written in a user-friendly style (with quotes etc) that will make it easy to edit for publication.

5   Marketers deal with a wide range of people and groups in the course of business. Each of these interpersonal encounters should be regarded as a contact, a source of further contacts and the basis of a network.

6

Objective	How can this be achieved via your relationships with media contacts?
• Produce good copy	Have a clear understanding of the media being used, such as readership profiles for the press
• Be reliable	Meet deadlines and provide information when asked
• Keep yourself informed about events	Seek out up-to-date information, with regular contact with your 'network'
• Be co-operative at all times	Respond appropriately when the media wish to check facts, conduct interviews or visit your organisation

7   Your notes may have included suggestions along the following lines. Joining craft classes (through one of the Guilds, or local education centres) to learn basics and make contacts: membership of societies/groups? Requesting briefings by staff (synergy of technical/marketing input). Chatting informally to customers: identifying Guild members for further contact. Asking Guilds for information (way of making contact + access to info). Request meeting with editors of Craft Journals (discuss possible editorial/advertising + pick brains on market) or request referral to others. Invite Guild Secretary and Committee to launch of Knitting Shop. Contact Guild Secretary to discuss possibility of discount for Guild Members (incentive). Ask Guild Secretary to recommend Guild member to give talk at launch, appreciation evening etc (defer to Guild expertise/credibility).

Now try Question 8 at the end of the Study Text

Part C
Organising and undertaking marketing activities

Planning and scheduling

Chapter topic list

1. Planning and control
2. Objective setting
3. Planning techniques
4. Co-ordinating techniques
5. Measuring and evaluating results

Syllabus content – knowledge and skills requirements

- 3.2 Identify alternative and innovative approaches to a variety of marketing arenas and explain criteria for meeting business objectives
- 3.4 Explain how marketing makes use of planning techniques: objective setting and co-ordinating, measuring and evaluating results to support the organisation

PART C ORGANISING AND UNDERTAKING MARKETING ACTIVITIES

Introduction

One of the learning objectives of the *Marketing in Practice* syllabus is that you should be able to 'apply planning techniques to a range of marketing tasks and activities', and the topic of this section of the syllabus is 'Organising and Undertaking Marketing Activities'.

In this chapter we consider a range of techniques that can be applied to various tasks – from your daily workload, to the preparation of advertising copy, to the organisation of an international conference!

On completion of this chapter, you should be able to:

- Appreciate the business objectives of marketing events
- Define objectives and set budgets for marketing events
- Utilise a number of simple planning and project management techniques
- Measure and evaluate the results of marketing events

1 Planning and control

FAST FORWARD

Planning is the process of deciding what should be done, by whom, when and how. It is essential for co-ordination and control, through which performance is monitored, measured against the plan and adjusted where necessary.

1.1 Planning

Planning allows individuals and units in business organisations to look ahead.

- The **objectives** for which they are responsible
- What **actions** will serve towards achieving those objectives
- How far they are being **successful** in achieving those objectives

1.2 Control

If planning is the process of deciding what should be done, **control** is the process of checking whether it has been done, and if not, doing something about it. The combined process of planning and control are known as a **control cycle**: Figure 9.1.

Figure 9.1: A control cycle

In more detail, the control cycle in management has six basic stages.

(a) **Making a plan**: deciding what to do and identifying the desired results.

- **Aims**
- **Objectives**, which must be achieved for the aims to be fulfilled
- **Performance targets and standards**
- **Specific short-term goals** for key tasks
- **Action plans**, specifying 'what, how, who, when, where and how much'

(b) **Carrying out the plan**, or having it carried out by subordinates.

(c) **Monitoring and measuring** actual results achieved.

(d) **Comparing feedback** on actual results against the plans.

(e) **Evaluating** the comparison, and deciding whether further action is necessary to ensure the plan is achieved. If results are worse than planned (negative feedback), the activity will have to be adjusted to get it back on course. If they are better than planned (positive feedback), it may be desirable to maintain the deviation from the plan, or to adjust the plan itself to take advantage of the situation.

(f) **Implementing corrective action** where necessary.

2 Objective setting

2.1 Criteria for meeting business objectives

> **FAST FORWARD**
>
> Five dimensions by which a plan can be **evaluated**:
>
> - Effectiveness
> - Efficiency
> - Economy
> - Elegance
> - Ethicality

The *Marketing in Practice* syllabus suggests that you should evaluate any potential marketing activity or opportunity (such as the events discussed in Chapter 10 and 11) according to whether it meets **business objectives**.

In general terms, there are certain attributes of a viable and suitable activity which can be measured and evaluated. Rather neatly, these can all be expressed as 'e' factors.

(a) **Effectiveness**. Does the activity/opportunity fulfil the company's objectives for serving the needs of its owners and its chosen market? Will it, for example, enhance market share, quality or profitability?

(b) **Efficiency**. Does the activity/opportunity allow the organisation to use its resources in such a way as to maximise benefit for cost, or return on investment? Will it, for example, involve low wastage rates, quick response to customer enquiries, completion of products to deadline or high productivity by staff?

(c) **Economy**. Does the activity/opportunity fulfil the company's financial objectives? Will it, for example, bring in the budgeted revenue or contribution, and/or fall within or below budgeted expenditure costs?

PART C   ORGANISING AND UNDERTAKING MARKETING ACTIVITIES

(d) **Elegance**. Does the activity/opportunity look and feel 'right' for the company? Will it, for example, enhance the image of the organisation, fit neatly with the market's needs, or create synergy?

(e) **Ethicality**. Does the activity/opportunity fulfil the company's sense of social responsibility and business ethics? Will it, for example, have low impact on the natural environment, make opportunities for minority group employees or promote socially responsible images/products?

In specific terms, you may well be evaluating the viability and appropriateness of a given event or activity against clearly defined goals and standards set out in the marketing department's policies, plans and budgets.

2.2 Setting SMART objectives

> **FAST FORWARD**
>
> **Operational objectives** should be SMART: specific, measurable, attainable, relevant and time-bounded.

'**Smart**' **objectives** are:

- **S**pecific
- **M**easurable
- **A**ttainable
- **R**elevant
- **T**ime-bounded

Examples

Increase sales volume by 5% in the year 2006 – 2007

Achieve and maintain for 5 years a 25% share of the domestic market for product x.

Exam tip

> In the June 2006 exam, you were asked to define the marketing objectives of a launch event (and how its success could be evaluated). The point is that a SMART object should make evaluation posible. The examiner complained that candidates listed the SMART criteria – but then didn't use them to produce specific measurable, attainable, relevant and time-bounded objectives. Don't make this mistake if objectives come up again!

Action Programme 1

List at least five SMART objectives for a product launch, trade exhibition or other marketing event.

Whatever the specific objective, the important thing is to *have* a specific objective!

2.3 Budgets

> **FAST FORWARD**
>
> **Budgets** are, essentially, SMART objectives expressed in financial terms.

Key concept

> A **budget** is a statement of desired performance expressed in financial terms: expenditure, revenue, profit and so on.

In practice, overall marketing budgets are often already set, or set based on last year's budget, or set as a percentage of projected turnover for the year. When you are evaluating or planning a marketing activity or event, the limits to your spending will probably be determined.

(a) **Regular or core marketing spend**, which maintains the marketing/selling cycle: catalogues, sales force support, agency retainers, PR.

(b) **Spend on individual products and services**, for launch and/or maintenance marketing.

(c) **Contingencies**. If you are lucky, there may be an amount to be used at the marketing department's discretion, for any new or unforeseen opportunities that crop up during the year.

The main **budgetary control tasks** can be summarised as follows.

- **Estimate all the costs** involved in the proposed event/activity
- Compare the estimated total cost with anticipated **returns, benefits and objectives**
- Establish that the estimated total cost is within the departmental **expenditure budget**
- **Monitor actual expenditure** against the budget
- Compare actual total cost against **actual returns**

Exam tip

> You may be given a number of tasks for which some rate card, fee and other costings are provided, and then asked to draw up a budget. More importantly, you may be asked to assess the viability of various marketing opportunities and options, based on costs *and* anticipated returns, benefits and objectives. This is usually a feature of the compulsory Part A questions of this paper – so make sure you get some practice!

Budgeting is covered in Part E of this Study Text. The above paragraphs should enable you to put it in the context of objective setting and control. Always take into account the **cost/budget implications** of any marketing event that presents itself.

3 Planning techniques

FAST FORWARD

> Basic steps in **work planning** include:
>
> - The establishment of priorities (considering tasks in order of importance for the objective concerned)
> - Scheduling tasks

3.1 Prioritising

A piece of work will be **high priority** in the following circumstances.

(a) **If it has to be completed by a deadline**. The closer the deadline, the more urgent the work will be.

(b) **If other tasks and people depend on it**: if the scheduling of advertisement media depends on a market research report, the first task will be to compile or obtain the report. Begin at the beginning!

(c) **If it is important**. There may be a clash of priorities between two urgent tasks, in which case relative consequences should be considered: if an important decision or action rests on a task (for example, a report for senior management, or correction of an error in a large customer order) that task should take precedence over the preparation of notes for a meeting, or processing a smaller order.

Key concept

> A **deadline** is the end of the longest span of time which may be allotted to a task: in other words, the last acceptable date for completion.

3.2 Scheduling

Key concepts

> **Activity scheduling** provides a list of activities – or task sequence in the order in which they must be completed.
>
> **Time scheduling** specifies the timescale or start and end times and dates for each activity in a task sequence or action plan.

Determining the time that it will take to do a task is easy if it is a **routine task** that you do regularly. Simply keep a note of how long it takes you, on average. With **non-routine** tasks, particularly substantial ones, it can be far more difficult to determine how long to allow. You can ask someone with more experience than you, or you might be able to break the new task down into smaller stages whose duration you can more easily estimate.

Time schedules can be determined by two main methods.

(a) **Forward scheduling** starts with a given starting time/date and adds estimated times for each stage of the task (allowing for some which will be undertaken simultaneously by more than one person) to decide the estimated completion time/date. This method is useful for routine tasks and projects for which no definite deadline has been set.

(b) **Reverse scheduling** starts with the target completion time/date or deadline, and works backwards through the estimated time for each stage of the task, determining the latest start timed for each stage and for the task as a whole, which will enable you to meet the deadline. This is often used in marketing where target dates for conferences, launches and campaigns are already fixed.

Whichever method is used, bear in mind that task times will only be estimates. You may wish to build in some extra **'slack' time**.

- You will then be less likely to fall behind.
- If you do fall behind on one task, you will have some catch-up time built in.

3.3 Planning aids

FAST FORWARD

> **Planning aids** include lists and checklists, action plans and diaries, charts and precedence networks.

3.3.1 Lists

Lists are useful ways of identifying and remembering what needs to be done, and of monitoring how far you have got. If you do not do this already, try it once: you will be hooked, and your daily productivity will shoot up.

A **checklist** is simply a list which allows for ticking or 'checking' off each. Again, it may or may not reflect the order in which you actually perform the tasks. You may simply have a column to put ticks against each task, or you may want to have a space for times/dates on which you started or finished the activity, or even for stages of the activity (for example, where a particular document is at a given date) – or elements of all of these.

As an example, here is a checklist for an advertising manager preparing deadlines for a number of press advertisements.

9: PLANNING AND SCHEDULING

Ad	Due date	Writer	Designer	Photo-grapher	Film	Print	Proofed	Sent?
Times	3/9	21/8	22/8	24/8	30/8	-	2/9	✓
Standard	3/9	22/8	23/8	26/8	30/8	-	2/9	✓
A5 classified	7/9	29/8	30/8	-	-	-	4/9	✓
Leaflet A	12/9	10/8	12/8	15/8	-	2/9		
Leaflet B	13/9	2/9	3/9					

Action Programme 2

Suppose you are the advertising manager's assistant. She has fallen ill on the 5th September, and has asked you to take over the ad and leaflet production. 'I've left you my work checklist,' she says. 'You can work from that.' You find on her desk the checklist given as our example above.

(a) What can you tell from the checklist?
(b) What does this suggest about the usefulness of checklists?
(c) What tasks that you have to perform in your own work might benefit from the same approach?

3.3.2 Action plans

Action plans set out a programme of work or action, including time scheduling. Our example of a checklist for an advertising manager was a kind of action plan.

The following is another example, for the writing of a report.

	Activity	Days before due date	Target date	Date begun	Date completed
1	Request files	6	3/9		
2	Draft report	5	4/9		
3	Type report	3	6/9		
4	Approve report	1	8/9		
5	Signature	1	8/9		
6	Courier	0	9/9		

3.3.3 Timetables

The same information could be formatted as a timetable or diary entry. You may already be using such methods to timetable your studies. Timetables and diaries have several benefits.

- Remind you of key times and dates
- Remind you to make necessary advance preparations
- Help you allocate your time effectively

PART C ORGANISING AND UNDERTAKING MARKETING ACTIVITIES

Action Programme 3

Here is a timetable/diary page for the week of the 3rd to 9th September. Enter the schedule given in Paragraph 3.3.2 as an action plan, as you would do an appointments diary. Consider how you would highlight the due date.

SATURDAY 3 / SUNDAY 4	WEDNESDAY 7
MONDAY 5	THURSDAY 8
TUESDAY 6	FRIDAY 9
Week commencing 3 SEPTEMBER S 3 S 4 M 5 T 6 W 7 T 8 F 9	

3.3.4 Bar charts

Longer-term schedules may be used to show the following.

(a) The **length of time** to be taken for scheduled events or activities.

(b) The **relationship between events or tasks** – for example, whether they take place at the same time or in sequence. This can be particularly useful for identifying where excessive or clashing demands are being made. You may have scheduled two tasks at once, or scheduled a task over a period when you planned a holiday.

(c) The **relationship between planned and actual** task duration or output.

The following is a simple example of a **bar chart** in the form of a year planner, in this case, a general plan for a fashion retail outlet.

	J	F	M	A	M	J	J	A	S	O	N	D
New year sale	▭	▭										
Spring stock in		▭	▭									
Summer fashion preview				▭								
Summer sale								▭	▭			
Closed for refitting						▭						
Extra staff											▭	▭
X on holiday								▭				
Y on holiday		▭						▭				

3.3.5 Gantt charts

Another widely-used form of chart, which is used to show progress as well as schedule, is the **Gantt chart**, developed by H L Gantt for progressing the building of US Navy ships during the First World War. A Gantt chart is like the horizontal bar chart used above, but each division of space represents both an amount of time and an amount of work to be done in that time. Lines or bars drawn across the space indicate how much work is scheduled to be done and/or how much work has actually been done. The more work, the longer the line or bar.

Exam tip

> The Pilot paper and December 2002 exam asked you to produce a Gantt chart for the planning of a marketing event. You might also have chosen to use a bar or Gantt chart in December 2003 to illustrate the timing of media bookings as part of your 'media plan'. In general, if you see the word 'schedule', it might be worth asking yourself if a chart such as the one above might be a professional and efficient way of conveying the data.

The advantage of such a chart is that you can see the **relationship between time spent and amount done**. You can compare amounts produced in one week or month, say, with those in another (by the relative lengths of the bar or line). You can, similarly, compare amounts scheduled to be done with those actually done.

PART C ORGANISING AND UNDERTAKING MARKETING ACTIVITIES

The information below, about planned work and actual progress, is set out in a Gantt chart.

Day schedule	Daily schedule (units)	Cumulative in the day (units)	Work done work done (units)	Cumulative (units)
Mon	100	100	75	75
Tues	125	225	100	175
Wed	150	375	150	325
Thu	150	525	180	505
Fri	150	675	75	580

Daily schedule and work actually done

Monday	Tuesday	Wednesday	Thursday	Friday
----→100	----→125	----→150	----→150	----→150
→75	→100	→150	→180	→75

- - - - → Scheduled work
———→ Work done

Action Programme 4

Look at the Gantt chart above.

(a) What information is clearly shown by the chart? (Is it more obvious how production is doing on the chart than on the tabulated data from which it was drawn?)

(b) What further Gantt chart might be helpful for the manager of this work, which can be drawn from the data given?

(c) Draw the Gantt chart you have suggested.

(d) What information is most usefully provided by this new chart?

[*Key skill for Marketers: Presenting information*]

4 Co-ordinating techniques

4.1 Project planning

FAST FORWARD

The organisation of marketing activities and events is often approached on a **project** basis.

Co-ordination involves the solving, allocating and scheduling of the various resources and activities required to complete a complex task. In this section, we will look at some of the more advanced techniques used in **project management**.

Key concept

A **project** is an undertaking, often cutting across organisational and functional boundaries, and carried out to meet specific goals within cost, schedule and quality objectives.

A **project plan** aims to ensure that the project objective is achieved within the requirements of quality, cost and time.

(a) **Breaking the project down** into manageable units of activity, and determining the sequence of, or relationships between, those units or tasks.

(b) **Estimating the resources** (materials, money, time and so on) required for each unit.

(c) **Sequencing and scheduling** each unit in the most appropriate way for co-ordinated performance.

4.1.1 Breaking the task into stages

Breaking a project down into its component parts is called establishing a **work breakdown structure** (WBS) for the project.

- Discovering exactly what work must be accomplished
- Determining the resources required
- Sequencing and co-ordinating the work done

The work breakdown can be expressed in a checklist, bar chart, or Gantt chart, as discussed in section 3 above.

4.1.2 Procedures

Some projects are already set up as a neat sequence of tasks, or **procedure**, reflecting the order in which tasks need to be performed. Where this sequence is not immediately obvious, it can be 'mapped' using a **network**. A simple network shows which activities need to be completed before others. In the example below, the squares or 'nodes' denote activities, and the arrows show logical sequence and precedence.

Consider the diagram above as a plan for going away on holiday.

Activity 1 = Reserving your holiday place by phone

Activity 2 = Booking travel insurance

Activity 3 = Renewing your passport

Activity 4 = Sending in a completed booking form. (This follows a reservation and requires details of insurance cover.)

Activity 5 = Obtaining a travel visa. (This can't be done until you have a valid passport.)

Activity 6 = Collection of tickets (for which you need to have made a written booking).

The advantage of such a method is that (unlike a checklist) it allows you to show where a number of activities need to be done at roughly the same time (like activities 1, 2 and 3 above).

PART C ORGANISING AND UNDERTAKING MARKETING ACTIVITIES

4.2 Network analysis

FAST FORWARD

More complex projects may require **network analysis** or **critical path analysis (CPA)** in order to sequence and schedule tasks accurately.

Key concept

Network analysis is a term for project planning techniques which aim to 'map' the activities in a particular project, and the relationship between them, including:

- what tasks must be done before others can be started
- what tasks could be done at the same time
- what tasks must be completed on schedule if the completion date for the whole project is not to slip: the critical tasks.

The most commonly used form of network is called an **activity-on-arrow diagram**, because activities are represented by an arrowed line, which runs between one event (start or completion of the activity) and another. Events are depicted by a node, or circle.

Hence in the following example we map activity A, which starts at a certain point (event 1) and ends at a certain point (event 2).

Let us tackle a more complex example. Suppose your work breakdown structure comprises six activities: we will call them activities A–G.

(a) Activities A and B can start together

(b) You have to have done activity B before you can do activity C

(c) Once activity A is completed, activities D and E can start, at the same time

(d) Activity F follows on from activity D

(e) Activity G will be completed at the same time as activity F, to end the project. However, activities C and E must be completed before G can commence.

Action Programme 5

Do not look at the network diagram below. Read (a)–(e) above again. Working from left to right, draw the network diagram showing activities A–G and events 1–6.

Now uncover our solution.

4.2.1 Critical path analysis (CPA)

More information can be added to a network diagram, to describe not just what happens next, but when it should happen, and how long the whole project will take if each activity takes as long as it is supposed to. This technique is called CPA, or **critical path analysis**. If Activity A takes three days, it is shown like this.

Let us say, building on our original A-G network, that:

Activity   A takes 3 days
           B takes 5 days
           C takes 2 days
           D takes 1 day
           E takes 6 days
           F takes 3 days
           G takes 3 days.

Our network would be as follows.

Let us assume that you have all the resources you need to carry out the above project as drawn: in other words, you have enough workers to do activities A and B at the same time, and so on. The shortest possible time in which you can complete the project is 12 days. See if you can work out why.

Each of the 'routes' of arrows from the first event to the last event is called a **pathway**.

Action Programme 6

List all the pathways in the network above, and add up how many days each path will take to reach event 6.

The shortest possible duration for the project is 12 days. This is the duration of the longest path (AEG), not the shortest! The activities on the longest path determine the deadline for the whole project, because if one of them runs over time, the whole project will run over time. They are therefore critical activities, and the path on which they sit is called the **critical path**. We show the critical path on a network by drawing double or thicker lines between the events on that path.

PART C ORGANISING AND UNDERTAKING MARKETING ACTIVITIES

4.3 SOST + 6M

FAST FORWARD

SOST + 6M is an overall framework for planning marketing events.

One planning technique that may be used for planning marketing events is known as **SOST + 6M**. We have already covered some of its aspects earlier in this chapter, but this framework provides a useful way of drawing the ideas together.

Situation ⎫   **M**en
Objectives ⎬ **M**oney
           ⎪   **M**achines
Strategy ⎬ **M**aterials
Tactics   ⎭ **M**inutes
               Measurement

- **Situation.** What are the circumstances the company finds itself in?
- **Objectives.** What are the company's objectives in this situation?
- **Strategy.** How is the objective going to be achieved?
- **Tactics.** What are the operational details of the decided strategy?

Consideration of the above elements will result in an outline plan, which can be carried out by organising the resources indicated by the 6Ms.

- **Men**, or human resources skills and expertise
- **Money.** What is the budget?
- **Machines.** Equipment may be needed.
- **Materials.** This may include sample products or brochures.
- **Minutes.** Time is a precious resource and needs to be carefully planned, or scheduled.
- **Measurement.** What criteria will be used to evaluate progress and success, and how will they be monitored and reviewed:

Exam tip

The December 2005 exam made 20 marks available for producing an 'event plan ... using a suitable event planning model' for a cultural festival (about which you had ample data). The examiner indicated that SOST + 6M was the appropriate model. (Even better, if you were able to add a GANTT chart or precedence network to illustrate the planning schedule.) A similar question was set in December 2006, this time specifying SOST + 6M as the model to use for a conference plan. The examiner's main complaint in this case was that the objectives given were not SMART: note that the SMART model is taken for granted as part of SOST + 6M!

5 Measuring and evaluating results

5.1 Project monitoring

> **FAST FORWARD**
>
> **Bring forward systems** are used to schedule follow-up actions.

Control over work must be maintained to ensure that jobs do in fact reach completion, and if those jobs involve various tasks over varying periods, planning will be necessary to keep track of future events, deadlines and results. Systems which provide for this are called **bring forward** or **bring up** systems. Anything which needs action at a later date (and therefore may get forgotten) should be processed in this way:

- Checking on progress of an operation
- Checking completion when the deadline is reached
- Checking payments when they fall due
- Retrieving files relevant to future discussions, meetings, correspondence.

Checklists are useful, as we suggested earlier, for monitoring what has been done and what has not. Diary systems may also be used. A reminder may be put in the diary or timetable for the relevant day, to check 'task x completed?', 'payment received?', 'response received to letter ref: IO/cw2?', 'one week left for revision'. If you use card index or concertina files, you could slip a card or note into the sequence or appropriate date section, for checking on the day.

5.2 Evaluating marketing activity

> **FAST FORWARD**
>
> Various **targets and standards** may be used to monitor and evaluate the effectiveness of marketing activity.

There are various systems for measuring the effectiveness of marketing activity (which will be discussed in more detail in Part E).

(a) There may be **annual targets** (sales, budgets, expenditure budgets etc) against which performance can be measured.

(b) **Moving standards** (such as monthly sales targets) allow the same performance measurement on an on-going control basis.

(c) **Diagnostic standards** monitor how the market is responding to the marketing activity, to give continuous performance feedback (eg via electronic point of sale information or market research).

Diagnostic feedback may be obtained by:

- Monitoring output against the marketing plan
- Measuring volume and/or growth of sales
- Comparing marketing activities (and/or sales) this year against last year
- Monitoring market share, and any year-on-year changes
- Monitoring customer complaints, returns or repeat sales and recommendations
- Gathering research on customer satisfaction, awareness, response to marketing
- Measuring the accuracy of budgets and schedules
- Comparing sales figures (and/or enquiries, size of contacts base and so on)
- Measuring direct responses (coupons returned, calls to response lines)

PART C ORGANISING AND UNDERTAKING MARKETING ACTIVITIES

Chapter Roundup

- **Planning** is the process of deciding what should be done, by whom, when and how. It is essential for co-ordination and control, through which performance is monitored, measured against the plan and adjusted where necessary.

- Five dimensions by which a plan can be **evaluated**:
    - Effectiveness
    - Efficiency
    - Economy
    - Elegance
    - Ethicality

- **Operational objectives** should be SMART: specific, measurable, attainable, relevant and time-bounded.

- **Budgets** are, essentially, SMART objectives expressed in financial terms.

- Basic steps in **work planning** include:
    - The establishment of priorities (considering tasks in order of importance for the objective concerned)
    - Scheduling tasks

- **Planning aids** include lists and checklists, action plans and diaries, charts and precedence networks.

- The organisation of marketing activities and events is often approached on a **project** basis.

- More complex projects may require **network analysis** or **critical path analysis (CPA)** in order to sequence and schedule tasks accurately.

- **SOST + 6M** is an overall framework for planning marketing events.

- **Bring forward systems** are used to schedule follow-up actions.

- Various **targets and standards** may be used to monitor and evaluate the effectiveness of marketing activity.

Quick Quiz

1. Give examples of non-operational and operational goals of a business.
2. Define efficiency and effectiveness.
3. Explain what is meant by forward and reverse scheduling.
4. What is the advantage of the Gantt chart for scheduling?
5. What is the 'critical path' in a network diagram?
6. Give three examples of diagnostic standards for evaluating marketing activity.

9: PLANNING AND SCHEDULING

Answers to Quick Quiz

1. Stated goals (non-operational) are often not the same as operational (for businesses, usually financial) goals. Operational examples: to increase sales volume by 5% next year; to increase profitability by 10%; to reduce staff absenteeism by half. Non-financial objectives might include: to develop markets in untouched international countries; to gain a reputation as a responsible employer or being environmentally sound.

2. Efficiency – does the organisation operate in such a way as to gain the maximum advantage from all its resources? Effectiveness – does the business achieve what it sets out to do?

3. Forward scheduling starts from now and by estimating the time each task will take arrives at a completion date. Reverse scheduling starts from the date by which the whole activity must be completed and breaks this down into stages by which each subtask must be completed.

4. The key advantage is that you can see the relationship between time spent and the amount done.

5. The critical path (on a network diagram) represents the longest sequence; this is the most critical, as it determines the overall project duration.

6. A full list is given in section (c) in Paragraph 5.2.

Action Programme Review

1. (a) To obtain pricing comparisons with three major competitors with market share over 10%.

   (b) To identify five potential distributors and/or agents for our product in South Africa.

   (c) To demonstrate our new product to 1,000 potential customers in the UK.

   (d) To obtain 500 sales leads in the north-eastern region.

   (e) To obtain editorial coverage in two national newspapers or regional newspapers with total circulation of 20 million readers in the seven days following the event.

   (f) To meet 10 new media contacts in television and radio.

   (g) To take advance sales orders to a value of £10,000.

   (h) To increase the mailing list of potential customers by 2,000 names.

2. (a) Studying the manager's checklist shows that you don't need to worry about the ads: they are finished and sent off. Leaflet A is at the printers, and has been for three days: it still needs to be proofed and sent off before the 12th – a week to go. Leaflet B seems to be at the designers – with just over a week to go: it is clearly falling behind and will need watching: in particular, the photography seems to be held up and will have to be dealt with first.

   (b) Checklists are particularly helpful in the event that you have to hand a task over to someone else for completion.

   (c) You might have suggested shopping lists or things to do in general – or points to be covered in an essay (a very useful planning habit to get into!).

PART C ORGANISING AND UNDERTAKING MARKETING ACTIVITIES

3   The action plan for dealing with the tasks identified in Action Programme 3 is as shown below.

SATURDAY 3 Request files SUNDAY 4 Draft report	WEDNESDAY 7
MONDAY 5	THURSDAY 8 Approve report. Signature to report.
TUESDAY 6 Type report	FRIDAY 9 REPORT DUE Courier
Week commencing 3 SEPTEMBER S S M T W T F 3 4 5 6 7 8 9	

4   (a)   The Gantt chart shows clearly that production is slightly behind schedule on Monday and Tuesday, spot on on Wednesday, better than planned on Thursday, but well short on Friday.

   (b)   It would be helpful to see how the cumulative production measured against the cumulative schedule, since daily comparisons are up and down.

   (c)

Monday	Tuesday	Wednesday	Thursday	Friday
- - - ▶100	- - - - - ▶225	- - - - - - ▶375	- - - - - ▶525	- - - - - - ▶675
▶75	▶175	▶325	▶505	▶580

   (d)   It is easy to see that the final weekly total output is well down on schedule.

5   The solution is given in the text.

6   There are three paths, as follows.

   ADF   = 3 + 1 + 3 days   = 7 days
   AEG   = 3 + 6 + 3 days   = 12 days
   BCG   = 5 + 2 + 3 days   = 10 days

> Now try Question 9 at the end of the Study Text

Event management

Chapter topic list

1. Marketing organisation
2. Meetings and conferences
3. Shows, exhibitions and trade fairs
4. Events, stunts and corporate hospitality
5. The international dimension

Syllabus content – knowledge and skills requirements

- 3.1 Describe the scope of individuals' roles in marketing; meetings, conferences, exhibitions, outdoor shows, outlet launches, press conferences
- 3.2 Identify alternative and innovative approaches to a variety of marketing arenas and explain criteria for meeting business objectives
- 3.3 Demonstrate an awareness of successful applications of marketing across a variety of sectors and sizes of business
- 3.6 Explain how an organisation should host visitors from other cultures, and organising across national boundaries

PART C ORGANISING AND UNDERTAKING MARKETING ACTIVITIES

Introduction

There are three basic dimensions to marketing organisation.

- **How to organise** (planning, co-ordination, administration and control techniques)
- **What to organise** (what aspects of a given event need organising)
- **In what contexts** (what types of event you might be required to organise)

In this chapter, we address what to organise in a range of contexts. In Chapter 9, we looked at planning and control techniques, or how to organise. One of the key aspects to be organised for any event is the **venue** or where the event will take place. We will tackle this separately, in Chapter 11.

1 Marketing organisation

> **FAST FORWARD**
>
> **Organising** means 'giving an orderly structure to' or 'making arrangements for' a set of things or events. Marketing activities which require organisation include meetings and conferences, press conferences, trade shows and exhibitions, launch events, publicity stunts and corporate hospitality.

Just about everything covered in the *Marketing in Practice* syllabus involves organisation! It is the basis for all efficient activity.

In this chapter, we look at the orderly structure to be developed, and arrangements made, for various marketing activities and events. These range from sales meetings to trade exhibitions to product launch parties and publicity stunts. Essentially, they are opportunities for communication:

(a) **Face-to-face communication** between people involved in the marketing process, such as marketing staff, suppliers, distributors, customers, the media and/or general public.

(b) **Public relations**, including media relations, customer relations and employee relations.

(c) **Personal promotion** of an organisation and its product/services. Often, a first direct encounter – launch or introduction – between a product and its potential market.

Exam tip

> A range of event management tasks may be set in the exam. In the December 2002 exam, you had to draw a Gantt chart for *planning* the event (some of the requirements of which were given). In June 2003, the focus was on *promotion* of an event. In June 2004, you were asked to draw up guidelines for a client on how to organise a conference. Nearly the whole December 2005 paper focused on venue selection, promotional support and relationship management for an event (a cultural festival: ie the event was the product/service – not merely a marketing tool!) Both June and December 2006 exams featured planning and promotion of events: a launch event and hosting an international conference respectively. Think as widely as you can through the issues involved. What difference might it make if (as in the June and December 2006 scenarios) visitors would be coming from overseas?

2 Meetings and conferences

2.1 Meetings

> **FAST FORWARD**
>
> **Marketing meetings** include a range of formal and informal discussions for the purposes of: project management; sales management; sales/service pitches or presentations; and negotiations.

Meetings are an organised form of face-to-face communication. In a marketing context, they will mainly include the following.

(a) **Project meetings**, bringing together people involved in a marketing project for briefing, planning, creative brainstorming, problem solving, reporting on progress, or post-project analysis and feedback. Such meetings may be small and relatively informal, involving a working team. If they involve representatives from other organisations or units (interdepartmental management meetings, or meetings with agency executives or consultants, say) they will require greater organisation in order to ensure the efficient gathering of participants and conduct of business.

(b) **Sales meetings**, bringing together the sales team or teams for briefing, motivation, training and/or reporting back from the field. Sales meetings are often used to present new products, marketing plans and sales targets to the sales force, both to inform and (if possible) to enthuse them about the upcoming sales period. Sales meetings are especially important if sales representatives do not work out of the organisation's premises: they offer an opportunity to reinforce team identity and to allow representatives to get to know the marketing team and each other. The venue, dates and frequency of such meetings will require particular attention, in order to avoid disruption to sales activity, and to ensure that information and support are given at the most relevant and helpful time.

(c) **Introduction or 'pitch' meetings**, in which suppliers present their products/services to potential clients/customers. An advertising, PR or market research agency, for example, may make a presentation and show its portfolio to those responsible for selecting and retaining such services. The marketing organisation may hold a similar meeting with retail outlet buyers, to introduce new or existing products.

(d) **Negotiations**. Formal relationships, collaborations and transactions are often conducted face-to-face, in order that mutual benefits can be hammered out with full feedback from all parties.

2.2 Organisation of meetings

> **FAST FORWARD**
>
> Basic elements of **meeting organisation** include: venue/date/time; agenda; information; facilities; and follow-up.

Whatever the purpose of a meeting, small or large, formal or informal, the following aspects will need to be organised.

(a) **Venue, date and time**. The convenience of all parties will need to be considered, as well as suitability for the meeting's purpose.

   (i) Is the venue equipped with the space and facilities required by the meeting? (This will be discussed in detail in Chapter 11.)

   (ii) Is the date timely: does it allow decisions to be reached and action taken by deadlines or target dates?

   (iii) The venue will need to be booked (even if it is your company's meeting room).

   (iv) Notification of the meeting to participants. Relevant people will need to be informed of the date, time and venue, what they will need to bring with them, how to get there and so on. This may include guest speakers or presenters who will need to be booked and briefed in advance.

(b) **Agenda and objectives**. Some notice needs to be given so that participants know what the meeting is about, what preparation they need to do, what information they need to gather and so on. At the very least, a list of objectives/topics should be available or drawn up at the meeting itself. This may also include a schedule of meeting session times and breaks.

(c) **Preparation of information**. If a presentation is to be given, information will need to be gathered and other material (visual aids, new product samples or prototypes) sourced and collated. Think through the agenda carefully. Most meetings will encourage the asking of questions, so relevant information sources should be available for reference. You may also consider name-tags for larger numbers of participants who do not know each other.

(d) **Facilities**. Depending on the purpose of the meeting, you may need to organise:
- Seating arrangements
- Equipment (TV, video or other visual aids, projectors, flip charts)
- Refreshments
- Other amenities (such as parking or overnight accommodation)

(e) **Follow-up**. Someone needs to take notes of minutes of the meeting, so that follow-up action can be taken. Minutes are also a record and confirmation of what was discussed and so may be circulated to participants along with notes.

Action Programme 1

What information would you need to prepare for a meeting of sales representatives prior to the launch of a new product? (Think about the need to educate and to support/motivate the sales team.)

2.2.1 Liaising with an external venue

If the meeting is held at your business premises, you may have access to many of the facilities required in-house. If you are organising a meeting at another venue – a hotel, restaurant or conference centre, say – you will need to liaise with the venue staff.

(a) State your **requirements** clearly.

(b) Allocate **responsibility** for sourcing various requirements.

(c) Check that your requirements are being met, according to specification, schedule and **budget**.

2.2.2 'Bells and whistles'

The amount and type of organisation required for a meeting will depend on the number of participants involved, the formality or informality of the meeting, the activities to be performed and the facilities required.

The purpose and participants of the meeting will also dictate the degree of sophistication and presentation required: a departmental team meeting will be less concerned with image-creation and hospitality than a meeting with clients to negotiate a major promotional collaboration. There are many creative opportunities to make a meeting into a PR event, but you need to be aware that 'bells and whistles' cost money, as do external venues and services.

(a) Check the **marketing budget** for general items (such as printing or entertainment) under which some meetings-related expenditure might be allocated).

(b) Check for, or draw up, a budget for regular and important special meetings, such as sales meetings and client pitches. Make sure that you can **justify the expenditure** by anticipated returns (improved sales performance, new accounts).

(c) **Record and monitor** all expenditure on meeting organisation for budgetary control and post-meeting evaluation.

2.3 Conferences

FAST FORWARD

The organisation of a **conference** will cover much the same ground as for a meeting, but the larger number of participants, longer duration and more varied agenda will require more features.

Key concept

The term '**conference**' can be used interchangeably with 'meeting'. 'Conferring' simply means 'meeting for discussion'. However, it often implies a much larger gathering of people.

For example:

(a) A **sales conference** is a larger and less frequent version of a sales meeting, involving a gathering of the regional or national sales force, annually or seasonally (prior to relevant selling cycles).

(b) A **trade conference** is a gathering of participants over a day or several days, to attend a schedule of meetings, seminars or lectures, workshops and other activities relevant to their trade or profession.

2.3.1 Organising a conference

The organisation of a conference will cover much the same ground as for a meeting, but the larger number of participants, longer duration and more varied agenda will require more features.

(a) **Longer notice and more comprehensive briefing** on the agenda, schedule and preparation requirements.

(b) **Advertising and promotion** of the conference or **invitation** to it, if it is open to a wider public.

(c) **Organisation of transport and overnight accommodation** for participants, or guidance on how they can make their own arrangements.

(d) More complex, and long-range **planning and co-ordination** of guest speakers and presentation materials.

(e) Organisation of **social, recreational or educational activities** and presentations, in addition to meetings. This may include dinners and parties, shows and sporting facilities, tours of relevant sites and local attractions and conference merchandise (T-shirts, pens, information packs). These are designed to attract delegates to the conference and to promote the organiser's image and facilities.

Hosting or sponsoring a conference for the trade, or on an issue of relevance to it, is a public relations exercise on a major scale. You may also be called upon to organise attendance at a conference for members of your department, in which case, the basic checklist applies.

- Budget
- Transport bookings/schedules
- Accommodation bookings/details
- Information/preparation/equipment required
- Pre-planned appointments/schedule

2.3.2 Tele- and video-conferencing

Bear in mind that there are cost-effective long-distance alternatives to face-to-face meetings.

(a) **Tele-conferencing** is a meeting held via the telephone. Modern telephones allow for multi-party link up (conferencing) and also speaker facility, so that all participants in a room can hear and speak. This is a common option for short, relatively informal meetings where travel and associated costs of a face-to-face meeting cannot be justified.

(b) **Video-conferencing**, via live video connection or web-cast, adds visual and non-verbal communication, effectively allowing a 'face-to-face' meeting without travel time or cost. PC systems also allow data sharing on-screen and via modem, enabling participants to bring to the meeting video, audio, graphic and text information which can be viewed and accessed by everyone.

2.3.3 Press conferences

> **FAST FORWARD**
>
> **Press conferences** are used to brief journalists. They should be reserved for genuine announcements of major importance or newsworthiness.

Key concept

> A **press conference** or **news conference** is a meeting called at a prescribed time and place, to brief journalists and/or issue a statement on a particular subject, and allow journalists to ask questions and take photographs.

The essential point about a press conference is that you are asking the media to come to you. Such conferences should be used sparingly, being reserved for genuine announcements of major importance or newsworthiness. (Journalists become cynical of organisations which call conferences on minor matters or pure self-promotion.) You might consider a news conference if, for example, you were launching a public campaign, releasing a special report or study commissioned by your organisation, or announcing a major policy change.

Organisation of a press conference includes the following.

(a) **Adequate notice** given to media contacts and news editors. Media invitations or brief press releases should give details of the conference, including a sufficient idea of its subject to act as an incentive to attend.

(b) Selection and set-up of an appropriate **venue**. However attractive your corporate headquarters for PR purposes, consider whether its location will draw the right journalists and have the necessary equipment.

- Powerpoints for TV crews and access to telephone links
- Sufficient seating
- Some form of platform and microphones for spokespeople

(c) Selection and briefing of an appropriate interview co-ordinator or **chairperson**.

(d) Written **briefing material** and **visual aids** for use and release at the conference.

(e) Provision of **refreshments**.

(f) **Timing** of the conference to suit relevant journalists.

- Not too close to media deadlines: late afternoon will usually rule out morning newspapers and TV
- Not too distant from deadlines: Monday morning is unlikely to attract Sunday papers.

(g) Ensuring that ensuing media coverage is **monitored** and reported back to the organisation.

3 Shows, exhibitions and trade fairs

FAST FORWARD

Shows, exhibitions and trade fairs offer opportunities for public relations, promotion, networking and competitor research.

Exhibitions and trade fairs (for example, the Ideal Home Exhibition, the Boat Show or the Frankfurt Book Fair) offer several opportunities.

(a) **Public relations** (both to visitors and via media coverage, taking advantage of the interest generated by the exhibition organisers).

(b) **Promoting and selling** products/services to a wide audience of pre-targeted potential customers, particularly where demonstrations (eg of technical innovations) or visual inspection (eg clothes or motor cars) are likely to influence buyers.

(c) **Networking** within the industry and with existing clients.

(d) **Testing the response** to new products.

(e) **Researching competitor products** and promotions.

(f) **Researching suppliers' products** and services and making contacts along the supply chain.

Marketing at Work

Exhibition open for Olympic Games contract opportunities

Austrade took a trade mission to Beijing's Stadia China 2004 Exhibition in a bid to gain more 2008 Olympic contracts for Australia.

The exhibition, timed to coincide with the finalisation of the Olympic venue tendering process and the beginning of construction of the new National Stadium for the Games, targeted opportunities for sports stadiums and related sports and leisure facilities in China.

Austrade provided a Business Matching Centre for Australian companies to position themselves to win more supply contracts.

Business delegations from China's provincial and municipal sports administrations visited the exhibition. These included officials from BOCOG, other agencies involved with the Olympic Games and event organisation and the State General Administration of Sports.

3.1 Considering exhibiting

FAST FORWARD

Exhibiting is a demanding and expensive exercise, which should only be undertaken after research and cost-benefit analysis.

Most industries are catered for by at least one annual or bi-annual exhibition in the UK, as well as internationally. The events themselves are set up by **exhibition organisers** who are responsible for booking and preparing the venue, registering participants and organising seminars and events, issuing catalogues of stand-holders and events, providing stand construction services, organising lounges, amenities and catering facilities, access and parking, power and lighting, promotion and press coverage.

3.1.1 Research

The first steps for the marketing co-ordinator are to:

(a) **Research** what fairs/exhibitions are available and relevant.

(b) **Contact** each show manager or contact person for a 'show pack' or whatever details are available. These should include: how many people attend the show; where from and in what jobs/sectors; who the exhibitors are; what spaces/stands and facilities are available to exhibitors and at what cost; what transport and accommodation is available to exhibitors and at what cost.

(c) **Research the experience**, competence and asset-backing of the exhibition organisers. If it does not look as if they have the money or organisation and communication skills to make a success of a major logistical and promotional exercise, be cautious!

3.1.2 Cost-benefit analysis

Exhibiting is expensive!

- Site fees, stand construction and display (estimated 66% by the Exhibition Industry Federation)
- Staff costs, including opportunity cost of staff being withdrawn from their normal sales work (22%)
- Promotion and entertainment of visitors (12%)

Marketing at Work

New media is having an impact on the exhibitions industry. The Internet can be used to attract visitors to shows and for post-show marketing via e-mail.

In addition, some exhibitors are using webcast technology to broadcast their shows live on the Internet. While this is not the same as being there, such facilities are still good for communicating useful information about exhibited products, with online visitors able to view just the stands they are interested in.

The director general of the Association of Exhibition Organisers says: 'The growth of exhibitions will go hand in hand with the growth of electronic media'. Visitors can use the Internet to book exhibition tickets, flights, hotel rooms and meetings.

A **budget** should be drawn up to cover all costs associated with going to the show/exhibition. This should be compared with forecast revenue from the show in order to assess the show's viability. After the event, the show's **profitability** can be evaluated in the same way.

However, it should be recognised that your objectives for a particular show may not solely be sales revenue. You may want to find a distributor in a new international market, or to raise awareness of your brand with the trade press, or to introduce your product to a new market. Such achievements may take time to 'ripen' into confirmed sales. In the Exhibition Industry Federation survey, the average time to convert an exhibition lead to a sale was seven months, and in some cases, two years or more.

Action Programme 2

(a) Carry out the steps outlined in Paragraph 3.1.1 for an industry sector you are involved or interested in. Swap information with other students, if available.

(b) Draw up a rough budget for a stand and any facilities and services offered. Compare this (partial) exhibition expenditure with the number and suitability of the target attendees. Would you go ahead with the exhibition?

[*Key skill for Marketers: Using Financial information and metrics*]

3.1.3 Booking considerations

At the time of booking a stand or space, you will have to decide on several issues.

(a) The **size** of your site. This will depend on the number and nature of products you wish to display, whether you want entertainment/meeting space for your exclusive use, the relative importance of the particular show, and your exhibition budget.

(b) The **location** of your site. It needs to be accessible for the flow of visitors. It needs to be in a relatively-targeted and labelled sector for your business, among others in your field but not in the shadow of strong competitors.

(c) The **design** and **construction** of your site. Exhibition organisers generally offer a range of basic prefabricated or modular stand designs and related services which they can have set up for you. If you wish to use their services, you may have to specify your requirements for shelving, lighting, power and telephone points, water/heating facilities, fire extinguishers, floor covering, furniture, flowers/plants and so on. Cleaning services and insurance may also be offered.

(d) The **information** you will provide for the exhibition catalogue, press pack and signage.

3.2 Planning and preparation

FAST FORWARD

Basic organisational considerations include:

- Guest list
- Invitation or advertising and response monitoring
- Choice of venue, date and time
- Notification of the purpose/objectives of the event
- Planning of seating, facilities and amenities
- Catering and other services
- Provision of promotional/supporting information
- Booking and briefing of guest speakers/presenters
- Booking of transport and accommodation (if required) of participants
- Budgeting for all of the above

Exhibitions can be a huge logistical exercise, taxing your organisational skills to the utmost! They require planning well in advance – and then compress a lot of activity all at once into a very hectic period.

PART C ORGANISING AND UNDERTAKING MARKETING ACTIVITIES

There are a number of areas in which **advance planning** will pay off.

(a) **Stand design, display and services**. As we mentioned above, specialist stand contractors can set up the structure, fixtures and fittings of a stand to your specifications, but you need to have considered what your needs for display and facilities will be.

    (i) What **space** will be required for uncluttered access and vision, and for storage, confidential negotiations and meetings?

    (ii) What **furniture** is required for meetings, storage, display?

    (iii) What items will you want **displayed or demonstrated**? How will you transport them to the exhibition site? (There are specialist exhibition movers especially for overseas exhibitions, where export regulations must be observed.)

    (iv) What decorative items will project the desired **image** of your organisation?

    (v) What **stationery** (order books, price lists, visitors books) will you require to do business on the stand?

    (vi) What **services** will you require for operating the stand, such as cleaning, rubbish removal, security and provision of refreshments? You will also need to contract with the transporters, constructors and suppliers to dismantle the stand at the end of the exhibition.

(b) **Stand staffing**

Trade show networking and selling is hectic, intense and tiring. You will need to arrange for a rotating roster of stand staff, including a Stand Manager to organise the stand and liaise with exhibition organisers, reception staff, sales staff, technical staff (if the product requires expert demonstration or advice) and multilingual export staff.

(c) **Accommodation and transport for personnel**

A large exhibition can absorb available transport and accommodation even in a major city. If you are outside your home area, ensure that you have booked transport to the exhibition city, hotel or other accommodation and also any hire cars required, well in advance.

(d) **Pre-arranged meetings and visits**

In order to maximise your return on investment, ensure that you hit as many of your target audience as you can. Make a 'hit list' of key customers, suppliers and agents (from your database or from the pre-circulated list of exhibitors and attendees).

    (i) Invite them to visit your stand. Give directions, incentives such as prize draws or free samples, and if possible, make definite appointments.

    (ii) Supply their details to your sales staff, who can arrange to go and visit them.

Exhibition checklist

- ☐ Book space and pay direct
- ☐ Draft and supply catalogue/signage information
- ☐ Design stand/lighting/fixtures and fittings
- ☐ Order lighting, flooring, furniture, shelving, and storage
- ☐ Order water, power, heating, telecom, drainage
- ☐ Order fire extinguisher, check safety regulations
- ☐ Insure stand and exhibits

- ☐ Organise products/brochures/display materials for exhibit
- ☐ Arrange delivery/export of large items, and return
- ☐ Contract for stand cleaning, plant/flower supply and maintenance, security
- ☐ Plan staffing of stand
- ☐ Plan VIP appearances
- ☐ Arrange transport and accommodation of staff, VIP's
- ☐ Design and prepare promotional literature, signage, incentives to visitors
- ☐ Gather stationery and equipment for use on stand
- ☐ Invite customers/prospects, arrange meetings
- ☐ Arrange for photography, prepare press releases
- ☐ Order stand catering/refreshments
- ☐ Brief stand personnel; prepare task lists, rosters

3.3 At the exhibition

During the **set-up** period before the exhibition, you will work with contractors and your own staff to check that all the structures, fixtures, fittings and services associated with the stand are in place and functioning correctly.

Day-to-day **administration** of the stand will include:

- Appointment making, communications, offering refreshments
- Providing information, screening and routing 'serious' prospects
- Distributing leaflets or running competitions
- Recording all visits and sending visitors away with information

Action Programme 3

'The visitors to your stand will form their opinion on your company and its products more by their perception of you, than the stand or its contents.'

Take the time to think about the following issues. What effect could they have on visitors?

Behaviour	Effect on visitors
The way you conduct yourself on the stand	
The way you approach visitors	
The way you describe your product/service	

3.4 After the exhibition

Once an exhibition is finished, the stand will need to be dismantled, and its various components sent back where they came from.

The most important stage of the exhibition is **follow-up**.

(a) The contact information gained needs to be input to the organisation database and immediately utilised, even if it is only an e-mail to thank the contact for the visit.

(b) All promises made during the show (to send out literature or make a sales call) must be fulfilled as soon as possible.

4 Events, stunts and corporate hospitality

> **FAST FORWARD**
>
> A variety of **promotional events**, **stunts** and **corporate entertainments** may be used for applications such as product or outlet launches, corporate communication and key relationship building.

Although the territory of **promotional events**, **publicity stunts** and **corporate entertaining** is fairly well trodden, there is room for a high degree of creativity. The syllabus for *Marketing In Practice* requires you to 'develop an awareness of successful applications across a variety of sectors and sizes of business' (including 'alternative and innovative approaches'). Students should share their own experiences and compare and contrast different approaches.

Action Programme 4

Start to develop your awareness now!

(a) Buy, borrow or look in the library for a copy of *PR Week*, plus the trade journal of whatever sector you are interested in. Check the media pages of the reputable newspapers. Start a cuttings file.

(b) Select a major sporting event or venue near you, contact the Corporate Hospitality Department or ticket agency and ask for any information they may have on corporate packages.

(c) Collect any invitations *you* receive to promotional events, (yes, this may mean *joining* those mailing lists you usually avoid) and attend as many as you can.

(d) Swap cuttings and stories with other students.

[*Key skill for Marketers: Improving own learning and performance*]

4.1 Product and outlet launches

> **FAST FORWARD**
>
> **Product and outlet launches** may be accompanied by a range of promotional activities (advertising, special offers, press releases, merchandising), but they are also often the occasion for a social gathering.

Examples of launch events include:

- **A preview or private viewing** by press and key clients and contacts, (often used by fashion companies, art galleries and movie distributors)
- A **speech or presentation** by a VIP as the centrepiece of a meal or party
- A **themed party**, reflecting the nature of the product or brand
- An **official opening or unveiling ceremony**

10: EVENT MANAGEMENT

Exam tip

> A range of tasks was set in the June 2006 exam around the organisation of a launch event, including: invitations, guidance for event staff; issues in dealing with overseas guests; and a news release describing the event's success. Read questions carefully for both topic and format requirements!

4.1.1 Purposes of launch events

The purpose of a launch event may be:

(a) **To attract media coverage.** This is particularly effective if VIP or celebrity guests are present, or if the event itself is newsworthy (unveiling a genuine innovation, or imaginative in its venue or theme).

(b) **To raise the PR or industry profile of the organisation** by inviting a wide range of potential contacts.

(c) **To build relationships with existing customers or clients** by involving them in company celebrations.

(d) **To give key customers or trade buyers a chance to preview and pre-order** new products.

(e) **To reward staff, suppliers and distributors** who have worked on the launch.

4.1.2 Organisation of launch events

Each event will have its own individual requirements, depending on its purpose, size, budget and style. However, the following will generally need attention.

(a) **Guest list**

Checklists of categories of people to be considered will help to ensure the right mix for the purpose of the event, including general and trade press and media, existing customers, style leaders and celebrities, suppliers and distributors, staff and community figures.

(b) **Invitations**

These should go out weeks in advance, and replies should be requested. In order to estimate numbers, particularly for high profile, smaller and catered events, it may be necessary to follow up those who do not respond. For a large event, anticipate a high dropout rate.

The style of invitations is an important PR exercise in itself: use your creativity to intrigue or impress, or to tie in with the product or event theme.

(c) **Venue**

This will be discussed in detail in Chapter 11.

- Availability
- Suitability/size
- Facilities
- Access
- Budget

(d) **Catering**

Unless you are having a very small informal gathering in your own premises, it is advisable to use professional caterers, or a catered venue. Caterers can supply a wide range of buffet foods and drinks, waiter service and hire of crockery and glasses. Lay out refreshments away from the main exhibition/presentation area, but spread about to keep guests circulating.

(e) **Staffing**

Ensure that you have welcomers and refreshment servers as well as information providers, order takers and an event co-ordinator.

(f) **Photography**

If you cannot persuade a press photographer to be present, or would prefer to control the images yourself, hire a photographer. (An interesting photo with a good caption written on the back may be sufficient to secure a feature in a newspaper or magazine.)

(g) **Promotional material and give-aways**

Depending on the purpose and status of the event, you may wish to make available product catalogues or brochures, samples or themed branded party gifts.

Action Programme 5

The Needle Works

You decide that the opening of the new knitting department needs to be celebrated and promoted with a launch event of some kind. Jot down some ideas on what sort of event you might have; where; whom you invite; and how and what you might provide for your guests. For each idea, note what costs will have to be taken into account. Make your ideas as creative as possible, given the need to keep costs fairly low.

4.2 Publicity stunts

FAST FORWARD

A **publicity stunt** is any event calculated to attract the attention of the media. It needs to be amusing or whimsical, unusual, highly visual and of local or topical interest to their audience.

From the organisation's point of view, a publicity stunt also needs to be relevant to the aims of press coverage: potential customers should remember the **product,** not just the event!

The organisation of publicity stunts needs to include the following.

- The **event itself** (time, location, participants, props and costumes)
- **Notification** of the public and press/media that the event is taking place

Other events include:

(a) **Promotional tours** by artists, recording artists or authors, giving interviews, readings/performances and signing copies of product for sale

(b) **Award ceremonies** and celebrations for staff, or in collaboration with other organisations in an industry

(c) **Public seminars** (or a tour of speaking engagements), promoting an organisation's expertise

Exam tip

You may be asked for your suggestions for 'other promotional and marketing tools' (as well as advertising) to support a new launch. When given such a wide brief, don't forget 'events' as an option.

4.3 Corporate hospitality

Corporate hospitality involves entertaining by an organisation for the purposes of:

- **Building or cementing relationships** with key clients
- **Rewarding and motivating** key suppliers
- Encouraging **networking** and informal communication
- **Showing a presence** at major sporting or cultural events

Large scale corporate entertaining at sporting and cultural events is often handled by **agencies**, who purchase a block of tickets and sell them on to companies as part of a hospitality package including a marquee, box or hospitality room, drinks and food and event programmes. (Larger companies may own a permanent box or block of seats at stadiums and theatres, and use on-site catering services.) For a small company with no particular status requirements, ordinary ticket purchase and on-site catering may be sufficient.

If you book an event (concert, rugby international, football, golf, tennis) through an agency, the price per head is likely to be high, so you will need to plan the guest list and attendance carefully.

- There is likely to be a set number of places which need to be filled: have a reserve list.
- Try and find people who will be interesting to each other and of a similar status.
- Invite guests verbally at first, to get the date in their diaries: then follow up.
- Monitor responses, and invite reserve-list replacements as soon as possible.
- Send reminders a week before the event with tickets and details.
- Arrange all requirements for transport, parking, accommodation.
- Liaise with agency staff to ensure that catering and other services are in hand.
- Brief the hosts on the list of guests, their company and position.

There will usually be a separate **budget allocation** for hospitality events. The return on investment on such entertaining is not always readily quantifiable, since there are many other factors in customer loyalty and favour, but there may well be industry norms and expectations to live up to.

Marketing at Work

Corporate hospitality (also known as event marketing) needs to become more targeted and focused. Some £330 million is spent on event marketing annually, but it is not necessarily money well spent. A recent survey found that, out of 77 UK companies, only 34% evaluated such events against their objectives, and 72% cited personal management preferences as important factors when choosing what event to stage. Corporate hospitality should instead be regarded as an important part of the marketing mix, and accountable in the following areas:

- Have we seen a growth in business?
- Have we seen improved relationships?
- Have we got direct orders from it?
- Has it opened up new lines of communication?
- Has it been something we can build on?

Marketing Business, April 2000

Exam tip

The June 2005 exam took an interesting angle on this topic by asking you to evaluate a proposal to use a train (since your organisation was a railway) as a venue for corporate hospitality events. A similar scenario was set for the use of a Transportation Museum in December 2006. How would you *promote* the venue? How might you *evaluate* it as a business entertaining option? A useful reminder to consider these syllabus topics from the point of view of the promoter – as well as that of the potential buyer/user!

5 The international dimension

> **FAST FORWARD**
>
> **International organisation** is complicated by factors including:
>
> - language
> - law and custom (culture)
> - import/export requirements
> - currency
> - travel requirements
> - time differences
> - unknown media
> - length of communication lines

5.1 Organisation across borders

The organisation of international events involves several additional factors.

(a) **Language**

As organiser, you may have to communicate with guests, venues and service providers for whom English is not a first language. You can overcome these difficulties.

(i) Work through an international agency, or branch of your organisation with representatives in the other country.

(ii) Employ a translator/interpreter to prepare or mediate communications or find a colleague who speaks or writes the language in question.

(b) **Currency**

Members of your organisation going abroad for meetings or exhibitions may need to be equipped with appropriate local currency, travellers cheques or credit facilities.

Fluctuations in exchange rates should be taken into account when checking foreign currency expenditure against pound-sterling budgets.

(c) **Travel arrangements**

International travel is more complex.

(i) Travel itineraries, including airport transfers, flexible ticketing options, allowance for checking in times and time differences

(iii) Travel insurance

(iii) Travel documentation. Some countries require travel visas and a letter of confirmation that the person is travelling on company business, as well as a valid passport.

(iv) Medical precautions and vaccinations, which need to be planned well in advance of departure

(v) Longer lines of communication. Travellers would be provided with all schedules, itineraries, details of arrangements and if possible local contact numbers in the event of problems.

(d) **Import/export arrangements**

Sending products and promotional materials overseas (or receiving them from overseas) for exhibitions and other events can be complicated, because of:

- Customs documentation
- Lead time required.

International freight services and exhibition consultants may be an option.

(e) **Time differences**

E-mail and fax are the most effective means of communication where events are to be organised in different time-zones.

(f) **Local law and customs** (cultural factors)

Check with embassies, trade delegations, consultancy services or local contacts, about such matters as the role and safety of women, consumption of alcohol, dress codes, the content of printed matter, business etiquette and religious sensibilities.

(g) **Distance**

Since you are not on the spot to monitor and supervise arrangements, briefings, instructions and confirmations will be more important when organising events overseas, whether directly or through intermediaries.

Exam tip

> The December 2002 exam asked you to plan a celebration event for all the retailers of a company in Africa. It was up to you to note: (a) The African setting (what constraints may that put on your plans if you are a student from London or Hong Kong?) and (b) the fact that the retailers come from a range of African nations (will they need help with accommodation? what venue will provide ease of access?)

5.2 Hosting visitors from other countries

Similar considerations to those outlined above apply to hosting overseas clients, suppliers or agents who visit your office or marketing events.

(a) Visitors may need your **support**, as local organiser, with transport and accommodation arrangements, as well as advice on visas and currency requirements.

(b) You may need to provide an **interpreter** for visitors who are not fluent in English.

(c) Be aware and respectful of the **cultural norms and values** (including business and social customs) of your visitors. In the Far East, for example, hospitality requires the host to offer gifts to the guest, and this is not to be interpreted as a bribe. In other countries, 'baksheesh' or 'oiling the wheels of industry' is the norm. Negotiation and conflict resolution styles differ according to culture. Age and gender incur differing degrees of respect. Body language and eye contact have different connotations.

(d) Be aware or ask about **religious or cultural requirements** in regard to diet, Sabbath observance and other matters.

(e) Remember that visitors may be new to your city or country as well as to your organisation, and may welcome scenic as well as factory **tours**. Opportunities for sightseeing and local entertainment may be highly appreciated.

(f) Be very clear, in advance, whose organisation is **responsible** for the arrangements and expense of the visit.

It may be helpful to act as, or appoint, a **permanent host**, guide or liaison person to accompany or keep in regular touch with foreign visitors and to co-ordinate their various travel and business arrangements.

PART C ORGANISING AND UNDERTAKING MARKETING ACTIVITIES

> **Action Programme 6**
>
> Make a list of the (a) corporate areas/cities and (b) tourist sights you would wish an important overseas client to see on a three-day visit to your company/country.

Exam tip

> The December 2005 and June 2006 exams specifically addressed this topic, with marks available for identifying key issues in receiving and hosting artists and visitors from different national and cultural backgrounds. Specifically *cultural* issues were tested in December 2006.

5.3 Cultural factors in international events

Culture is 'the collective programming of the mind which distinguishes the members of one category of people from another' (*Hofstede*, 1991). It is – broadly – 'the way we do things around here.'

Culture includes customs and norms of behaviour, artefacts (things made by a society), rituals (symbolic activities such as ceremonies) – and also the underlying values, beliefs and assumptions which share them and give them their meaning.

Some examples of cultural issues relevant to event management (and indeed, marketing in general) include:

(a) **Linguistic differences** and abilities, affecting the extent to which communication will be understood.

(b) **Social customs** around matters such as: mixing social and business conversations; the importance of hospitality; the acceptability of gift-giving; the importance attached to conventional 'manners' and so on.

(c) **Communication styles**: formality/informality in the way people deal with each other; the acceptability of displays of emotion; the importance of 'face' or public respect. Such factors impact on the ways in which people handle conflict, negotiation and so on.

(d) **Body language**: different non-verbal cues are used in different cultures; 'personal space' requirements vary. Such factors can inadvertently cause offence.

(e) **Business norms and practices**: formalities (eg exchange of business cards) may be a respect issue; attitudes to gifts and hospitality may vary; the extent of 'movement' expected in negotiations may differ; and so on.

(f) **Social values and roles**: eg the role of women in business or respect for age/seniority.

(g) **Religious observances**: eg Sabbath days, prayer times, dietary restrictions, clothing customs.

Chapter Roundup

- **Organising** means 'giving an orderly structure to' or 'making arrangements for' a set of things or events. **Marketing activities** which require **organisation** include meetings and conferences, press conferences, trade shows and exhibitions, launch events, publicity stunts and corporate hospitality.

- **Marketing meetings** include a range of formal and informal discussions for the purposes of: project management; sales management; sales/service pitches or presentations; and negotiations.

- Basic elements of **meeting organisation** include: venue/date/time; agenda; information; facilities; and follow-up.

- The organisation of a **conference** will cover much the same ground as for a meeting, but the larger number of participants, longer duration and more varied agenda will require more features.

- **Press conferences** are used to brief journalists. They should be reserved for genuine announcements of major importance or newsworthiness.

- **Shows, exhibitions and trade fairs** offer opportunities for public relations, promotion, networking and competitor research.

- **Exhibiting** is a demanding and expensive exercise, which should only be undertaken after research and cost-benefit analysis.

- **Basic organisational considerations** include:
    - guest list
    - invitation or advertising and response monitoring
    - choice of venue, date and time
    - notification of the purpose/objectives of the event
    - planning of seating, facilities and amenities
    - catering and other services
    - provision of promotional/supporting information
    - booking and briefing of guest speakers/presenters
    - booking of transport and accommodation (if required) of participants
    - budgeting for all of the above

- A variety of **promotional events**, **stunts** and **corporate entertainments** may be used for applications such as product or outlet launches, corporate communication and key relationship building.

- **Product and outlet launches** may be accompanied by a range of promotional activities (advertising, special offers, press releases, merchandising), but they are also often the occasion for a social gathering.

- A **publicity stunt** is any event calculated to attract the attention of the media. It needs to be amusing or whimsical, unusual, highly visual and of local or topical interest to their audience.

- **International organisation** is complicated by factors including:
    - language
    - law and custom (culture)
    - import/export requirements
    - currency
    - travel requirements
    - time differences
    - unknown media
    - length of communication lines

Quick Quiz

1. What special considerations apply to the organisation of sales team meetings?
2. What are an 'agenda' and 'minutes' of a meeting?
3. Outline the procedure for calling a press conference.
4. What considerations dictate the desirable size and location of an exhibition stand?
5. What costs of participating in exhibitions need to be budgeted for?
6. Give four examples of events that might be organised for a product launch.
7. What is a 'publicity stunt' and what makes it effective?
8. What is a 'hospitality package'?
9. What are some of the arrangements that need to be made for international travel?
10. Give four examples of cultural differences that might be taken into account when hosting overseas visitors.

Answers to Quick Quiz

1. Sales meetings must not interrupt sales activity and should give information and support at an appropriate time.
2. An agenda (Latin for 'things to be done') is a list of various items of business at a meeting. The minutes are a written record of the discussion and/or decisions of a meeting.
3. Give adequate notice and select time appropriate for publication deadlines; select a venue with necessary facilities; brief a co-ordinator; prepare written briefing or visual aids; arrange refreshments; feedback to the organisation afterwards.
4. Size: number and nature of your products; meeting space required; need for prominence. Location: flow of visitors; relative position of competitors; need for prominence.
5. You need to consider site fees, staff costs, promotion and the entertainment of visitors.
6. The four examples given in the text are: presentations, themed parties, an unveiling ceremony and a preview.
7. A publicity stunt is any event calculated to attract the attention of the media. It is effective when it reinforces your message in a novel, entertaining and memorable way.
8. A hospitality package is a set of benefits to enable your customer to best enjoy corporate hospitality – for example, entry to an exclusive enclosure, box seats or hospitality rooms.
9. Language issues, currency, itineraries, import and export arrangements, time differences, local law and customs, and the fact that all of these have to be negotiated at a distance.
10. Four examples of cultural differences you need to consider are religion, social custom, business customs and language.

Action Programme Review

1 Information for a sales meeting might include: market research reports, budgets and forecasts, sales support materials (order forms, brochures), new product prototypes and/or samples for demonstration, mock-ups of promotional/ad campaigns, media schedules and promotion/PR plans, training manuals (if required).

2 Just do it! If you struggled to find details of relevant trade shows and exhibitions, did you try trade journals? Perhaps it was the wrong time of year for the exhibition to be advertised. There are also published directories of national and international trade shows and exhibitions. Or, try your local chamber of commerce, or business advisory service. Better yet, tap your networks, or check some websites: practise those research skills!

3

Behaviour	Effect on visitors
The way you conduct yourself on the stand	Will they approach, or stay away?
The way you approach visitors	Will they take the time to listen to you or run away?
The way you describe your product/service	Will they be interested enough to become a firm lead?

4 This is the only way to broaden your thinking.

5 Your ideas might have included aspects along the following lines (but don't let our suggestions limit your thinking).

Venue: In new wool department (opportunity to browse; impact of colour wools, can take pre-orders) – no venue cost

OR

Local tapestry/craft museum? (unusual – but hire cost + staff costs to liaise with curator etc)

Event: Sunday brunch (not evening, to include older customers, out of town customers)
- croissants, sandwiches
- Bucks fizz/orange juice
- catering cost (also crockery/glass hire) *relatively* inexpensive food type
- exhibition of knitted work } Supplied *free* by wool manufacturers
- demonstrations } (promoting own brands)

Invite: Staff (hosts), suppliers, editors of craft magazines, local radio, all regional customers and *all* customers who requested knitting information (even if not expected to come). (Mail costs)

Invitations: Simple card with multicoloured wools knitted through (minimal material cost + staff time).

Gifts/incentives: Prize draw on entry to win a kit. (Cost of kit.)

Introductory 5% discount on launch purchases? (Discount cost.)
Information leaflets

PART C ORGANISING AND UNDERTAKING MARKETING ACTIVITIES

6   Your answer will depend on your organisation and its location. Bear in mind that this is an important client, so (s)he may be worth investing some time and money in entertaining, but also that (s)he is on a business trip.

> Now try Question 10 at the end of the Study Text

Venue selection

Chapter topic list

1. Venue appraisal
2. Suitability
3. Synergy
4. Making recommendations

Syllabus content – knowledge and skills requirement

- 3.5 Appraise and select a venue, based on given criteria and make appropriate recommendations

Introduction

As we saw in Chapter 10, the venue of some marketing events in which the company may wish to participate are chosen by external event organisers: trade conferences, shows and exhibitions and some corporate hospitality packages.

In this chapter, we consider the evaluation and selection of a venue for events where this is at the company's discretion: product launches, parties, customer events, publicity stunts, meetings and conferences.

We will discuss a number of standard and more creative (and/or expensive) possibilities: you should continue to swap experiences and ideas with fellow students, and to keep an eye out for opportunities yourself. From the outset, bear in mind that the most appropriate place for the informal planning meeting of your sales team may be your office meeting room, with no special facilities laid on!

1 Venue appraisal

FAST FORWARD

A **venue** is the appointed place for a meeting, concert, sporting fixture or other event. It may be a dedicated entertainment/event venue or a premises which can be adapted to the theme of an event.

1.1 Gathering venue information

Dedicated entertainment and event venues such as conference centres, large hotels, sports stadia, theatres and exhibition centres promote themselves to event organisers, through:

- Specialised **directories** and source books for event organisers
- The **catalogues** of hotel and conference centre chains (such as the Forte Group)
- Entries in business **directories** and yellow pages
- **Information packs** available on request
- Event management **consultants**.

Thinking 'outside the box', however, you might also gather venue information by contacting any potential venue you find interesting: zoos, art galleries, National Trust properties and other such sites will often have information on hire and event management services available. (If not, don't be afraid to break new ground!)

Action Programme 1

Begin to compile you own venue directory file. Make a list of categories that you would find useful (start with your present job, then think beyond): Conference, Prestige, Themed, Sports and so on. As you gather notes and brochures, tag each with the relevant category. (Build towards an index card-file or binder.)

Once you have gathered, or are aware of, a wide variety of venues, you can match the requirements of a particular event with the attributes of a number of venues to select the best fit.

There are two broad criteria for selecting a venue for a marketing event.

- Suitability
- Synergy

We will look at each in turn.

2 Suitability

FAST FORWARD

Suitability of a venue may be assessed using the acronym 'ASFAB': Access, Size, Facilities, Availability, Budget.

Exam tip

'Criteria for selecting a venue' is a classic exam topic. You should take account of the content of this section and note down its key features as a ready-made checklist.

The examiner also suggests the acronym ASFAB:

- ☐ Access
- ☐ Suitability/size
- ☐ Facilities
- ☐ Availability
- ☐ Budget

'Access' may seem like a small consideration but it featured prominently in the December 2003 scenario, where you were asked to assess the suitability of a small marina as a conference venue. The examiner pointed out that – although students used the ASFAB acronym – they paid insufficient attention to detail. The marina is 'situated at the end of a narrow country lane' – hardly suitable for large equipment trucks or mass vehicular access/parking! If you're going to use an acronym, make sure you take careful account of each point, in relation to the scenario.

Suitability means fitness for an intended purpose and appropriateness for an occasion. Your particular event may have many different criteria and constraints: a suitable venue will meet as many of them as possible.

2.1 The size or capacity of the venue

How many people are on your list of guests or participants? How many people does the venue hold? This may be defined by various factors.

- Seating capacity (for example, in a lecture hall, restaurant, theatre or cinema)
- Accommodation capacity (in a hotel or residential conference centre)
- Space and comfort (in a room where people will be standing)
- Accessibility and lines of sight (in a gallery, exhibition hall or shop)
- Safety and fire regulations (which limit numbers, so as to allow emergency exit)

Cost, atmosphere and PR considerations suggest that you should not select a much larger venue than your numbers require. (A small group of people in a large room feels awkward and looks like a disappointing turnout, even if everyone expected has come.)

(a) Hotels and Conference Centres have meeting rooms and auditoria of various sizes and styles.

(b) 'Private party' areas can be roped or screened off in otherwise public restaurants, theatres or museums.

The price charged by a large venue may reflect economies of scale, but it may also reflect the wide range of services and facilities available. Do not pay for what you will not use.

2.2 The location of the venue

Where are the majority of your guests/participants based? Will they find the venue convenient to get to? This may not be a critical consideration in the case of a sales meeting, which participants have to attend. However, if you need to **attract guests**, factors concerning convenience will be important.

(a) **Proximity** to where many of your guests are likely to be at the time of the event

(b) **Accessibility**. You will need to evaluate the availability of public transport, road access and parking facilities.

For a small, special event, however, do not let inaccessibility put you off, if the remoteness of the venue is of benefit in other ways. Minibus or coach hire may be worthwhile to transfer guests to a gathering in a remote country location for golf, or a house-party style event. More innovative alternatives can also be arranged, where the costs of doing the unusual are considered worthwhile.

The venue should also be located conveniently for the purpose of the event. If you want to show customers a new outlet or showroom, or give suppliers and agents a tour of your plant or warehouse facilities, any associated meetings or entertainment will be most efficiently held at or near the site in question.

> **Exam tip**
>
> In December 2004, you were asked to outline criteria for selecting a venue for a 'franchise roadshow' for a new 'chocolate and coffee' franchise. In December 2005, you had to outline *non-financial* factors to be considered in choosing (*between two given*) venues for a cultural festival visited by 100,000 people! In June 2006, you also had to calculate costings for two very different venues for a launch event as part of the compulsory Part A question. If you work through the ASFAB framework, bear in mind that you still need to **contextualise**. Think NOW how you'd go about it. Venue selection comes up regularly in one form or another.

2.3 The status and style of the venue

Despite 'star rating' systems, status, style and degrees of comfort and luxury are highly subjective matters. The level of formality of a venue, its comfort and amenities, decor, style of service, dress codes and so on project a powerful image, with which your event will be associated. The image of the venue should be matched to the following.

- The desired image and status of the organisation or the product or brand
- The tastes, age and status bracket of the guests
- The purpose and style of the event (business-like, entertainment, social networking)

Action Programme 2

What sort of marketing events might you hold at:
(a) a branch of McDonalds?
(b) the Ritz tea-rooms?
(c) a country bed and breakfast hotel?
(d) a prominent city night-club?
(e) an outdoor adventure centre?

2.4 Facilities

Some of the main facilities your event might require include the following.

(a) **Conference/meeting facilities**, including suitable furniture, presentation equipment, staging or sound systems, communications centre and secretarial support services.

(b) **Catering facilities or services**, ranging from drinks and snacks to full-scale buffet or sit-down banquet.

(c) **Accommodation**, for longer conferences and events. Consider what type of accommodation, and what standard of comfort and presentation your guests require.

(d) **Recreational activities**. Conferences are often opportunities to reward staff and to encourage team-building by offering leisure facilities.

(e) **Disabled access** and facilities: ramps, lifts and wheelchair access.

Outdoor venues and events will require additional attention to:

- **Shelter** (especially in the event of bad weather)
- **Toilet facilities**
- **Safety**, for example, if sporting or adventure activities are involved.

The **house rules** of a venue should also be checked. Conference centres owned by church organisations, for example, often prohibit alcohol on the premises. If you require non-smoking, or smoking facilities, you will need to check.

Bear in mind that any services and facilities lacking from an otherwise ideal venue may be sourced for you by the venue organisers. Event management is a jigsaw puzzle, not just a checklist!

2.5 Cost

All of the above criteria have cost implications. As we discussed in Chapter 9, you need to start the venue selection experience with some clear ideas.

(a) A clear set of **objectives** for your event, including any financial benefits you expect to accrue from it.

(b) An **expenditure budget** in proportion to the financial and non-financial returns expected from the investment.

(c) An **event concept and plan** which places the venue specification in the context of the objectives and budget.

The venue is not the only cost of an event. Balance what you need your venue to offer with the constraints an expensive venue will place on the rest of your event budget. If your clients genuinely expect to be entertained at a five-star level, you may have to indulge them. It is however possible to transform the most inexpensive venue into a high-impact event through creativity in concept, decoration and imported services.

This is where synergy comes in.

Action Programme 3

The costs of exhibiting at Trade Fair A and Trade Fair B during August 20XX were as follows.

	Trade Fair A		Trade Fair B	
	£'000	%	£'000	%
Stand design and hire	70	35	50	20
Stand promotion	30	15	125	50
Hospitality and literature	90	45	50	20
Stand staffing	10	5	25	10
	200	100	250	100

Required

Show the costs for the trade fairs in pie charts.

[*Key skill for Marketers: Presenting information*]

3 Synergy

> **FAST FORWARD**
>
> **Synergy** (2 + 2 = 5) is where the venue itself adds value to the event through:
> - incentive/attraction
> - impact/memorability
> - PR/media value
> - association of ideas to the organisation/product/brand
> - encouraging collaboration
> - building on existing relationships and familiarity

Key concept

> **Synergy** is a scientific principle whereby the whole is greater than the sum of its parts. This can be simply put as: 2 + 2 = 5.

Synergy implies that the venue not only satisfies certain necessary conditions for an effective event, but adds something to the event's effectiveness. In business terms, **the venue itself adds value** and there are several ways in which it can do this.

- Adding **attraction**, or incentive to people to attend
- Adding **impact** or memorability to the event
- Adding **PR/media value**, newsworthiness or media interest
- Adding **association**, linking the organisation, product or brand with the event in the participants' and audience's minds

3.1 Creative thinking

Attraction, impact and PR/media value can be contributed by a venue, through:

- Originality
- Whimsicality
- Visual impact
- Topical associations or links

3.2 Association of ideas

Synergy often occurs by lateral thinking, so **associative links** or **common themes** between event and venue not only aid originality but help to draw attention and memory to the event/product/brand. Some venues are naturally themed for synergy with products: museums and art galleries for design/art products, for example, or embassies for products linked with foreign countries. Other associations may be more specific: showing a pure wool fashion range in a shearing shed, say, or promoting an all-star basketball team at the Planetarium.

3.3 Building on relationships

Another form of synergy is in **building relationships** which enlarge the image or audience of both parties. The venue and event organiser may find possibilities for collaboration on joint PR and promotion, to their mutual benefit. A venue may negotiate a special rate in order to gain from the PR potential of a high profile event.

3.4 Building on familiarity

Synergy may come from familiarity. An event for **existing customers**, for example, might justifiably be held at the company's premises or regular entertainment venue, to capitalise on:

- Associations with a history of successful transactions
- The ease and security of familiar surroundings
- The strong projection of corporate image
- The customer's sense of acknowledgement, belonging and involvement
- The customer's habit of making purchases in that environment.

A product or press launch which needed extra impact to attract the media, on the other hand, would require greater originality.

Action Programme 4

Brainstorm, by association of ideas, some possible venues for the following events.

(a) The press launch of a book called 'The Wild West'.

(b) Launch of the new season's designs by an exclusive boutique jeweller to existing high-spending customers.

(c) A party for your sales representatives and outlet contacts to celebrate the outstanding success of your 'G.I. Fred' Action Man toy.

(d) A seminar on 'Doing Business in the Commonwealth', sponsored by your organisation for the business community.

4 Making recommendations

> **FAST FORWARD**
>
> You may be asked informally for your thoughts on venues, or you may be required to research and evaluate a number of options for a formal report or presentation.

Your recommendations should be set out and structured according to whatever instructions you are given. However, a useful general format is as follows.

PART C ORGANISING AND UNDERTAKING MARKETING ACTIVITIES

VENUE SELECTION FOR (EVENT)

Event: (Brief description of the event type and size, intended audience.)

Objectives: (Key aims of the event: media coverage, sales generated, leads generated, business transacted, staff rewarded)

Budgetary constraints: (Total expenditure budget available, if set)

VENUE 1	VENUE 2 (Alternative option, if required)
Venue: (name)	*Venue:*
Location:	*Location:*
Concept: (Venue type/theme associations, possible synergy)	*Concept:*
Capacity:	*Capacity:*
Style: (Image/status/comfort level)	*Style:*
Facilities & Services: (relevant to needs of event)	*Facilities & Services:*
Transport/access:	*Transport/access:*
Key advantages: (relevant to needs of event. Opportunity for synergy)	*Key advantages:*
Disadvantages: (facilities/service lacking and needing to be supplied. Any drawbacks)	*Disadvantages:*
Cost: (Estimates based on event plan/brief)	*Cost:*
Recommendation: (Venue 1 or 2, if required)	

Exam tip

The December 2005 exam allocated 8 marks (and June 2006, 12 marks) for recommending a choice between two possible venues, and justifying your decision. Obviously, for only 8 marks (about 15 minutes), you wouldn't be able to work through this format: remember to be flexible – and to do no more (although certainly no *less*) than the question asks for.

11: VENUE SELECTION

Action Programme 5

The Needle Works

Using the above format, write a report or prepare a presentation evaluating the venue(s) you briefly proposed in Action Programme 5, Chapter 10. (Make up any details you wish or take the opportunity to do some live research, if such a venue exists.) Recommend a venue, if appropriate.

[*Key skill for Marketers: Presenting information*]

This is the basic data required for a well-argued recommendation. If you were giving a presentation, or submitting a formal report, you might include visual aids.

- Photographs of the venue and its facilities
- Maps showing location, access, parking

You might also submit the full information pack and rate card of the recommended venue.

Exam tip

> One of the proposed assessment tasks for *Marketing in Practice* is a *presentation* to be given on *venue selection* for:
>
> - a product launch and/or
> - an event for existing customers.
>
> You might like to practise, or make notes for a variety of such presentations. Research an actual venue and present it as a recommendation to fellow students or to a friend: get feedback on whether you 'sold' your recommendation effectively. Alternatively, give a presentation on 'How to select an event venue': you might want to make this more memorable: try headings such as 'Suitability, Synergy, Size, Status, Style, Site, Service and Safety'! Or ASFAB: Access, Suitability/size, Facilities, Availability, Budget.

Chapter Roundup

- A **venue** is the appointed place for a meeting, concert, sporting fixture or other event. It may be a dedicated entertainment/event venue or a premises which can be adapted to the theme of an event.
- **Suitability of a venue** may be assessed using the acronym 'ASFAB': Access, Size, Facilities, Availability, Budget.
- **Synergy** (2 + 2 = 5) is where the venue itself adds value to the event through:
    - incentive/attraction
    - impact/memorability
    - PR/media value
    - association of ideas to the organisation/product/brand
    - encouraging collaboration
    - building on existing relationships and familiarity
- You may be asked informally for your thoughts on venues, or you may be required to research and evaluate a number of options for a formal report or presentation.

Quick Quiz

1. Where can an event organiser find out about available venues?
2. How is the size or capacity of a venue defined?
3. What does a 'convenient' location involve?
4. Give three examples of special requirements for outdoor venues?
5. Give three examples of qualities of a venue that might attract media interest.
6. Write out a checklist for data in support of a venue recommendation.

Answers to Quick Quiz

1. A list of information sources is given in Paragraph 1.1.
2. Your answer should have included: seating capacity, accommodation capacity, standing capacity, accessibility and limits prescribed by fire and safety regulations.
3. A location must be: accessible for staff/delegates; comfortable for your guests; offer all necessary facilities; convey your message – and fall within the budget constraint.
4. These requirements are primitive: toilets, shelter and safety!
5. Media interest will be aroused by: good photograph opportunities (visual impact); originality (newsworthiness to readers); topical associations or links (ties in with other stories).
6. You should refer to the checklist provided in Paragraph 4.

Action Programme Review

1 This will be a valuable resource for your career as well as for assessment of your competence in this area of the *Marketing in Practice* syllabus!

2 The following are just some suggestions to guide your thinking.

   (a) A McDonalds might be hired out for a kid's party (PR for charitable donation?) or for an informal cheap sales team lunch meeting (especially if the product was American or pop-culture) – or even for a product launch.

   (b) A product launch or preview for older, wealthier customers/clients, or a formal PR seminar/presentation.

   (c) Accommodation for sales/marketing staff at a nearby conference or exhibition or a buyer meeting for a new 'bed and breakfast' guide.

   (d) Launch party for ABC1 market, celebrities, media: fashion or entertainment product.

   (e) Team-building for sales/marketing staff. Inter-corporate challenge (media stunt, charity sponsorship). Press launch for new sports shoes or deodorant?

3

Trade Fair A
- Stand staffing 5%
- Stand design and hire 35%
- Hospitality and literature 45%
- Stand promotion 15%

Trade Fair B
- Stand staffing 10%
- Stand design and hire 20%
- Hospitality and literature 20%
- Stand promotion 50%

4 Again, these are just ideas: don't let us stifle your creativity!

   (a) A wild west theme park, a film set, a rodeo, the bison enclosure at a zoo.

   (b) The jeweller's own premises, the Tower of London (crown jewels), the Fabergé section of the V & A Museum, Covent Garden hospitality room.

   (c) A paint-ball centre or laserdome (good team-building).

   (d) The Commonwealth Centre (in London) or particular country's delegation (eg Australia House) or Tourist Bureau.

5 If you used a live venue, keep this report for your portfolio – it will contain useful information.

Now try Question 11 at the end of the Study Text

Part D
Co-ordinating the marketing mix

Advertising media

Chapter topic list

1. Advertising
2. Media selection
3. Press
4. Radio
5. Television
6. Other media
7. Advertising on the Internet
8. Media scheduling
9. The printing process

Syllabus content

- 4.1 Select media to be used based on appropriate criteria for assessing media opportunities, and recommend a media schedule
- 4.3 Explain the process for designing, developing and producing printed matter, including leaflets, brochures and catalogues

PART D CO-ORDINATING THE MARKETING MIX

Introduction

In this chapter, we look at above-the-line advertising media.

(a) We will start by outlining the general criteria involved in media selection

- Criteria by which the effectiveness and efficiency of media can be evaluated
- How the major media can be compared with each other

(b) We will then look at each of the major media in turn, and at how opportunities to advertise in each can be evaluated.

(c) Finally, we will focus on the scheduling of media: how to plan the frequency, duration/size and number of advertisement for maximum impact.

In Chapter 13, we will look at below-the-line activities, PR and collaborative sales promotion. You should also be able to draw on your studies for the *Marketing Fundamentals* and *Customer Communications* modules.

1 Advertising

FAST FORWARD

Advertising is 'any paid form of *non-personal* presentation and promotion of ideas, goods or services by an *identifiable* sponsor'. (American Marketing Association).

Promotion is generally divided into broad areas.

(a) **Personal** (direct marketing, network marketing and the use of sales representatives)

(b) **Impersonal**, which can be further divided up.

- **'Above-the-line'** methods, such as media advertising
- **'Below-the-line'** promotions or negotiated sales incentives
- **Point of sale**: in-store promotional messages and displays
- **PR and publicity**: 'free' transmission of the promotional message
- **Informational methods**, such as printed catalogues, brochures and leaflets

Key concepts

Above-the-line promotion is advertising placed in paid-for media, such as the press, radio, TV, cinema and outdoor sites. The 'line' is one in an advertising agency's accounts, above which are shown its earnings on a commission basis, from the buying of media space for clients.

Below-the-line promotion involves product-integral and negotiated sales incentives, such as packaging, merchandising, on-pack discounts and competitions and so on. (Agency earnings on a fee basis are shown below the 'line' in their accounts.)

2 Media selection

FAST FORWARD

Media selection should be made in accordance with the organisation's **advertising objectives** on the following criteria.

- The size of the audience/circulation
- The type of audience (in relation to the target audience)
- The opportunity of the audience to use the medium
- The effort required to use the media
- The audience's familiarity with the medium
- The selectivity/segmentation allotted by the medium
- The suitability of the medium's technical characteristics for the message
- The suitability of the medium's perceived function for the message
- The cost-effectiveness of the medium
- The medium's susceptibility to testing and measurement

The general criteria for selecting a medium to convey the promotional message to the appropriate audience are as follows.

- The advertiser's specific **objectives** and plans
- The **size of the audience** which regularly uses the medium
- The **type of people** who form the audience of the medium
- The **suitability** of the medium for the message
- The **cost** of the medium in relation to its ability to fulfil the advertiser's objectives
- The susceptibility of the medium to **testing and measurement**

The planning of an advertising campaign includes:

(a) The identification of the **target audience**: Who are they? Where are they? Which demographic group do they fall in? What are their interests, media consumption habits, buying patterns, attitudes and values?

(b) The specification of the **communication** or promotional message: What do you need to say, and in what way, in order to impact on the audience in such a way as to achieve your marketing goals?

(c) The setting of **targets**: What is the marketing goal to which the advertising can contribute? What do you expect the ad to achieve and at what cost? What aspects of the audience's thinking or behaviour do you wish to change, and how will you recognise and measure that change if and when it occurs?

2.1 The size and type of the audience

Each medium reaches a certain number and 'type' (demographic group, market segment, interest group) of people. There is a trade-off between the size and relevance of the available audience.

(a) General-interest, national mass-market medium (such as a national newspaper or television) will have the largest **circulation figures**, but may not reach the highest percentage of a particular market segment.

(b) **Segmentation** may be possible through the scheduling and placing of ads in large-scale media (for example, in special-interest sections or supplements in the press, or by programme preference in TV).

(c) **Targeted media** may reach a smaller population, but a higher percentage of the target audience.

- **Local or regional media** (in the catchment area)
- **Specialist magazines** and journals related to the target audience
- Media which fit the **'media habits'** of the target audience

PART D CO-ORDINATING THE MARKETING MIX

Action Programme 1

Brainstorm a list of media which might be suitably targeted (by factors in the media themselves, or in the media habits of the target audiences) for advertising the following products/services.

(a) A local garage offering car service, maintenance and parts
(b) An up-market restaurant
(c) A software package for use by accountants (based on UK law and regulation)
(d) A new brand of washing powder
(e) A microchip for use in engineering applications

2.1.1 Influences on the effective audience

Hearne (1987) suggests that the effective audience of a medium and therefore the competitiveness of different media is influenced by the following factors.

(a) **Opportunity to use the medium**. The potential audience will not be able to use TV during working hours, or magazines while driving, or cinema over breakfast. Radio in the morning and TV in the evening have bigger effective audiences.

(b) **Effort required to use the medium**. People usually use the medium that will cost them least effort. Print media require the ability to read and concentrate: television is comparatively effortless.

(c) **Familiarity with the medium**. People consume media with which they are familiar: hence the survival of print media, since the education system is still predominantly print-orientated. Electronic media are, however, gaining ground.

(d) **Segmentation by the medium**. The print media currently has the greatest capacity for segmentation into special-interest audiences. Commercial television segments to a limited extent through programming, and cable/satellite television to a greater extent, through the proliferation of channels. Some media only charge in proportion to the segment you are targeting, which is more cost effective than paying for the full circulation.

Action Programme 2

What opportunity, effort and familiarity issues might you consider when appraising the following media?

(a) A newly launched radio station
(b) Daytime television
(c) Posters on buses
(d) Web pages

In addition, you should be aware that major issues are emerging for conventional media arising from factors such as:

(a) **Digital video recorders**, which allow viewers to electronically fast forward through ads when recording TV programmes

(b) Changing media consumption habits. Teenagers have been found, for example, to **multi-task** while consuming media: listening to an i-Pod while reading a magazine and watching TV, say! The media is said to be increasingly **fragmented**.

2.1.2 Media research

> **Media research** is designed to provide data on circulated audience reach and media habits.

Media research is designed to provide advertisers with detailed information on the size and composition of the audience for relevant media and the reading and viewing habits of the different types of people and so on. Media planners (the people in advertising agencies who plan how to deploy the main-media advertising budget) use as much reliable research data as they can obtain. Here are some examples.

(a) The National Readership Survey or JICNARS (Joint Industry Committee for National Readership Surveys) for major newspapers and magazines

(b) BARB (the Broadcasting Audience Research Bureau Ltd) for television

(c) RAJAR (Radio Joint Audience Research) for radio

(d) JICPAS (Joint Industry Committee for Poster Advertising Surveys) for posters

A marketing organisation may also wish to commission or carry out its own research into the media habits of its customers and potential customers.

2.2 The suitability of the medium for the message

Certain media 'do' certain things better than others. You might need to bear this in mind:

(a) **The technical characteristics of the medium**. The success of a medium depends on its ability to identify and offer the benefits which its technical characteristics are best suited to provide: television for images and demonstrations; cinema for fantasy, visual impact; radio for music and participation; print for detailed information.

(b) **The perceived function of the medium**. Media users look to different media to perform different functions in their lives: information/education (world news, local events, specialist instruction) or entertainment (music, sport, escapism, community contact). These perceptions of a medium's functions and strengths will influence the orientation of its audience towards advertising messages.

(c) **The impact/realism of the medium**. One of the strengths of television is the impact to be derived from its realistic merging of sight and sound.

2.3 Cost and value for money

> **Cost comparisons** are usually made on the basis of 'cost per thousand' (people reached, or impacts).

Cost in itself is not a helpful criterion (unless it rules out a medium by virtue of its exceeding the spending budget). What advertisers need to know, in order to compare and evaluate media meaningfully, is the following.

- How many relevant people are reached?
- How many times and how effectively?
- For how much?

The conventional criteria of value for money measurement is: **cost per thousand people reached** by a medium. If an advertisement in a newspaper with a circulation of 2 million readers costs £7,000, the cost per thousand is £3.50.

'Cost per thousand' is a common **inter-media comparison**-measuring device. However, it is only a crude measure, which does not take everything into account.

(a) The **targeting or relevance** of the audience reached by different media (or in different issues or time slots)

(b) The **potential impact** of an advertisement in different media (its size or length, colour or black and white, positioning in the publication or programme schedule, proximity to competing ads)

(c) **Extended or repeated exposure** to the ad (if people use the medium frequently, or pass it on to friends)

(d) **Selective exposure** to the ad (for example, people may not read the whole paper or magazine, or may leave the room during TV commercials)

The different media have their own methods of allowing for these factors when promoting their effectiveness to advertisers, and we will look at some of them – such as television ratings – later in this chapter.

Action Programme 3

What is the cost per thousand of the following media, and what other factors would you take into account when comparing them?

(a) The Morning Post (local newspaper): circulation 20,000. Cost per column centimetre: £4.00 and you want a 5c.c. classified ad.

(b) The Weekly (a national trade magazine) circulation 900,000. Cost per colour page (only size available): £2,000 (rate card).

(c) Radio Fab: reaches 30% of its catchment area of 210,000 adults. Minimum package of 20 15-second ads costs £700.

[*Key skill for Marketers: Using financial information and metrics*]

2.4 Susceptibility to testing and measurement

Testing or measuring the effectiveness of advertisements is the only sure way to know what 'works' in terms of gaining a response. The same ad run in different media can demonstrate the comparative effectiveness of the media, while different ads (size, position, timing, layout, response methods, headlines) in the same media can indicate the most effective form of the promotional message.

Some media are better for testing ads than others and if this is important to you, you will need to ask yourself the following questions.

(a) How **quickly** do I want our tests to yield results? (A daily publication produces response more quickly than a weekly.)

(b) How **effectively** does the medium allow me to elicit direct responses? (Will it carry a direct-response coupon, or memorable telephone number?)

(c) Will I be able to **attribute** increased enquiries/sales to their source in a particular ad? (Coded coupons or web hit tracking, for example).

Exam tip

> There are a variety of advertisement-focused questions in the examiner's repertoire. Questions include:
>
> - The costing of alternative advertising media/strategies (using data given) to justify a choice (December 2002)
> - Producing guidelines for colleagues on 'how to select advertising media' (December 2002)
> - Producing briefing notes for radio adspace salespeople, on the advantages and disadvantages of radio advertising compared to newspapers, TV and outdoor media (June 2003)
> - Producing a media plan, showing how you could spend a given budget over a given period to best effect, justifying your decisions (December 2003)
> - Producing a media plan for local area advertising of a railway (using data given) and then recommending media that could be used to extend the campaign nationally (June 2005)
> - Describing the advantages and disadvantages (for a particular campaign) of TV, radio, cinemas, magazines and other specified media (December 2005)
> - Preparing and justifying a media plan for a special event, and suggesting how its success could be evaluated (December 2006)
>
> This is a core topic: get to grips with the basics – and practise applying/testing them in a variety of contexts.

2.5 A general comparison of major media

The following are some of the ways in which you might usefully evaluate advertising media.

Medium	Advantages	Disadvantages
Newspapers (daily metropolitan / national)	<ul><li>'Mass' medium: large audience in single exposure</li><li>Targeted sections (auto, home, computers etc)</li><li>Reader navigation: seeking news, information</li><li>Short lead time for production: accept ads 24-48 hours before publication</li><li>Flexibility of ad size</li><li>Tangibility of ad (can be torn out and kept)</li><li>Multiple readers/users</li><li>Allows detailed information (prices, phone numbers etc)</li><li>Allows (still) images</li><li>Allows response mechanisms (eg captions)</li></ul>	<ul><li>Circulation does not mean readership: wasted circulation paid for</li><li>Print/image reproduction of variable quality</li><li>No exclusivity: ad may be next to competitor's</li><li>Costs loaded for preferred positions</li><li>Short life-span of news</li></ul>
Newspapers (local/free)	<ul><li>Low cost</li><li>Geographical targeting</li><li>High local readership</li><li>Special sections (especially local real estate, entertainment etc)</li></ul>	<ul><li>Circulation of free papers/weeklies not always monitored/audited</li><li>Variable editorial content</li><li>Subject to weather and junk mail rejection if letterbox dropped</li></ul>

Medium	Advantages	Disadvantages
Magazines	- High circulation (major titles) - Targeted audiences (special) - High quality reproduction (colour photography etc) - Potential high prestige - Reader motivation (selection, subscription) - Long shelf life and multiple use/readership - Tangibility, detail, images, response mechanisms (see newspapers)	- High costs of production - Hyper-segmentation (by interest and geography, may be insufficient circulation to support local outlets) - Long lead times: copy/artwork required 1 – 3 months before publication, can be inflexible
Television	- 'Mass' medium: large audience at single exposure, almost universal ownership/access - Detailed monitoring of exposure, reach, viewer habits - Allows for high degree of creativity - Realism: impact of sound + sight + movement - High-impact visual images reinforce retention - Allows demonstration - Flexibility as to scheduling - Allows association with desirable products	- Most expensive of all media costs - High production costs - Lack of selectivity (except via programming) of audience - Lack of opportunity: does not reach commuters/workers - Long lead times for booking and production: penalties for withdrawal: inflexibility - Passive, unmotivated audience: 'zapping' by video fast-forward and remote controls erodes reach
Radio	- 'Mass' medium: wide coverage/access - Audience selectivity (local/regional) programme style/variety/content) - Opportunity: radio is portable – in-home, in-car, on public transport, shops, offices – even jogging - Function: high usage for morning news, home 'companionship', background - Personal (and potential for participation) - Highly competitive costs of air time and production - Can be backed by personal DJ promos	- May be passive 'background' noise: low attention, retention - May be 'cluttered' by announcers/DJ promotions - Sound only: no tangibility (pressure on retention of message), no shelf-life or 'pass on' circulation, no demonstration, no coupons, limited details

Medium	Advantages	Disadvantages
Outdoor media (poster sites bus stops, buildings etc)	• Flexible: sites, duration of lease • Comparatively low cost • Opportunity: exposure to commuters, shoppers	• Difficulty of verification of exposure/response • Subject to weather • Opportunity: site specific • No audience selectivity (except by site)
Cinema	• Glamorous • High impact (large size, highly visual, loud sound, high quality) • Captive audience (no TV 'zap' factor) • Can segment by local area	• High cost • Opportunity: site/time specific • Poor verification of response • Limited number of people reached per exposure
Internet	• Principally sight, but with sound and colour further possibilities are developing • Interactive, permitting direct response • Able to track audience movements • Message permanent, and can be downloaded	• Generally poor viewership • Consumer confidence in security low (but improving) • Possible to direct audience to information, but can be difficult to gain large audience without support from other media • Not yet a mainstream media with broad customer appeal • Speed of access depends on sophistication of technological link • No universal computing language yet agreed

3 Press

FAST FORWARD

Press or print media include:

- **Newspapers**: daily and weekly, morning and evening, national and regional
- **Magazines**, periodicals and journals; general appeal, special interest and trade

3.1 Circulation and readership figures

The **Audit Bureau of Circulation (ABC)** provides audited figures of the actual circulation of major newspapers and magazines. This figure is often the basis of advertising rates. It offers only partial information.

(a) There may be many **more readers than purchasers**. People may pass a publication on to others to read, or it may be perused by many people in dentists' waiting rooms or hairdressers. It is the estimated **readership** that interests the advertiser. The **Readership Survey** publishes the average readership per issue.

(b) Readership data is also available on what **types of reader** consume various publications, with what frequency and in what manner (all the way through or some sections only).

3.2 Types of press ads

> **FAST FORWARD**
>
> Print media offer classified, semi-display, display, advertorial and loose-insert advertising options.

Print media offer different types of advertising.

(a) **Classified advertising**. The classified sections of publications offer small spaces for text-only ads. The advantage is that classified space is very cheap, and the publication usually typesets the ad for you. The disadvantage is the difficulty of attracting attention with so much competition and so little space: icons, headline, styles and impactful/incentive copy are required to make an ad stand out.

(b) **Semi-display advertising** allows you to use borders, typographic features and illustrations to attract attention (although on a crowded page, white space and simplicity may be more effective). Small ads in the Yellow Pages are a good example.

(c) **Display advertising** offers further opportunity for creativity: the advertisers design and provide their own artwork or film, constrained only by the technical specifications (size, colour) of the publication. Full-colour magazine ads are a good example. 'Long copy' advertisements break the usual simple visual style of display advertising by including lots of detailed information.

(d) **Advertorials** are advertisements presented as edited copy, in order to take advantage of the perceivably objective authority of editorial matter. Features on health and beauty, advice, house and garden are often advertisements for the products and services 'reviewed' or 'recommended'.

(e) **Loose inserts or 'drop outs'** are printed leaflets (produced by the advertiser) inserted into magazines and newspapers. They usually work out 4 or 5 times more expensive than advertising space – but draw up to 5 or 6 times as many responses as a full-page advertisement.

Marketing at Work

Car manufacturers often use **long copy display** ads for their cars. Full-page advertisements include detailed technical specifications and engineering drawings of the cars' driving and safety features. Such extensive copy is often effective for very expensive products, because it provides sufficient information to support an expensive purchase decision – and to justify or rationalise the purchase as a 'good' decision, not merely based on desire or snobbery.

Contrast this with purely visual display ads – often with no copy at all.

3.3 Press ad rates

Print media is bought in **column inches** (or centimetres) or standard **page divisions** (quarter, half or full page, or 'junior' page). The cost/rate differs.

- The **size** of the ad
- The number of **colours** in the ad and the production quality of the publication
- **Position** of the ad for which a premium may be charged
- The **readership** number of the publication
- The **potential for readership** targeting or niche marketing
- The **prestige** of the publication and the spending power of its readership.

3.4 Positioning press ads

Media research into **'traffic per page'** (the reading and noting of different pages in a print publication) suggests the following.

- **Early pages** are read more than late pages (depending on editorial content)
- **Right-hand pages** have higher noting scores than left-hand pages
- **Pages opposite relevant or popular editorial content** do better than pages opposite other advertising and less read editorial content.

Cover space is particularly sought after because of its high visibility, and usually also because the covers are printed on better quality paper for colour production. The outside front cover is likely to be most expensive, followed by outside back, inside front (especially if opposite the contents page) and inside back.

3.5 Scheduling of press ads

> **FAST FORWARD**
>
> **Scheduling** is a combination of **reach or exposure** (how many of the right type of people see the ad) and **frequency** (how many times people see the ad).

With press advertising, an ad may need to be repeated:

(a) if the ad is **small** (and may not be noticed by all readers at one exposure)
(b) if the publication is **high circulation** (so the ad may not be noticed by all readers)
(c) if the product or ad is **interesting** (and will therefore continue to attract attention).

Even so, the **law of diminishing returns** operates with repeated exposure: Figure 12.1. As the ad reaches a higher proportion of the relevant audience, more often, the rate of response levels off. **Awareness** of the company or offer increases with repetition, but the **rate of direct response** to individual ads (via coupon or response line) falls: the 'easiest' prospects have already been reached.

(*Source:* The Institute of Direct Marketing, cited in Jay, 1998)

Figure 12.1: The law of diminishing returns

The best **time** to place an ad depends on many factors: seasonal selling cycles (summer/winter, Christmas), relevant editorial content (special features or supplements), and even different days of the week and times of day (encouraging working hours, evening or weekend purchases).

PART D CO-ORDINATING THE MARKETING MIX

4 Radio

> **FAST FORWARD**
>
> The perceived function and image of **radio** is an important factor in the response to radio advertising.

Radio is a personal and 'intimate' medium which encourages relationship and trust: according to the Radio Advertising Bureau (www.rab.co.uk), people are more likely to believe what they hear on radio than what they see on television. Local radio has a particularly close 'community' image. National radio stations are aimed more at a particular type of listener.

Radio tends to form the **background** to other activities. This enables it to have a wide reach (since it can be listened to while driving, working, jogging), but also lessens listeners' attention to and retention of advertising messages. The lack of visual images is also a disadvantage, but can be overcome by different techniques: the use of dialogue, mood, drama, humour and curiosity.

Radio ads are usually bought in series of 15 second or 30 second '**slots**'. Because of the high 'portability' of radio, there may be a wider range of off-peak scheduling opportunities.

Exam tip

> A radio station was itself the subject of the June 2003 paper: it's worth remembering that promotional media also have to promote themselves! The scenario also raised interesting questions about whether other media are 'competitors' – or promotional avenues and potential collaborators. You were asked to consider how the radio station and local newspapers could 'work together' and run 'joint promotions'.
>
> Get used to 'crossing areas of the syllabus'. While you're thinking about how ICT is used in promotion, think how an ICT company might promote itself. And so on …

4.1 Listenership figures

RAJAR (Radio Joint Audience Research Ltd) release quarterly reports showing what percentage/volume of the population listens to commercial radio, at what times and for how long, with breakdowns for each radio station. Around 25% of the UK population listens to national commercial radio, and 50% to local commercial radio, in the course of a week, for an average 15 hours per week. Over 70% of 15 – 34 year olds listen to commercial radio and almost the same proportion of business people and housewives with children.

Although such figures do not indicate whether people hear or take in any ads that may air during their listening hours, there are several positive indicators that radio can perform well in this respect.

- **Prompted recall of radio ads** is 80% of that of TV ads.
- Radio listeners report that they **do not generally switch stations** when ads come on.
- An average-weight campaign on radio will reach each consumer **four times a week**.
- **Talk-back radio** has a high response rate, even late at night.

5 Television

> **FAST FORWARD**
>
> Because of the high exposure, glamour and audio-visual impact of **television**, it has become the favoured medium for launching new products, raising brand awareness and building brand loyalty.

The **Independent Broadcasting Authority (IBA)** controls commercial TV (and radio) in the UK, and licenses a number of regional companies.

Because of the **high exposure**, **glamour** and **audio-visual impact** of television, it has become the favoured medium for launching new products, raising brand awareness and building brand loyalty, re-positioning brands and also motivating the employees and supply chain partners of the advertising organisation. (This perception is encouraged by advertising agencies, whose **commission** on TV airtime is many times higher than on print space and other media.)

A major recent trend is in the development of **direct response TV advertising**, in which the viewer is given a telephone number and invited to call for more information or to place an order. This used to be perceived as down-market and American, but research now shows that it promotes an image of the organisation as organised, financially sound and willing to be readily accessible to customers. Direct response advertising has also enabled detailed measurement of the effectiveness of ads on different stations, at different times, in different formats.

5.1 Viewership figures

As with radio, it is a complex matter to access not just how many sets are owned and switched on at particular times, but how many people are actually watching – let alone consciously taking in what is being transmitted.

The size of the television audience for a given programme (and advertising) is measured in **ratings**: rating points, or **TVRs**. One TVR point represents 1% of all homes which have a TV set in the region to which the programme is broadcast. Ratings are used by TV stations to monitor the popularity of their programmes, and to set advertising rates. The advertiser pays for the number of TVRs allocated to given advertising spots.

(a) A programme with 20 TVRs is seen by 20% of homes with a TV. This is the number of people who will (in theory) see an ad once.

(b) If you placed an ad in four programmes, each with a rating of 20 TVRs, you would achieve 80 TVRs. However, some homes might have seen the ad all four times, while others may have missed it altogether. You need to distinguish between reach and **frequency** (the number of times the ad is run, and therefore the number of **opportunities to see** it, or OTS).

(c) **Gross Rating Points (GRPs)** are a measure of probable **reach** multiplied by probable **frequency**. If you buy 280 GRPs, about 70% of households should have four opportunities to see your ad.

(d) **Target Audience Rating Points (TARPs)** measure reach and frequency against specific demographic audiences, across a wide range of criteria (geographic, gender, age, socio-economic bracket). These are the most effective guide for advertisers, since they allow the media planner to devise a schedule which will deliver the largest relevant audience for the available budget: the gross cumulative exposure of the campaign to the target audience can be assessed on the standard cost-per-thousand basis.

> **Key concepts**
>
> **Reach** refers to the size of the audience which is exposed to an ad, both net (number of people reached) and gross (including cumulative multiple exposures)
>
> **Frequency** refers to the number of times an ad is run, opportunities to see (OTS) the ad; or 'impacts'
>
> **Ratings** are measurements of television audiences, which multiply reach by frequency (or OTS) to give the probable coverage and repetition of an ad, with (TARPS) or without (GRPs) breakdown by demographic criteria.

The lowest cost per thousand is not necessarily the best schedule. One recommendation is the purchase of at least 250 – 300 TVRs, giving 70% coverage and a minimum of 4 OTS, in order to make a TV campaign worthwhile.

Statistically valid and helpful for comparison as ratings are, they still give only limited information: they count 'pairs of eyes', not responsiveness to ads. Detailed **qualitative media research** is required to indicate people's media habits.

- **Leaving the room** during commercial breaks
- Using the **remote control** to change channel to avoid ads
- **Videoing** TV programmes and fast-forwarding through commercial breaks (particularly using digital recording devices)

Further testing will be required to gauge **awareness and recall** of specific ads.

Marketing at Work

The concept of **retail media** is based on the idea that supermarkets and shopping centres offer advertisers a captive audience at a time when it is especially receptive to sales messages.

This has already triggered the advent of supermarket media such as car-park posters, trolleys with panel ads and ads printed on the back of receipts.

It is now being recognised that **shopping centres** are effectively a major media channel in their own right.

- Street furniture (including shopping centre furniture) has become a major category in 'outdoor' advertising.

- 'Experimental' advertising and promotion is a major growth sector, turning in-centre advertising from one-way messaging to two-way 'brand experiences'. 'Its about creating **branded experiences** which people *choose* to engage with; that little bit of magic which can brighten up the shopping experience. Once engaged, it's then possible to establish a dialogue, exchange information – which includes sampling.' Examples of experimental promotion include: a cooking demonstration/show by Electrolux kitchenware; a lounge kiosk for vodafone; and a Galatic Handball competition for Colorado lynx.

- Shopping centres support media buyers in matching promotions to demographics, supplying shopper segment and 'traffic' (store visits, browsing habits etc) information.

Why the hype? 'The answer lies somewhere between media fragmentation, advertisers' desire to get closer to the cash register, the fact that audiences are already in a shopping mindset, and massive footfall.'

(*Ad News*, 19 May 2006)

5.2 Scheduling TV ads

In addition to TARPs, which suggest where and when to schedule ads in order to reach an optimum number of target viewers an optimum number of times, the advertiser should consider the following.

(a) **Daytime audiences** are more responsive. Direct responses to TV ads are greatest between 12 noon – 2pm and 2pm – 4pm on weekdays.

(b) Audiences show greater recall of ads at the **beginning** of a long commercial break. The more ads they see, the lower the recall of each.

(c) Audiences tend to watch through commercial breaks in the **middle of TV programmes**, because they do not want to miss any of the programme. However, viewers are reluctant to take action in response to ads during the programme, so direct-response ads are more successful during **end breaks** (Most people respond within 15 minutes of the ad spot.)

(d) While most advertisers use 30-second ads, **90-second** or even two minute ads can be more effective (as with long-copy press ads) especially for complex or expensive products.

(e) Very short (**10 second**) ads can also be effective, and offer much higher TARPs for the available budget, since you can get more exposures. However, the greater impact of longer commercials usually offsets the reduced TARPs which longer ads deliver.

(f) Repetition of ads increases TARPs, but is subject to the law of **diminishing returns**. It is essential for the message to sink in, but people easily become habitual and cease to notice or be motivated by the ad. One strategy is to have a **set of related ads** which can be rotated, reinforcing but varying the message.

Action Programme 4

All other things being equal, and subject to detailed research, at what time of day, or in what kind of programme, might you advertise the following products on TV?

- Shoe polish
- Home disinfectant
- Car repairs
- Chat/introduction lines

6 Other media

6.1 Outdoor media

> **FAST FORWARD**
>
> **Poster advertising** is one of the oldest media for consumer goods advertising. Size and visibility of the sites are the main consideration.

Poster sites on walls, hoardings and bus shelters can be leased for a fee per calendar month. In addition, many vehicles (buses, trucks and taxis) now carry external advertising, and some are tailor-made to do so (advertising 'floats'). Trains and buses also offer internal advertising positions. Size and visibility of the sites are the main consideration.

Marketing at Work

Transit media in South Africa

It is predicted that turnover in the outdoor advertising industry could rise to R1-billion in five years.

Outdoor advertising currently claims 4.28% of the total adspend in SA annually, compared with adspend of 5% to 11% in developed countries.

The areas of transit media, including trains, taxis, buses and moving billboards on trailers, have a 16.34% share of the outdoor advertising expenditure.

As the economy develops and more people are absorbed into the workforce, so the numbers of commuters – the transit media audience – increase. ...

With 80% of the population dependant on public transport and much of the country's rural areas without electricity, transit and alternative media are taking advertising to a much broader demographic market. ...

SA is one of the first countries in the world to have developed transit media and the country is leading its growth.

Worldwide, the outdoor advertising industry is worth about R80-billion.

Bridge (2004)

For Polish speakers, another interesting site, showing examples of outdoor media in Poland is: www.mediadoran.pl.

6.2 Cinema

> **FAST FORWARD**
>
> **Cinema advertising** takes advantage of high audio-visual impact and a captive audience but still requires a high quality and entertainment value.

Cinema advertising best suits 'lifestyle' products.

- **Branded consumer goods** with high style and profile, aimed mainly at young adults (such as jeans and alcohol)
- **Local services** in the area of the cinema (particularly restaurants)

6.3 New media

> **FAST FORWARD**
>
> A wide range of **electronic and non-traditional media** (including CD-ROM, text messaging and the Internet) is now used, particularly to access the youth market.

Technology has widened the range of advertising media to include the following.

(a) **Videos** including informational instructional videos and advertising accompanying entertainment videos

(b) **Teletext** (usually via sponsoring of relevant types of information which the target audience might access)

(c) **Enhanced CD and CD-ROM** (especially for selling merchandise related to the information or entertainment contained on the CD)

(d) **Websites**. Internet shopping and other transactions are on the increase. Websites with product/service information and related links vary in sophistication, but can provide an attractive **audio-visual and interactive** experience of promotional messages. In addition, they offer an opportunity for customers to access basic information which they might be reluctant to ask about over the phone.

(e) **Web advertising**, such as banner and pop-up ads, which contain a simple message designed to make users click on the link to the advertiser's website.

(f) **SMS advertising**, using mobile phone text message (a huge growth area in youth marketing)

(g) **Computer accessories** as advertising media: mouse pads, screen savers, mobile phone ring tones and so on.

Marketing at Work

Orion Books in the UK became the first publisher to use video advertising on ATM cash machines. Orion ran 10-second film adverts to promote *Promise Me*, by Harlan Coben, on 28 London-based ATM machines in May 2007.

7 Advertising on the Internet

FAST FORWARD

The **Internet** has become a medium for carrying advertising in its own right.

The same principles that we have already discussed in this chapter, centred around **matching medium to audience**, still apply. Companies need to be sure that the web provides the right environment and audience profile to meet marketing objectives.

Marketing at Work

Online advertisements are becoming ever more attention seeking. Animation, video and audio are moving the field beyond the normal banner advert. A company called *Eyeblaster.com* has facilitated the development of brash and noisy online advertising. The new formats are giving scope for greater creativity.

Newspapers, which invested heavily in putting their content online, are at the forefront of experimenting with the new formats to attract advertising revenue to their sites.

The use of interactive banner adverts is also increasing, adding value to the advertisement by providing services such as:

- Entering a destination to show the cheapest fare
- Filling in an e-mail address to receive further information

7.1 Links to a corporate site

The most common form of web advertising occurs when the advertiser uses a range of sites to drive visitors to a corporate site.

Portal (eg Yahoo!) → *Corporate Website*
General news service (eg Sunday Times) → *Corporate Website*
Special interest site (eg lifestyle magazine) → *Corporate Website*

Source: www.marketing-online.co.uk

Companies are still learning what works with web advertising, and what does not. There are two basic types of promotion associated with the Internet.

PART D CO-ORDINATING THE MARKETING MIX

(a) **Online promotion** uses communication via the Internet itself to raise awareness. This may take the form of links from other sites, targeted e-mail messages or banner advertisements.

(b) **Offline promotion** uses traditional media such as TV or newspaper advertising to promote a website address (URL).

Exam tip

> You were expected to know this distinction between on-and off-line promotion of a website, in the December 2005 exam.

7.2 Banner advertising

FAST FORWARD

> **Banner advertising** is a common form of on-line promotion, used to drive traffic to a corporate site.

Key concept

> A **banner advertisement** is 'a typically rectangular graphic displayed on a web page for purposes of brand-building or driving traffic to a site. It is normally possible to perform a click through to access further information from another website. Banners may be static or animated'. Banner adverts can be targeted at a particular audience.
>
> *Source: www.Marketing-online.co.uk*

Here are some examples of banner advertisements.

Action Programme 5

Imagine that you are investigating the likely revenues from advertising on a website you are helping to set up. Why would you expect an organisation to want to pay for banner advertising on your web page?

Marketing at Work

In virtually every category, particularly high-consideration products and services, more and more customers are going online to perform critical tasks and meet their needs throughout the sales cycle. ...

Most online advertising is fundamentally flawed, and arguably getting worse. The most basic examples are the countless message-based banners bombarding customers across the Internet. The worst culprits are the pop-ups and -unders that have proliferated in recent years. Let's not even mention spam. What's the solution? People read magazines and watch TV. They use the Internet. Create something they can use.

Where do you start? **Think about why your customers are going online**. What can you provide that helps them to get things done? What would help meet their specific needs (emotional, functional and so on) and enable them to move forward in the sales cycle? Whatever it is, provide that information – or better yet utility – within the advertising itself. Make it so good your customers seek to interact with your advertising because they can get things done.

Once you've created advertising that your customers can actually use, make sure to deploy it where they actually need it on the Internet. Find those contextual spots, whether a search engine or a highly relevant media property, where customers want to pull information, content and functionality from your brand. More importantly, execute all of this in a manner that invites rather than invades.

(Johnson, 2004)

Banner advertising can generally be placed through a traditional agency. It is typically paid for according to the number of users who view the web page. Cost is calculated as **cost per thousand ad impressions**.

7.3 Other online advertising methods

> **FAST FORWARD**
>
> Increasingly sophisticated methods are being used to target the vast Internet audience, using search-engine listings, pay-per-click advertising and e-mail marketing.

These include:

(a) **Promotion in search engines and directories** (such as Yahoo). Your company may want to have its company website listed when a user types in a specific keyword, such as 'office equipment'. To achieve this, your website should be registered with each of the main search engines (Yahoo, MSN, Infoseek, Netscape, Excite, Google, for example). Search-engine placement is a major issue in on-line promotion.

(b) **Links from other sites**. This involves making sure that your site is linked to as many related sites as possible. There is a major new trend towards 'pay-per-click' advertising, where the advertiser only pays the host when a user clicks on the link.

(c) **Using e-mail** for advertising new products directly to customers (on a permission-marketing basis).

8 Media scheduling

> **FAST FORWARD**
>
> **Media scheduling** requires a mix of:
> - reach
> - repeat exposure, or frequency, and
> - cost-effectiveness, in relation to
> - specific media objectives.

Having taken the decision on which media to use, they need to be scheduled so that they are used at the right time. We have already discussed most of the issues in media scheduling as we described each of the major media.

To summarise, an **efficient media schedule**

- Balances maximum **reach** and maximum **repeat exposure**
- To the most **specific target audience**
- At the lowest, or budgeted **cost per thousand**
- In accordance with specific **media objectives**

Media software packages have been compiled by media buyers and agencies, which contain detailed readership/audience breakdowns by demographic group of each programme on each channel and each supplement of each newspaper.

The mix of **reach and repetition** within time and budget parameters is infinitely variable. It may be concentrated over a short period of time or in peaks and troughs, or evenly spread over a long period. It may be spread over multiple media, to capture wide coverage, or a limited number of targeted media, to secure maximum repeat exposure.

With adequate research data, the schedule should be supported by an estimate of **reach and frequency**: the number and type of people who will have the opportunity to see each advertisement booked on the schedule, and how many times.

A simple format for a media schedule might be as follows.

Proposed Advertising Campaign

1 Media Rationale

Product/service:

Budget: £_____ (approx)   *[if known]*

Target Audience: *[target demographic/ geographical groups]*

Timing of campaign: *[period during which advertising will run]*

Objectives/Special instructions: *[direct response mechanisms, if any; support measures, such as manned response lines; target responses/results]*

Media selection: *[Media selected, + reasons/criteria: circulation, targeting, timings available, costs]*

2 Advertising Schedule

Media details and placement	Day	Week commencing:							Total	@ rate	Cost
Month		(m)				(m)					
Date		(d)	(d)	(d)	(d)	(d)	(d)	(d)			
[Publication 1]											
[eg] 30 x 5cm – front half	Tue			1					150	15.00	2,250
+ 10% loading									%	10	225
[Publication 2]											
30 x 5cm – page 7	Thu	1				1			300	16.35	4,905
+ £4 right loading										4.00	1,200

Media details and placement	Day	Week commencing:								Total	@ rate	Cost
Month		(m)				(m)						
Date		(d)	(d)	(d)	(d)	(d)	(d)	(d)	(d)			
[Radio Station 1]												
30 sec 30 x 30 sec												
Mon-Fri 8-9.30pm	Wk/c	1				1				2	1,500	3,000
[Radio Station 2]												
30 sec 15 x 30 sec												
Mon-Fri 8-9.30pm	Wk/c		1				1			2	1,000	2,000
[TV Station]												
30 sec 4-6pm	Sun		2	2		2				6	800	4,800
30 sec 7.30-8.30pm	Sun		1	1						2	1,400	2,800
30 sec 5.30-6.00pm	M-F				1					1	1,500	1,500

3 **Summary of Costs**

Press: £

Radio: £

Television – Time: £

Monitors: £

Total: £

Exam tip

You may be given basic circulation and rate card details for a number of newspapers (morning, evening, daily, weekly and free) and radio stations (new and established), plus creative estimates for artwork production, and asked to prepare an outline media schedule, including costs, to support a new service launch. You may also have to use the information on the availability of media opportunities and costs to appraise the viability of the launch in different regions.

The examiner noted in his report to the December 2003 paper that 'prepare a media schedule' often crops up 'in some guise or other' – and it came up in both June and December 2004, in June 2005 and in December 2006. Be prepared! And be prepared to justify any schedule you propose, in terms of timing, reach, impact and so on of the media chosen.

In December 2003, you were asked to allocate a small budget of £2,000, and in June 2005, £5,000 (specifically for *local* area advertising). A selection of media costings was given to help you. The examiner noted that students *assumed* they should use all the options given – thereby spreading the budget very thinly. The information given in a scenario is intended to guide you in making evaluations and choices: use it to 'weed out' unsuitable options, or to focus your time/budget on areas of maximum impact. Don't assume that every option presented to you in the scenario 'must be' a good one! (In June 2004, for example, you were asked to advertise a night club: the examiner considered Sunday morning media a poor choice as it would be too late for the Saturday night peak time.)

9 The printing process

> **FAST FORWARD**
>
> Key processes in **managing printing tasks** include: formulating job specifications; gathering price quotations; and checking pre-press and sample proofs.

9.1 How much do you need to know?

Printing is highly technical and involves a great many variables and decisions. Fortunately, **buying print related services** does not require a full and detailed grasp of all the process and machinery involved, nor even all the terminology.

- You must have a clear and specific idea of what you want to achieve and at what cost
- You should establish a good working relationship with a printer
- You should get a range of price quotations based on job specifications
- You need to formulate a clear and specific contract with the selected printer

In practice, you may be dealing with a marketing services agency which will handle the print management of a job for you. You may have a creative department in your own organisation, which will be able to supply you with the necessary technical specifications, and will already have embedded most of them in the artwork, film or discs which the printer will use.

If you are dealing direct with printers, you will often find yourself dealing with a sales representative, who may be little more technically expert than you are at the early stage of your print management career.

Printers are often delighted to educate their clients: it makes their job easier too.

(a) Most printers are happy to give **samples** of different weights and styles of paper. Some have comprehensive sample packs including different folds and finishes. You can also ask for a mock-up (using blank pages) of the format and size of booklet, catalogue or leaflet you are considering, so you can check total weight.

(b) Printers supply a **range of information** about their services and the machinery they use. Some have prepared simple guides to print processes and terminology.

(c) Most printers are happy to give a **guided tour** of their facilities.

In addition, there are manuals and short courses on print management, price guides (useful reference tool) and other sources of reference information.

Exam tip

> Much of this syllabus area would be difficult to assess via examination or case study without a large amount of data being provided: it is more likely to be part of a skills audit, as an area of competence. However, a case study may require you to be aware of:
>
> (a) The various relationships required by the production of printed matter and their communication/co-ordination requirements
>
> (b) What information you would need to acquire in order to manage a print task
>
> (c) What printed items are *available* as promotional tools
>
> (d) Which you might *recommend* as generally cost-effective, given basic design parameters

Action Programme 6

The Needle Works

You have realised that while direct marketing, using your customer database, is an efficient means of reaching the needlecraft market, you do not yet have a direct access to the less familiar knitting market. With the launch of the new knitting department imminent – on the 3rd September – you decide to look into the possibility of some local advertising. You gather the following information.

Local Newspapers	Circulation	Cost per column cm	
The Evening Gazette	90,000	£10.00	(£2 loading for front half)
The Morning News (Mon – Sat)	30,000	£ 4.50	(5% loading for right hand page)
The Community Weekly (free)	70,000	£ 5.00	(10% loading for position in weekly 'Events' section)

The *Evening Gazette* is the main paper for business and young people, sold extensively at commuter stations and on the streets after 5pm. The *Morning News* is the more traditional paper, mainly delivered to homes and sold in newsagents during the morning. The *Community Weekly* is distributed free to letterboxes on Wednesday mornings and contains local news and events.

Local Commercial Radio

'Home Sound'. Media pack shows catchment area 300,000 adults weekly: station penetration audited at 30 net ratings points. The station is mostly a talk and easy listening station. Ads sold as package of 20 x 15 second slots (5 peak, 15 off-peak) for £750. Off-peak hours are weekday mornings 10.00 – 12.00 and afternoons, 2.00 – 4.00pm and Sunday afternoons 12.00 – 4.00pm. 'Home Rock', is the sister station with a pop/rock music format. Penetration audited at 20 adult rating points, of which 80% are in the 18 – 24 age bracket. The ad rates and packages are the same as Home Sound.

Posters

Poster sites are available per calendar month at local bus stops (£150) on a hoarding outside the Post Office (£100) and in the underground station (£200).

You want to run a campaign for three weeks: weeks commencing Monday 15th, 22nd and 29th August (the launch is on Saturday 3rd September). You have an overall budget of £2,000 for the campaign.

Draft a proposed campaign schedule, with a budget of £3,000 over two weeks.

Chapter Roundup

- **Advertising** is 'any paid form of *non-personal* presentation and promotion of ideas, goods or services by an *identifiable* sponsor'. (American Marketing Association).
- **Media selection** should be made in accordance with the organisation's **advertising objectives** on the following criteria
    - The size of the audience/circulation
    - The type of audience (in relation to the target audience)
    - The opportunity of the audience to use the medium
    - The effort required to use the media
    - The audience's familiarity with the medium
    - The selectivity/segmentation allotted by the medium
    - The suitability of the medium's technical characteristics for the message
    - The suitability of the medium's perceived function for the message
    - The cost-effectiveness of the medium
    - The medium's susceptibility to testing and measurement
- **Media research** is designed to provide data on circulated audience reach and media habits.
- **Cost comparisons** are usually made on the basis of 'cost per thousand' (people reached, or impacts).
- **Press or print media** include:
    - Newspapers: daily and weekly, morning and evening, national and regional
    - Magazines, periodicals and journals; general appeal, special interest and trade
- Print media offer classified, semi-display, display, advertorial and loose-insert advertising options.
- **Scheduling** is a combination of **reach or exposure** (how many of the right type of people see the ad) and **frequency** (how many times people see the ad).
- The perceived function and image of **radio** is an important factor in the response to radio advertising.
- Because of the high exposure, glamour and audio-visual impact of **television**, it has become the favoured medium for launching new products, raising brand awareness and building brand loyalty.
- **Poster advertising** is one of the oldest media for consumer goods advertising. Size and visibility of the sites are the main consideration.
- **Cinema advertising** takes advantage of high audio-visual impact and a captive audience but still requires a high quality and entertainment value.
- A wide range of **electronic and non-traditional media** (including CD-ROM, text messaging and the Internet) is now used, particularly to access the youth market.
- The **Internet** has become a medium for carrying advertising in its own right.
- **Banner advertising** is a common form of on-line promotion, used to drive traffic to a corporate site.
- Increasingly sophisticated methods are being used to target the vast Internet audience, using search-engine listings, pay-per-click advertising and e-mail marketing.
- **Media scheduling** requires a mix of:
    - reach
    - repeat exposure, or frequency, and
    - cost-effectiveness, in relation to
    - specific media objectives.
- Key processes in **managing printing tasks** include: formulating job specifications; gathering price quotations; and checking pre-press and sample proofs.

Quick Quiz

1. How can media be selective or targeted?
2. What does 'cost per thousand' not take into account as a measure of cost effectiveness?
3. What are the advantages and disadvantages of (a) cinema and (b) poster advertising?
4. What is 'pass on' readership, and why is it important?
5. Which are the most effective positions for press ads?
6. What advantages does radio have over TV for advertising?
7. What are TARPs, what do they tell the advertiser, and what *don't* they tell the advertiser?
8. How long should a TV ad be, and how often should it be repeated?
9. List three uses of websites and the Internet as an advertising medium.
10. What makes an efficient media schedule?

Answers to Quick Quiz

1. Selection of media is based on the best way of getting the message to the target audience. You need to know the strengths and weaknesses of the various media and match them with your audience profiles, resources and budget. A targeted audience is a selection already identified as being interested in your product. However, you may have to be more ingenious to reach the interested few than in appealing to a mass market.

2. The answer to Action Programme 3 gives full information. In summary you must consider coverage, target audience, and repeat exposures.

3. Cinema advantages: glamorous, high impact, captive audience, local. Cinema disadvantages: high cost, time specific, poor verification of response, limited number of people per exposure. Posters advantages: flexible sites, duration, low cost, exposure to shoppers and commuters. Posters disadvantages: difficulty of verification of response; weather, site specific and little audience selectivity.

4. Pass on readership is where a printed item (typically a magazine) is read by successive people (perhaps in a waiting room). It gives your advertisement a much longer shelf life and massively increases reach.

5. The covers, inside and out, because of the prestigious presentation. Also early in the publication, alongside popular editorials and on right hand pages, where they are more likely to catch the eye.

6. Radio is a cheaper medium, which often enjoys a captive audience (drivers/housewives employed in other tasks). Listener loyalty means that consumers are likely to hear an ad several times a week. Radio listeners do not have a fast forward control or flit to other stations during commercial breaks.

7. Target Audience Rating Points. See Paragraph 5.1.

8. It depends on your message. Ads of a minute and a half or longer can be valuable for complex product. 10 second ads can be similarly effective. Repeated exposure is good – up to a point, where the ad becomes habitual and hardly noticed.

9. Online advertising methods: promotion through search engines; banner advertising and using e-mail to target customers. Internet advertising can involve creation of your own website or using those of related organisations.

10. Refer to the list provided in Paragraph 8.

PART D CO-ORDINATING THE MARKETING MIX

Action Programme Review

1. (suggestions only)
   - (a) Local radio (in car), bus stop, poster sites (driver visibility), local paper 'Auto' section.
   - (b) Local cinema (evening session, adult-appeal film), local paper 'Food' section, Good Food Guide (regional listing), local radio (classical music/news programmes?)
   - (c) UK Accountancy journals (various), Underground Station posters in financial districts, direct mail.
   - (d) Commercial TV (especially daytime for housewives, poster sites (shopper visibility), women's and household magazines. (Assuming mainly female buyer decision.)
   - (e) Trade (engineering journals, Research/home website of inventor.

2. (a) Opportunity and effort are good with radio: effortless background, portable etc. Familiarity may be a constraint where station newly launched: listeners may not want to switch from old favourites, may not be able to recall frequency.
   - (b) Daytime TV: minimal effort and good familiarity with regular users, but limited opportunity if target audience includes workers/school-age commuters.
   - (c) Bus posters: minimal effort (depending on size, length of copy, sight lines: can be a strain to read bus posters), good familiarity, good opportunity because moving around (outside posters) but limited by bus users only (inside).
   - (d) Web pages: high effort (to search, wait, use hypertext queries etc, requires technological know-how) improving familiarity (biased towards young computer-literate), limited opportunity by virtue of technology, access and expertise required.

3. (a) 5cm ad x £4.00 = £20 per ad to reach 20,000 people = £1 per thousand
   - (b) £2,000 to reach 900,000 people = about £2.20 per thousand
   - (c) £700 to reach (30% x 210,000 =) 70,000 people = £10 per thousand (net)

   The local newspaper is cheapest per thousand, but may not offer the coverage required by the advertiser: the magazine is not only high circulation and national, but the space offered is larger and in colour, for greater impact (if relevant). It is a trade magazine – which may (or may not) fit the target audience of the advertiser. The radio spots seem expensive per thousand but these are the net number of potential listeners: in effect, there will be repeat exposures over the package of 20 ads, so the figure for cumulative impacts may well be higher. (If only half of the 70,000 listeners heard the ad 3 times, and the rest once, for example, the impacts would be 140,000 and the cost per thousand £5.)

4. (a) Assuming mainly professional male buyers, next to business news, news or evening/weekend sports.
   - (b) Assuming mainly female buyers/decision makers, daytime (cost effective), home/lifestyle programmes, prime time soaps (eg for launch).
   - (c) Assuming car-owner buyers, not during commuting hours: driving/car programmes, motor sports, home/lifestyle (women buyers).
   - (d) Assuming single buyers, late-night television.

5. Two main reasons:
   - (a) They hope that the customer will click on the advert and be exposed to more detailed information.
   - (b) All visitors to the web page will see the advert, noting it either consciously or subconsciously.

6 PROPOSED ADVERTISING CAMPAIGN: KNITTING DEPT. LAUNCH

Media Rationale

Product/Service:	New knitting department (launch Sat 3 Sept)
Budget:	£2,000
Target Audience:	Women 30+ in local area
	Additional weighting to women 45+, knitters
Timing of Campaign:	3 weeks
	WK/C 15, 22, 29 August
Objectives/Special Instructions:	Advertising to generate:
	(a) personal enquiries re knitting products/services (address only: no telephone response)
	(b) attendance on launch day (target 500 customer visits)
Media Selection:	The *Community Weekly* (£1.43 per thousand) was selected as cheap space with relatively high audience relevance: older women tend to read community news, especially when delivered free. Wednesday a good day for Saturday event.
	Evening Gazette (£2.20 per thousand) higher circulation and lower c/p/t than *Morning News* (£3.00 per thousand), but the target audience favours morning papers plus smaller circulation encourages repeat exposure.
	Radio was selected as good value. *Home Rock* ruled out as inappropriate for target audience. *Home Sound:* 30% x 3000,000 = 100,000 *net* audience (£7.50 per thousand *net* + cumulative exposures: TARPs to be confirmed).
	Posters: convenient shopper reminder: target audience uses bus and post office, both local.

Advertising Schedule

Media details & placement		Day	W/C August			Total no	@ Rate	Cost
			15	22	29			
Community Weekly								
2 x 10cm	Semi-display – Events' section +10% load	Wed	1	1	1	60 %	£5.00 10	300 30
Morning News								
2 x 10cm	Semi-display – +5% load	Tues + Sat	2	2	2	120	£4.55	540 27
Home Sound								
15 sec	20 x 15 sec							
[Peak] Mon-Fri 8-10am		M-F	2	1	1	5	750	750
[Off Peak] Mon-Sat 10am-12pm								
Poster site [one month]								
A1 – Bus stop A764		-	1			1	£150	150
A1 – Post Office Site B.3		-	1			1	£100	100
								£1,897

Now try Question 12 at the end of the Study Text

13: Promotional activity

Chapter topic list

1. PR and promotions
2. Sales promotion
3. Trade promotion
4. Point of sale
5. PR and publicity
6. Collaborative programmes
7. Promotion on the Internet
8. Integrated learning

Syllabus content – knowledge and skills requirement

- 4.2 Evaluate promotional activities and opportunities, including sales promotion, PR and collaborative programmes

Introduction

In Chapter 12, we looked at **above-the-line** promotional activity. In this chapter, we discuss the range of promotional activities which fall '**below-the-line'**. These are activities for which there is no cost of media space, and in which there is usually some form of negotiated incentive or augmented offer to the consumer. Again, you should be able to draw on your studies for *Marketing Fundamentals* and *Customer Communications* in this area.

1 PR and promotions

FAST FORWARD

PR and sales promotion are increasingly used as part of the promotional mix.

Twenty years ago, **promotional incentives,** such as gift samples, coupons, prize draws, competitions, on-pack offers and collaborative programmes (get a free X cola when you buy a Y burger or rent a Z video), were considered as short-lived sales boosters. However, it has now been recognised that such campaigns can have long-term effects on consumer buying patterns and attitudes, and promotions marketing is a discipline in its own right, with agencies capturing a significant proportion of marketing budgets.

PR or public relations is now recognised to have significant advantages for carrying specialist messages to target audiences which are not sensitive to advertising, and for managing corporate communications and image in general.

Exam tip

It's vital to note that 'promotion' (in the sense of 'the promotion mix') is a wider concept (embracing all forms of *customer communications*: advertising, direct marketing, personal selling and so on) than 'promotion' (in the sense of **'sales promotion'**). If you get a question like 'How can the promotional mix be used to ...?' (as in June 2006), this refers to both above- and below-the-line methods and ICT equivalents. If you get a question like 'How can you run joint promotions ...?' (as in June 2003) you may narrow your thinking to sales or trade promotions – but state this assumption clearly, if you're making it!

The December 2004 exam explicitly asked how the *'rest* of the promotional mix' could be used to support a particular *'sales* promotion'. Define all terms clearly ...

The examiner repeatedly notes this pitfall in exam reports – and its determined to keep testing it until students have got the message! *Sales* promotion techniques were specifically tested in both the June and December 2005 exams and again in December 2006: in each case you had to recommend three techniques that could be used to promote specified services/events.

Meanwhile, don't neglect consumer and trade *sales* promotions as one of the tools in your mix!

2 Sales promotion

2.1 Sales promotion mechanisms

FAST FORWARD

The purpose of **sales promotion** may be to increase short-term sales volume, encourage repeat purchase, encourage customer loyalty, encourage new product trial or brand trial, convey information, convey a positive PR image, extend media coverage, extend the database, motivate salespeople and distributors or attract and motivate purchase influencers.

Different types of promotion are effective in achieving different objectives.

Purpose	Examples
• Increase short-term sales volume	Free gifts or discount coupons with purchase Two-for-one offers
• Encourage repeat/multiple purchase	Collectible coupons towards more substantial gifts Multiple entries in prize draws/competitions
• Customer loyalty incentive/reward programmes	Coupons/vouchers for subsequent visits
• Product launch, encourage new product trial or alternative brand trial (weaning away from competitors)	Money-off coupons Free samples and in-store trials Demonstrations of new products Free gifts with new products (eg magazines)
• Convey and embed information	Competitions with questions based on product information
• Convey a positive brand/corporate image	Purchase incentives linked to charitable donations, equipment for schools
• Extend media coverage with 'free' space	Samples/give always supporting product reviews (press, radio) competitions: space to explain rules, prize (product)
• Extend database	Coupon returns, competition entries, phone responses giving name/address details (plus high awareness)
• Motivate supply chain	Consumer promos as 'push' technique to support retailer Gifts/prize draws/competitions to motivate sales force and/or retailers Discount/awards schemes
• Motivate influencers (journalists, reviewers, style leaders)	Advance sampling/demonstration/showing of new/improved products

Note that all the above purposes are to do with **generating profitable sales**.

Action Programme 1

Visit your local supermarket, and spend some time identifying the various types of sales promotion you encounter.

This is a useful exercise 'on the ground' to enhance your everyday awareness of sales promotion techniques. Having begun such a programme of primary research, you will have a better understanding of relevant secondary sources: the analysis of promotional collaborations and campaigns in the marketing trade press and media sections of newspapers.

[*Key skill for Marketers: Improving own learning and performance*]

We will look at some of the main techniques in turn.

PART D CO-ORDINATING THE MARKETING MIX

2.2 Bonus and discount offers

FAST FORWARD

> **Common promotional mechanisms** include coupons, premiums, bonus packs, rebates, samples, demonstrations, games and competitions, gifts, merchandising and events.

2.2.1 Coupons

Key concept

> **Couponing** is a fairly straightforward approach whereby the purchaser obtains a coupon – incorporated in the product packaging or labelling, or as an attached or separate printed item – which offers some incentive or bonus: a discount or free gift, say.

Couponing is a simple strategy for encouraging **repeat or volume purchases**, since they offer a benefit on the next purchase of the same item, or another specific item, or on a certain cumulative volume of purchases.

You should be familiar with promotions that require the consumer to send in a certain number of wrappers, labels, bar-codes, tokens or bottle caps/ring pulls. They are often used by soft-drink and confectionery marketers, particularly since free gifts for children tend to have a higher perceived value than their actual cost.

Coupons are also useful as one-off **incentives** supporting press advertising, overcoming inertia and attracting bargain hunters. Cinemas, museums and galleries, for example, often offer money off ticket prices via cut-out coupons in the press. Hairdressers, take-away food and video rental outlets similarly offer vouchers on products and services. You should be able to think of many other examples.

2.2.2 Premiums

Key concept

> **Premiums** are offers of a product or service free, or at a specially discounted price, usually for a limited time, in order to induce or trigger purchase of (usually another) product.

Premiums may be offered through coupons, or through product packaging or advertised 'write-in' schemes or retailer administered promotion at point of sale.

Premiums are useful for **boosting sales of the 'parent' product** in the short-term, by motivating a purchase decision (free garlic bread with every special large pizza, say). They can also be used to get consumers to try the premium or give-away product itself. So, for example, you might get a sample jar of a newly-launched coffee blend when you buy a large jar of the market-leading blend.

Premiums are most effective when there is a natural **synergy** between the parent product and the give-away, and when the give-away has some perceived value, but not too much. A free pen with personal organiser, or honey 'twister' spoon with jar of honey, or drinking glass with premium spirits are examples of well-judged premium promotions.

Marketing at Work

One of the most celebrated **disasters in sales promotion** was the 1992 joint Hoover/Your Leisure offer of two free flights (to Europe and the US) to any customer who spent a minimum of £100 on its products. Spot the mistake! Leonard Hadley, Chairman of Hoover's US parent company, Maytag, had to admit that the offer was like 'a bad accident ... you can't determine what was in the driver's mind'. The promotion attracted more than double the anticipated applications, leading to the dismissal of three senior managers and a £19 million provision to cover the costs. The promotion had not been insured against unforeseen demand. The bargain was just too good. And the second-hand vacuum cleaner market would take a long time to recover from the over-supply!

2.2.3 Bonus packs

Bonus packs provide extra product for the same price. They work on the same principle as premiums, but offer more of the same product (rather than another product) as the incentive. This is usually done via **product packaging**, in order to keep the process simple. It advertises itself by messages such as '10% extra' or '12 for the price of 10'. You will often see a dotted line or different coloration on the packaging to show the extent of the bonus.

Bonus packs can be particularly effective:

(a) To **lure consumers from competing brands** without discounting or altering your price. Bonuses are effectively a discount, without being a discount: people don't usually resent removal of the offer in the way that they would a return to higher prices.

(b) Where competing brands are largely **undifferentiated**, so that consumers will buy whichever one offers value for money at the time.

2.2.4 Rebates

Rebates, or 'cash back' offers are a form of delayed bonus, and an alternative to up-front discounts.

2.3 Samples and demonstrations

2.3.1 Sampling

Sampling is a technique based on giving consumers an opportunity to try your product for free. This is a kind of hands-on advertising.

(a) **Motivates** people to try a new brand (curiosity and lack of cost or risk can overcome the inertia of habitual use and apathy)

(b) **Convinces** people of product claims and benefits that they may not have believed through advertising alone

(c) Is particularly effective in **launching** new and innovative products, the benefits of which may be hard to convey

(d) **Converts** customers of other brands which is important where market share is hotly contested

Sampling may be implemented:

- At **retail** outlets
- As part of a **direct mail** or letterbox drop campaign
- As part of a **'home trial'** programme
- As part of an agency-negotiated **Mass Consumer Sampling** exercise.

2.3.2 Demonstrations

Demonstrations work on the same principle as sampling for more **expensive and complex** products or services. Demonstrations showing how easy and versatile a food processor is to use, for example, attract interest and overcome potential sales objections. Demonstrations are effective in launching new products which are perceived as complex, difficult or risky to use – or the effects of which (in the hands of an expert) are particularly spectacular. ('Miracle' cleaning fluids and vacuum cleaners are often demonstrated on this basis, because no consumer is going to risk creating the kind of carpet stains the demonstrator can use.)

2.4 Competitions and games

Consumer competitions are now a major area of promotion. Competitions can be run using a variety of media incentives and an infinite variety of themes. Prizes offered can be an attractive incentive for a large number of consumers to try a product, make repeat purchases or send in mailing list details without involving huge outlay from the promoter. In addition, if consumers have been motivated to enter a competition, their general awareness of the product or organisation will be high, and competition 'losers' will be well primed for a direct-mail special offer of the product.

Competitions may be automatic entry (for example, prizes for the 'thousandth shopper' in a particular department store), or participative (where people have to send or ring in entries). Some of the many competition formats in regular use include the following.

(a) **Prize draws** where people send or ring in contact details (with or without answers to questions), and the first name (or correct answer) 'drawn' at random wins. This is a popular approach, because it requires little effort on the part of the organiser or entrant, for potentially high rewards. (Telephone competition lines often make a profit in their own right, via special premium-charge phone lines.)

(b) **Games** of skill or luck: for example, promotional scratch cards, bingo, puzzles, lotteries.

(c) **Participative contests**: for example, story-writing competitions, recipe competitions, photo competitions.

(d) **Informational competitions**. People may be asked to complete a quiz based on information to be researched (often used in travel and encyclopaedia/educational resource promotions) to whet the appetite. Alternatively, the questions may be based on product information supplied or to be researched by product inspection or trial. Questions such as 'in 25 words or less, complete the following sentence: 'I love Brand X because...' are often used because they provide useful feedback (and even advertising ideas).

Action Programme 2

Devise a creative competition concept to promote:

(a) candied fruit peel
(b) The Needle Works' store
(c) a range of new travel guidebooks
(d) a brand of household detergent

The number and value of **prizes** offered says a great deal about the organisation, although nobody expects charities to give away the same prizes as car manufacturers. The latter may give away a top of the range car or a foreign holiday to the top winner while charities may give away a small number of relatively low-value items (like food hampers). Promotional merchandise (branded T-shirts or baseball caps) may be given away in their hundreds as a promotional tool. Think about the competitions you have seen, or even entered.

2.4.1 Planning sales promotion competitions

The acronym 'COMPETE' may be used as a checklist for planning effective sales promotion competitions.

- Co-sponsors — Plan any collaborations with retailers or other promoters
- Objectives — Know what message the competition is intended to send and what results it is intended to produce

- Mechanics — How will the competition be delivered, entered and judged? Plan the logistics of entry handling and prize distribution
- Prizes — Decide the number and value of prizes to attract consumers and reinforce the product concept
- Expenditure — Budget costs and time
- Timing — Will the competition counteract seasonal laws or competitor promotions? How far away should the closing date be, before momentum is lost?
- Evaluation — What criteria will be used to define the competition's success?

Marketing at Work

As an example of how promotional offerings can be tailored for **synergy with the brand**, consider cereal maker, Kellogg's.

- Special K, aimed mainly at 18-35 year old women who care about health and fitness, did a promotion offering a free hour with a personal trainer, and a pedometer.
- Sugar Puffs, on the other hand, are marketed to children, so the offer was a free swim voucher.

Professional Marketing, Feb 2005

2.5 Gifts and merchandising

A wide variety of free gifts or purchasable merchandise can be used to promote products and brands, creating brand recognition and in many cases an extra 'medium' or space for advertising messages. Specialist agencies exist to source promotional gifts and merchandise for trade and consumer promotions. Some of the most popular include branded coasters, keyrings, mouse mats, computer screen savers on CD ROM, calendars, pens and pencils, baseball caps, T-shirts, beer mats, carrier bags, book marks ... you name it!

Action Programme 3

We dare you to come up with another 30 ideas for promotional merchandise! (There are at least that many already in use ...)

2.6 Events

A range of the kind of promotional events we discussed in Chapter 9 – launch parties, technical or discussion seminars, conferences, publicity stunts, entertainments, previews – are also included in sales promotion activities, since they are often opportunities not just to attract media interest and make contacts, but to showcase products. Just as an example, real estate developers often use informational seminars (which people pay to attend) on 'Wealth building through real estate investment' or 'What is negative gearing?' to demonstrate their expertise and generate client relationships. Record labels similarly host discos, and publishers readings, to showcase their products to willing audiences.

3 Trade promotion

> **FAST FORWARD**
>
> **Trade promotions** may be used as 'push' techniques to sell products into distribution outlets.

Bear in mind that not all promotions are aimed at consumers: some may be aimed at selling into ('push') or motivating retailers, distributors, sales force and trade/industry customers. We discussed some trade promotions in the chapter on developing supply chain relationships (Chapter 7).

Trade promotions include:

(a) **Monetary incentives** such as increased trade discounts (increased margins on the product), allowances, extended credit or other favourable finance plans, extended warranty on products, performance bonuses for sales people

(b) **Joint advertising** and promotion, sharing advertising and other costs with the dealer or retailer

(c) **Point-of-sale support** from display materials, information, merchandising

(d) **Competitions and awards** for salespeople or dealers/distributors

(e) **Business gifts** linked to sales or purely relational (eg diaries, calendars, alcohol and other items traditionally given at Christmas)

(f) **Consumer promotions** promoted to retailers as aggressive 'pull policy'

(g) Gifts, competitions, events and information offered at **trade shows and exhibitions**

(h) **Corporate hospitality**: key trade partners invited to sporting and entertainment events

4 Point of sale

> **FAST FORWARD**
>
> **Point of sale materials** may be supplied to retailers to support product displays and induce purchase decisions in-store.

Key concept

> The **point of sale** (POS) is the place (usually in-store) where goods are bought and paid for. By extension 'point of sale' refers to promotional materials displayed in-store to stimulate purchase decisions.

Point of sale material includes:

- **Product housing or display casing**, such as metal or plastic racks, carousels
- **Posters and showcards** (self-standing cardboard posters or images)
- **Mobiles** (ceiling-hung objects or display cards)
- **Shelf tags** and '**wobblers**' (attention grabbers attached to shelves)
- **Counter-standing leaflet dispensers** with promotional or informational handouts
- **Bookmarks, balloons, branded carrier bags**
- **Interactive kiosks**

Most point of sale material is **produced by manufacturers/suppliers** for use by retailers. It should be:

- **Attention-grabbing**
- **Easy to assemble** and used by retailers
- **Small enough** not to obstruct aisles or take up too much room
- **Compatible** with the retailer's own store design/display plans
- **Durable** enough for the period of the promotion

Offering POS material is a significant 'push' factor, indicating that the supplier is serious about highlighting its product and selling through to consumers.

5 PR and publicity

We have already introduced 'public relations' as a discipline, attitude and body of skills in Chapter 8, where we suggested that every employee of an organisation is practising public, or employee, relations as a representative of the organisation. Here, we will look briefly at some of the main PR activities that have not yet been discussed, and will suggest how PR activity can be monitored and evaluated.

Exam tip

> The December 2005 exam made ten marks available for recommending any three 'public relations activities' to gain awareness among the target audiences of a cultural festival. (When you see 'awareness' as the criteria for a campaign in general, think advertising and PR! But remember, advertising *isn't* a PR activity!) The examiner particularly appreciated answers which recommended *targeted* strategies, such as gaining media coverage in specialist or special-interest media used by the target audiences: try and be as realistic and sophisticated in your thinking as possible!

5.1 Securing media coverage

FAST FORWARD

> **PR methodologies** include media relations, press releases, photo calls, product submission for offers and reviews, press conferences and offering expert spokespersons, in order to secure 'free' media coverage.

Media coverage in editorial articles, product reviews and news items is free promotion, but it is only 'promotion' if the coverage is **positive**. Companies make news for all the wrong reasons, and despite the old saying that 'there's no such thing as bad publicity' – there probably is. When Perrier mineral water was found to contain tiny amounts of a toxic chemical after an accident in the bottling plant, there was an avalanche of headlines, of which the most memorable were 'Eau dear' and 'what a fiasceau'.

5.1.1 Advantages and disadvantages of coverage

The advantages and disadvantages of coverage may be summarised as follows.

Advantages

- **Raise awareness** of your brand, message or image among a wider audience
- Generate **word-of-mouth** about your product
- **Get your message read**/listened to more carefully than advertising
- Have the effect of implied **endorsement or recommendation**
- **Support** advertising and sales promotion campaigns

Disadvantages

- You cannot **control** the content of editorial matter
- Journalists are interested in their own objectives (circulation and ratings)
- Mistakes and shortcomings are usually more newsworthy than successes

5.1.2 Guidelines for obtaining coverage

In order to have a chance of securing coverage you will have to do the following.

(a) **Build up a network of media contacts** (or use a PR or media relations agent). Cultivate contacts regularly, and make notes on each contact.

(b) **Send out media releases** alerting journalists to anything you can make newsworthy.

(c) **Send photographs**, or notify media of **photo calls** where possible. Print media are much hungrier for usable images (with suitable captions) than stories.

(d) **Add supporting incentives**. Magazines, local newspapers and radio stations are often happy to offer their readers special offers and competitions, which secure related explanation/description space.

(e) **Hold press conferences**, only in cases where something genuinely newsworthy can be revealed.

(f) **Offer products for trial and review,** if you are confident that they can stand up to scrutiny and possibly comparison with competitors.

(g) **Offer relevant spokesperson and 'experts'** for interview, comment or consultation on product-related areas. Offer technical articles to trade journals, for example, or publish informational booklets in order to gain a profile as an expert commentator or analyst.

Ensure that whoever undertakes media relations, and particularly live interviews, knows what they are doing!

(a) Know the angle, audience and style of the medium/publication/programme and journalist they will be talking to or writing for.

(b) Be on guard, however friendly, informal and 'off the record' the discussion may seem.

(c) Make the most of the opportunity to enhance the organisation's image of expertise or personality, and to get the message across.

Much of this activity is labour-intensive. In order to make best use of time and money, try and *target* media that are most relevant to your objectives and audiences, rather than merely using a scatter-gun approach.

5.2 Sponsorship

FAST FORWARD

Sponsorship has offered marketing avenues for organisations which are restricted in their advertising, or wish to widen their awareness base among various target audiences.

One way of gaining profile and publicity is **sponsorship**. Marketers may sponsor local groups or school teams, all the way up to national and international sporting and cultural events and organisations for a variety of purposes.

- Awareness creation in the audience of the sponsored event
- Media coverage generated by the sponsored event
- Opportunities for corporate hospitality at sponsored events
- Creation of a positive image among employees and the community

Sponsorship has offered marketing avenues for organisations which are restricted in their advertising, or wish to widen their awareness base among various target audiences. Examples include tobacco sponsorship of sporting events. There is wide corporate involvement in mass support sports such as football, while opera, concerts and orchestras tend to be sponsored by financial institutions and prestige marketing organisations.

When **evaluating sponsorship opportunities**, you need to be aware that there will be costs of supporting advertising and PR over and above the basic sponsorship costs. Advertising on team shirts, programmes and hoardings may or may not be included in the sponsorship package of benefits.

When **offering sponsorship opportunities**:

- Describe the event/organisation to be sponsored in terms which are relevant to the potential sponsor's objectives

- Highlight competitor sponsorship or credible current/past sponsors to emphasise the value of sponsorship
- Show how the event/organisation (and its promotion) will reach and appeal to the potential sponsor's target audience, to emphasise potential PR benefits to the sponsor
- Specify what is required of the sponsor (amount of funding or other support) and what package of benefits is available in return
- Emphasise mutual benefits of the relationship.

Exam tip

> The December 2005 exam asked you to draft a letter to potential sponsors, 'selling the benefits of involvement' with a cultural festival. The examiner specifically required 'selling the benefits' in question – and gave few marks for answers which didn't do this! The examiner also recommended ending such a letter with 'a robust or persuasive "call to action"' – not just a passive 'if you are interested, please call'. Take the advice!

5.3 Other PR methodologies

FAST FORWARD

> **Other methods** include a wide range of information programmes targeted at specific audiences: employees, government, public, financial media, trade and so on.

A wide range of public relations (government relations, financial relations, public information) vehicles is available. The following are some of the more common examples, some of which we have touched on already.

- Media packs
- Informational literature: brochures, booklets, books
- Annual, financial, market research and other reports
- Newsletters and bulletins (internal and external)
- Video, audio or CD ROM packages
- Seminars, conferences, demonstrations
- Trade shows, exhibitions and fairs
- Product placement (use of the product identifiably in video, TV, cinema and novels)
- Tours, open days, factory/office visits
- Submissions, reports and lobbying of government
- Educational packs for schools/colleges
- Corporate entertainments and special events
- Staff conferences, communication programmes

Marketing at Work

Nissan in the US is planning to plant around 200,000 sets of keys in pubs, concert halls and public facilities as part of a 2007 stunt marketing campaign. The attached key chain will read: "If found, please do not return. My next generation Nissan Altima has an intelligent key with push-button ignition, and I no longer need these."

Action Programme 4

Start collecting examples of:

(a) editorial articles which quote representatives of named commercial organisations

(b) named or visibly identified brands (watches, cars, soft drinks) in movies and TV programmes

(c) lists acknowledging sponsors of the programmes of sporting and entertainment events, or in their names. Note their impact, memorability, frequency and credibility.

5.4 Evaluating the effectiveness of PR

FAST FORWARD

The **results of PR activity** should be measured against defined purposes and objectives.

The purposes of a given PR initiative may be one or more of the following.

(a) To **support and augment advertising** and sales promotion by securing credible product endorsement or review of products, and media coverage of launches, surveys, newsworthy events, competitions and special offers.

(b) To **reach specialist audiences** which are not sensitive to advertising, but appreciate information: for example, by educational programmes in schools, technical briefings in medical and scientific markets, marketing research to industry bodies or government.

(c) To **manage communications with stakeholders** on sensitive or controversial issues, and to minimise the damage caused to sales and corporate image by crises.

(d) To **influence specific strategic audiences** where threats or opportunities exist (for example, government lobbying).

(e) To **inform and motivate** the trade and **supply chain** about a new product or promotion.

(f) To **improve communication and morale** among employees.

(g) To **educate the community** or market about issues relevant to the product or service, raising consumer awareness of needs or problems which it answers.

Media coverage can be easily monitored using cuttings or media monitoring agencies, where this is a measure of effectiveness. However, where possible, the achievement of objectives should be the criterion: because PR is often perceived as 'free' and its results as invisible, it is too easy for costs to escalate without detailed justification.

Some useful measures include the following.

(a) Define the **key messages** that will fulfil the specific objectives of the programme, and use media monitoring, feedback, customer/audience research and communication audits.

- Reach the target audience
- Correctly convey the message, resulting in the desired attitudes and awareness.

(b) Monitor appropriate **performance measures** for the specific objectives, to assess whether PR programmes have any effect. Does employee turnover fall following the introduction of employee communications? Is awareness of product-related issues higher in consumer focus groups following a publicity campaign? Have sales recovered following a crisis management exercise? Expect to see some results.

However, it should be recognised that public relations can be a long-term process of education, attitude change, and relationship building. A realistic time-scale for return on investment should be established in the light of the organisation's strategic goals.

Exam tip

> The examiner has shown increasing interests, in recent years, in testing candidates' knowledge – not just of how to implement promotional methods, but how marketers and customers might *evaluate the effectiveness* of these methods. How might clients evaluate a corporate hospitality initiative (June 2005)? How might you evaluate the effectiveness of sales promotion techniques (June 2005)? How might you evaluate an advertising campaign (December 2006)? Think about these aspects for *any* technique you recommend.

6 Collaborative programmes

FAST FORWARD

> **Collaborative promotional programmes** (often negotiated by promotional agencies) exploit the synergy available to non-competing, compatible products or organisations, by sourcing premiums, prizes and gifts, reinforcing marketing messages, sharing audiences, lending credibility and sharing costs.

6.1 Exploiting synergistic relationships

One of the most popular ways in which sales promotions can augment the offer to the consumer is by exploiting synergistic relationships with other products or marketing organisations. (Remember, synergy is the effect whereby 2+2=5.) There are various ways in which synergy can be obtained.

(a) One organisation may source **premiums**, **competition prizes** and **gifts** from other marketing organisations so that both benefit from the exposure and purchase incentives. Disney cartoon figures have long been merchandised as special offers with kids' meals at McDonalds, for example. Prestige cars, luggage and other brands are often used as competition prizes.

(b) Non-competing products in the same or related markets might **reinforce each other** (for example, promoting a stir-fry cookbook and a non-stick wok in a joint competition or premium offer). You get best use out of the one product by also purchasing the other, and if they can be purchased together (or are identified with each other), other brands may be ignored.

(c) Non-competing products with **different customer** bases can be jointly promoted to create cross-over between their respective audiences. Loyal customers of a video store may be persuaded to try the brand of cola or snack food offered free with rental. Loyal customers of that cola or snack food may be persuaded to use that video store because of the free offer.

(d) **Product placement** is a collaborative programme, because it allows the entertainment's producers to source costumes and props while the suppliers of product gain potential high-impact exposure. James Bond's choice of car and watch seldom go unnoticed.

(e) Non competing products or organisations can collaborate in informational or educational promotions to offer the consumer their **cumulative expertise or knowledge**, or one can offer **credibility** or expertise to another in exchange for exposure to its audience. Banks and youth magazines often give away promotional booklets of 'Exam tips' to students at revision time, 'in association with' exam experts such as study guide publishers.

(f) The **costs** of promotion and other collaborative programmes can be shared.

Marketing at Work

In May 2006, it was announced that Walt Disney had ended its 10-year **marketing alliance** with McDonald's. Various reasons given for the move include:

- The 'family friendly' Disney group wanted to distance itself from fast food and its highly-publicised links to childhood obesity [rumours from US industry sources: denied by McDonald's]
- McDonalds' desire to have greater flexibility and options in its 'entertainment relationships' [McDonalds' media statement]
- Both McDonalds' and Disney, which agreed the parting was mutual; said McDonalds' products would still be available in Disney's theme parks and that the two companies would still work together on other promotions. For example, Disney was open to potential McDonalds' promotions targeting adults!

B&T, 12 May 2006

6.2 Planning and organising collaborative promotions

FAST FORWARD

The issues involved in collaborative promotion can be complex. Creativity, ingenuity, wide networks and persuasive skills may be required to locate and put together synergistic partnerships that everyone will trust to bring mutual benefit.

Introductions and negotiations are often carried out by promotional agencies, but you may approach or be approached by other organisations direct.

Exam tip

The June 2003 exam explicitly asked you to write a letter proposing collaboration in promotion between two potential competitors. Bear in mind, though, that collaborative promotion may be a useful synergistic tool in the promotion mix: consider it as an option in any scenario. (You were given the option of solo or collaborative sales promotion activities in December 2006: the examiner was disappointed that candidates neglected the possibilities.)

As a co-ordinating exercise, collaborative programmes require the following.

(a) Detailed **negotiation** and agreement of objectives, responsibilities, schedules and costs
(b) Regular **communication** between promotional partners, agencies and suppliers of creative and other services required
(c) Provision of all **information, copy, photographs and samples** required for advertising, packaging and POS displays
(d) Rigorous **monitoring of progress** and checking of all details (especially those prepared by other parties) for correctness and conformity with agreed objectives
(e) **Monitoring** of the promotion, its **logistics** (eg competition entry handling) and **results**, especially if controlled by the other party

When considering the merits of a proposed collaborative programme you should think about the following.

- What is the potential **exposure** to our target audience?
- **What will they think** of this partnership?
- Will they **recognise** us within the collaboration?
- Is there any **threat** to our brand?
- Are our **marketing objectives** being met?

Marketing at Work

i-Pod and U2

Two well-known entertainment brands – band U2 and Apple's i-Pod – were **cross-promoted** in a worldwide 2004 campaign.

'U2 exudes everything Apple wants to stand for – and vice versa,' says Joseph Jaffe, president of Jaffe marketing consultancy. 'Independence, creativity, self-expression, and authenticity.'

The pairing scored with music fans. Following its exclusive release on Apple's iTunes Music Store, U2's *How to Dismantle an Atomic Bomb* went on to top the iTunes sales charts for weeks after its late-November debut. Offline the album launched at the top of the US pop charts, selling almost twice as many copies as U2's last US release did during its first week – a success that rescued the band from the purgatory of 'classic rock' status.

For this, U2 and its Interscope/Geffen/A&M label credit iTunes and the $20 million TV campaign Apple undertook to back the partnership. (U2 agreed to appear in the ads for free.) As Bono put it, 'We want our audience to have a more intimate online relationship with the band, and Apple can help us do that.'

Thomas Mucha, 'Silhouettes & Synergy', *Business,* Jan/Feb 2005

Action Programme 5

The Needle Works

Following the success of your co-promotion with your supplier Threadlines, you decide that collaboration with related organisations can:

(a) widen the audience for your marketing message beyond your current customer base (without paying full advertising costs)

(b) reinforce The Needle Works' prestige and expert image among craft consumers.

Relations with the Craft Guilds have not yet improved, but you review your network contacts. See if you can come up with some ideas to discuss with one or more of those contacts for a collaborative promotion which will have benefit for the exposure and sales of both (or all) parties, and will also have PR potential for media coverage and wider interest (to save on advertising costs).

7 Promotion on the Internet

> **FAST FORWARD**
>
> The **Internet** can be used for a broad range of promotional applications, including direct marketing; sales promotion; customer loyalty programmes; media and public relations; relationship marketing; partnership development; customer service; market research; and corporate identity.

The Internet can be used for a broad range of promotional applications.

| Advertising | - Dedicated corporate websites, banner/button advertising, ranking on Internet search engines (to increase site exposure)
- The forecast global penetration of the Internet over the next few years would give it a significantly larger audience than any of the television networks, print media outlets or other advertising vehicles
- Studies show that brand awareness increases some 5% after using banner advertising |
|---|---|
| Direct marketing | - E-mail messages sent to targeted mailing lists (rented, or developed by the marketing organisation itself)
- 'Permission marketing' (targeting consumers who have opted to receive commercial mailings) |
| Direct response advertising | - Immediate contact (information/transaction facilities) to follow up customer responses to TV/radio/print advertising |
| Sales promotion | - On-line prize draws and competitions
- On-line discounts (offset by lower transaction costs)
- Downloadable or e-mailed discount vouchers |
| Customer loyalty programmes | - Value-added benefits that enhance the Internet buying experience
- User home page customisation
- Virtual communities (chat rooms etc)
- Free e-cards/SMS messages |
| Media/press relations | - Online media/press kits
- E-mailed media releases
- 'About us' and 'contacts' pages
- Technical briefings and articles on key issues |
| Pubic relations | - 'About us' and 'FAQ' (frequently asked question) features
- News bulletins (eg for crisis or issues management)
- Publicity/information for sponsorships, exhibitions and events
- Sponsorship of popular/ useful information sites |
| Relationship marketing | - Customisation of Web pages and targeting of offers/promotions
- E-mail follow-up contacts
- E-zines: special interest newsletters published on the Web, or distributed by e-mail direct to subscribers and mailing lists |
| Grass roots marketing | - Generating word of mouth promotion and recommendation among customers
- Online chat or message board forums and 'introduce a friend' schemes/incentives
- **Viral marketing** (so-called because it simulates the way a virus works!): giving visitors communication tools which they send to others, requiring them to visit the site: eg electronic postcards, greeting cards and links ('Send this page to a friend') |

| Direct distribution | - Of products (through online shopping) and services (including access to information databases)
- Products can be **ordered** via the Net
- Some can also be **delivered** via the Net, by downloading direct to the purchaser's PC: examples include music, computer software, Clipart, product catalogues and instruction manuals |
|---|---|
| Partnership development | - Strategic promotional collaborations with synergistic content-specific sites or 'portals' (search engines, Web directories or other high-traffic sites such as Yahoo! or MSN) |
| Customer service and technical support | - E-mail contact
- FAQs (frequently asked questions)
- Access to databased information
- Online messaging or voice interruption for interactive support |
| Market/customer research | - Gathering information on customers and visitors for the purposes of market segmentation, personalisation/customisation of future contacts
- Site monitoring
- Online or e-mailed feedback questionnaires and surveys |
| Corporate identity | - Website and e-mail messages must be designed to create a unified and coherent marketing message alongside all other marketing messages for **marketing synergy** |

Action Programme 6

Smith and Chaffey (2001) suggest five benefits of promotion on the web. See if you can complete the table with some ideas of your own.

Benefit	How?
Sell – Grow sales	
Serve – Add value	
Speak – Get closer to customers	
Save – Save costs	
Sizzle – Extend the brand	

Marketing at Work

THE ALAMO
Ofoto is proud to bring you photos from the upcoming Touchstone Pictures movie, "The Alamo"

view album

© 2004 Touchstone Pictures

ofoto A Kodak Company

Save 20%* when you spend $10, and get a FREE movie ticket courtesy of Ofoto!

Visit Ofoto today and save 20% on everything from prints and one-of-a-kind photocards to frames and photo albums. And get a movie ticket with any purchase while supplies last**.

Use this code when you order to get your ticket: ALAMO20

join now   sign in

* Save 20% offer expires on 4/30/04. Does not apply to shipping costs, film processing, applicable sales tax, or Kodak Mobile Service Subscription. One coupon redemption per customer. Cannot be combined with other offers in one order. No substitutions, transfer rights or cash equivalents will be given.

** In order to receive MovieCash good for a free movie ticket, you must make a purchase at Ofoto using the coupon code ALAMO20 between 3/26/04 and 4/30/04. For those that qualify, MovieCash will be mailed out to eligible customers the week of 5/3/04 via USPS while supplies last. Cannot be combined with other offers. No substitutions, transfer rights or cash equivalent will be given.

(www.ofoto.com)

8 Integrated learning

This syllabus focuses on sales promotion, PR and collaborative programmes – three areas in which a marketing assistant is perhaps most likely to be involved. However, you are expected to draw on your learning about promotional activity from *Customer Communications* and *Marketing Fundamentals* as well, including techniques such as direct marketing and personal selling (which came up in the December 2006 exam). Make sure you have this content under your belt.

13: PROMOTIONAL ACTIVITY

Chapter Roundup

- PR and sales promotion are increasingly used as part of the promotional mix.
- The purpose of **sales promotion** may be to increase short-term sales volume, encourage repeat purchase, encourage customer loyalty, encourage new product trial or brand trial, convey information, convey a positive PR image, extend media coverage, extend the database, motivate salespeople and distributors or attract and motivate purchase influencers.
- **Common promotional mechanisms** include coupons, premiums, bonus packs, rebates, samples, demonstrations, games and competitions, gifts, merchandising and events.
- **Trade promotions** may be used as 'push' techniques to sell products into distribution outlets.
- **Point of sale materials** may be supplied to retailers to support product displays and induce purchase decisions in-store.
- **PR methodologies** include media relations, press releases, photo calls, product submission for offers and reviews, press conferences and offering expert spokespersons, in order to secure 'free' media coverage.
- **Sponsorship** has offered marketing avenues for organisations which are restricted in their advertising, or wish to widen their awareness base among various target audiences.
- **Other methods** include a wide range of information programmes targeted at specific audiences: employees, government, public, financial media, trade and so on.
- The **results of PR activity** should be measured against defined purposes and objectives.
- **Collaborative promotional programmes** (often negotiated by promotional agencies) exploit the synergy available to non-competing, compatible products or organisations, by sourcing premiums, prizes and gifts, reinforcing marketing messages, sharing audiences, lending credibility and sharing costs.
- The issues involved in collaborative promotion can be complex. Creativity, ingenuity, wide networks and persuasive skills may be required to locate and put together synergistic partnerships that everyone will trust to bring mutual benefit.
- The **Internet** can be used for a broad range of promotional applications, including direct marketing; sales promotion; customer loyalty programmes; media and public relations; relationship marketing; partnership development; customer service; market research; and corporate identity.

Quick Quiz

1. Give examples of promotions designed (a) to encourage new product trial and (b) to enlarge the promoter's database.
2. What are premiums most useful for, and when are they most effective?
3. Why is sampling effective at converting customers of other brands?
4. Outline the 'COMPETE' formula for consumer competitions.
5. Give three examples of trade promotions.
6. What are the attributes of effective POS material?
7. What are the benefits and drawbacks of getting 'free' publicity?
8. What are the purposes of sponsorship?
9. Give four examples of collaborative promotions: one premium, one competition, one offering cross-over audiences and one based on expertise/prestige.
10. Describe some types of web promotion.

PART D CO-ORDINATING THE MARKETING MIX

Answers to Quick Quiz

1   (a) money-off coupons, free samples, demonstrations
    (b) coupon returns, competition entries, phone responses

2   Premiums are the offer of a product or service free/discounted for a limited time. They are intended to encourage future purchase or to lure customers away from an undifferentiated brand.

3   Curiosity and lack of cost or risk can overcome the inertia of habitual use or apathy.

4   This is explained in Paragraph 2.4.1.

5   Monetary incentives, joint advertising, point-of-sale support. A full list is given in Paragraph 3.

6   You should have the five points listed in Paragraph 4.

7   Lack of control; conflicting interests between media/organisation; often negative publicity makes a juicier story.

8   Refer to the bullet points in Paragraph 5.2.

9   You should be vigilant for examples of your own. Some examples might be McDonalds with a give-away toy based on a Disney character (premium), a wok with a competition to win a related prize (perhaps a cookbook) (competition), a video rental outlet promoting snack food (cross-over) and an expensively produced technical manual on tyres, such as one produced by Dunlop Australia.

10 Refer to the table in Paragraph 7.

Action Programme Review

1   Some of the promotional tools you may have encountered are: on-pack coupons, discount vouchers, on-pack competitions and prize draws ('look out for the Special Packs/Bottles...'), in-store trials, tastings and demonstrations, free gifts and product samples (often with magazines), two for the price of one or free sample combo packaging, point of sale displays, vouchers and coupons with special offers printed on the back of your till receipt, special offers on selected products, prize draw entry forms, free recipe booklets for food products, store credit cards or loyalty schemes. You'll be amazed how much sales promotion is out there! (You might also like to consider whether or how far your buying behaviour is influenced by it...)

2   Just some suggestions.

    (a) A cake decorating competition, using candied peel, or a recipe competition using candied peel. Promoted on pack and by POS leaflets and ads: purchase required. Winning entries to be made and published in a range of promotional ideas/recipe cards. The winners to be given a gourmet weekend for two or cordon bleu cookery course; runners up to be given Jane Asher's Cake Decorating book.

    (b) The Needle Works might similarly promote (in-store) a tapestry design competition. The winning designs to be made up as Tapestry Kits (profits to be given to charity) and the tapestry to be stitched. Winning designer acknowledged in all publicity, plus royalty on design and prize (weekend in Normandy to see Bayeux Tapestry?).

    (c) Possibly a travel photo competition, or a less participative geography quiz, based on identifying photos from the new Guides (so entrants have to buy, borrow or at least inspect them). Prize: air miles or a camera or photography course: not too high price tag.

    (d) A simple prize draw, for which bottle 'crowners' (neck-hanging coupons) need to be sent in with contact details: purchase incentive. Widely advertised plus on-pack information. Prize: six months' use of household cleaning service or luxury holiday.

3   For example: balloons, towels, ashtrays, matchbooks, yo-yos, toy figures, directors' chairs, umbrellas, can coolers/holders, stickers, scarves, ties, badges, sports jackets, credit card holders, wallets, penknives, playing cards, footballs, rulers, notepads, sports bags, cigarette lighters, outdoor pub umbrellas, jewellery, seat covers, litter bins, glassware, mugs, torches. Keep going!

4   You must develop 'radar' for this kind of thing.

5   Whatever ideas you came up with check them against the 'brief' you set yourself. We have developed the idea we floated in Action Programme 2. The Needle Works could run a collaborative tapestry design competition with a suitable partner: a national craft gallery or design council might see its PR potential (expressing the community's aspirations and identity) and would lend the promotion credibility – and a wide relevant mailing list, educational programme and other communication avenues. The Needle Works would gain exposure, and later revenue from merchandising (selling the design as a pattern, kits and so on): both parties could merchandise postcards or posters of the finished tapestry, and perhaps educational videos on 'The Making of the Tapestry'. There would be highly photogenic publicity opportunities as the winning designers were announced and given prizes, and on an on-going basis as the tapestry took shape and was finally presented to the public, and then toured round galleries and public institutions. Costs would have to be investigated and cost-sharing negotiated. In order to take full advantage of the spin-off sales potential, the Needle Works would probably need to have moved out of its local retail niche and into wider sales via mail order catalogue and perhaps Internet – but these initiatives should probably be on the agenda anyway.

6

Benefit	How?
Sell – Grow sales	Wider distribution Wider product range
Serve – Add value	Extra benefits from online transactions (eg discounts) Dialogue/feedback
Speak – Get closer to customers	Track customers, ask them questions, online interviews
Save – Save costs	Printing and postage reduced, for example
Sizzle – Extend the brand	Create brand awareness and involvement through interactive content

Now try Question 13 at the end of the Study Text

Mix decisions 14

Chapter topic list

1. Price
2. Place
3. Product
4. The extended marketing mix
5. ICT and the new marketing mix

Syllabus content – knowledge and sills requirements

- 4.4 Analyse the impact of pricing decisions, and role of price within the marketing mix
- 4.5 Describe the current distribution channels for an organisation and evaluate new opportunities
- 4.6 Describe how organisations monitor product trends
- 4.7 Explain the importance of the extended marketing mix; how process, physical aspects and people affect customer choice
- 4.8 Explain the importance of ICT in the new mix

Introduction

So far in Part D of this Study Text – Co-ordinating the Marketing Mix – we have concentrated on one of the four Ps – promotion. The *Marketing in Practice* syllabus suggests a promotional bias, particularly since, at a practical level, much of the material on promotional activity may be new to you.

It may seem that we have therefore set ourselves (and you) a somewhat Herculean task in covering the other three Ps of the mix – plus its 'extensions' – all in one chapter. But there is good news.

(a) You will be building substantially on the knowledge gained from *Marketing Fundamentals*.

(b) For this module, a practical co-ordinatory approach is required. We confine ourselves to the areas listed in the syllabus.

(c) These practical, co-ordinatory tasks largely involve the gathering, evaluation and presentation of information, which we covered in detail in Chapters 1-4 of this Text.

1 Price

1.1 The role of price in the mix

FAST FORWARD

Price can be defined as a measure of the value exchanged by the buyer for the value offered by the seller. It is an important part of the perceived quality and differentiation of the offer, and as such must be integrated carefully into the marketing mix.

Key concept

Price can be defined as a measure of the value exchanged by the buyer for the value offered by the seller. It may be, for example, expressed as fees, fares, tuition or rent.

Price is important within the marketing mix.

(a) It influences profitability at the 'top line', by generating revenue, rather than at the 'bottom line' by striving to control costs (like place, product and promotion).

(b) It has an important role in differentiating products and organisations in a market. Pricing strategies are used to gain and maintain competitive advantage.

(c) It is part of the overall product offer, its perceived value to the buyer, and the image of the producer/seller. Price must therefore be consistent with the other elements of the marketing mix.

Marketing at Work

Customers like clear and concise messages that are easy to understand, so that they can make well-informed decisions. Confusing information may make them move to 'simpler' rivals.

Thomson, Britain's biggest tour operator, was investigated over **misleading pricing** after it launched a new way of selling package holidays in early 2002.

It proposed charging for 'optional' extras such as in-flight meals and hotel transfers – and it was calculated that these extras could cost a typical family of four up to £100 on top of the basic price. Comparisons with other operators were more difficult. Other extras included guaranteeing families that they could sit together, reserving window or aisle seats, and increased baggage allowances.

Thomson said that it is merely responding to an increasing trend among travellers to plan their own holidays and use the low-cost airlines, a trend accelerated by the Internet. Customers could now 'personalise' their trips and only pay for what they want. But it was argued that lack of price clarity could lead to cynicism and rejection of the product.

In the absence of other information, customers tend to judge **quality** by price. A rise may be taken to indicate improvements, a reduction may signal reduced quality, for example through the use of inferior components or a poorer quality of raw material.

The ultimate objective of pricing is to produce the level of sales required to fulfil the organisation's marketing and financial objectives.

- **Maximising profits**, or the returns on assets or investments
- **Maintaining or increasing market share** or customer base
- **Market penetration**: getting a new product adopted and accepted quickly
- **Increasing short-term sales volume** (eg through discounted pricing)

The **price sensitivity** of customers (that is, the extent to which price is an incentive or disincentive to purchase) should have been analysed prior to strategic price setting. Your tasks in regard to price might consist of monitoring this sensitivity: analysing the effect of price setting or changes on buying behaviour and sales.

1.2 Price sensitivity

> **FAST FORWARD**
>
> **Price sensitivity** varies according to market and personal variables, and can be measured as the **price elasticity of demand**.

Research on price sensitivity of customers has shown the following.

(a) Customers have a good concept of a 'just price' – a feel for what is about the right price to pay for a commodity.

(b) Unless a regular purchase is involved, customers search for price information before buying, becoming price aware when wanting to buy but forgetting soon afterwards.

(c) Customers will buy at what they consider to be a bargain price without full regard for need and actual price.

(d) For consumer durables it is the down payment and instalment price rather than total price which is important to the buyer.

(e) In times of rising prices the price image tends to lag behind the current price, which indicates a resentment of the price increase.

Price sensitivity will vary amongst purchasers. Those (like trade buyers) who can pass on the cost of purchases will be least sensitive and will respond more to other elements of the marketing mix. For example, the business traveller will be more concerned about the level of service and quality of food in looking for an hotel than price. In contrast, a family on holiday are likely to be very price sensitive when choosing an overnight stay.

Price **perception** is important in the ways customers react to prices. For example, counter-intuitively, customers may react to a price increase by buying *more*.

- They expect further price increases to follow
- They assume the quality has increased
- The brand takes on a 'snob appeal' because of the high price

1.3 Monitoring the effect of pricing decisions

FAST FORWARD

The **effect of price changes** can be assessed using quantitative and qualitative data on sales performance, contribution, consumer attitudes and competitor/supplier/distributor reactions.

There are various quantitative and qualitative methods of measuring the factors discussed above.

(a) **Quantity** of products sold in comparable periods before and after the price change can be compared. Changes in quantity sold during a temporary promotional price offer can also be measured.

(b) The **contribution** to fixed cost and profit made by the product (sales revenue *minus* variable costs) can be compared at the old and new price.

(c) You could use a **market test** to estimate the effect on demand of a price change. This would involve a change of price in one region and a comparison of demand for the brand with past sales in that region and with sales in similar regions at the old prices. This is a high risk strategy.

(d) A **direct attitude survey** may be used to test buyers' reactions to price changes. **Pricing research** is notoriously difficult, especially if respondents try to appear rational to the interviewer or do not wish to offend him or her. Usually there is a lack of realism in such research.

Action Programme 1

Product X sold 1,300,000 units in the year 200X, at the price of 28p per unit. Variable cost per unit was 16p. In the year 200Y, the price of product X went up to 32p per unit and 1,100,000 units were sold at the same cost per unit. What is the effect of the price increase?

[*Key skill for Marketers: Using financial information and metrics*]

The reactions of suppliers, distributors and competitors will also need to be monitored.

(a) **Suppliers** may attempt to negotiate higher rates for their products or services if they perceive that the organisation has raised its prices.

(b) **Distributors** may deal with a range of suppliers, and are concerned with their own profits. If they feel product price rises are squeezing their profit margins, or cash flow, they may reconsider stock levels.

(c) **Competitors'** reactions to a price change are particularly important. Responsive price changes can be monitored through published price lists and advertising, suppliers and distributors and customers.

1.4 Other price-related issues

At a co-ordinating level, the marketing department will also have to give attention to the following.

(a) **Competitor pricing** will have to be monitored.

(b) Pricing decisions will have to be accurately and effectively **communicated to customers and consumers**, in all advertising and informational literature. Gathering, checking and cross-checking price data is one of the essential tasks in promotional co-ordination (especially for large-scale catalogues). The way prices are expressed may have an influence on purchase decisions, particularly in direct marketing. Prices must be easy to understand (how many customers will understand '£24.99 non net'?) and easy to calculate (how many customers will have a calculator to hand to add VAT or percentages for postage and packaging?).

(c) **Market research** may disclose pricing issues: customer perceptions or gaps in market segments related to prices. These should be input into pricing decisions.

(d) **Promotional proposals** may involve discounts, premiums and bonuses. These should be regarded as strategic pricing issues, since they represent an adjustment to the price positioning of the product.

Action Programme 2

What might (a) a price reduction and (b) a price rise suggest to buyers, and what would then help to *counteract* the expected incentive or deterrent effect on sales?

Exam tip

Both sets of exams in 2006 required calculation of the effect of price increases (based on percentage increases and their effect on sales): these are classic number questions, so be prepared. More interestingly, the examiner complained that candidates' ideas for sales promotion seem to focus on price reductions – with no consideration of the effect on profitability. Beware the temptation to recommend costly, profit-eroding solutions!

2 Place

FAST FORWARD

Place is concerned with the selection of distribution channels and logistics.

Key concept

'**Place**' as an element in the marketing mix is largely concerned with the selection of **distribution channels** to deliver the goods to the consumer, and with the **storage** and **physical distribution** of goods (**logistics**).

We have already discussed some elements of the marketing co-ordinator's role.

- Developing **business relationships** down the supply chain
- Promoting products to distributors by **'push' techniques** or trade promotions
- Supporting distributors via **'pull' promotions** to consumers

In addition, the marketing co-ordinator may have to monitor the effectiveness of current distribution channels and new opportunities.

2.1 Evaluating current distribution channels

FAST FORWARD

Channels of distribution should be evaluated for effectiveness, efficiency and economy, level of customer service, degree of controllability and quality of business relationship.

Criteria which may be used to evaluate distribution channels and logistics

(a) **Effectiveness** in getting products to customers (ie sales) and in performing each of the distributive functions that leads to sales

(b) **Efficiency and economy** in terms of the costs of distribution

(c) **Level of service** offered to customers, supporting loyalty and repeat sales

(d) **Degree of control** achieved over the distribution channel, where desired for competitive advantage or integration of marketing effort up to the point of sale

(e) **Degree of co-operation or conflict** with the distributor (channel dynamics)

> **Exam tip**
>
> A question in December 2002 asked you to draft a response to a **retailer** who has approached your firm with a view to join your retail network (basic relationship/PR/ front-line skills) *and* to state what information you would need about the retailer and the market for your product in its country, before you made a decision to work with them (investigating distributor and investigating market opportunities). Another example of a question crossing over syllabus areas: stay flexible in your thinking!
>
> Similar questions were set about choosing and managing **franchisees** in December 2004.

2.1.1 Effectiveness

The measure of effectiveness will depend on specific objectives and criteria appropriate to the processes and channels used. **Sales** made through the distribution channel, however, are a key indicator:

- Compared month-on-month or year-on-year to show growth or decline trends
- Compared for different channels, to show which are more effective than others

2.1.2 Efficiency

Cost of distribution is one of the key factors in selecting distribution channels. Intermediaries may reduce the costs of selling for the manufacturer by **bearing or sharing the costs** of stockholding, transportation and display. In addition, manufacturers may receive payment more quickly from intermediaries than by selling direct to the consumer.

Distribution costs should be monitored.

- Cost savings should be being obtained, compared to estimated costs of other channels.
- Costs should be in line with negotiated and budgeted expenditure.
- The channel should be cost-efficient.

2.1.3 Level of service

Customer service is a key source of competitive benefit, and therefore a key objective of distribution systems. It may include factors such as:

- The availability of, and charges for, installation, repair and after-sales service
- Readiness to take back and quickly re-supply defective goods
- The preparation of orders delivered with correct contents and in good condition
- Lead time from placement of an order to delivery
- Choice and flexibility in product specifications, size of order accepted and ordering convenience
- The availability of product information and/or demonstration
- A customer service orientation in front line staff.

Such factors are part of the offer to the customer, and responsibility for them should be clearly apportioned by negotiation between manufacturers and intermediaries, and monitored. If the manufacturer has a service policy of re-supplying faulty goods, the willingness of a retailer to mediate the return and exchange should be ascertained.

2.1.4 Degree of control

Manufacturers may wish to **control or dominate** a distribution channel:

(a) Ensuring that its policies with regard to pricing, promotion and sales service are carried out, and its marketing message is integrated all the way to the point of sale

(b) Maintaining closer contact with consumers and sources of marketing information

(c) Gaining competitive advantage by having exclusive distribution through major retailers or distributors.

2.1.5 Degree of co-operation or conflict

As business relationships, channels are subject to conflicts of interest, culture, priorities and personalities. Attention will need to be given to **channel management** where negotiations and problem-solving take up an unacceptable amount of managerial time, or result in lost sales (for example, though lack of co-operation on promotions or point-of-sale display).

2.2 New opportunities in distribution

There are opportunities to be exploited in distribution.

(a) Offering EDI (**electronic data interchange**) enables a firm to cut lead times for orders. This can be a source of differentiation.

(b) Distribution has a **branding effect**. Distribution can be a central and explicit part of a brand's identity, such as First Direct (Midland Bank's telephone banking subsidiary).

(c) Distribution might become part of the **marketing information** system. Retailers (through using scanning technology) probably know more about customers than manufacturers.

Changes and new opportunities, from direct mail order marketing or Internet marketing to retail outlet refitting and re-siting, should be evaluated.

Action Programme 3

The Needle Works

From your knowledge of The Needle Works so far, how effective is its present distribution strategy, and what new opportunities might profitably be exploited?

3 Product

3.1 What is a product?

FAST FORWARD

A **product** is a package of benefits.

Key concept

A '**product**' is a **package of benefits**, although we tend to think of it as a 'thing' with 'features'.

The package of benefits includes:

(a) A **physical aspect**, which relates to the components, materials and specifications (colour, size etc.) of the product: for example, a size 12 pullover made of 100% pure wool in a natural colour

(b) A **functional aspect**, which is a statement of how a product performs and for what purpose it is likely to be bought: the wool pullover may give warmth and comfort

(c) A **symbolic aspect**, which represents the qualities the product suggests to, or confers upon, the buyer: the '100% pure wool' label may represent quality, status or ecology (as a natural rather than synthetic product).

The overall package for the marketer includes:

- Product specifications and materials
- Product design or styling
- Product functions and benefits
- Product packaging
- The range of products in a 'line', and additions to or deletions from it.

There are many strategic issues in product planning, positioning, branding and portfolio management. However, at the co-ordinatory level, you are most likely to be involved in the following.

(a) **Monitoring product performance** over time, through the product life cycle, and in relation to competitors.

(b) **Monitoring product trends**: new products entering the market, existing products becoming fashionable (or becoming fashionable again) and product modifications by competitors.

(c) **Co-ordinating product-related promotional activity:** launch marketing, market testing and consumer research, promotional packaging (special offers/competitions on pack) and so on.

3.2 Monitoring product performance

FAST FORWARD

> **Product analysis** can be used to determine how successfully a product or product line is performing.

Product performance can be monitored and analysed using:

- Sales and profit/contribution figures
- Feedback from sales reps and retailers
- Customer research, (questionnaires, feedback forms, attitude surveys, perceptual mapping)
- Records of customer complaints, warranty claims
- Comparative competitor and market data
- Product life cycle (PLC) and Boston Consulting Group (BCG) Growth Share models, which show how sales, profitability and market share of a product can be expected to change over time

Marketing at Work

McDonald's fast food restaurants are slashing their burger menus across Europe to make way for a **new range** of healthier foods including chicken salads and chopped fruit.

Launched today in the UK, Salad Plus has been dubbed McDonald's 'most significant menu change' in its 30-year history.

The move follows the chain's decision last week to phase out 'super-size' fries and drinks in the US and is a major attempt to fight for the £445 million-a-year prepared salad market.

McDonald's, which has come under increasing pressure from anti-obesity campaigners who claim the company encourages an unhealthy lifestyle, will overhaul menus in 16 European countries by slashing its line-up of burgers for chicken salads, yoghurts and chopped fruits. The chain has already successfully introduced a premium salads range in the US.

Denis Hennequin, executive vice-present of McDonald's Europe, said the company was also working with nutritionists on a 'smart labelling' system which should be ready by the end of the year.

www.mad.co.uk: 9 March 2004

As we discussed in Part A of this Text, the quantitative data can tell you 'how' a product is doing, but not 'why': some qualitative data on consumer perceptions will need to be gathered to analyse trends which may present potential threats and opportunities.

3.3 Monitoring product trends

> **FAST FORWARD**
>
> **Product trends** may be prompted by technical, social, political, economic or environmental factors, as well as by the progression of the product life cycle.

This should form part of the environmental scanning discussed in Part A of this Text.

(a) To indicate opportunities for new products in order to anticipate or keep pace with consumer needs and wants, technological capability and/or competitor activity

(b) To indicate the need to modify existing products, positioning or promotion, for the same reasons.

We can talk about product trends because products alter in consumers' perceptions, competitive position and technological up-to-dateness with time.

The word 'trend' has also come to be used to describe 'fashions' and this is also a feature of product perception and buying patterns.

(a) **Technological development** can prompt buying (and supply) trends. As microchip technology gets cheaper and more sophisticated, for example, there has been increased miniaturisation of electronic products (from computers to calculators and watches), and trends toward more sophisticated and higher-quality audio-visual reproduction (supporting fashions like the i-Pod).

(b) **Social-cultural factors** can prompt fashions and fads, such as increased consumption of wine with meals in the UK (supported by exposure to Europe and an expanding world-wide range of choice) or a preference for 'green' and ethical products (eg free range eggs).

(c) **Economic and political factors** prompt trends based on disposable income, tax efficiency and attitudes towards financial responsibility. The market for small, fuel-economical cars, for example, is growing steadily at the expense of large and luxury models.

There is undoubtedly value in gathering environmental data in order to identify trends. However, there are limitations to the ability of apparent trends to 'predict' the future. Change is a complex phenomenon and it is possible to oversimplify the model underlying an apparent trend.

This is not to say that marketers should not use their 'antennae' for marketing opportunities! If you have an instinct that a certain product area or innovation is going to be The Next Big Thing – speak up! But be aware that this does not make for accurate R & D budgeting or sales forecasting. In real life – as in the *Marketing in Practice* assessment – you will usually need to justify any product recommendations you make.

PART D CO-ORDINATING THE MARKETING MIX

Action Programme 4

The following is a *perceptual map* plotting consumer respondents' views on different brands of toilet tissue, asked whether they found it 'strong' or 'weak' to handle, and 'soft' or 'harsh' to the touch.

How would you report on the performance of Brand X, as its marketing co-ordinator?

Note that product trends are not just about new product opportunities. The energy and effort invested in adding new products and brands to the portfolio is seldom mirrored by the identification and weeding out of weak and declining, redundant and non-'fitting' products. Effective marketing co-ordination means directing resources to profitable activities: beware product proliferation or sentimental attachments to 'dead horses'.

3.4 New product testing

At a preliminary stage the **concept** for the new product should be tested on potential customers to obtain their reactions. It is common to use the company staff as guinea pigs for a new product idea, although their reaction is unlikely to be typical. But it is difficult to get sensible reactions from customers. Consider the following examples.

(a) New designs for wallpaper. When innovative new designs are tested on potential customers it is often found that they are conditioned by traditional designs and are dismissive of new design ideas.

(b) New ideas for chocolate confectionery have the opposite problem. Potential customers typically say they *like* the new concept (because most people like chocolate bars). However, when the new product is launched it is not successful because people continue to buy old favourites.

A working **prototype of the product**, which can be tried by customers, can be used for **product testing**. This stage is also very useful for making preliminary explorations of production costs and practical problems. We need to have some idea of whether the product could be produced in sufficient quantities at the right price were it to be launched. The form the product test takes will depend very much on the type of product concerned. The best advice seems to be that to get realistic responses the test should replicate reality as clearly as possible.

(a) If the product is used in the home, a sample of respondents should be given the product to use at home.

(b) If the product is chosen from amongst competitors in a retail outlet (as with chocolate bars) then the product test needs to rate response against competitive products.

(c) If inherent product quality is an important attribute of the product then a 'blind' test could be used in which customers are not told who is producing the new product.

(d) An industrial product could be used for a trial period by a customer in a realistic setting.

3.5 Product-related launch and promotion activity

Bear in mind the following.

(a) A **'new' product** can be one that opens up an entirely new market, one that replaces an existing product, or one that broadens the market for an existing product.

(b) An **'old' product** can become 'new' if it is introduced to a new market, is packaged in a different way, or is promoted in a different way.

4 The extended marketing mix

FAST FORWARD

The 'added elements' of the **extended marketing mix** are:

- People
- Processes
- Physicals

These are particularly relevant to **service marketing**, and are sometimes called the 'service marketing mix'.

Exam tip

Questions have been set in December 2002, June 2003, December 2003 and June 2005 along the lines of: *'How can the full (or extended or service) marketing mix be used to ...?'* Aside from focusing on the purpose stated, in your answer, you really need to take in the words 'full' and/or 'extended'! The examiner noted: 'This is the seven Ps. Candidates who thought this was about four, five or three Ps were obviously at a disadvantage!' Better candidates use the 7Ps as a framework, within which they make *specific proposals:* eg signage or uniforms (for Physical Evidence), staff training (for People), automated call answering (for Processes) and so on. Look out, also, for phrases such as 'the *rest* of the extended marketing mix' – if some elements have already been dealt with or specifically excluded: focus on the RIGHT Ps!

The examiner is making this increasingly clear, to help you avoid the pitfalls. In December 2005 and both exams in 2006, questions referred to 'the **THREE** elements of the service marketing mix (people, process and physical evidence). Don't rely on this though: be alert!

4.1 People

People are an important ingredient in the marketing mix and environment (as Part B of this Text should have indicated).

(a) The market itself consists of people, with different (or similar, within market segments) needs, values, attitudes and disposable income. Marketing involves attempting to understand people's needs and behaviour.

(b) Suppliers, distributors, business contacts and competitors are people: doing business involves building relationships.

(c) Marketers, salespeople and customer service personnel are people.

The importance of employees in the marketing mix is particularly important in **service marketing**, because of the **inseparability** of the service from the service provider: the 'creation' of the service and 'consumption' of the service generally happen at the same moment, at the interface between the server and the served. Front-line staff must be selected, trained and motivated with particular attention to customer care and public relations.

In the case of some services, the physical presence of people actually performing the service is a vital aspect of customer satisfaction: think of clerks in a bank, or personnel in catering establishments. The staff involved are performing or producing a service, selling the service and also liaising with the customer to promote the service, gather information and respond to customer needs.

Arguably, however, all members of the organisation are involved in 'marketing': all personnel should have the skills, motivation and attitudes to do their jobs to a professional standard as a 'quality workforce', and should be rewarded and valued accordingly. This means concrete policies and continuous development.

- Policies of selection
- Programmes of training
- Standard, consistent operational practices
- Standardised operational rules
- Effective motivational programmes
- Managerial appointments
- The attractiveness and appropriateness of the service offer
- Effective policies of staff reward and remuneration

4.2 Processes

Processes are the way in which marketing tasks are carried out. Efficient processes can become a marketing advantage in their own right. If an airline, for example, develops a sophisticated ticketing system, it can offer shorter waits at check-in or wider choice of flights through allied airlines. Efficient order processing not only increases customer satisfaction, but cuts down on the time it takes the organisation to complete a sale.

Issues to be considered include the following.

- Policies, particularly with regard to ethical dealings (a key issue for many consumers)
- Procedures, for efficiency and standardisation
- Automation/computerisation of processes
- Queuing and waiting times
- Information gathering, processing and communication times
- Capacity management, matching supply to demand in a timely and cost effective way
- Accessibility of facilities, premises, personnel and services

Such issues are particularly important in service marketing, because of the characteristic of '**heterogeneity**': because of the number of factors and different people, involved, it is difficult to standardise the service offered. The quality and precise specifications will vary with the circumstances and individuals.

(a) Establishing service standards and objectives, as far as possible
(b) Co-ordinating staffing levels to smooth out fluctuations in demand
(c) Managing customer contact points, to avoid unnecessary queuing and facilitate information-giving

Services are also innately **perishable**: a doctor's services may be put off, but not really 'kept until later' – still less an information request or seat on a bus. Services have a specific, often narrow, window of opportunity. This factor, too, creates a need for process planning for adequate staffing levels, without wasteful over-manning for efficient work flow.

4.3 Physicals

Physical elements include:

- Tangible evidence of purchase
- The corporate and purchase environment

Again, this is particularly important in service industries, because of:

- The **intangibility** or lack of physical substance involved in service
- The **lack of ownership** of services

These factors make it difficult for consumers to perceive, evaluate and compare the qualities of service provision, and may therefore dampen the incentive to consume.

Issues of intangibility and ownership can be tackled by making available a tangible symbol or representation of the service 'product' or ownership, and the benefits it confers. Tickets, programs and merchandise for entertainment, certificates of attainment for educational services and customer loyalty, discount or credit cards are all 'cues' representing the service available and a history of past positive experiences.

Alternatively, the physical evidence may be incorporated into the design and specification of the service environment involving the building, location or atmosphere to:

- Convey the nature of the service involved
- Transmit messages and information
- Imply aesthetic qualities, moral values or other aspects of a corporate image
- Reinforce an existing image
- Reassure about the professionalism and security of the business
- Engender an emotional reaction in the customer.

Such environmental factors include finishing, decor, colour scheme, noise levels, background music, smells and ambience.

Marketing at Work

'So-called **4S stores** are retail outlets that deal in the sales, spare parts, services and surveys of particular brands of cars. The potential market is huge for incoming enterprises able to offer the best *services contracts* under this sector of the market.

'Mazda's sales centre at Meilinguan in Shenzhen is one example. A clean and neat maintenance area, modern equipment and management, highly professional ambience, impressive service facilities, ample supply of spare parts and swift follow-up services make it a favourite location for car owners.

'4S stores are also intensifying competition on the Chinese mainland. Consumer demand is diversifying and people are becoming more demanding with the products and services they pay for. The old dealership system can no longer meet market and consumer needs.

PART D CO-ORDINATING THE MARKETING MIX

'The emergence of 4S stores is apparently the answer to these needs. 4S stores seem to help cultivate consumers' faith in particular brands and increase their sales.

'Mr Zhang, a traditional car dealer, admitted that his company's recent drop in sales was due to competition from 4S stores. It seems to suggest that conventional car dealers fail to provide the kind of personalised "quality service" that 4S stores have to offer.

'Car sales have close profit margins and dealers mainly rely on after-sale service for their profits. After selling a car, they have to woo buyers into bringing it back for maintenance by offering a better service.'

Lou (2004)

Action Programme 5

What physicals could be provided by:

(a) a provider of adventure sport activities?
(b) a provider of tourist information services?
(c) a provider of travel services?
(d) a TV rental provider?

5 ICT and the new marketing mix

FAST FORWARD

Even with the advent of **information and communication technology (ICT)**, the marketing mix still provides a sound framework for generating marketing strategy. According to Chaffey (2002) 'the Internet provides many new opportunities for the marketer to vary the marketing mix'.

5.1 ICT in the marketing mix

The following are some examples of the use of ICT in the marketing mix.

Product
- www.Barbie.com has games online that involve styling the dolls. The most popular choices are fed through to new product development.
- Product information can be provided by analysing consumer queries. EasyJet has a detailed set of FAQ's, compiled from the hundreds of thousands of online questions it receives.
- Outline information may itself be the product, eg with online databases or access to information via mobile phones.

Price
- In theory, prices are more easily compared between many suppliers using the Internet.
- Offering differential pricing for products purchased over the Internet has become commonplace. EasyJet offered a £5 discount on flights booked online.

Place
- The Internet and mobile telephone technology has enabled worldwide and remote access to products and services.
- E-commerce and m-commerce empower customers to order, pay for and monitor the delivery of products themselves: a form of direct marketing, cutting out layers of the supply chain.

Promotion
- We looked in detail at the Internet as a promotional tool in Chapter 13.

Marketing at Work

The web division of Sainsbury's has launched a kitchen appliance shop which it claims is part of a strategy to move further into non-food **online retail**.

The new channel can be accessed through the Sainsbury's To You site and offers a database of 4,000 product lines.

'Supermarkets have changed, becoming more of a one-stop shop,' said online director Toby Anderson. 'We plan to turn Sainsbury's online store into more of a general retail business. The web division has elastic walls and we're able to provide a wider product range.'

Sainsbury's aims to offer lower prices than rival retailers, and promises to deliver goods in five to seven days.

'The range will only be available online so we'll have lower overheads and we're prepared to accept a lower profit margin,' said Anderson.

New Media Age, 5 March 2004

5.2 ICT in the extended marketing mix

> **FAST FORWARD**
>
> The **service** elements of the marketing mix are as important in the virtual world as they are in the physical world.

The **People** element of the marketing mix refers to the how an organisations' staff interact with customers and other stakeholders. Some of these interactions can be automated. Examples include:

- **Autoresponders**, which automatically generate a response when an e-mail is received.
- **E-mail notifications**, which update customers on the status of their order.
- **Call-back facility**, whereby customers fill in their phone number on a form and specify a convenient time to be contacted.
- **Frequently Asked Questions** (FAQ).
- **On site search engines**, to help customers find what they're looking for quickly.

Interactivity is essential when considering ICT and the extended marketing mix.

Process	Speed of website access, via search engines
	Fast access to related links
	Stable website that does not break down
	Ease of navigation
	Increasing options for e-commerce and m-commerce = self-service purchase and payment transactions.
Physical evidence	Design and layout of the website
	Content and pictures easy to understand
	Pre-paid phones cards (and variants) as proof of e-transactions
People	Interactivity via personalised e-mail
	Virtual communities created with mobile phones and Internet chat rooms, discussion boards etc
	Customer care and technical support lines

In addition, physical evidence in the form of *printable* confirmations and vouchers may be important particularly for less accustomed users, who feel insecure with 'virtual' records of transactions.

PART D CO-ORDINATING THE MARKETING MIX

Action Programme 6

How could a company use the Internet to:

• Undertake market research?	
• Generate sales leads?	
• Offer after-sales support?	
• Improve staff performance (and thereby customer satisfaction)?	

[*Key skill for Marketers: Using ICT and the Internet*]

In summary, here are some ideas to consider: Figure 14.1.

Product
- Online support
- Clearly designed website
- Interactivity
- Focused on the 'surfer'
- New products (eg i-Pod)

Place
- Electronic distribution
- E-mail
- Networked computers to improve communications
- Supply chain (e-procurement)
- Use of laptops

People
- Innovative
- Technically competent

Use of ICT in the marketing mix

Price
- Online secure payment by credit card
- Personal billing
- Ease of comparison by consumers

Process
- New technologies eg broadband, 3G mobile phones, WAP
- Integrated databases for customer relationship management

Promotion
- Web banners and pop-ups
- Web page sponsorship
- Web newsletters and updates
- Site imagery
- Online offers

Figure 14.1: The cybermarketing mix

Exam tip

> There will almost certainly (December 2002, June and December 2003, June and December 2004) be a question such as: *'How can the firm use ICT to …?'* Like all questions on this paper, you need to:
>
> - Broaden your thinking – to include ICT applications in all 7Ps of the mix and all aspects of ICT (Internet, mobile phone, SMS, fax, digital TV/radio, database interrogation)
> - Narrow your thinking – to answer the purpose set, in the context given.
>
> As usual, a mnemonic may help to marshal your thoughts. (The examiner recommends Smith and Chaffy's Ss: 'Speak, Sell, Serve, Save, Sizzle' – if this doesn't ring a bell, see Action Programme 6 of Chapter 13.) However, it cannot substitute for contextualisation/application! Make practical, cost-effective, tactical proposals.

Chapter Roundup

- **Price** can be defined as a measure of the value exchanged by the buyer for the value offered by the seller. It is an important part of the perceived quality and differentiation of the offer, and as such must be integrated carefully into the marketing mix.

- **Price sensitivity** varies according to market and personal variables, and can be measured as the price **elasticity** of demand.

- The **effect of price changes** can be assessed using quantitative and qualitative data on sales performance, contribution, consumer attitudes and competitor/supplier/distributor reactions.

- **Place** is concerned with the selection of distribution channels and logistics.

- **Channels of distribution** should be evaluated for effectiveness, efficiency and economy, level of customer service, degree of controllability and quality of business relationship.

- A **product** is a package of benefits.

- **Product analysis** can be used to determine how successfully a product or product line is performing.

- **Product trends** may be prompted by technical, social, political, economic or environmental factors, as well as by the progression of the product life cycle.

- The 'added elements' of the **extended marketing mix** are:
  - People
  - Processes
  - Physicals

  These are particularly relevant to **service marketing**, and are sometimes called the 'service marketing mix'.

- Even with the advent of **information and communication technology (ICT)**, the marketing mix still provides a sound framework for generating marketing strategy. According to Chaffey (2002) 'the Internet provides many new opportunities for the marketer to vary the marketing mix'.

- The **service** elements of the marketing mix are as important in the virtual world as they are in the physical world.

PART D CO-ORDINATING THE MARKETING MIX

Quick Quiz

1 Outline how (a) a market test and (b) attitude surveys can be used to evaluate the effect of pricing decisions.

2 What measures of the effectiveness of a distribution channel might you consider?

3 What factors are prompting widespread changes in distribution methods?

4 How can product performance be monitored?

5 Give an example of product trends prompted by each of the PEST factors.

6 How can consumer response to a new product be pre-tested?

7 Explain the terms 'inseparability', 'intangibility' and 'perishability' as applied to service marketing.

8 What measures should be considered to manage (a) people, and (b) processes for consistent customer service?

9 Give examples of how ICT can be used in the marketing mix.

Answers to Quick Quiz

1 See (c) and (d) of Paragraph 1.3.

2 Effectiveness; efficiency and economy; level of service; degree of control; degree of co-operation or conflict.

3 Electronic data interchange; branding; information gathering (see Paragraph 2.2)

4 A list of suggestions is given in Paragraph 3.2.

5 Political: disposable income, tax. Environment: green sympathies, protection of the natural world. Social: fashions and must-haves, or ethical concerns. Technological: ease of production, range of possibilities.

6 Pre-testing should aim to replicate the real use of the product as much as possible with a prototype. Blind testing is an alternative.

7 Inseparability: the service cannot be separated from the service provider. Intangibility: lack of physical substance; Perishability: the opportunity for the service exists in time and if not used, is lost.

8 People: see the list of issues in Paragraph 4.1. Processes: a list of issues is given in Paragraph 4.2.

9 See Paragraphs 5.1 and 5.2 for ideas.

Action Programme Review

1. Quantity sold has gone down by 200,000 units, representing £64,000 of sales revenue. However, *contribution* by Product X is as follows.

   Year 200X   1,300,000 × (0.28 − 0.16) = £156,000
   Year 200Y   1,100,000 × (0.32 − 0.16) = £176,000

   An increase of £20,000 in contribution

2. (a) A price reduction may mean: the item is about to be superseded by a later model; the item has some fault and is not selling well; the firm is in financial trouble and may not stay in business to supply future parts/service; the price may come down even further, so it will pay to wait; the quality has been reduced.

   (b) A price increase may mean: the item is 'hot' and may be unobtainable unless bought soon; the item represents unusually good value; the seller is greedy and is charging what the traffic will bear.

3. The Needle Works' current distribution system relies entirely on its retail store. This functions well within its geographical area and market: it is the largest space of its kind used in craft retail, carries a wide range of stock, and is regarded as a kind of 'superstore' in the market. The premises are perceived as a 'quality' setting, and encourage customer re-visit. As far as we know, there are no problems involved in inventory, transportation or warehousing: The Needle Works controls all these stages of the distribution process.

   However, there is a major shortcoming in the failure of the system to reach the wider geographical market for its products and services – which obviously exist, given the visitor/tourist sales. The Needle Works needs to consider

   (a) mail order; direct selling through a catalogue of its products and services
   (b) Internet promotion and/or selling.

   With a warehouse of its own (the capacity of which would need to be evaluated) and an efficient EPOS system in place, attention would need to be given to postage/freight costs of sending products direct to consumers, plus the capacity and training of staff to handle the increased volume and information requirements of orders. The catalogue and website would need to be designed and produced, but the costs are likely to be minimal compared to increased orders. The Needle Works could retain control over its image for quality and personal service, and provide the specialist information it may not trust to intermediaries.

4. You would be fairly pleased that your brand was perceived as one of the strongest available. You would, however, worry slightly that people found it harsh to the touch: people who want a soft tissue, and are less worried about strength, are presumably buying Brands A, B or C. You would also be a bit concerned that people see little to choose between your Brand X and competing Brands Y and Z: it may come down to price on the supermarket shelves. However, you would be delighted to see that a great opportunity exists for a soft and strong toilet tissue: there is no competition there at the moment, and if people are buying Brand A for its softness, how much more eagerly they will buy Brand X if it were sold on 'softness – with strength'!

5. (a) A photo or video of the activity is a common one, or perhaps merchandise such as a T-shirt or baseball cap.

   (b) A map or brochure, guide book or souvenir.

   (c) An itinerary or ticket.

   (d) A rental schedule, reminder card, customer card.

6

• Undertake market research	• Create an online focus group
• Generate sales leads	• Channel all website enquiries to the sales team
• Offer after-sales support	• Respond promptly to enquiries – set up a page featuring FAQs
• Improve staff performance (and thereby customer satisfaction)	• Set up online (via intranet) product information, to make sure all staff know about products and services

Now try Question 14 at the end of the Study Text

Part E
Administering the marketing budget (and evaluating results)

Understanding marketing budgets

Chapter topic list

1. Budgeting and budgetary control
2. Marketing budgets
3. Administration of the budget
4. Flexible budgets
5. Accuracy of budgets
6. Computers and budgeting

Syllabus content – knowledge and skills requirements

- 5.1 Demonstrate an ability to manipulate numbers in a marketing context
- 5.1 Explain the process used for setting a budget

PART E: ADMINISTERING THE MARKETING BUDGET (AND EVALUATING RESULTS)

Introduction

In this chapter, we look at the related processes of:

(a) **Setting budgets**: the process of forecasting expenditure and revenues for given activities or areas of activity (especially in marketing); and

(b) **Budgetary control**: the process whereby managers investigate any differences between budgeted and actual results, so that corrective action can be taken if necessary.

1 Budgeting and budgetary control

1.1 Introduction to budgets

FAST FORWARD

Budgets are the concrete components of what is known as a **budgetary control system**.

Exam tip

The senior examiner has said that he does not want this section of the syllabus to strike terror into the hearts of students and lecturers. You do need to have an appreciation of costs, how they are apportioned, and how cost effective are marketing activities. As such, basic manipulation of figures is essential. You may need to present a budget for a proposed promotional exercise.

Businesses must concentrate on their objectives if they are to be successful. Having established a long-term corporate plan, management should develop a co-ordinated short-term plan which will steer the business towards long-term goals. This is usually done using **budgeting**, a process which draws together the necessary actions and co-ordinates the activities of management, with a master budget as an end result.

The organisation should gain from the actual preparation process, as well as from the budget itself.

However tightly an organisation may wish to control its expenditure, conditions change and budgets may have to change with them. A strong local campaign by a competitor, for example, may require you to change your priorities away from national advertising and match their local focus. Budgets should be **flexible**.

1.2 The purpose of budgetary control systems

FAST FORWARD

Such a system essentially ensures communication, co-ordination and control within an organisation.

Communication, **co-ordination** and **control** are general objectives of budgetary control systems. Specific objectives include the following.

(a) **To ensure the achievement of the organisation's objectives**

Objectives for the organisation as a whole, and for the marketing department as a unit within the organisation, are set. Quantified expressions of these objectives are then drawn up as targets to be achieved.

(b) **To compel planning**

This is probably the most important feature of a budgetary planning and control system. Planning forces management to look ahead, to set out detailed plans for achieving the targets for each department, operation and each manager and to anticipate problems.

(c) **To communicate ideas and plans**

A formal system is necessary to ensure that each person affected by the plans is aware of what he or she is supposed to be doing.

(d) **To co-ordinate activities**

The activities of different departments of the organisation need to be coordinated. This concept of co-ordination implies, for example, that the production budget should be based on sales expectations.

(e) **To provide a framework for responsibility accounting**

Budgetary planning and control systems require that managers are made responsible for the achievement of their budget targets. For the marketing manager, this is likely to mean that he or she must not overspend!

(f) **To establish a system of control**

Control over actual performance is provided by the comparisons of actual results against the budget. Departures from budget can then be investigated.

(g) **To motivate employees to improve their performance**

The interest and commitment of employees can be retained via a system of feedback of actual results, which lets them know how well or badly they are performing.

1.3 Types of budget planning

> **FAST FORWARD**
>
> Depending on how the organisation is managed, marketing (and other) goals may be set at different levels.

There are three types of budget planning for a marketing budget, depending on how the organisation is managed.

(a) **Top-down planning** involves the setting of goals for lower management by higher management.

(b) **Bottom-up planning** exists where employees set their own goals and submit them to higher management for approval.

(c) **'Goals down-plans up'** planning is a mixture of the two styles, whereby top management sets overall goals and employees lower in the organisation hierarchy then set plans for achieving those goals. This type of planning is well suited to the formulation of sales budgets.

2 Marketing budgets

> **FAST FORWARD**
>
> A **marketing budget** is a financial plan for a defined period of time which will include planned expenditure and revenues connected with marketing activities.

The overall marketing budget is made up of a number of **individual budgets** that relate to individual plans associated with **different marketing activities and functions**. If the marketer can estimate the benefits – financial and otherwise – that a particular investment will bring then the feasibility of going ahead with that plan can be assessed.

Following an activity, marketers should **evaluate** the plan and determine whether it should be repeated or not. Any promotional activity that is planned takes place in the future, and it is possible that hidden costs may emerge, or the situation change so that the plan is not implemented as expected. The evaluation process should investigate whether any increased costs could have been prevented, or whether the activity was not as viable as initial calculations identified.

PART E ADMINISTERING THE MARKETING BUDGET (AND EVALUATING RESULTS)

2.1 The marketing plan

The marketing **plan** consists of several inter-related decisions.

(a) **Sales targets**: these must be set for each product and each sales division (with sub-targets also set for sales regions, sales areas and individual salesmen). Sales targets may be referred to as **sales quotas**.

(b) The **total marketing budget** must be set.

(c) Given an overall marketing budget, **resources must be allocated**.

- **Salaries** of salespeople
- **Above-the-line** expenditure (advertising)
- **Below-the-line** expenditure (sales promotion items, price reduction allowances)

(d) Expenditure on marketing will also be allocated to **different products or services** within the organisation's range. Some products might justify additional marketing expenditure whereas others, nearing the end of their life cycle, may lose a part of their previous allocation.

2.2 Why have a sales and marketing budget?

Budgeting for **sales revenue** and **selling costs** is plagued with uncertainty. The variables are so many and so difficult to estimate, even within a wide tolerance (largely because of competitive action and changing consumer habits and tastes), that both setting budgets and budgetary control on the marketing side are different from the more 'mechanical' approach which can be adopted with other budgets.

A sales and marketing budget is necessary for the following reasons.

(a) It is an element of the **overall strategic plan** of the business (the master budget) which brings together all the activities of the business.

(b) Where sales and other non-production costs are a large part of total costs, it is **financially prudent** to forecast, plan and control them.

(c) The uncertain nature of factors which influence selling makes the need for good forecasts and plans greater. If budgets are to be used for **control**, then where budget estimates are more uncertain, more budgetary control is necessary.

2.3 Setting a marketing cost budget

FAST FORWARD

> **Marketing costs** can be budgeted using percentage of sales, competitive parity or the objective/task method.

Unquantified value objectives (such as 'increasing sales') will make it difficult to:

- Assess whether the money was well spent and the objective was achieved
- Produce properly and specifically designed promotions.

There are a number of ways of setting marketing budgets.

(a) **Percentage of sales**. Research has shown that in the UK, some marketing budgets are fixed by some rule-of-thumb, non-scientific methods, such as the following.

- A percentage of the previous year's sales
- A percentage of the budgeted annual sales
- A percentage of the previous year's profit

There is no reason, however, why marketing costs should relate directly to either total turnover or profits. Given that large amounts of expenditure may be incurred on advertising, these arbitrary guesswork systems reveal an alarming lack of proper financial control.

(Empirical observation and testing, or mathematical models, can be used to estimate more accurately the effect expenditure has on sales.)

- (b) **Competitive parity**, ie fixing marketing expenditure in relation to the expenditure incurred by competitors. (This is unsatisfactory because it presupposes that the competitor's decision must be a good one.)
- (c) **The objective and task method**. The marketing task for the organisation is set and a budget is prepared which will help to ensure that this objective is achieved.

Wilmshurst (1999) says that 'one of the problems often associated with advertising is that the costs are all too obvious but the gains not very clear'. He suggests that this difficulty can be minimised if **clearly quantified objectives** are set out. He gives the following examples.

1. **To produce direct sales of £100,000**, ie orders are to be received from people replying directly to the advertisement totalling this amount or more.
2. **To increase the number of people who have knowledge** of specific features of the product or the company from 15 per cent of the population to 25 per cent.
3. **To produce enquiries from genuinely interested potential customers** at a cost of not more than £9.50 per enquiry.
4. To achieve a situation where at least **60 per cent of our target audience can 'recall'** an advertisement up to two weeks after it has appeared.

Another crucial factor is *resource availability*: 'how much do we have to spend?' This will have a fundamental influence on the type of marketing activities that can be carried out.

> **Exam tip**
>
> Most papers require basic calculations for Part A, using numerical data given to add up costs, calculate profits and work out the cost/profit implications of changes in strategy. The examiner reminds candidates that numerical information can also be conveyed in words ('one hundred members') – and that 'per week', 'per month' or 'per year' make a great difference to calculations, depending on what is required. There is no substitute for practice in this area!
>
> This area of the syllabus isn't just about number work, though. In December 2006, you were asked to describe three methods of setting a marketing budget, and recommend one for the scenario.

2.4 Example: marketing cost budget

The example below shows a typical marketing cost budget. Notice that in this example only the selling and agency commission vary directly with the level of sales.

Marketing cost budget

	£
Salaries and wages of marketing staff	X
Advertising expenses	X
Travelling and distribution costs	X
Market research activities	X
Promotional activities	X
Selling and agency commission	X
	X

2.4.1 Fixed and variable costs

Many cost items will be fixed, although, as we can see from above, there will be some variable costs such as sales commission, which varies directly with the level of sales. Some of the marketing budget will have to be prepared in conjunction with the sales budget since the level of sales anticipated will rely on marketing support. The balance of the budget may well be determined by the activity anticipated from new products which may be launched during the year, and which will need promotional support.

2.4.2 Direct and indirect costs

Direct costs are costs that are incurred directly as a result of carrying out marketing activity. (One way of looking at them is: do they come out of the marketing budget?) If you don't carry out any marketing, you don't incur any direct costs. These include media, print, agency fees and so on.

Indirect costs (or overheads) are costs incurred by the organisation that can be attributed to marketing activity, but which might still be incurred whether or not the activity was carried out. Examples include rents paid for marketing offices, costs of office equipment, salaries of support staff and so on.

- **Simple method costing** takes account only of direct costs, when estimating the cost of a given marketing activity.

    This is quick, simple and relatively easy to calculate: a good rule of thumb for comparing costs of various marketing options. (It is usually sufficient for an exam scenario.)

- **Complex method costing** takes into account direct and indirect costs. It is a more true and realistic picture of the total costs of marketing activity for the purposes of planning and evaluation. (A complex method costing may be twice the amount of a simple method costing for the same marketing activity ...)

We will cover costing in more detail in Chapter 16.

Exam tip

In June 2006, you had to distinguish between the direct and indirect costs of an event.

In the June 2004 exam you were asked to calculate:

(a) the **costs** (to an advertising agency) of performing work, and
(b) the **charges** made (by the agency to its client) for the work.

As the agency is a business, you were expected to note that there should be a difference between the two! Get to grips with these basic concepts.

2.5 Budgetary control

Once the plan has been implemented, the task of marketing management is to control the use of resources. Aspects of control include the following.

- Comparison of actual sales against the budget
- Comparison of actual marketing costs against budgeted levels (measuring effective cost control)
- Comparison of marketing costs against sales (measuring cost-effectiveness)
- Analysis of the profitability of individual products, and distribution outlets
- Strategic control, ie checking whether the company's objectives, products and resources are being directed towards the correct markets.

We will be looking at the evaluation of marketing decisions in Chapter 16.

The allocation of **direct selling costs** to products or type of outlet is fairly straightforward, but **indirect costs** must also be allocated. This aspect of cost allocation should be carefully considered when deciding whether to eliminate an unprofitable expenditure from selling or distribution.

(a) The cost of distributing goods to a distant area may seem unprofitable but if, by not selling the goods in this area, there will be **unused production capacity**, the products which are produced and sold will have to bear a higher proportion of fixed costs.

(b) The allocation of fixed selling costs to products may make a product seem unprofitable, but the product may still be making a **contribution** to those fixed costs.

Eliminating unprofitable selling and distribution expenditure is sound commercial practice. If the removal of one part of selling costs relieves a company of a cost which is higher than the contribution to profit gained from it, then this part of selling activity can and should be eliminated. The unavoidable fixed costs of production as well as selling and distribution should be taken into account in any such decision.

Action Programme 1

Does your organisation operate a budgeting system? Talk to various managers to find out what functions budgets perform in your organisation.

3 Administration of the budget

3.1 Responsibility for the preparation of budgets

Managers responsible for **preparing** budgets should ideally be the managers (and their subordinates) who are responsible for **carrying out** the budget. For example, the marketing manager should draft the marketing expenditure budget and marketing overhead cost centre budget.

3.2 Budget committee

> **FAST FORWARD**
>
> The co-ordination and administration of budgets organisation-wide is usually the responsibility of a **budget committee** (with the managing director as chairman).

Every part of the organisation should be represented on the committee, so there should be a representative from sales, production and marketing. Functions of the budget committee include the following.

- **Co-ordination** of the preparation of budgets, which includes the issue of the budget manual
- Issuing of **timetables** for the preparation of functional budgets
- Allocation of **responsibilities** for the preparation of functional budgets
- Provision of **information** to assist in the preparation of budgets
- **Communication** of final budgets to the appropriate managers
- **Comparison** of actual results with budget and the investigation of variances
- **Continuous assessment** of the budgeting and planning process, in order to improve the planning and control function

3.3 The budget preparation timetable

> **FAST FORWARD**
>
> The **principal budget factor** (or key budget factor or limiting budget factor) is the factor that limits an organisation's performance for a given period. It is often the starting point in budget preparation. In most organisations, this will be sales demand.

Let us now look at the steps involved in the preparation of a budget for The Needle Works. The step-by-step approach described here is indicative of the steps followed by many organisations. The budget committee may meet several times before an organisation's budget is finally agreed.

Step 1 **Communicating details of the budget policy and budget guidelines**

The long-term plan is the starting point for the preparation of the annual budget. Managers of the Needle Works responsible for preparing the budget must be aware of the way it is affected by the long-term plan so that it becomes part of the process of meeting the organisation's objectives. For example, if the long-term plan calls for a more aggressive pricing policy, the budget must take this into account.

Step 2 **Determining the factor that restricts output**

In most organisations the principal budget factor is sales demand. The Needle Works will be restricted from making and selling more and more of its products, because there would eventually be no further demand at a price which would be acceptable to the company. The interface between sales and production is fundamental since the function of the sales and marketing department is to provide for the needs of the customer whilst maximising the benefit to the business. If sales are the principal budget factor then the production manager can only prepare his budget after the sales budget is complete. A company may also have limited distribution and selling resources, for example.

Management may not know what the limiting budget factor is until a draft budget has been attempted. The first draft budget will therefore usually begin with the preparation of a draft sales budget.

There are occasions when budgeting does not begin with the sales budget, because there is a shortage of a key resource which prevents the business from selling as much as it could. For example, there could be a shortage of skilled labour, of raw materials or of machine capacity. In these situations there is a **limiting budget factor**. Budgeting would start by looking at the problem of how to maximise profits within the resource constraints.

Step 3 **Preparation of the sales budget**

We have already established that, for many organisations, the principal budget factor is sales volume. The sales budget is therefore often the primary budget from which the majority of the other budgets are derived.

Before the sales budget can be prepared a **sales forecast** has to be made. Sales forecasting is complex and difficult and might involve the consideration of a number of factors for The Needle Works.

- Past sales patterns
- The economic environment
- Results of market research
- Anticipated promotions
- Pricing policies and discounts offered
- Competition
- Changing consumer taste

On the basis of the sales forecast of the organisation, a sales budget will be prepared. This may be subdivided, possible subdivisions being by product, by sales area or by management responsibility.

Step 4 Initial preparation of budgets for The Needle Works

Budget	Detail
Goods stock budget	Decides the planned increase or decrease in finished stock levels
Product sourcing budget	Stated in units of each product and is calculated as the sales budget in units plus the budgeted increase in finished goods stocks or minus the budgeted decrease in goods stocks
Budgets of resources for production and design	**Materials usage budget** is stated in quantities and perhaps cost for each type of material used. It should take into account budgeted losses in production **Labour budget or wages budget** will be expressed in hours for each staff grade and in terms of cost
Overhead cost budgets	Production overheads Product sourcing overheads Design overheads Administration overheads Selling and distribution overheads
Raw materials stock budget	Decides the planned increase or decrease of the level of stocks
Raw materials purchase budget	Can be prepared in quantities and value for each type of material purchased once the raw material usage requirements and the raw materials stock budget are known
Overhead absorption rate	Can be calculated once the production volumes are planned, and the overhead cost centre budgets prepared

Step 5 **Negotiation of budgets with superiors**
This process continues until the final budget is presented to the budget committee for approval.

Step 6 **Co-ordination of budgets**
Remember that it is unlikely that the execution of the above steps will be problem-free. The budgets must be reviewed in relation to one another. Such a review may indicate that some budgets are out of balance with others and need modifying so that they will be compatible.

Step 7 **Final acceptance of the budget**
When all the budgets are in harmony with one another they are summarised into a **master budget**.

Step 8 **Budget review**
The budgeting process does not stop once the budgets have been agreed. Actual results should be compared on a regular basis with the budgeted results. The frequency with which such comparisons are made depends very much on the organisation's circumstances and the sophistication of its control systems but it should occur at least monthly. Management should receive a report detailing the differences and should investigate the reasons for the differences. If the differences are within the control of management, corrective action should be taken to bring the reasons for the difference under control and to ensure that such inefficiencies do not occur in the future.

The differences may have occurred, however, because the budget was unrealistic to begin with or because the actual conditions did not reflect those anticipated (or could have possibly been anticipated). This would therefore invalidate the remainder of the budget.

The budget committee, who should meet periodically to evaluate the organisation's actual performance, may need to reappraise the organisation's future plans in the light of changes to anticipated conditions and to adjust the budget to take account of such changes.

The important point to note is that the budgeting process does not end for the current year once the budget period has begun: budgeting should be seen as a continuous and dynamic process.

4 Flexible budgets

4.1 Fixed budget

FAST FORWARD

> The master budget prepared before the beginning of the budget period is known as the **fixed budget**.

The term 'fixed' means the following.

(a) The budget is prepared on the basis of an **estimated volume** of sales (or production), but no plans are made for the event that **actual volumes** may differ from **budgeted volumes**.

(b) When actual volumes of sales (or production) during a period become known, a fixed budget is not adjusted to the new levels of activity.

4.2 Flexible budget

FAST FORWARD

> A **flexible budget**, by recognising different patterns of costs and sales, is designed to change as volume of output or sales changes.

A **flexible budget** is designed to change to relate to the actual volumes in a period. Flexible budgets may be used in one of two ways.

(a) **At the planning stage**. For example, suppose that The Needle Works expects to sell 10,000 tapestry kits during the next year. A fixed budget would be prepared on the basis of these expected volumes. However, if the company thinks that sales might be as low as 8,000 units or as high as 12,000 units, it may prepare flexible budgets, at volumes of, say 8,000, 9,000, 11,000 and 12,000 units. This enables contingency plans to be drawn up.

(b) **Retrospectively**. At the end of each month or year, flexible budgets can be used to examine actual results achieved. Flexible budgets are an essential factor in **budgetary control**.

   (i) Management needs to know how good or bad actual performance has been. There must be a yardstick against which actual performance can be measured.

   (ii) Business is **dynamic**, and actual volumes of output cannot be expected to conform exactly to the fixed budget.

   (iii) For useful control information, it is necessary to compare actual results **at the level of activity achieved** against the results that would have been expected at this level of activity, which are shown by the flexible budget.

Action Programme 2

Explain what is meant by the terms 'fixed budget' and 'flexible budget' and state the main objective of preparing flexible budgets.

4.3 Example: flexible budgets

Suppose that The Needle Works expects sales of kits during the next year to be 9,000 units. The following historical records of cost are available.

Units of sales	Cost of sales
9,800	£444,000
7,700	£381,000

Management is not certain that the estimate of sales is correct because they believe that competitors are planning promotional campaigns that may reduce The Needle Works' sales by as much as 1,000 units. On the other hand, there is every chance that the promotions may backfire and attract customers to The Needle Works, pushing sales up by 1,000 units. They have therefore asked you for flexible budgets to be prepared at sales levels of 8,000 and 10,000 units. The sales price per unit has been fixed at £50.

If we assume that within the range 8,000 to 10,000 units of sales, all costs are fixed or variable, the fixed and flexible budgets would be based on the estimate of fixed and variable costs.

		£
Total cost of 9,800 units	=	444,000
Total cost of 7,700 units	=	381,000
Variable cost of 2,100 units	=	63,000

The variable cost per unit is therefore (£63,000 ÷ 2,100) = £30

		£
Total cost of 9,800 units	=	444,000
Variable cost of 9,800 units (9,800 × £30)	=	294,400
Fixed costs	=	150,000

The fixed budgets and flexible budgets might now be prepared as follows.

	Flexible budget 8,000 units £	Master budget 9,000 units £	Flexible budget 10,000 units £
Sales (× £50)	400,000	450,000	500,000
Variable costs (× £30)	240,000	270,000	300,000
Contribution	160,000	180,000	200,000
Fixed costs	150,000	150,000	150,000
Profit	10,000	30,000	50,000

5 Accuracy of budgets

FAST FORWARD

It is very important that budgets (especially the sales budget) should be **reasonable**, **realistic** and **accurate**. Seasonal variations, for example, should be recognised.

It is important that budgets should be as **accurate as possible**. Failure to present a sufficiently accurate budget would cause problems.

- Plans will be made on **false assumptions** of costs and profits
- Comparisons of actual results with the budget would give **meaningless information**

There are many practical difficulties in attempting to plan accurately, some of which cannot be overcome. Unnecessary inaccuracies, however, should be avoided. Seasonal variations should be carefully allowed for and individual cost items carefully budgeted.

5.1 Zero base budgeting

> **FAST FORWARD**
>
> **Zero-base budgeting** is a system of budgeting for the activities of an enterprise as if each activity were being performed for the first time.

One way in which many organisations ensure that inefficiencies are not concealed by the practice of 'adding on a bit' is by introducing **zero-base budgeting**. This was very well defined by Morden (1986).

> 'Zero-base budgeting (ZBB) is a formalised system of budgeting for the activities of an enterprise *as if each activity were being performed for the first time,* ie from a zero base. Essentially, a number of alternative levels of provision for each activity are identified, costed and evaluated.
>
> ZBB is based on the belief that management should be required to justify *existing* activities in exactly the same way as new proposals. Thus, established activities will have to be compared with alternative applications of resources.
>
> Zero-based budgeting takes away the *implied right* of existing activities to receive a continued allocation of resources.'

Up to 50% of large companies now operate some form of ZBB and are particularly likely to require it of business areas where measures of effectiveness are not easy, as is often the case with advertising expenditure.

6 Computers and budgeting

> **FAST FORWARD**
>
> Budgeting nowadays is usually **computerised** by using either a computer program or a spreadsheet package.

Budgeting used to be a dreaded task. You can imagine the complexity of the budgetary process which even small organisations have to undergo. Remember, also, that it is highly unlikely that the execution of the steps in the process will be problem free. Budgets will be out of balance with each other and will require modification so that they are compatible. The revision of one budget may well lead to the revision of all of the budgets. The manual preparation of a master budget and a cash budget in the real world would therefore be daunting to say the very least.

Computers, however, can take the hard work out of budgeting: a computerised system will have a number of basic advantages over a manual system.

Budgeting is usually computerised using either a computer program written specifically for the organisation or by a commercial spreadsheet package. Both methods of computerisation of the budgeting process will involve a mathematical model which represents the real world in terms of financial values. The model will consist of several, or many, interrelated variables, a variable being an item in the model which has a value. Once the planning model has been constructed, the same model can be used week by week, month after month, or year after year, simply by changing the values of the variables to produce new results.

A major advantage of budget models is the ability to evaluate different options and carry out **'what if' analysis.** By changing the value of certain variables (for example, increasing the annual pay award to the workforce) management are able to assess the effect of potential changes in their environment.

Computerised models can also incorporate actual results, period by period, and carry out the necessary calculations to **produce budgetary control reports**.

The use of a model also allows the budget for the remainder of the year to be adjusted once it is clear that the circumstances on which the budget was originally based have changed.

6.1 Spreadsheets

Most organisations do not have budgeting programs written for them but use **standard spreadsheet packages**. The idea behind a spreadsheet is that the model builder should construct a model in rows and columns format.

Advantages of using spreadsheet packages for budgeting are as follows.

(a) Spreadsheet packages have a facility to perform **'what if' calculations** at great speed. For example, the consequences throughout the organisation of sales growth per month of nil, $1/2\%$, 1%, $1^1/2\%$ and so on can be calculated at the touch of a button.

(b) Preparing budgets may be complex. Budgets may need to go through several drafts. Spreadsheets aid this process in that one or two figures can be changed and then the **computer will automatically make all the computational changes to the other figures**.

(c) A spreadsheet model will **ensure that the preparation of the functional budgets and master budget is co-ordinated**. Data and information from the functional budgets will be automatically fed through to the master budget model, ensuring that the master budget is a true reflection of the subsidiary budgets.

PART E   ADMINISTERING THE MARKETING BUDGET (AND EVALUATING RESULTS)

Chapter Roundup

- Budgets are the concrete components of what is known as a **budgetary control system**.
- Such a system essentially ensures communication, co-ordination and control within an organisation.
- Depending on how the organisation is managed, marketing (and other) goals may be set at different levels.
- A **marketing budget** is a financial plan for a defined period of time which will include planned expenditure and revenues connected with marketing activities.
- **Marketing costs** can be budgeted using percentage of sales, competitive parity or the objective/task method.
- The co-ordination and administration of budgets organisation-wide is usually the responsibility of a budget **committee** (with the managing director as chairman).
- The **principal budget factor** (or key budget factor or limiting budget factor) is the factor that limits an organisation's performance for a given period. It is often the starting point in budget preparation. In most organisations, this will be sales demand.
- The master budget prepared before the beginning of the budget period is known as the **fixed budget**.
- A **flexible budget**, by recognising different patterns of costs and sales, is designed to change as volume of output or sales changes.
- It is very important that budgets (especially the sales budget) should be **reasonable**, **realistic** and **accurate**. Seasonal variations, for example, should be recognised.
- **Zero-base budgeting** is a system of budgeting for the activities of an enterprise as if each activity were being performed for the first time.
- In **budgetary control** managers are held responsible for investigating differences between budgeted and actual results, and are then expected to take corrective action or amend the plan. Such a process is part of what is known as **responsibility accounting**.
- Budgeting nowadays is usually **computerised** by using either a computer program or a spreadsheet package.

Quick Quiz

1   What are the general objectives of a budgetary control system?
2   Describe some ways of setting marketing budgets.
3   What is the theory of diminishing returns?
4   What are the functions of a budget committee?
5   What is a flexible budget?
6   What are the advantages of using spreadsheet packages for budgeting?

Answers to Quick Quiz

1. The key objectives are summarised in Paragraph 1.2.

2. Top-down planning; bottom-up planning; goals down-plans up.

3. Advertising expenditure generates corresponding marginal revenue only up to a certain point – after which the benefits of the outlay diminish.

4. A list of functions is given in Paragraph 3.2.

5. A flexible budget, by recognising different cost patterns, is designed to change as volume or output or sales changes.

6. By automating the process; a master budget can be automatically updated by linked departmental budgets, scenarios can be worked out through 'what if?' queries, formulae and macros can perform consequential calculations; a standard format is easy to design which is easy to interpret.

Action Programme Review

1. This is a useful exercise in helping you to understand the importance of budgets and to recognise that resources are limited and must be allocated carefully.

2. Fixed budgets are based on estimated volumes of production and sales but do not include any provision for the event that actual volumes may differ from budget.

    A flexible budget is designed to change so as to relate to actual volumes achieved. This has two advantages.

    (a) At the planning stage, it may be helpful to know what the effects would be if the actual outcome differs from the prediction. This would enable contingency plans to be drawn up if necessary.

    (b) At the end of each month or year, actual results may be compared with the flexible budget as a control procedure.

> Now try Question 15 at the end of the Study Text

PART E ADMINISTERING THE MARKETING BUDGET (AND EVALUATING RESULTS)

Justifying the budget

Chapter topic list

1. Are marketers interested in numbers?
2. Overheads and contribution
3. The viability of marketing opportunities
4. The results of marketing mix decisions
5. Has the budget been well spent?

Syllabus content – knowledge and skills requirements

- 5.1 Demonstrate an ability to manipulate numbers in a marketing context
- 5.2 Explain the process used for apportioning fixed and overhead costs
- 5.3 Explain how organisations assess the viability of opportunities, marketing initiatives and projects
- 5.4 Prepare, present and justify a budget as the basis for a decision on a marketing promotion
- 5.5 Make recommendations on alternative courses of action
- 5.6 Examine the correlation between marketing mix decisions and results
- 5.7 Evaluate the cost-effectiveness of a marketing budget, including a review of suppliers and activities

PART E ADMINISTERING THE MARKETING BUDGET (AND EVALUATING RESULTS)

Introduction

In this chapter, we examine why marketers need to be able to use numbers – if only to talk to accountants! We look at how **costs** and **contributions** can be calculated in order to assess (and justify) the viability of opportunities and projects.

We also examine the results that may arise from mix decisions and the actions that management may take to amend them if results are not as expected or hoped.

1 Are marketers interested in numbers?

Marketing activities are generally undertaken with a view to increasing sales and (hopefully) profits – that is why most businesses are in business! How can marketing activities 'prove' themselves? A thorny problem – marketing budgets are often the most difficult to justify and the first to be cut – but in this chapter we look at some of the ways of assessing the viability of marketing opportunities by posing some key questions that should be asked of any significant marketing investment.

A company deploys its chosen marketing mix based, among other considerations, upon decisions of cost and budget constraints. No resources are infinite and each business has to make the best use it can of the resources available to it (money, time etc). The resulting mix may produce success or failure, leading to possible revisions of distribution channels or activities.

2 Overheads and contribution

FAST FORWARD

It is a fundamental part of marketing that the activity is undertaken so that **revenue less costs equals a profit**. It is important in the context of budgeting that we know what the costs are in order to perform our jobs properly.

Let us emphasise again why marketers need to have accurate and timely information on costs. The CIM's definition of marketing helps us focus on this.

> 'Marketing is the management process responsible for identifying, anticipating and satisfying customer requirements **profitably**.'

The basic principle of cost behaviour is that as the level of activity rises, costs will usually rise. It will cost more to have 20,000 promotional leaflets printed than it would cost for 10,000, for example.

2.1 What are overheads?

FAST FORWARD

Overheads are indirect costs, including the indirect costs of materials, labour and other expenses.

Key concept

An **overhead** is the cost incurred in the course of making a product, providing a service or running a department, but which cannot be traced directly and in full to the product, service or department. In other words: an indirect cost.

Overheads can be categorised as:

- Production overhead
- Administration overhead
- Selling overhead
- Distribution overhead

2.1.1 Production overhead

Key concept

Production overhead includes all indirect material costs, indirect wages and indirect expenses incurred in the factory from receipt of the order until its completion.

Examples of production overhead include the following.

(a) **Indirect materials** which cannot be traced in the finished product.

- Consumable stores, eg material used in negligible amounts

(b) **Indirect wages**, meaning all wages not charged directly to a product.

- Salaries and wages of non-productive personnel in the production department, eg foremen

(c) **Indirect expenses** (other than material and labour) not charged directly to production.

- Rent, rates and insurance of a factory
- Depreciation, fuel, power, repairs and maintenance of plant, machinery and factory buildings

2.1.2 Administration overhead

Key concept

Administration overhead is all indirect material costs, wages and expenses incurred in the direction, control and administration of an undertaking.

Examples of **administration overhead** are as follows.

(a) **Depreciation** of office administration overhead, buildings and machinery.

(b) **Office salaries**, including salaries of administrative directors, secretaries and accountants.

(c) **Other charges**: rent, rates, insurance, lighting, cleaning and heating of general offices, telephone and postal charges, bank charges, legal charges, audit fees.

2.1.3 Selling overhead

Key concept

Selling overhead is all indirect materials costs, wages and expenses incurred in promoting sales and retaining customers.

Examples of **selling overhead** are as follows.

(a) **Printing** and **stationery**, such as catalogues and price lists.

(b) **Salaries** and **commission** of salesmen, representatives and sales department staff.

(c) General advertising and public relations activity.

(d) Rent, rates and insurance of sales offices and showrooms, bad debts and collection charges, cash discounts allowed, after-sales service.

PART E ADMINISTERING THE MARKETING BUDGET (AND EVALUATING RESULTS)

2.1.4 Distribution overhead

Key concept

Distribution overhead is all indirect material costs, wages and expenses incurred in making the packed product ready for despatch and delivering it to the customer.

Examples of **distribution overhead** are as follows.

(a) Cost of packing cases.

(b) Wages of packers, drivers and despatch clerks.

(c) Freight and insurance charges, rent, rates, insurance and depreciation of warehouses, depreciation and running expenses of delivery vehicles.

2.2 Contribution

FAST FORWARD

The level of **contribution** made by a product is defined as the sales value *minus* the variable costs associated with the units produced. Contribution is what is 'left over' to pay for fixed costs of operation, such as rent.

The principles of analysing **contribution** are set out below.

Key concept

The level of **contribution** made by a product or portfolio of products is defined as the total sales value *less* the variable costs associated with the units produced. The 'contribution' is the contribution made to profits and fixed costs.

(a) **Fixed costs** (such as rent) **are the same**, no matter what the volume of sales and production. Variable costs vary with the volume of sales and production (eg the cost of additional materials, or sales force commissions).

(b) If the volume of sales rises by one item:

- **Revenue** will increase by the **sales value** of the item sold
- **Costs** will increase only by the **variable cost per unit**
- The increase in profit will therefore equal the **sales value minus variable costs**: the amount of **contribution** earned from the item.

(c) If the volume of sales **falls** by one item, the profit will fall by the amount of contribution earned from the item.

This all has a major impact on the marketing manager because of its implications to both **pricing** and **decision making**, so we will look at two simple examples.

2.3 Example: contribution

The Needle Works is considering making another product, the 'silver standard' frame, which will have a variable production cost of £11 and a sales price of £30. It also expects to spend £3 per unit on marketing the product. Fixed costs for each month will be £65,000 (administration, sales and distribution).

What is the contribution to fixed costs and the profit for the month if sales are as follows?

- 4,000 frames
- 10,000 frames
- 15,000 frames

Solution

First, we identify the variable costs and deduct them from the sales value to derive the **contribution**. We then deduct the **fixed costs** to arrive at **profit**.

	4,000 frames	10,000 frames	15,000 frames
Sales revenue	120,000	300,000	450,000
Variable costs			
Production	44,000	110,000	165,000
Marketing	12,000	30,000	45,000
Contribution	64,000	160,000	240,000
Fixed costs	65,000	65,000	65,000
(Loss)/profit	(1,000)	95,000	175,000
(Loss)/profit per unit	£(0.25)	£9.50	£11.67
Contribution per unit	£16.00	£16.00	£16.00

The conclusions which may be drawn from this example are as follows.

(a) The **profit per unit** varies at **differing levels of sales**, because the average fixed overhead cost per unit changes with the volume of output and sales.

(b) The **contribution per unit is constant** at all levels of output and sales. Total contribution increases in direct proportion to the volume of sales.

(c) The most effective way of **calculating the expected profit** at any level of output and sales is as follows.

- Calculate the total contribution.
- Deduct fixed costs as a period charge in order to find the profit.

(d) In our example, the expected profit from the sale of 17,000 frames would be calculated as follows.

	£
Total contribution (17,000 × £16)	272,000
Less fixed costs	65,000
Profit	207,000

You should be able to see the following.

- If total contribution exceeds fixed costs, a **profit** is made.
- If total contribution exactly equals fixed costs, the activity will **break even**.
- If total contribution is less than the fixed costs, there will be a **loss**.

Costing is very relevant to your studies and in practice.

(a) You may be faced with a situation where you must decide whether in the short term to produce one of two products.

(b) You may be the brand manager for a mature product which has not increased its sales volume for the several years. How would you assess the potential benefits for the company if you increased your promotional support and reduced the price? Look at the following example.

> **Exam tip**
>
> As an example, the June 2005 exam gave you detailed data on the different income sources and costs of a railway (a) in its previous form and (b) under a new franchise. You were asked to calculate the effects of the new (projected) passenger numbers, ticket prices and subsidies (income) and staffing changes (costs), by showing total income and costs under both structures.
>
> Similarly, in December 2005 you had to use data on two festival venues to compare the projected revenue (income), costs and therefore profit from each. This calculation was later used to support your recommendation of one venue over the other.

2.4 Example: evaluating options

The Needle Works' next door neighbour is Kestrel Cycles Ltd. It makes one type of mountain bike in addition to a range of conventional street cycles. Unfortunately their mountain bike sales have been languishing for the past three years, and management is considering the option of spending a one-off amount of £300,000 on extra advertising and dropping the unit selling price by £20 per bike to £150 for the coming year.

The bike has a variable product cost of £90 and current marketing costs of £5 per unit, which would continue to be spent. Sales for the coming year are expected to be 20,000 units with total fixed costs at last year's level of £250,000. The sales volume has been estimated by the marketing manager as a direct consequence of the increased advertising expenditure and reduced selling price. Sales last year were only 4,500 units.

Should management proceed? The analysis could be presented as follows.

	Last year £	Coming year £
Sales revenue	765,000	3,000,000
Variable costs		
Production	405,000	1,800,000
Marketing	22,500	100,000
Contribution	337,500	1,100,000
Fixed costs	250,000	250,000
Extra marketing expenditure	–	300,000
Profit	87,500	550,000
Profit per unit	19.44	27.50
Contribution per unit	75.00	55.00

As can be seen from the analysis, contribution per unit has decreased by £20 because of the decreased selling price. Profit per unit has increased because the overall increased revenues have more than compensated for the increased advertising costs. On the face of it, management will want to go ahead, but they may wish to see more evidence of the achievability of the sales forecast. The fact that break-even level (where contribution equals fixed costs) is now $\frac{£550,000}{55.00} = 10,000$ units to be sold may give cause for concern, as this represents a sales increase of 122% on last year. If sales 'only' doubled in the coming year (respectable enough in itself), then the company would make a loss on its mountain bikes, calculated as (9,000 units × £55 contribution) – 550,000 = £(55,000) loss.

Action Programme 1

The Needle Works

The Needle Works budget committee has asked you to allocate the marketing budget for next year. Albert Smith has already decided that the company can afford to spend £70,000 (not including your salary) on marketing costs in the coming year: 'It is 2.7% of our budgeted sales of £2.6 million, which seems a reasonable proportion. Anyway, we cannot afford to spend more.'

You are not entirely happy with this 'all-you-can-afford' approach but recognise that Albert Smith's approach to marketing should become more sophisticated when you can prove the effectiveness of the marketing budget.

Based upon some costings you have undertaken, you decide upon the following activities for the coming year.

Activity	Months	Cost per month
Newspaper advertising	January – December	£750
Local radio	January – December	£1,000
Promotional coupons	February and August	£5,000
Garden party at old people's home	July	£2,000
Discount sale	January – February	£10,000
Knitting class party	April	£2,500
Posters and point of sale material	January – December	£500
Stand at London Craft Show	October	£4,500
Frames giveaway competition	March	£4,000

Present these numbers on the following grid for submission to the budget committee.

PART E ADMINISTERING THE MARKETING BUDGET (AND EVALUATING RESULTS)

THE NEEDLE WORKS MARKETING BUDGET

ACTIVITY	Jan £	Feb £	Mar £	Apr £	May £	Jun £	Half 1 Total £	Jul £	Aug £	Sept £	Oct £	Nov £	Dec £	Half 2 Total £	Year Total £
Newspaper Advertising															
Local Radio															
Stand at London Craft Show															
Garden Party															
Class Party															
Promotional Coupons															
Discount Sale															
Posters, leaflets & point of sale material															
Frame giveaway Competition															
Total															

[*Key skill for Marketers: Using financial information and metrics*]

3 The viability of marketing opportunities

3.1 Marketing decisions

FAST FORWARD

Marketing managers must remember that their decisions will have **financial implications**.

It helps to be able to identify what the various types of decision facing a marketing manager might be.

(a) **Routine planning decisions**, for example budgeting. Budgeting decisions commonly analyse costs and revenues. They are also often concerned with how to make the best use of scarce resources.

(b) **Short-run problem decisions**, typically, unforeseen 'one-off' special decisions of a non-recurring nature, where the costs and benefits are all obtained within a relatively short period. For example, what price should be quoted in the tender for a contract?

(c) **Longer-range decisions**, meaning decisions made once and reviewed infrequently, but which are intended to provide a continuing solution to a continuing or recurring problem. They include decisions about selling and distribution policies. For example, should goods be sold through middlemen or direct to customers? What type of customer should the sales force attempt to attract? What should the company's discount policies be? Should a new product or service be launched?

(d) **Control decisions**. For example, should disappointing performance be investigated, given that the benefits expected must exceed the costs of investigation and control?

Pricing decisions are sometimes put into a category of their own, but pricing decisions span most of the range of decision categories above: routine pricing decisions are made at periodic price reviews, 'one-off' short-run pricing decisions might be made for specific jobs or contracts or to dispose of surplus stocks, long-range decisions about price must be made for services, products or product ranges and some control decisions might have to be made about prices (for example, are excessive discounts being allowed?).

Levels of marketing expenditure are often significant, and any marketing strategy will have to be evaluated accordingly. However, according to Keith Ward: 'levels of marketing expenditure ... are often subjected to far less rigorous financial evaluations than smaller financial commitments on more tangible assets.'

Treating marketing expenditure as a **cost** is probably appropriate for reporting considerations, but for **decision-making** purposes, there is an argument for analysing it, and controlling it, as if it were an **investment**. (For many marketing-led businesses, their most valuable assets are their brands – yet reducing expenditure on marketing is a tempting option to improve short-term profitability.)

Part of the strategic marketing plan, should be some form of quantitative analysis of the proposed investment. For example, assume the marketing department of The Needle Works chooses to spend £50,000 on re-positioning a product.

- How can a link between future sales and the £50,000 expenditure be established?
- What would happen if the money was not spent? Would market share fall?
- Would an alternative use of £50,000 be more valuable?

The benefits from marketing expenditure might sometimes be much less easy to quantify than, say, the cost savings on new equipment. Markets are an environment, where customers and competitors cannot be controlled. **Instability and uncertainty** are inherent within them.

PART E ADMINISTERING THE MARKETING BUDGET (AND EVALUATING RESULTS)

3.2 Relevant costs

FAST FORWARD

> The costs which should be used when assessing marketing opportunities are often referred to as **relevant costs**.

Key concept

> A **relevant cost** is a future incremental cash flow arising as a direct consequence of a decision.

Only costs which will **differ under the available options** should be considered. Say you, as marketing manager of The Needle Works, have already contracted to pay £1,000 for some full-page advertisements in the local newspaper. It is the newspaper's policy that this booking is not refundable if cancelled. You now might be trying to decide whether to advertise on local radio instead. The £1,000 already contracted to is irrelevant to the decision, because it will be incurred whether you decide to advertise on radio or not.

Exam tip

> The information on the marketing budget that we have presented so far is important, but it is equally important that you get used to dealing with numbers in the context of an examination question. Work carefully through the chapter on statistical information in *Customer* Communications, where number-handling skills are covered. Try the following exercise, which has been adapted from a question on the Specimen Paper when the *Marketing in Practice* module was first created.

3.3 Example: crunching the numbers

Bettacars is a rapidly expanding car repair, servicing and spare parts company with 200 branches throughout the UK. It offers a full range of guaranteed repairs and services to all mainstream makes of car and light commercial vehicle. They keep fast moving lines in stock, but have negotiated deliveries from all suppliers which ensure prompt turnaround of business.

Turnover is anticipated to reach £200 million in 2008, comprising:

50% routine servicing and fitting of tyre exhausts etc
25% general repairs
25% spare parts

Helix employ 200 people at their head office and has a team of 18 area managers, while the average branch employs 12 people.

Project 24

Petrol stations, convenience stores and some major supermarkets are moving in the direction of 24-hour opening. One of Bettacars' competitors has trialled 24-hour opening in the London area. The operations director is keen not to be left behind. It is estimated that for an increase in wage costs of 5%, an extra 10% could be added to turnover. Two branches, both located in the West Midlands, are keen to be the first to offer this new service.

The branch trading accounts are shown below.

BRANCH TRADING ACCOUNTS 2006-2007

£'000s

Branch	Turnover	Purchases	Fixed Costs	Wages	Contribution
711	1,975	1,005	475	260	235
718	900	500	280	190	(70)

> **INTERNAL MEMO STRICTLY CONFIDENTIAL**
>
> To: J. Brown, Marketing
> From: S. Smith, Operations
> Date: 12/5/2007
> Subject: **Project 24**
>
> Further to our recent discussions, District 7 appears an excellent pilot for 24-hour opening. Two branches should be opened on a trial basis, these being 711 Shirley and 718 Wolverhampton, details of each branch are given below:
>
> **711 Shirley**
>
> - Situated on main arterial road from Birmingham
> - Intense local competition (Halfords and Kwikfit)
> - Large affluent commuter population
> - Outlet revamped last year cost £200,000
>
> **718 Wolverhampton**
>
> - Located close to town centre on Ring Road
> - Inner city site, has suffered from theft
> - Due for refit January 2008
>
> I look forward to the Marketing Department assisting these two Branches.

MEDIA COSTINGS

Newpapers

Wolverhampton	Circulation	Cost per s.c.c.
Evening Echo	90,000	£9.50
Weekly Tribune (free)	75,000	£4.75
Morning News	30,000	£4.00
Shirley		
Gazette (free)	80,000	£5.25
Evening Post	40,000	£3.25
Weekend News	25,000	£2.50

Local radio

Wolf Radio (Wolverhampton) reaches 30% of its catchment of 230,000 adults each week. Package of 20 × 15 second slots (5 peak) costs £950.

Shirley Sound is a new radio station serving 100,000 homes set up three months ago. Costs for a 30 second slot is £50 peak, £20 off-peak (minimum 10 slots).

Posters

The Big Poster Co. have a range of sites from £100 p.c.m in close proximity to both branches.

Creative estimates

DRFC have estimated £200 creative development plus £600 production for a 20 × 3 ad.
Advantage would charge £250 for an ad up to 25 × 4.
All local papers offer free artwork.

PART E ADMINISTERING THE MARKETING BUDGET (AND EVALUATING RESULTS)

Use the above information to answer the following questions:

(a) One branch has to be put forward for an initial three-month trial. From the information given, which would you recommend and why?

(b) Prepare an outline media schedule for the trial period, showing costs.

(c) How would you propose supporting Project 24 over the next year, and what budget is required?

Solution

(a) Branch 711 has been selected based on the following criteria.

   (i) **Financial**

	711 Shirley £'000	Turnover up 10% £'000	718 Wolverhampton £'000	Turnover up 10% £'000
Turnover	1,975	2,172.5	900	990
Purchases	1,005	1,105.5	500	550
Fixed costs	475	475	280	280
Wages (up 5%)	260	273	190	199.5
Contribution/(loss)	235	319	(70)	(39.5)

   The above figures show that Shirley will make an additional contribution of £84,000 (£319,000 − £235,000), compared with losses recovered at Wolverhampton of £30,500.

   (ii) **Other reasons**

   (1) Shirley has recently had a refit

   (2) The location appears to be superior, with a large affluent commuter population and no reports of theft (unlike Wolverhampton).

   (3) Media costs are lower

(b) Before any media schedule can be devised, an appropriate **total promotional budget** needs to be set. On the limited amount of information available, the model we could use is **percentage of turnover**. A suggested figure is 6% of £1,975k, being £118,500, of which £17,850 will be used for the media launch.

   (i) **Justification for the size of budget**

   (1) The estimated increase in business could increase contribution

   (2) Need to reach a wide audience quickly

   (3) Need to increase revenue to help repay investment for site revamp

   (4) This pilot is an important strategic move for the group, therefore every assistance must be given to ensure its success

   Assumptions

   With the lack of information certain assumptions need to be made.

   (1) All newspapers are tabloid for cost purposes

   (2) Gazette and Weekend News are weekly publications and the Evening Post is six evenings

(ii) **Schedule**

The **timing** of this pilot is crucial to its success. We have chosen a three-week teaser campaign across all media. This will be followed by a one-month explosion of coverage in the weeklies, and 25˚× 4s on Friday in the evening paper, plus continuous peak slots on the radio. Finally, the campaign will settle down to a continuous drip in the print media and a small burst at the end on radio to reinforce the message.

Media	3 weeks Pre-Launch £	Month 1 £	Month 2 £	Month 3 £	Cost £
Shirley Sound					
25 slots @ £50	1,250				
60 slots @ £50		3,000			
30 slots @ £50				1,500	
					5,750
Gazette					
25 × 4 @ £525	1,575	2,100	1,050	1,050	5,775
Weekend News					
25 × 4 @ £250	750	1,000	500	500	2,750
Evening Post					
25 × 4 @ £325	975	1,300	650	650	3,575
					17,850

Posters, PR and production costs will be allocated from the rest of the promotional budget.

(c) **Support for Project 24**

Given the turnover of the company is estimated to be around £200 million by 2008 and the introduction of 24-hour working is estimated to add another 10% to turnover to bring it to £220 million, the selection of a marketing budget is crucial to the project's success.

(i) **Affordable approach**: what is left after all the costs have been deducted from profit.
(ii) **Competitive parity**: using your competitors spend as a guideline.
(iii) **Percentage of sales**: applying a rough percentage between 5-10% (as we saw above)
(iv) **Objective and task approach**: the money to achieve the objectives set.

On our first launch we used a percentage of sales. If we felt that was successful, a figure of 5% is not unrealistic. This will give us a budget of £11 million (ie 5% of £220 million), of which a large proportion would be spent on advertising. This size budget will not become available straight away, as rollout will take time. A sensible figure for the support needed over a quarter to support the new project should be in the region of £1.5million.

Once the launch period is over, the 24-hour service can be incorporated in all aspects of future promotions.

Choice of recommendations

The size of the budget gives us the flexibility to use both **local** and **national** advertising. Research has shown that national advertising, reinforced by local advertising, gives far greater response.

The cost of any meaningful TV campaign would be too costly and take all of the budget. With the advent of national commercial radio stations, supplemented by local ones, listening figures have continued to climb steeply. This would be a far better use of the budget, coupled to national/local press, national/local specialist magazines and business directories. This will give the project the **synergy** and **coverage** it needs.

In today's increasingly 24-hour society, other options need to be considered. The **Internet** is one such place. A website could enable people to purchase spare parts online as well as offering a booking-in service, with a map to show all the national sites.

4 The results of marketing mix decisions

Having costed various activities, decided that they were worthwhile, and set them up in an approved budget for the forthcoming year, it is time for the evaluation process to start.

After all this, the company may be in a position to decide whether or not its budget was well spent. This is not a black and white analysis, as the decisions will vary from company to company. One company may desire a 50% cut in the level of customer complaints after spending £2million on a new call centre. Another may expect to see sales double as a result of a £100,000 promotional coupon campaign. The two companies are spending their marketing budget with very different aims in mind.

Exam tip

Consider this advice from *Marketing Success* (May 2002).

'In order to make well-informed decisions about what to do, organisations need to learn lessons from the past. What worked well? Why did it work well? Can it be repeated?'

Evaluating marketing activities is not always something that many organisations do well. Even if it is done, the information may not be passed on or readily accessible for future planners.

Carry out some research in your own organisation, or one you know well. Find out:

- How exhibitions are evaluated – number of sales leads, customers contacted, new enquiries, publicity achieved.
- How the effectiveness of corporate hospitality is evaluated – response rate to invitations.
- How advertising results are measured – viewing rates, circulation figures, attitude surveys.
- How sales promotions are measured – increase in sales, coupons.

Do not forget the importance of qualitative evaluation, so look at how quantitative results are used. For example, the results from the exhibition may have been good, but were customers reporting that this was the last time they would attend because they were weary of exhibitions? Is this a lesson to be learnt? Success may not be repeatable next year.

Understanding why events and activities are successful is critical to whether they can be repeated. Measuring results and achievement of objectives is important, but evaluating why it happened is essential.

4.1 Uses of costing information

FAST FORWARD

Cost information is important in making mix decisions, because resources are always finite. It can also be used to evaluate results.

You may still be wondering why, as a marketer, the costing aspects are relevant to you: after all, your main focus is the **customer**, and you might regard an inward looking concentration on costs and production processes as evidence of a **product-orientated attitude**.

Let us remember again that the essence of marketing is that **customer needs are satisfied profitably**. In the long run, profit is achieved because sales revenue from goods and services exceeds the costs.

Cost information is also important in **marketing mix decisions** because resources are always finite.

(a) **Price decisions**. A product's cost might be a constraint on the marketer's freedom to adjust the price element of the marketing mix. It is true that many supermarkets sell 'loss leader' products to entice their customers to buy higher-priced goods, but on the whole **cost is a constraint**.

(b) **Product decisions**. When deciding whether or not to launch a new product, marketers might discover that the market price is far below the cost of making a particular product or service. The marketer may then have to redesign or reposition the product to make it cheaper.

(c) **Place decisions**. Distribution expenses can affect overall profitability. Cost information can enable marketers to discover which distribution channels are the most effective use of resources.

(d) **Promotion decisions**. The marketer's budget often includes the costs of advertising, sales promotion and so on. Cost information can suggest which media might be best employed.

Every marketing mix strategy will lead to a certain level of profit.

There are a number of benefits that a costing system can provide when evaluating mix results.

- The identification of profitable and unprofitable products and services
- Assistance in setting prices
- The provision of accurate stock valuations
- The analysis of changes in costs, volume and hence profit
- Assistance in planning, control and decision making (such as budgets and pricing)

Marketing at Work

The importance of marketers getting their heads round **accounting information** was emphasised in *Marketing Business*.

'From board representation through budget setting processes to effectiveness measurement, marketing and advertising come a poor second or third to other disciplines in finance directors' eyes ... Marketing directors simply must justify their activities in order to command the levels of expenditure they need.' The senior examiner has also commented: "we marketers must take on the accountants at their own game".'

PART E ADMINISTERING THE MARKETING BUDGET (AND EVALUATING RESULTS)

5 Has the budget been well spent?

FAST FORWARD

The decision as to whether or not the budget has been well spent will depend on individual **company objectives** for their marketing activities. Each activity may or may not have a quantifiable effect.

You put together a budget for The Needle Works in Action Programme 1. The overall budget was £70,000 which you spread between a range of activities. What are some measures of success that you could look for from each activity?

Taking each activity in turn, we could suggest the following.

Activity	Spend	Objective
Newspaper advertising	£9,000	Increase customer traffic by 5%
Local radio	£12,000	
Stand at London Craft Show	£5,000	Meet new suppliers and out-of-town customers
Garden party	£2,000	Public relations
Class party	£2,500	
Promotional coupons	£10,000	Increase sales in those months by £20,000
Discount sale	£20,000	To get rid of old season stock and increase customer traffic
Posters and leaflets	£6,000	To decorate store and encourage awareness
Frames giveaway	£4,000	To encourage customer traffic and sales

As you can see, not all of the activities have a quantifiable benefit attached to them. The two parties are mainly aimed at public relations, while the newspaper and local radio advertising is aimed at increasing customer traffic by a stated amount. The success or otherwise of this advertising could be measured by comparing the levels of visitors before and after the campaigns (by examining the visitors' book, for example). The total cost of the advertising, £21,000, could be compared with incremental sales (sales pre- and post-campaign).

The redemption of promotional coupons may be so successful (and expensive!) that you decide not to do it again because the cost outweighed the additional sales gained. A printer may become so expensive that you decide to go somewhere else.

Each activity may or may not have a quantifiable effect and you may be constantly revising your portfolio of activities, but the overall benefit of marketing budgeting and planning is likely to lead to increased awareness by customers and suppliers which will translate into additional sales at some point. It may not be in the same week, or even the same year, but without marketing planning it is unlikely to happen at all.

Exam tip

The December 2004 exam gave proposals for two different sales promotion options, with data on the proposed **price reduction** and estimated **increase in sales** at different levels of price reduction. From this data, you were required to calculate which option would yield the best results in terms of sales and profit.

Marketing at Work

Measuring the success of the strategy

Vodafone's sponsorship deal with Manchester United cost Vodafone £30 million over a four-year period. Vodafone clearly had to evaluate the effectiveness of this partnership in terms of its own marketing objectives. It did so in four ways:

- *General awareness* was measured through consumer research. For example, consumers were asked questions such as 'Did you know that Vodafone sponsors Manchester United?'

- The *impact* of phones and accessories was measured by charting ongoing improvements in sales.

- The success of *value added services* such as manUmobile was monitored in terms of the number of people registered and usage of the services.

- *Media evaluation* – Vodafone monitored TV and press coverage to measure the exposure of the Vodafone brand resulting from the sponsorship.

Keeping check in this way enabled Vodafone to assess whether or not it had made a wise strategic move in teaming up with Manchester United. Evidence strongly suggested that it had.

PART E ADMINISTERING THE MARKETING BUDGET (AND EVALUATING RESULTS)

Chapter Roundup

- It is a fundamental part of marketing that the activity is undertaken so that **revenue less costs equals a profit**. It is important in the context of budgeting that we know what the costs are in order to perform our jobs properly.
- **Overheads** are indirect costs, including the indirect costs of materials, labour and other expenses.
- The level of **contribution** made by a product is defined as the sales value minus the variable costs associated with the units produced. Contribution is what is 'left over' to pay for fixed costs of operation, such as rent.
- Marketing managers must remember that their decisions will have **financial implications**.
- The costs which should be used when assessing marketing opportunities are often referred to as **relevant costs**.
- **Cost information** is important in making mix decisions, because resources are always finite. It can also be used to evaluate results.
- The decision as to whether or not the budget has been well spent will depend on individual **company objectives** for their marketing activities. Each activity may or may not have a quantifiable effect.

Quick Quiz

1. What is the CIM definition of marketing?
2. What is an overhead?
3. What is contribution?
4. Give an example of a fixed cost.
5. Why might the benefits from marketing expenditure be difficult to quantify?
6. What benefits does a proper costing system provide?
7. Give an example of how cost information can help with a 'place' decision.
8. What might be the marketing objective behind a retailer having a discount sale?

Answers to Quick Quiz

1. This should be ingrained! 'Marketing is the management process responsible for identifying, anticipating and satisfying customer requirements profitably' (CIM).

2. An overhead is a cost incurred in the course of making a product, providing a service or running a department which cannot be traced directly and in full to the product, service or department.

3. The contribution made to profit and fixed costs, which equates to total sales value less the variable costs associated with the units produced.

4. For example, a lithographic printer's make ready charge which is the same whether the print run is long or short.

5. Not all activities have a quantifiable benefit attached to them and they are performed in an uncertain and unstable environment. Because direct benefits cannot always be demonstrated, marketing budgets can be a tempting target for a short-term cost cutting exercise.

6. Resources are always finite and a proper costing system enables better decisions as to their use.

7. Marketers can make decisions as to which distribution channels are the most cost effective.

8. To get rid of old season stock and increase customer traffic.

PART E ADMINISTERING THE MARKETING BUDGET (AND EVALUATING RESULTS)

Action Programme Review

1

THE NEEDLE WORKS MARKETING BUDGET

ACTIVITY	Jan £	Feb £	Mar £	Apr £	May £	Jun £	Half 1 Total £	Jul £	Aug £	Sept £	Oct £	Nov £	Dec £	Half 2 Total £	Year Total £
Newspaper Advertising	750	750	750	750	750	750	4500	750	750	750	750	750	750	4500	9000
Local Radio	1000	1000	1000	1000	1000	1000	6000	1000	1000	1000	1000	1000	1000	6000	12000
Stand at London Craft Show							-				4500			4500	4500
Garden Party				2500			2500							-	2500
Class Party							-	2000						2000	2000
Promotional Coupons		5000					5000							-	2500
Discount Sale	10000	10000					20000		5000					5000	10000
Posters, leaflets & point of sale material	500	500	500	500	500	500	3000	500	500	500	500	500	500	3000	6000
Frame giveaway Competition			4000				4000							-	4000
Total	12250	17250	6250	4750	2250	2250	45000	4250	7250	2250	6750	2250	2250	25000	70000

Now try Question 16 at the end of the Study Text

Question and Answer bank

QUESTION BANK

1 Orientation

You are a marketing assistant for a small college of further education currently experiencing a declining number of students. You have been in your position for twelve months and you realise that the college is product orientated.

In an effort to communicate the concept of a marketing orientation you feel that you must write a report to the principal of the college detailing the following.

(a) The difference between product orientation and market orientation, citing examples of each
(b) The steps involved in establishing a marketing orientation approach
(c) The anticipated benefits to the college of introducing such a marketing approach

(15 marks)

2 Databases and market research

You are the new marketing manager for a local market gardener who supplies fruit and vegetables to retailers throughout the region, but uses an outdated card system for its database. Write a report to the Director outlining the benefits of electronic database marketing.

(20 marks)

3 In-house research

Your company has decided to bring all of its marketing research activity 'in house' because it is felt that to give knowledge of the company's products and plans to outside organisations is too risky in the commercial sense. Previously the company has used market research agencies to carry out 'ad hoc' marketing research as needed.

You have now been given the task of drawing up a list of the tasks that will have to be undertaken by the new marketing research department.

(20 marks)

4 Report on company capabilities

For a number of years a small group of friends have pursued their interest in making hand-made Arts and Crafts style beds. The combination of their design and wood-turning has resulted in many requests for beds for friends. Others have encouraged them to go into business full-time, pointing out that a significant opportunity exists for custom-made beds. Produce a report which analyses the likely strengths and weaknesses of this new company's internal capabilities relative to this marketing opportunity.

(20 marks)

5 Marketing teamwork

As the marketing manager for a wholesale market gardening company which is expanding into the retail side of the business, opening up two new garden centres in the region, you have to ensure that the key players involved in the expansion will work effectively together.

What steps should you take to ensure the team works effectively? **(20 marks)**

6 Non-verbal communication

(a) You are the marketing manager for a chain of hotels. You have been asked to write a short article for the company newsletter about the role of front line staff in marketing the company. In particular, you are asked to use the article to explain the importance of non-verbal communication in dealing effectively with customers. Use examples to illustrate the points you are making.

(12 marks)

(b) Write a memo for circulation to all reception staff about the effective use of telephones. In particular, you should focus on the appropriate way to deal with incoming calls, the transfer of calls and message taking.

(8 marks)

(20 marks)

7 Advertising agencies

(a) List briefly the process in selecting an advertising agency.
(b) What role does an advertising agency play in developing an advertising campaign?
(c) Outline a typical agency structure.

(15 marks)

8 Negotiations

You have been asked to write an article outlining the win/win strategy you could adopt when negotiating with another organisation.

(20 marks)

9 Control, planning and evaluation

Little Fingers plc manufactures and retails a wide range of children's games and toys. Recently the following memorandum was circulated to all Little Fingers staff.

INTERNAL MEMORANDUM

To: All staff, all departments
From: The Managing Director

Each year this company spends 5% of turnover on marketing activities. Despite this high level of expenditure we have little feedback on their effectiveness. In order to encourage more monitoring and evaluation we will be offering a prize for the best suggestions for appropriate marketing control, planning and evaluation procedures in project management.

You decide to enter the competition. Prepare a report which explains different approaches to marketing, control, planning and evaluation. Provide details of how these approaches should be implemented.

(20 marks)

10 International event management

You are the assistant marketing manager for an international engineering company with subsidiaries all over the world. They have just launched a new product and a sales conference has been arranged by the marketing manager. You have been asked to produce a checklist that takes into consideration all the factors that may be of interest and necessity for the international delegates who are attending the conference in the UK.

(20 marks)

11 Venue appraisal

You are a marketing assistant for a medium-sized industrial company and the marketing manager has given you the task of compiling a checklist on "How to select a suitable venue" to be included in a handbook he is compiling.

(20 marks)

12 Media choice

You are the recently appointed marketing manager for a large car dealership with ten branches located throughout a promotional region. This region is served by a commercial television company and a separate independent radio company. There is one evening newspaper, and several weekly free newspapers. Your advertising spend is likely to be just over £1 million. Write a memorandum to your M.D. comparing the strengths and weaknesses of the different media available with specific reference to advertising new and used cars.

(20 marks)

13 Magazine sales promotion

You are the promotions manager at a magazine publisher which produces a range of consumer specialist titles sold primarily via the news-stand. Produce an outline report for your marketing director, recommending and justifying how sales promotion techniques could be used to attract new readers and retain existing readers.

(20 marks)

14 Price

(a) Explain why price is important within the marketing mix.
(b) What is meant by elasticity of demand?

(10 marks)

15 Market research for new product launch

You are a newly appointed as a marketing manager in a publishing company and have been given specific responsibility for a new product launch. Your organisation wants to introduce a new magazine aimed at the teenage female market as identified as part of last year's strategic review. In this respect you have been given a budget of £30,000 to conduct further market research prior to the launch. Explain how you would plan and conduct this research. You are required to give the specific stages in your research plan, explaining your chosen options.

(20 marks)

16 Flexible budgets

Forecast sales for a new product line have been estimated at 10,000 units per annum. Selling prices have been discussed at £100 per unit, £150 per unit and £200 per unit. Fixed costs associated with the product are budgeted at £50,000 per annum. Variable costs are budgeted at £10 per hour of direct labour and £40 per unit produced in material costs. It takes two hours of direct labour to assemble and pack the units for delivery. Each unit sold will incur delivery costs but these will be recouped from the customer in full and are forecast to make an additional contribution of £10 per unit sold.

(a) Prepare a budget for each price level that clearly shows sales, cost of sales, contribution and net profit.

(b) In addition flex the budget to show what would happen if the sales forecast is only 80 per cent accurate.

(20 marks)

ANSWER BANK

1 Orientation

To: College Principal
From: A N Student
Date: June 200X
Subject: Market orientation

Contents

(a) The difference between product and market orientation

(b) The steps involved in establishing a marketing orientated approach

(c) The anticipated benefits to the college of introducing such an approach

(a) **Difference between product and market orientation**

The college will be **product orientated** if it displays the following characteristics.

(i) Courses designed and delivered without reference to market trends and customer needs
(ii) Limited use/adoption of MKIS systems
(iii) Short-term, reactive view to changes in the marketing environment
(iv) Lack of customer-focused systems and processes
(v) Organisation structure focused upon courses and not customer and market issues

The college will be **market orientated** if it displays the following characteristics.

(i) Course design and development clearly focused upon market trends and evolving customer needs

(ii) Flexible modes of course delivery and opening hours

(iii) Organisation structure and systems designed with a customer focus and not an internal organisation focus

(iv) Empowerment of staff to deliver excellent customer service

(v) Culture of change with limited bureaucracy

(b) **The steps to establish a marketing orientated approach**

(i) The philosophy that lies behind a marketing orientation must be embraced with a genuine belief and **commitment by the senior management** of the college.

(ii) The college will need substantially to upgrade its current student **information system** to provide more than just name, address and course records. Company and other key stakeholder information should also be accessible within the system.

(iii) The college **structure** will need to be revised if it is to achieve increased level of market and customer orientation. The structure should include **customer related** functions and roles and not those which just to satisfy internal organisation needs.

(iv) The college **culture** must be adapted to suit the more customer focused environment. The organisation and its employees will need to redefine current practice and functions, towards increased co-operation, autonomy and flexibility.

(v) Improved **internal communication** systems need to be designed to ensure all employees are kept informed of college activity and plans. Communication systems should facilitate **feedback**.

(vi) A programme of **customer care training** should be planned for all members of staff and targets agreed. This training should be provided on an ongoing basis.

(vii) An agreed system of **monitoring and control** should be implemented to ensure that any deviations or shortfalls from the desired standards can be actioned.

(c) **Benefits**

Several benefits will emerge as a result of the college changing from a product to marketing orientation. Some of these will not occur in the **short term** but will have a significant impact on the colleges performance and competitiveness **longer term**.

(i) The college will develop a sharper **competitive edge** clearly focused on the market and customers' needs.

(ii) Its perceived **image** in the local community will be changed from being seen as fairly staid to being more dynamic.

(iii) Increased **revenue** will be generated from courses positioned in growing markets.

(iv) The college will be seen to be more **responsive** to local education needs.

(v) Courses and programmes will be **tailored and targeted** and thus be seen as having more relevance.

(vi) **Recruitment** will become more effective through better targeting. As a direct result the college should retain more students to completion of programmes and continuing with further programmes.

(vii) **New course developments** can be developed in closer line with **market needs** and evaluated more effectively in terms of the colleges mission and goals.

Whilst this change from product to marketing orientation will involve significant commitment in terms of **time and resource**, the long-term benefits will be considerable.

2 Databases and market research

To: A. Director
From: A. Marketing Manager
Date: June 200X
Subject: Benefits of electronic database marketing

The objective of this report is to outline the contribution that a **marketing database** could make to the development and support of our business.

According to the **Institute of Direct Marketing** a marketing database is 'a collection of all available information of past, present and prospective customers, structured to achieve maximum usefulness'. The real value of a marketing database lies in its ability to be an invaluable aid in **decision making** and **communications strategy** development. The database can be used repeatedly, so reinforcing the point that it is four times more expensive to gain a new customer than it is to retain an existing one.

Database marketing is a customer-orientated approach to marketing, and its special power lies in the techniques used to harness the capabilities of computer and telecommunications technology. Building accurate and up-to-date profiles of existing customers would enable the company to increase its market share by:

(a) Increased customer retention by staying close to the target audience through better targeting and contact

(b) Better use of resources and cost reduction due to less duplication of information handling

(c) Better decision making through quality management information.

The database may be used to meet a variety of objectives with numerous advantages over traditional marketing methods.

- Focusing on prime prospects
- Evaluating new prospects
- Cross-selling related products
- Launching new products to potential prospects
- Identifying new distribution channels
- Building customer loyalty
- Converting occasional users to regular users
- Generating enquiries and follow-up sales
- Targeting niche markets

An effective database can provide the following **management information**.

(a) **Usage patterns** eg reasons for account closures/loyal repeat customers/seasonal or local purchase patterns/demographic purchase patterns and purchase patterns in response to promotional campaigns

(b) **Evaluation of marketing activities** eg response rates

(c) **Segmentation analysis** to ensure accurate targeting

(d) **Account analysis** eg value or product type

(e) Updated **market research information**

A database can only be as effective as the information which is input. This means that **accurate data is essential** and this will require investment of time and effort to ensure that both data capture and data entry are accurate. **Variables** which could be considered for inclusion are name, address, telephone number, gender, age occupation, services used, frequency of use, time of day of visit etc.

The **customer database** could be maintained through our new **EPOS system** in which all our purchasing data would be automatically updated, **transaction documents** such as order forms, invoices and customer account records, any customer care **feedback** questionnaires which are now distributed to all our customers and the new customers who visit our stalls at the shows and exhibitions we attend.

In conclusion, the development of a marketing database would take **time and money**. Consideration needs to be given as to whether we develop our own database or whether we purchase an **off-the-shelf package** and then set about tailoring it to our specific requirements. Overall, a marketing database has the potential to provide us with invaluable data regarding a wide range of marketing and consumer issues, as well as providing us with a tool for **competitive advantage**.

I look forward to discussing the contents of this report next week at our scheduled meeting.

3 In-house research

Marketing research can cover all of the marketing activities undertaken by an organisation. The **objective** of marketing research is to understand the **problems** and identify the level of **effectiveness** of this activity. Market research focuses upon the identification of **needs**, and market **opportunities** and **threats** facing an organisation.

The extent of the tasks that will have to be undertaken by the new marketing research department will be dependent upon the type of organisation and its current level and sophistication of research activity. Working on the assumption that the organisation invests substantially in marketing research, the following list of tasks would be paramount.

Market research

- Customer/consumer surveys (qualitative and quantitative)
- Market trends analysis
- Marketing environment analysis (SLEPT factors)
- Market share analysis
- Geodemographic analysis

Such data can be obtained from both primary and secondary sources. A decision would have to be made as to the level of sophistication required of such research and whether the in-house team has the appropriate skills.

Product research

- Brand perception/image studies
- Packaging and product design studies
- New product development research
- Test marketing
- Comparative studies between competitive products

Promotion research

- Promotion effectiveness (ie recall)
- Sales impact of promotional activity
- Corporate image
- Publicity generated
- Media research
- Sales force effectiveness

Distribution research

- Sales performance analysis
- Service delivery performance
- Costs/profitability studies
- Dealer satisfaction studies
- Location analysis
- The analysis of packaging for transportation and shelving
- Dealer advertising requirements

The **costs** of such a marketing research operation would have to be investigated. Additional investment would be required in **marketing information systems** and staffing levels. The required level of **expertise** may not be available in-house.

An estimation of the **time** and **resources** needed to effectively complete the range of marketing research indicated would need careful consideration.

4 Report on company capabilities

To: Bed Makers
From: A Consultant
Date: June 200X
Subject: Strengths and weaknesses

Introduction

This report reviews, in table format, the company's perceived strengths and weaknesses with regard to its internal capabilities for exploiting the opportunity for custom-made beds.

Strengths and weaknesses analysis

Area	Strengths	Weaknesses
Corporate management and organisation	Friends with a common interest Experience of working together Flexible, innovative responsive Willing to seek advice	No MD No formal structure No corporate objectives
Financial	None apparent	Need capital investment High risk borrowers Lack of expertise
Personnel	Enthusiastic/motivated Work well as a team	Assumed lack of investment and marketing experience No formal relationships
Production	Possess necessary skills Have necessary tools Make to order	No experience of higher volumes Might need new equipment
Marketing strategy	Niche marketing	No formal strategy Responsive rather than proactive No planning system No control systems
MkIS	Initiative	No formal MkIS No factual knowledge of market sizes and trends, buying motives etc.
Product	Custom built Good design High quality	None apparent
Price	Negotiable Potentially premium	No formal costings
Promotion	Recommendation Exhibitions/Fairs Trade/Arts and Crafts Magazines	No promotional skills No promotional budget No agency
Place	Some existing space (production) Direct delivery	No showroom space? No office?

Conclusion

Although the proposed new company has a number of important strengths, there is an almost equal number of weaknesses.

Following Kotler's recommendations, the strengths and weaknesses should be scored and their degrees of importance assessed so as to facilitate **prioritisation**. For example, it seems clear that product design and craftsmanship skills would have both a high score and a high importance, and should therefore be ranked as a major strength. However, lack of finance, lack of marketing skills and lack of market knowledge would rank as major weaknesses. Worked through in this way, it would seem major weaknesses exceed major strengths. Issues arising are as follows.

(a) It is unlikely that sufficient **funding** could be attracted without a formal business plan (I would be pleased to assist in producing one).

(b) Should the new company **outsource** marketing/sales/distribution so as to exploit better its design/production skills?

(c) I propose a **management team** is elected from the group to further the group's interests.

5 Marketing teamwork

Marketing managers have to try to ensure that with the coming together of people from different disciplines a good **working relationship** is maintained to achieve objectives.

A good working relationship in this context means prompt and willing service, co-operation, co-ordination, communication and teamworking in which all parties achieve mutual respect, conflict resolution and opportunity for job satisfaction.

This is essential as team members rely on each other for **information** or input in order to fulfil objectives, for example interaction between **internal** and **external** promotion managers, interaction between managers of **different departments** in the company, and interaction between administration staff and management. General courtesy and respect at all times can be rewarded in times of crisis when favours may be needed (eg individuals being prepared to work an extra thirty minutes to ensure a deadline is met and objectives are achieved).

Objectives of team management

The overall objectives of the team should be agreed and clearly understood. The manager must obtain feedback to ensure that people not only think they understand the objectives, but really do so.

Team building

The team should go through the **group formation** process as quickly as possible. **Barriers** should be broken down, differences aired and the team move into its productive stage as quickly as possible. This is an on going process.

- Keep in contact
- Be dependable
- Work on shared values and interests
- Show willing
- Socialise but behave appropriately
- Avoid or mend conflict
- Show respect for other people's beliefs and values
- Maintain a net balance of benefit

Options

All options for achieving objectives should be examined. A common way of doing this is brainstorming. If everyone is encouraged to contribute you get the most out of all the members of the team.

Strategies and tactics

The team must then set out in detail how these objectives are to be achieved. The style that is adopted depends on your personality and the personality of those in the team, the work situation and relationship, the urgency of the decision, the importance of other people's commitment to the solution, the organisation and its culture.

Measurement

Methods of measuring progress should be agreed relating directly to the objectives.

Timescales and reviews

Timescales for the project and for review points should be set. The general progress of the team's activities need to be monitored.

Meetings

The usual way of monitoring progress is the team meeting. These act as a forum for discussion and joint decision making. They allow feedback on individual progress, support and ideas from other members. Grievances and problems can be aired and solved.

Control

The team must have a degree of flexibility and should be able to adapt activities as circumstances change.

In conclusion, many factors can affect the overall success of the group. The size will influence its ability to communicate. The relationships, personalities and experience of the members will also have an impact on the team's effectiveness. The objectives of the team and any time constraints will both influence the way in which members relate to each other. Generally a lot can depend on the encouragement and motivation the team members receive from the leader.

6 Non-verbal communication

(a) **Body language**

Body language shows people how we feel.

Consciously or not we will communicate with our movements and respond to the body language of others. If they smile we react - usually with another smile. We also observe the **behaviour** of others. If you have watched any docu-soaps such as 'Airline' you will doubtless have noted the body language of particular front line staff.

With such staff in mind it is easy to see a connection between front-line staff and **effective customer care**

Good initial eye contact demonstrates your interest in the client and allows staff to pick up on the client's mood - they may be relaxed, frustrated or demanding. One of the aspects of our job is to note this and make an appropriate **response** - body and words!

For example:

'Have you had a difficult journey?'

'I'm sorry to hear that'

'Would you like to .... '

However, one of the interesting things about our work is that every customer is an individual and needs **individual care**. Our training recognises this. For instance, we speak to old and young differently - we also use different body language. Sometimes it is appropriate to move closer to someone - frequently it is not! In this respect we need to be aware of **cultural differences**.

The subject has been studied by anthropologists such as Desmond Morris. He started with animals at London Zoo - but we are not that different. We have all developed postures and gestures, movements and personal habits to make a full range of **statements** about ourselves.

At work it is important that we ensure that these statements and personal body language are used skilfully, to add to the level of customer care which is reflected in all aspects of our work as a service-led industry.

(b) **MEMORANDUM**

To: All reception staff
From: Ava Lines, Marketing Manager
Date: June 200X
Subject: **Effective use of telephones**

In order to help ensure that we are maintaining the highest possible standards, I have drafted this memorandum to highlight three key areas in the **effective use of telephones**.

Your responses would as usual be most welcome. Remember our aim is to maintain our **competitive edge**.

(i) **Incoming calls**

Key points are as follows.

(1) **Interpersonal skills** and sensitivity to each caller

(2) **Identification** and greetings

- Audible, clear
- Use company **guidelines**

(3) Establish nature of call and name of caller

(ii) **Transfer of calls**

(1) Inform/agree with caller need to transfer
(2) Follow **correct procedure** - including explanation to caller of what you are doing
(3) **Maintain contact** until caller has been transferred

(iii) **Message taking**

(1) Use notepad

(2) Receive message

- Time
- Name of caller
- Intended recipient
- Outline of nature of call
- Response given to caller

(3) Check back important details with caller

(4) Reassure caller that message will be passed on

(5) Ensure that it is!

Remember, please let us know how you feel we might improve these procedures.

7 Advertising agencies

(a) **Selecting an agency**

Stage 1 - Research

Criteria for selection

(i) Advertising your company has admired
(ii) Recommendation
(iii) Use of professional associations and marketing journals to profile the ideal agency
(iv) Identify several agencies that may fit your requirements

Stage 2 - Fine screening

(i) Write to the agency for literature
(ii) Arrange a visit to the agency
(iii) Produce a simple checklist of the characteristics you are looking for in an agency
(iv) Take it with you on the visit, ticking where the agency meets your brief
(v) Reduce the agency list down to three

Stage 3 - Brief

(i) Prepare advertising brief which is presented to the agencies
(ii) Invite agencies to present credentials and outline proposals for campaign
(iii) Impose time limit for presentation of proposals

Stage 4 - Presentation

(i) Presentations to take place over no more than 2 days on your premises
(ii) Keep the decision team small
(iii) Each team member to score each agency

Stage 5 - Decision time

(i) Use your score sheet to guide your decision
(ii) The sheet isn't an exact science - so include instinct, based on the compatibility with your own team, how they view us

Finally, discuss the **contractual details** with the successful agency.

(b) If an organisation uses an advertising agency, the development of the advertising campaign is usually a joint effort, with the agency performing functions such as copywriting, artwork, technical production and the formulation of the media plan.

The use of an agency provides an organisation with highly skilled **specialists** who are generally more objective than the firm's employees and have more experience in advertising.

(c) While different types and sizes of agencies will have different structures, what is listed below serves as a guideline.

Account executive

This is a person who is dedicated to a particular group of clients or in some cases an individual client. They are responsible for **communications** such as attending meetings, writing reports and generally **liasing** between the client and the agency.

Planning department

These individuals are responsible for the **analysis and interpretation** of market research reports which they have commissioned.

Creative department

These are the 'ideas' people and deal with words and pictures.

Media department

This is where they plan what **media** are to be used and buy the space on radio, television, magazines etc.

Production department

This is the department which is actually responsible for making the advertisement. Often there is an element of **subcontracting** here, as studios, camera crew and actors may be required.

Traffic department

This deals with getting the artwork or film to the magazine or TV station. When the promotional campaign involves a number of media this process becomes complicated because accurate timing is crucial.

8 Negotiations

All our lives we have been involved with **negotiations**. As a child we negotiated what time we would come home from a party, or the amount of pocket money we would receive.

One of the most direct examples of **communications** with customers and suppliers involves negotiation. This can involve gaining a discount for a run of adverts through to complex negotiations of a contract.

The aim of negotiating is not necessarily to get the best position for your organisation at the expense of the other party, but to view it as an exchange which is mutually beneficial. This is desirable if the relationship is to flourish.

The matrix below outlines the possibilities during negotiations.

	Buyer Win	Buyer Lose
Seller Win	Both are winners	Buyer loses
Seller Lose	Seller loses Buyer wins	Both parties lose

A basic win-win approach to negotiations is as follows.

(i) **Set the scene**. The participants should be relaxed and comfortable, possibly meeting beforehand to break the ice.

(ii) Agree the negotiating **procedure**. Then map out, in advance, what the needs and fears of both parties are.

(iii) Define your **desired outcome**, for example, 'If I can pay £500, it would be ideal, but I'd settle for £600. Above £700, it's just not worth my while.'. Start with the best case, leaving room to fall back. However keep sight of your goal.

The bidding must be realistic. A too high or low initial bid could offend the other party.

(iv) Look for mutual or trade-off benefits. For example, you could offer an early right hand page for a run of ads in exchange for pre-payment. Never agree a concession without securing a concession in return. Always offer something valuable to your customer, like the example above, that is cheap for you.

(v) Spell out the positive benefits to the other party and support them in saying 'yes' to your proposals by **making it as easy as possible**. Offer to supply **information** or help. Emphasise **areas of agreement** and common ground.

(vi) **Overcome negativity** by asking questions such as:

- 'What will make it work for you?'
- 'What would it take to make this possible?'

(vii) **Overcome side-tracks** by asking questions such as:

'How is this going to get us where we need/want to go?'

(viii) Be hard on the problem but soft on the person. **Work together** on problem solving (eg by using flip chart or paper to make shared notes).

(ix) Be **flexible**. A 'take it or leave it' approach breaks relationships. However, saying 'no' repeatedly to sales people is a good way of finding out just how far below the list price they are prepared to go! Make, and invite, reasonable counter offers.

(x) Be **culturally sensitive**. Some markets thrive on 'haggling'. Some cultures engage in a lot of movement up and down the bargaining scale (eg Asian and Middle Eastern), while others do their homework and fix their prices (eg German). In the former cultures, much emphasis is placed on building relationships and extending hospitality before getting down to terms.

(xi) **Take notes**, so the accuracy of everyone's recollection of what was proposed and agreed can be checked.

(xii) **Summarise and confirm** the details of your agreements to both parties by memo, letter, contract and acknowledge a mutually positive outcome. **Monitor** the agreement to ensure it is going to plan.

Experience, knowledge and expertise count in negotiation, but it is essential that the person negotiating is **well briefed** and thoroughly prepared. He or she needs to know the extent of their **authority** and the limits they can go to, as this is vitally important even in a win-win approach.

9 Control, planning and evaluation

To: E. Funne, Managing Director
From: A. Hopeful, Marketing Assistant
Date: June 200X
Subject: Suggestions for appropriate marketing control, planning and evaluation procedures in project management.

Introduction

It is recommended that the following steps need to be applied to ensure appropriate planning, control and evaluation in project management.

Budgeting control

(a) Estimate all **costs** involved in the event.

(b) Compare the estimated total cost with anticipated **returns**, **benefits** and **objectives**.

(c) Establish that the estimated cost is within the departmental expenditure **budget**.

(d) As the plan goes ahead, **monitor actual expenditure** against the budget and query any discrepancies.

(e) **Compare** actual total cost against actual returns.

Marketing objectives

Marketing objectives should show clearly where we want to be. Without knowing clearly where we want to be, we cannot possibly establish whether or not we are getting there. Objectives should be achievable, given market conditions and resources.

Project plan

(a) Break the project down into **manageable units of activity**, ensuring the correct sequencing of tasks for co-ordinated performance and achievement of the overall project objective.

A **network map** can be usefully applied when the sequence is not immediately obvious.

A **critical path** can be further developed from the network map to describe not only what should happen when but how long the whole project will take.

By using such a technique, the shortest possible timescale for a project can be identified, because the longest path determines the deadline. Once you have identified the estimated activity durations, you can start scheduling the earliest start date for each activity. The result is a detailed and effective schedule.

(b) Estimate the **resources** required; materials, money, time etc for each unit, as far as is practically possible, so that costs can be monitored and controlled.

Action plans and **timetables** are effective ways of reminding you of key times and dates and can help you **to allocate** time effectively. For long-term schedules charts are useful and can be referred to by all personnel involved in a project. The Gantt chart is particularly useful, not only in scheduling tasks but in evaluating planned work and actual progress.

Measuring and evaluating results

It is essential that tasks are **monitored** for deadlines, problems, and co-ordination. Tasks can get forgotten and the following procedure can help ensure objectives are reached.

- Check on progress of an operation
- Check completion when a deadline is reached

- Check payments when they fall due
- Retrieve files necessary for future meetings and correspondence

Evaluating marketing activity

(a) Performance can be measured against annual **targets** - sales, budgets, expenditure

(b) **Moving standards** allow performance measurement on an on-going **control** basis eg monthly sales targets.

(c) **Diagnostic standards** can be monitored to assess how the market is responding to any marketing activity eg through market research. Such **feedback** may include output against the marketing plan, comparing marketing activities to the previous year, measuring the accuracy of budgets and schedules etc.

In conclusion, in a fully marketing orientated company everyone is involved directly or indirectly in marketing and therefore in marketing evaluation. Discussion and comments should be encouraged both at meetings and through suggestion boxes to improve procedures. All staff should be asked for their opinions and those of others outside the company.

More specifically, formal marketing **evaluation and control** procedures should be the responsibility of the marketing director, implemented downwards through marketing, sales and retail personnel. Advertising, PR and marketing research agencies would also play a part in the evaluation process.

I would be pleased to clarify any of the above points if necessary.

A Hopeful

10 International event management

I will assume that the Marketing Manager will have produced a schedule and checklist for the conference venue itself, and that the international delegates will already be aware of the venue, date, time and the purpose of the event. They should also have information on speakers, schedule of meetings, and breaks.

The following criteria will be checked for the international delegates.

(a) Have the **English translators** been booked, and confirmed their attendance?

(b) Make it clear with the delegates that they are being invited to the conference as part of their employment with the company and they are not expected to pay for their hotel and travel expenses.

(c) Travel visas arranged if necessary and any letters of confirmation that delegates are travelling on company business.

(d) All travel itineraries have been dispatched and confirmed by the delegates.

(e) Transport booked for the airport collection and delivery of delegates to the hotel accommodation. Alternatively, if travelling independently, have they received detailed instructions for getting to their hotel and conference venue?

(f) Has the welcome meeting been arranged at the hotel with the interpreters confirming their attendance? Host personnel are trained and ready to hand for general assistance.

(g) Ensure the following:

  (i) All delegates are aware of the social events and outings (this encourages networking and can be a time when new ideas emerge for later discussion).

  (ii) Currency exchange/credit facilities are available at the hotel

  (iii) All international business and social customs are acknowledged, and religious and cultural requirements are known eg particular foods or consumption of alcohol.

11 Venue appraisal

Before an organisation books a space at an exhibition, the following points must be checked off to ensure suitability.

(a) **Organisers**

- Are they a reputable organisation?
- Do they belong to any association?

(b) **Venue**

- Is it a good venue?
- Has it the right status to be compatible with our goods and services?
- Is it in the right position to attract a good attendance?
- Does it have adequate space and size?
- Is it convenient to get to and easy for transporting exhibits to and from?
- Does it have adequate facilities?
- Does it comply with health and safety regulations for the anticipated numbers?
- If the venue is outdoors, has it suitable shelter if it rains?

(c) **Facilities**

- Are the guests suitably catered for, ie food, bar or accommodation near by?
- Have they the appropriate sound systems, presentation equipment, Internet facilities, along with other furniture like seating for staff and guests?
- Are the basic necessities like water, electricity and gas readily available?

(d) **Cost**

- Is the exhibition compatible with our marketing objectives?
- Does it fall within our budget?
- What returns do we expect after the event?
- What is the cost per square metre and could you negotiate depending on size?
- What are the estimated costs to design the stand, staff it, print sales literature and entertain customers?

(e) **Publicity/PR**

- How are the visitors to be attracted to the venue?
- Do they have a press office on site?
- What follow up publicity is going to take place?
- Are there any associated events like film/video shows in which we could take part?

(Please note. To ensure maximum coverage during the exhibition, early liaison with the exhibition press office is advised.)

(f) **Build-up and knock-down**

- Is there sufficient time to build the stand and take it down?

… ANSWER BANK

12 Media choice

Memorandum

To: Managing Director
From: Keith Reed
Date: June 200X
Subject: Advertising new and used cars
Strengths and weaknesses of different media.

As new marketing manager, I am summarising the strengths and weaknesses of different media to enable the most effective expenditure of our £1,000,000+ advertising budget.

Although our marketing objectives and strategy are not yet finalised, this memo gives you some preliminary thoughts on media selection. Operating in a highly competitive market means that we have to select our media mix carefully. This may mean some change from previous activities, but this is required if we are to maintain our excellent image and aggressive sales drive.

Medium	Strengths	Weaknesses
TV	High visual impact Wide coverage Low cost per thousand Ideal for launch of new models Allows demonstration Possible co-operative ad opportunity	Expensive production costs Expensive lump sum outlay Unsuitable for used cars Long lead time for booking Zapping away from commercial breaks using remote control
Radio	Drive time radio shows – right audience Mass medium – large audience at a single exposure Low cost per thousand Radio is portable Low production costs Used by car buyers	Office hours shows not right audience Sound only – pressure to retain message No shelf life Competition use it a lot
Papers (free and paid)	Targeted sections – motor section and special motoring features Good audience range Quick and responsive Possible links with local franchises Combine with leaflets Free auto papers available in supermarkets and petrol stations	Circulation doesn't mean readership Paid for newspapers expensive cost per thousand Free papers cheaper, but could lack quality in terms of content Free auto papers on stands not delivered to the home
Posters	Commuters and car drivers audience	Cannot get detailed information across
Direct mail	Low cost per order Good targeting tool since the database can track existing customers, lapsed customers and those about to buy a car	Low season

ANSWER BANK

Conclusion

We should concentrate on regional evening papers and selected weeklies for both new and used cars at present. However, our TV region is becoming more flexible on rates for regional customers, and some of our competitors are moving onto radio as well as into the recent free auto papers.

Therefore, we really must look at the whole **database** facility with a view to examining a major re-investment in a hybrid **marketing system** which links sales staff, sales, complaints, customers buying patterns, and enquiries.

We can also control our media usage next year, as I will be instigating a media analysis which will reveal the media cost per enquiry and cost per order of every sale we achieve. This may well change our media selection in the future.

13 Magazine sales promotions

Report

To: Marketing Director
From: Promotions Manager
Date: June 200X
Subject: Sales promotions techniques

1   **Introduction and objectives**

1.1 Following our discussion last week I thought it might be useful for you to be aware of some of the ideas my department is considering regarding suitable **sales promotions** for our publications. The following provides a brief definition and an outline of suggested sales promotion techniques.

1.2 The **Institute of Sales Promotion (ISP)** defines sales promotion as 'a range of tactical marketing **techniques**, designed within a **strategic marketing framework**, to **add value** to a product or service, in order to achieve a specific sales and marketing **objective**'.

Sales promotions fall into three categories: those aimed at **trade**, **salesforce** and **consumers**. I will concentrate on those designed to stimulate consumers, although this strategy will have trade repercussions, because when magazine sales increase there will be a knock on effect for our advertisers.

1.3 The objectives of such a campaign would be to encourage **new customers** whilst reinforcing benefits to our **existing customers**. This is based on the Pareto principle whereby 80% of our business is derived from 20% of our customers. This strategy will also provide opportunities for **cross selling** across titles.

Promotional variations will depend on a number of factors: the **nature** of the publication and its readers, **frequency** of publication and **purchase cycle** (whether a publication is one that readers will be interested in for a period of time, such as a lifestyle magazine, or one that may be bought for a specific purpose, such as *What Mortgage?*).

Before selecting one or more of the techniques outlined below we need to determine our **objectives**, as different promotional methods may be more suitable than others. The key applications of promotional techniques are as follows.

- To add appeal to the **brand** and thus enhance its image
- To encourage trial or repeat **purchase**
- To defend the product from **competition**
- To encourage **customer loyalty**
- To increase **market penetration**

2 **Potential sales promotion techniques**

I have deliberately only selected a few of our titles for this exercise. These are: Gardening Today, Knitting for Your Family, You and Your Pet, and Ms.

2.1 **Free products**. These could include seeds or gardening gloves with our gardening magazines, knitting or sewing needles, samples of petfood, small paperbacks etc.

2.2 **Competitions**. These need to be linked to the publication's readership. Prizes could include tickets to exhibitions, a quantity of plants, wool, animal food for a year, a holiday etc. This strategy will also allow for the collection of data which may be used in a direct marketing campaign.

2.3 **Subscription offers**. Upon taking out an annual subscription, readers could be entitled to the following: a gardening video, a knitting book, reduced pet insurance, free cosmetics.

2.4 **Pricing**. Discounting would involve reducing the price on some or all of the titles in order to stimulate demand and increase circulation. There needs to be careful **analysis** of likely increases in circulation before this approach is adopted, along with a consideration of the impact on profitability.

2.5 **Coupons**. These could be offered in conjunction with campaigns being conducted by advertisers.

2.6 **Extra product**. A larger than normal issue for the same price. This could take the form of a supplement such as a guide to pruning, knitting patterns for Christmas, a health guide for your pet or a seasonal fashion supplement.

3 **Conclusion**

3.1 Sales promotions can be considered to be short term in the sense that they can boost sales and attract new customers, but they are highly valid techniques in this highly competitive market. The key to success with these promotions is to ensure **synergy** with the publication and the readership. Selection factors will include cost effectiveness balanced with high perceived value for our readers.

14 Price

(a) Price is important within the marketing mix because it influences **profitability** by generating **revenue**, unlike all the other elements in the mix that generate costs. Quite often, price is the only aspect a marketer can change quickly in response to **demand** or combat a **competitor**. So it has an important role as a **competitive tool**, helping to **differentiate** products and organisations. However, price must be **consistent** with other elements of the mix since it contributes to the overall image of the product.

In the absence of other information, customers tend to judge **quality** on price, and an organisation cannot hope to offer an exclusive quality product at a low price - the price must be consistent with the overall product offer.

The ultimate **objective** of pricing is to produce the **level of sales** required to fulfil the organisation's **marketing and financial objectives**.

(i) **Maximising profits**. This means maximising the returns on assets or investments.

(ii) Maintaining or increasing **market share** involves increasing or maintaining the **customer base**.

(iii) **Market penetration**. Getting a new product adopted and accepted quickly, in order to speed up the initial phase of the product's life cycle, by setting a low price to stimulate growth.

(iv) **Market skimming**. This involves setting a high initial price for a new product, if the new product to the consumer has a high value (Sony Play station, CD players etc). Once **economies of scale** come on line and **demand** increases, prices generally fall.

(v) Increasing short-term sales volume, by promotional **price cuts**, **discount** offers and **bonuses**.

Price setting is a complex process and needs to be carefully planned in conjunction with all the other elements of the marketing mix.

(b) **Elasticity of demand**

Elasticity of demand is the **responsiveness of demand** for a product to **changes in its price**.

(i) If **demand changes drastically** in response to a small change in price, then demand is said to be very **elastic**.

(ii) If **demand changes very little** or not at all in response to a small change in price, then demand is said to be **inelastic**.

Price elasticity is measured as:

$$\frac{\text{\% change in sales demand}}{\text{\% change in sales price}}$$

(1) When elasticity is greater than 1 (elastic), if the price is lowered, total sales revenue would rise because of the large increase in demand. If it is raised, total sales revenue would fall because of the large fall in demand.

(2) When elasticity is less than 1 (inelastic), if the price is lowered, total sales revenue would fall, because the increase in sales volume would be too small to compensate for the price reductions. If it is raised, total sales revenue would go up in spite of the drop in sales quantities.

Marketing management needs to be able to estimate the likely effects of price changes on total revenue and profits. Price elasticity of demand gives precision to the question of whether the firm's price is too high or too low.

15 Market research for new product launch

The following report outlines the market research plan to be conducted prior to the launch of our new magazine aimed at teenage females.

Research conducted last year revealed the UK female teenage market as a viable new market for our magazine publications. The secondary research carried out at this time has defined a **demographic** and **psychographic** profile of our target market.

The following plan has been developed for pre-launch into the market to define the most successful **product** characteristics, **pricing** and **advertising** support. As a wealth of secondary research has already been gathered, this plan will focus entirely on primary **sources of information**.

The stages of the research plan are as follows.

- Define the research objectives
- Ascertain the best methods for obtaining the information
- Collect the data
- Process the data
- Make recommendations
- Implement the recommendations

Research objectives

Research objectives must be devised to be specific, measurable, actionable, reasonable and timescaled (**SMART**). Suggested objectives for the research are as follows:

- To investigate attitudes to **magazine content and layout** styles amongst the target group, to discover the most appropriate product mix
- To investigate attitudes to **advertising message and content** amongst the target group to discover the most appropriate advertising mix.
- To quantify **media consumption** of the target group
- To investigate attitudes to **magazine pricing** amongst the target group.

Method for obtaining information

Focus groups

A group of six to ten respondents from the target group will be engaged in a group discussion with a moderator. The sessions will be recorded or videoed for later analysis. Props will be used, such as advertising visuals, magazine layouts etc.

Reasons for choice of method

(a) This method has been chosen because it is a cost effective way of gathering respondent data, leading to a larger number of respondents being involved within the budget.

(b) The recording of focus groups allows more in depth analysis of the discussion.

(c) There are potential legal and /or moral implications surrounding street recruitment of this target group.

Collect the data

The first issue to consider is that of sampling. Although we have defined demographic and psychographic profiles of the target group, it is recommended that we address geographic considerations for the sample. Previous research projects have used specific city locations in the North, Midlands and South East of the UK to mirror the UK population. It is suggested that this research uses the same locations.

Respondents will be recruited through snowballing techniques which could be achieved through schools and colleges within the target areas. We must also consider the legal and moral implications of respondent recruitment. We will need to gain parental permission and possibly parental accompaniment for the respondents.

Process the data

Discussions will be captured on video. Transcripts of discussions will be produced and qualitative analysis techniques applied to the results.

Recommendations

The results will be written into a report format and a presentation given to company directors and marketing management.

Resource/costs/timing issues

We do not have the in-house expertise to conduct a research project of this type. A research brief will be written and submitted to two external marketing research companies. Previous experience would suggest that the budget of £30,000 will finance recruitment, data collection, analysis and reporting of 15 focus groups. The likely timescale for this project is two months from the awarding of the contract.

16 Flexible budgets

(a)

Forecast sales (units)	10,000	10,000	10,000
	£	£	£
Selling price	100	150	200
Direct labour per unit	20	20	20
Direct materials per unit	40	40	40
Unit contribution	40	90	140
Delivery costs recovery	10	10	10
Total contribution	50	100	150

Budget at each price level

Forecast sales (units)	10,000	10,000	10,000
	£	£	£
Sales revenue	1,000,000	1,500,000	2,000,000
Cost of sales:			
Direct labour	200,000	200,000	200,000
Direct materials	400,000	400,000	400,000
Contribution	400,000	900,000	1,400,000
Delivery costs recovery	100,000	100,000	100,000
Total contribution	500,000	1,000,000	1,500,000
Fixed costs	50,000	50,000	50,000
Net profit	450,000	950,000	1,450,000

(b) Flexed to 80% budget at each price level

Forecast sales (units)	8,000	8,000	8,000
	£	£	£
Sales revenue	800,000	1,200,000	1,600,000
Cost of sales:			
Direct labour	160,000	160,000	160,000
Direct materials	320,000	320,000	320,000
Contribution	320,000	720,000	1,120,000
Delivery costs recovery	80,000	80,000	80,000
Total contribution	400,000	800,000	1,200,000
Fixed costs	50,000	50,000	50,000
Net profit	350,000	750,000	1,150,000

List of Key Concepts and Index

KEY CONCEPTS

Above-the-line promotion 218
Activity scheduling 168
Administration overhead 307

Banner advertisement 234
Below-the-line promotion 218
Brief 131
Budget 166

Capability profile 63
Collaboration 120
Competitor analysis 69
Conference 185
Confidentiality 111
Conflict 96
Contribution 308
Co-operation 96
Co-ordination 88
Couponing 248
Crisis communication 150
Customer care 106

Database 24
Deadline 167
Demography 38
Discrimination 91
Distribution overhead 308

Frequency 229

Internet 12
Interpersonal skills 94
Issues management 150

Marketing audit 62
Marketing research 7

Network analysis 174
Networking 153
News conference 186

Overhead 306

Place 271
Point of sale 252
Politics 90
Premiums 248
Press conference 186
Price 268
Primary data 8

Product 273
Production overhead 307
Project 172
Psychography 38
Pull 139
Push 138

Qualitative research 8
Quantitative research 8

Rapport 94
Ratings 229
Reach 229
Relevant cost 314

Secondary data 8
Segmentation 37
Selling overhead 307
Synergy 208

Team 98
Time scheduling 168

INDEX

6M, 173
80/20 principle, 33

Above-the-line advertising media, 126, 218, 246, 292
Account director, 133
Account executive, 131, 133
Accounting, 87
Accuracy, 177
Accuracy of budgets, 299
ACORN, 38
Action plans, 169
Activity-on-arrow diagram, 174
Administration overhead, 306, 307
Advertising, 218, 240
Advertising agency, 122, 127
Advertising schedule, 236
Advertising Standards Authority, 150
Advertorials, 226
Age, 39
Agency brief, 131, 142
Agency costs, 136
Agency structure, 133
Agendas, 90
Agents, 137
AIO, 38
Alliances, 90
Annual targets, 177
Assisting visitors, 109
Association of ideas, 208
Attitude, 148
Audio-visual impact, 228, 240
Audit Bureau of Circulation (ABC), 225
Audits, 11
Audits of Great Britain (AGB), 12
Authority, 89
Award ceremonies, 194

Bar chart, 170
BARB (the British Audience Research Bureau), 221
Barcodes, 12
Bases for segmentation, 37
Behaviours, 89
Below-the-line, 126, 246, 292
Blocking groups, 90
Body language, 337
Bonus packs, 249
Boston Consulting Group, 274
Bottom-up planning, 291
Bought-in reports, 11
Brainstorming, 98, 148, 183

Brand identity, 128
Brand management, 86
Brand names, 128
Branded consumer goods, 232
Brief, 131
Briefing, 122
Bring forward, 177
Buchanan and Hyczynski, 5
Budget committee, 295
Budget co-ordination, 297
Budget policy, 296
Budget preparation timetable, 296
Budget review, 297
Budgetary control, 184, 290, 298, 302
Budgeting, 290, 295, 342
  computers, 300
Budgeting control tasks, 167
Budgets, 63, 166, 178, 184, 188, 299
Business cards, 155
Business databases, 40
Business Monitor, 10
Business networks, 153
Business objectives, 165
Buying trends, 33

Capacity, 205
Catering, 193
Chartered Institute of Marketing, 62
Checklist, 168, 177
Cinema, 232
Circulation, 219, 225
Citizen's Charter Complaints Task Force, 106
Classified advertising, 226
Client service, 64
Cliques, 90
Coca Cola, 70
Cohesive groups, 100
Collaborating, 120
Collaborative programmes, 257
Column inches, 226
Common themes, 208
Communication, 89, 100, 107, 219
Community, 146, 157
Community relations, 127
Compete, 250
Competitive advantage, 27
Competitive effectiveness, 63, 64
Competitive parity, 293
Competitor analysis, 69, 71
Competitor Intelligence System, 69
Competitor pricing, 64, 270
Competitor response profile, 71

Competitors' products, 72
Complaints, 106
Computer database packages, 24
Computers, 300
   budgeting, 300
Conference centre, 184
Conferences, 185
Confidentiality, 110
Conflict, 96
Consideration, 121
Consultancy, 50, 122
Consumer panels, 11
Consumers, 146, 157
Contact database, 31, 155, 157
Contacts, 153
Contacts planning, 40
Contingencies, 167
Contracts, 121, 149
Contribution, 308
Control, 164, 294
Control decisions, 313
Control, planning and evaluation, 342
Co-operation, 100
Co-operative working, 87
Co-ordinating techniques, 172
Co-ordination, 88
Co-ordinator, 98
Core marketing spend, 166
Corporate Christmas cards, 156
Corporate hospitality, 192, 195
Corporate identity, 261
Corporate relations, 127
Corrective action, 165
Cost, 207
Cost behaviour, 306
Cost per thousand, 221, 229, 236
Cost/budget implications, 167
Costing system, 319
Couponing, 248
Coupons, 248
Courtesy, 107, 150
Cover space, 227
Creative brief, 131
Creative service, 128
Crisis communication, 151
Critical path, 175, 342
Critical path analysis (CPA, 175
Cross-selling, 26
Cultural assumptions, 56
Cultural differences, 56, 149
Cultural requirements, 197
Culture, 89, 198

Customer choice, 88
Customer database, 25, 27, 38, 52
Customer feedback, 63
Customer information, 29
Customer orientation, 86
Customer relationship management, 34
Customer research, 261
Customer retention, 26
Customer service, 261, 272
Customer service orientation, 272
Customers, 72, 106
Customs, 197
Cuttings, 256
Cyber research, 12

Data, 24
Data manipulation, 25
Data Protection Act, 41
Data Protection Principles, 42
Data security, 41
Data storage, 24
Database, 13, 24, 25, 66, 192, 332
Database information, 40
Database packages, 24, 25
Daytime audiences, 230
Deadline, 167
Dealers, 137
Decision making, 27, 308
Demographic segmentation, 38
Demographics, 12, 38, 56
Demonstrations, 249
Depth interviews, 52
Desk research, 8, 72
Diagnostic feedback, 177
Diagnostic standards, 177
Diaries, 50, 55
Direct discrimination, 91
Direct Mail Services Standards Board, 41
Direct marketing, 41, 64, 127, 128, 260
Direct Marketing Association, 32
Direct Marketing Press, 32
Direct observation, 55
Direct response advertising, 229, 260
Direct sales service providers, 137
Direct selling costs, 294
Directories, 10
Directory of Directors, 72
Disability Discrimination Act, 91
Discrimination, 91
Disney, 257
Distribution channels, 120, 136, 271
Distribution outlet, 138

Distribution overhead, 306, 308
Distribution research, 8, 334
Distributors, 137, 147, 270
Do-it-yourself research, 50
Drucker, Peter, 5
Duty, 90

Economy, 165
EDI, 273
Editorial articles, 253
Effectiveness, 165, 271
Effectiveness of marketing activity, 177
Efficiency, 150, 165
Efficiency and economy, 271
Electronic point of sale information, 177
Electronic recording systems, 55
Elegance, 166
E-mail, 112
Employee relations, 128
Engineering, 87
Enhanced CD and CD-ROM, 232
Environmental scanning, 13, 65
EPOS, 29
E-procurement, 140
Equal opportunities legislation, 91
Equal or peer role, 89
E-relationships, 111
E-sourcing, 140
Ethical behaviour, 149
Ethicality, 166
Evaluating marketing activity, 177
Event concept, 207
Events, 251
Exhibition checklist, 190
Exhibition organisers, 187
Exhibitions, 187
Expenditure budget, 207
Expense budgets, 292
Expertise, 150
Express terms, 121
Extended marketing mix, 8, 71, 277, 283
External agencies, 49
External appraisal, 65
External visitors, 108
Eye contact, 107
E-zines, 260

Facilities, 184
Familiarity, 220
Family Expenditure Survey, 10
Family life cycle (FLC), 38
FAQs, 111

Fast-forwarding, 229
Feedback, 100, 122, 165
Field experiments, 55
Field research, 8
Finance, 87
Financial relations, 127
Finisher, 99
First Direct, 273
Fixed budget, 298, 302
Flat file, 25
Flexible budget, 298, 350
Flow of work, 135
Focus group, 52, 53, 349
Follow up, 26, 156, 184, 192
Forecasts, 63
Formality, 107
Forward scheduling, 168
Four Ps, 8
Franchises, 137
Friendly Martian, 54
Full service, 127
Functional budget, 295
Functional department, 98
Functional relationships, 89

Games, 250
Gantt chart, 171
Gifts, 251
Global virtual teamworking, 115
Goals, 100
Goals down - plans up, 291
Good Food Guide, the, 73
Government, 10
Government relations, 127
Grass roots marketing, 260
Greeting people, 107
Gross Rating Points (GRPs), 229
Group decision-making, 99
Group discussions, 53
Groupware, 13
Guest list, 193

Health and safety legislation, 90
Hearne, James, 220
Heterogeneity, 278
High circulation, 227
Hoover, 248
Hospitality package, 195
Household survey, 10

Image, 146, 157

Impact of Computerised Sales And Marketing Systems In The UK, 26
Implementer, 99
Implied terms, 121
Incentives, 248
Incomplete information, 6
Indirect materials, 307
Indirect wages, 307
Industrial markets, 40
Influence, 89, 94
Influencing skills, 95
Information, 5
Information needs, 109
Informational competitions, 250
Innovation, 88
Inseparability, 278
Institute of Direct Marketing, 52
Institute of Public Relations, 146
Intangibility, 279
Inter-media comparison, 222
Internal customer concept, 88
Internal data, 63
Internal data records, 9
Internal marketing audit, 62
Internal promotion, 88
International sources, 56
Internet, 12, 14, 56, 66, 73, 233, 259
Internet discussion groups, 154
Internet marketing, 273
Interpersonal relationships, 90, 94
Intranet, 13
Investigating customers, 33
Invitations, 193
Issues management, 151

JICNARS (Joint Industry Committee for National Readership Surveys), 38, 221
JICPAS, 221

Key relationships, 91
Keyword search, 66
Kotler, 85, 86

Laboratory experiments, 55
Language, 196
Language barriers, 56
Launches, 192, 199
Law of diminishing returns, 227, 230
Leads, 155
Leaflet dispensers, 252
Legal relationships, 90
Lifestyle analysis, 38

Lifestyle categories, 38
Limiting budget factor, 296
List brokers, 32
Listenership, 228
Lists, 168
Local or regional media, 219
Local radio, 228
Local services, 232
Localised virtual teams, 114
Location, 206
Log files, 56
Long copy advertisements, 226
Longer-range decisions, 313
Loose inserts, 226
Lose-lose, 96
Loyalty programmes, 260

Machines, 176
Magazine sales promotions, 346
Magazines, 225, 240
Mail Order Protection Scheme, 41
Mailing list, 31, 43
Major media, 218, 223
Management by objectives., 292
managing your manager, 97
Manufacturing, 87
Market intelligence, 13, 137
Market orientation, 331
Market penetration, 269
Market research, 7, 63, 153, 177, 334
Market researchers, 127
Market test, 270
Marketing and the small firm, 93
Marketing budget, 166, 184, 291, 292, 302
Marketing business, 319
Marketing capabilities, 63
Marketing concept, 86
Marketing databases, 26, 332
Marketing decisions, 7, 19
Marketing expenditure, 313
Marketing information system, 64
Marketing mix, 33
Marketing objectives, 63, 342
Marketing opportunities, 33
Marketing orientation, 5, 63, 85
Marketing performance, 63
Marketing research and planning, 7, 40
Marketing services, 126
Marketing strategy, 62
Marketing support, 127
Marketing teamwork, 336
Master budget, 297

Materials, 176
Matrix organisation, 86
McDonalds, 206, 257
Measurement, 176
Measuring and evaluating results, 342
Media, 146, 157
Media coverage, 193, 253
Media habits, 219
Media only service, 127
Media planners, 221
Media rationale, 236
Media relations, 127, 254, 260
Media releases, 253
Media research, 221
Media selection, 218, 219
Media software packages, 236
Meetings, 182
Men, 176
Merchandising, 251
Microsoft Access, 24
Midland Bank, 273
Minutes, 176
Mobiles, 252
Money, 176
Monitor-evaluator, 99
Motivation, 100
Moving standards, 177

National food survey, 10
National mass-market medium, 219
National newspaper, 219
Need to know principle, 111
Negotiating strategies, 124
Negotiation, 122, 183
Negotiation of budgets, 297
Network, 173
Network analysis, 174
Networking, 72, 87, 93, 153, 187
New media, 127, 232
News items, 253
Newsgroups, 12
Newspapers, 223, 225, 240
Non-government sources of information, 10
Non-verbal communication, 337

Objective and task method, 293
Objective setting, 165
Objectives, 49, 164, 176, 207
Observation, 55
Offer and acceptance, 121
Official statistics, 10
Online advertising, 235

Online promotion, 234
On-line transaction processing, 32
Opportunities, 67
Opportunities to see, 229
Organisation, 5, 176
Organising, 182, 199
Other secondary sources, 72
OTS, 229
Outdoor media, 231
Outdoor venues, 207
Overheads, 306, 307

Pace and lead, 156
Page divisions, 226
Parent product, 248
Pareto's law, 33
Participative contests, 250
Pathway, 175
PC Contacts Management database, 155
People, 278
Peppers and Rogers, 40
Pepsi, 70
Percentage of sales, 292
Perception, 269
Performance, 64
Performance data, 63
Performance measures, 256
Perishable, 279
Perrier, 253
Personal contact, 107
Personal interviews, 51
PESTLE, 66
Photo calls, 254
Photography, 128, 194
Physicals, 279
Pitch meetings, 183
Place, 136, 271
Place decisions, 319
Planning, 164, 290
Planning techniques, 167
Plant, 99
Point of sale, 248
Politics, 90
Portfolio, 126
Position, 226
Postal surveys, 51
Poster advertising, 231, 240
Posters, 252
Potential for readership, 226
Power, 89
PR consultancies, 127
PR crisis, 150

PR methodologies, 255
PR/media value, 208
Premiums, 248
Preparation of budgets, 295
Presentation, 16, 211
Press, 225
Press ad rates, 226
Press ads, 226
Press conferences, 186, 254
Press relations, 127, 260
Press/media coverage, 72
Pressure groups, 90
Prestige, 226
Price, 268, 347
Price decisions, 319
Price research, 7
Price sensitivity, 269
Pricing decisions, 313
Pricing research, 270
Primary data, 8
Primary sources, 9, 65
Principal budget factor, 296, 302
Print media, 225, 240
Printing, 238
Priorities, 167, 178
Prioritising, 167
Private viewing, 192
Prize draws, 250
Procedures, 89, 173
Processes, 278
Procter & Gamble, 5
Product, 273
Product decisions, 319
Product development, 41
Product endorsements, 128
Product housing, 252
Product launches, 64
Product life cycle, 274
Product management, 86
Product mix, 64
Product or production orientation, 85
Product packaging, 248, 249
Product performance, 274
Product placement, 128, 255, 257
Product research, 7, 334
Product reviews, 253
Product support, 138
Product testing, 276
Product trends, 275
Production overhead, 306, 307
Productivity, 88
Professionalism, 150

Profile, 155, 193
Profit, 306, 322
Profitable customers, 64
Project, 342
Project management, 172
Project meetings, 183
Project monitoring, 177
Project plan, 173
Project teams, 98
Projective techniques, 54
Promotion, 218
Promotion agencies, 127
Promotion decisions, 319
Promotional activities, 127
Promotional budget, 33
Promotional collaboration, 137
Promotional communication, 151
Promotional events, 192
Promotional incentives, 246
Promotional material, 194
Promotional messages, 147
Promotional proposals, 271
Promotional support, 138
Promotional tours, 194
Psychographic segmentation, 38
Public concerns, 151
Public relations, 88, 127, 182, 253, 260
Public sector organisations, 106
Public seminars, 194
Publicity stunts, 192, 194, 199
Published information, 10
Pull, 122
Purchase analysis, 12
Purchasing, 87
Push, 122
Push and Pull activity, 138

Qualitative media research, 229
Qualitative research, 8, 16, 52, 56
Quality, 269
Quality circles, 98
Quality control, 88
Quantitative data, 9
Quantitative research, 8, 15
Questionnaire, 50, 63

R & D, 87
Race Relations Act 1976, 91
Radio, 228
Radio Advertising Bureau, 228

RAJAR (Radio Joint Audience Research), 221, 228
Rapport, 94
Rating scales, 56
Ratings, 229
Raw data, 15
Reach, 227, 240
Reach and frequency, 236
Reach and repetition, 236
Readership, 225
Readership survey, 225
Rebates, 249
Receiving visitors, 107
Reception procedures, 108
Reciprocity, 156
Recommendations, 154
Recorded data, 55
Recording devices, 50
Records, 25
Relational database, 25
Relationship marketing, 260
Relevant cost, 314
Remote control, 229
Repeat exposure, 236
Repeated exposure, 222
Report on company capabilities, 334
Representing the organisation, 147
Research, 72
Research and development, 64
Research objectives, 349
Research planning, 48
Resource-investigator, 99
Response rates, 52
Responsibility accounting, 291
Responsiveness, 229
Retailers, 72, 136
Return on investment, 64
Reverse scheduling, 168
Right-hand pages, 227
Risk, 7, 19
Ritz, 206
Roles, 89
Ros Jay, 227
Routine planning decisions, 313

Sales budget, 292, 296
Sales conference, 185
Sales meetings, 183
Sales promotion, 127, 260
Sales revenue, 64
Sales targets, 292
Sales/promotion research, 7

Sampling, 249
Scheduling, 167, 168, 178, 227, 240
Scheduling of media, 218
Scheduling TV, 230
Search engines, 12
Seasonal selling cycles, 227
Secondary data, 8, 12
Secondary sources, 9, 57, 65
Segmentation, 37, 219, 220
Selective exposure, 222
Selling overhead, 306, 307
Semantic differential scales, 56
Semi-display advertising, 226
Sentence completion, 55
Service, 106
Set of related ads, 230
Seven Ps, 8
Sex Discrimination Acts 1975 and 1986, 91
Sexual harassment, 91
Shaper, 98
Shelf tags, 252
Short-run problem decisions, 313
Show material, 53
Situation, 176
Smart objectives, 166
Social contacts, 154
Social responsibility, 149
Social status, 38
Socio-economic group, 39
SOST, 176
Sources of data, 49
Sources of information, 9
Specialist, 99
Specialist magazines, 219
Specific target audience, 236
Sponsorship, 128, 254
Spreadsheets, 301
Staffing, 194
Stakeholders, 256
Star rating systems, 206
Status, 206
Strategy, 176
Strengths and weaknesses, 334
Structural relationships, 89
Structure, 89
Structured questionnaire, 50
Study and discussion groups, 98
Suitability, 204, 205
Summary of costs, 237
Superpanel, 12
Suppliers, 270
Supply chain, 63, 256

Surveys, 10
Synergistic relationships, 257
Synergy, 204, 208, 248

Tables, 25
Tactics, 176
Target audience, 64, 219, 256
Target Audience Rating Points (TARPs), 229
Targeted marketing, 37
Targeted media, 219
Targets, 219
Team, 98
Team briefings, 98
Team decisions, 99
Team identity, 183
Team performance, 100
Team worker, 99
Teamworking, 98
Technical characteristics, 221
Technology, 232
Telemarketers, 29
Telemarketing agencies, 137
Telephone surveys, 51
Telephones, 338
Teletext, 232
Television, 219, 228
Television Consumer Audit, 12
Testing, 222
The Institute of Direct Marketing, 227
Thematic apperception tests (TAT tests), 55
Themed party, 192
Third person, 54
Threats, 67
Time, 227
Timetables, 169
Top-down planning, 291
Trade associations, 10
Trade audits, 12
Trade conference, 185
Trade fairs, 187
Trade promotion, 252
Traffic per page, 227
Transaction processing, 40
Trend analysis, 12
Trigger words, 56
TVRs, 229

Unethical behaviour, 149
Unsolicited mail, 41
Unstructured questionnaire, 50

Value for money, 221

Venue, 182, 193, 204, 212
Venue selection, 210
Videoing, 229
Videos, 232
Viewership, 229
Viral marketing, 260
Virtual team, 115
Volume purchases, 248

Ward, Keith, 313
Web advertising, 233
Web sites, 12
Websites, 30
Web-sites, 232
What if analysis, 300
Who's Who, 72
Wholesalers, 136
Wilmshurst, 130
Win-lose, 96, 124
Win-win, 96, 125, 340
Wobblers, 252
Word association, 54
Word of mouth, 151
Work breakdown structure (WBS), 173
Work role, 89
Working relationship, 84, 101
Written brief, 50

Yearbooks, 10

Zero base budgeting, 300

CIM – Professional Certificate in Marketing: Marketing in Practice (8/07)

REVIEW FORM & FREE PRIZE DRAW

All original review forms from the entire BPP range, completed with genuine comments, will be entered into one of two draws on 31 January 2008 and 30 July 2008. The names on the first four forms picked out on each occasion will be sent a cheque for £50.

Name: _____ **Address:** _____

_____

_____

How have you used this Text?
(Tick one box only)

☐ Self study (book only)
☐ On a course: college_____
☐ With BPP Home Study package
☐ Other _____

Why did you decide to purchase this Text?
(Tick one box only)

☐ Have used companion Kit
☐ Have used BPP Texts in the past
☐ Recommendation by friend/colleague
☐ Recommendation by a lecturer at college
☐ Saw advertising in journals
☐ Saw website
☐ Other _____

During the past six months do you recall seeing/receiving any of the following?
(Tick as many boxes as are relevant)

☐ Our advertisement in *Marketing Success*
☐ Our advertisement in *Marketing Business*
☐ Our brochure with a letter through the post
☐ Our brochure with *Marketing Business*
☐ Saw website

Which (if any) aspects of our advertising do you find useful?
(Tick as many boxes as are relevant)

☐ Prices and publication dates of new editions
☐ Information on product content
☐ Facility to order books off-the-page
☐ None of the above

Have you used the companion Practice & Revision Kit for this subject?   ☐ Yes   ☐ No

Your ratings, comments and suggestions would be appreciated on the following areas.

	Very useful	*Useful*	*Not useful*
Introductory section (How to use this text, study checklist, etc)	☐	☐	☐
Introduction	☐	☐	☐
Syllabus coverage	☐	☐	☐
Action Programmes and Marketing at Work examples	☐	☐	☐
Chapter roundups	☐	☐	☐
Quick quizzes	☐	☐	☐
Illustrative questions	☐	☐	☐
Content of suggested answers	☐	☐	☐
Index	☐	☐	☐
Structure and presentation	☐	☐	☐

	Excellent	*Good*	*Adequate*	*Poor*
Overall opinion of this Text	☐	☐	☐	☐

Do you intend to continue using BPP Study Texts/Kits/Passcards?   ☐ Yes   ☐ No

Please note any further comments and suggestions/errors on the reverse of this page.

Please return to: Glenn Haldane, BPP Professional Education, FREEPOST, London, W12 8BR

CIM – Professional Certificate in Marketing: Marketing in Practice (8/07)

REVIEW FORM & FREE PRIZE DRAW (continued)

Please note any further comments and suggestions/errors below.

FREE PRIZE DRAW RULES

1. Closing date for 31 January 2007 draw is 31 December 2006. Closing date for 31 July 2007 draw is 30 June 2007.
2. Restricted to entries with UK and Eire addresses only. BPP employees, their families and business associates are excluded.
3. No purchase necessary. Entry forms are available upon request from BPP Professional Education. No more than one entry per title, per person. Draw restricted to persons aged 16 and over.
4. Winners will be notified by post and receive their cheques not later than 6 weeks after the relevant draw date. List of winners will be supplied on request.
5. The decision of the promoter in all matters is final and binding. No correspondence will be entered into.